THE AMERICAN LAW INSTITUTE

THE WTO CASE LAW OF 2008

LEGAL AND ECONOMIC ANALYSIS

This book is the sixth report of the American Law Institute (ALI) project on World Trade Organization Law. The project undertakes yearly analysis of the case law from the adjudicating bodies of the WTO. These studies cover a wide range of WTO law: this volume focuses on the year 2008. Each case is jointly evaluated by well known experts in trade law and international economics. The contributors critically review the jurisprudence of WTO adjudicating bodies and evaluate whether the ruling 'makes sense' from an economic as well as a legal point of view, and, if not, whether the problem lies in the interpretation of the law or the law itself. The Studies do not cover all issues discussed in a case, but they seek to discuss both the procedural and the substantive issues that form the 'core' of the dispute.

HENRIK HORN, Professor of International Economics, is Senior Research Fellow at the Research Institute of Industrial Economics (IFN), Stockholm. He is a member of the Editorial Board of the *World Trade Review* and is a member of the Centre for Economic Policy Research. He has previously worked for the Economic Policy Research and Analysis Division of the World Trade Organization, and has been a judge on the Swedish Market Court (supreme court for competition law).

PETROS C. MAVROIDIS is Edwin B. Parker Professor at Columbia Law School, Professor at the University of Neuchatel, and a member of the Centre for Economic Policy Research. He was previously Chair of Competition Law, EUI, Florence, and a member of the Legal Affairs Division of the World Trade Organization.

THE AMERICAN LAW INSTITUTE

THE WTO CASE LAW OF 2008

LEGAL AND ECONOMIC ANALYSIS

Edited By

HENRIK HORN

AND

PETROS C. MAVROIDIS

CAMBRIDGE
UNIVERSITY PRESS

CAMBRIDGE UNIVERSITY PRESS
Cambridge, New York, Melbourne, Madrid, Cape Town,
Singapore, São Paulo, Delhi, Tokyo, Mexico City

Cambridge University Press
The Edinburgh Building, Cambridge CB2 8RU, UK

Published in the United States of America by
Cambridge University Press, New York

www.cambridge.org
Information on this title: www.cambridge.org/9780521154017

© The American Law Institute 2010

First published 1999

A catalogue record for this publication is available from the British Library

Library of Congress cataloguing in publication data

ISBN 978-0-521-15401-7 Paperback

CONTENTS

Foreword

Since 1923, The American Law Institute, a private organization with more than 4,200 lawyers, judges, and professors as members, has sought to influence American and transnational law by recommending principles and rules that contribute to social and economic progress. The law of world trade, still in an early stage of development, will benefit from analysis by distinguished experts. For that reason, the ALI has sponsored books describing and constructively criticizing all the important decisions rendered by the Appellate Body of the World Trade Organization since 2001. This volume, the sixth in our series, considers decisions issued in 2008.

The subjects of the legal disputes discussed in this year's volume seem abstruse and sometimes amusing: bananas, Thai shrimp, upland cotton, and so forth. But an economically integrated world must have coherent, predictable, and fair rules governing trade. In just its second decade, the WTO has made progress, but its work can only be helped by careful study.

The six volumes analyzing WTO decisions are only one part of the ALI's effort to contribute to the law of world trade. In 2008, we published *The Genesis of the GATT*, by Professors Douglas A. Irwin, Petros C. Mavroidis, and Alan O. Sykes. Teams are now at work on two volumes that we expect to publish in 2011: one on the treatment of border instruments in the GATT and one on the National Treatment provision of Article III of the GATT. For The American Law Institute, it is an innovation to have our effort led by two non-Americans, Professor Henrik Horn of the University of Stockholm and Professor Petros Mavroidis of the University of Neuchatel and Columbia University in New York. It is also new for us to publish work, all portions of which are the product of cooperation between professors of trade economics and professors of trade law.

We appreciate the assistance of the experts who met in Geneva to discuss earlier drafts of this work and of other experts who have sent helpful comments to the authors. We are even more indebted to Professors Horn and Mavroidis for their high-quality leadership and to the authors they persuaded to contribute to this book. Finally, we thank the Jan Wallander and Tom Hedelius Foundation and the Milton and Miriam Handler Foundation for financial support that makes this important work possible.

LANCE LIEBMAN
Director
The American Law Institute

Introduction

HENRIK HORN AND PETROS C. MAVROIDIS

This volume contains eight reports on the World Trade Organization (WTO) case law of 2008, written in the context of the American Law Institute (ALI) project *Principles of World Trade Law: The World Trade Organization* (WTO). The project seeks to provide systematic analyses of WTO law based on both economics and law. Each report is written jointly by an economist and a lawyer, and each discusses a different WTO dispute. The authors are free to choose the particular aspects of the dispute they wish to discuss. The aim is to determine for each dispute whether the Appellate Body's (or occasionally the Panel's) decision seems desirable from an economic and a legal point of view, and, if not, whether the problem lies in the interpretation of the law or the text itself.

Earlier versions of the papers were presented at a meeting in Geneva in June 2009, and we are very grateful for the comments provided by the discussants Kamal Saggi, Joost Pauwelyn, Frieder Roessler, and Marco Bronckers. We would also like to thank the other meeting participants for providing many helpful comments, and the WTO for providing a venue for the meeting.

It deserves emphasis that the existence of the project is due to the efforts and commitment of Professor Lance Liebman, Director of the ALI. We have also benefited greatly from the support of ALI President Emeritus Michael Traynor and ALI Deputy Director Elena Cappella. Moreover, we sincerely thank Nina Amster, Judy Cole, Todd Feldman, Sandrine Forgeron, and Marianne Walker of the ALI's staff for providing, as always, very efficient administrative and editorial help. Finally, we are extremely grateful for financial support from The Jan Wallander and Tom Hedelius Research Foundation and the Milton and Miriam Handler Foundation.

Let us turn to the contents of the volume. **Schropp** and **Palmeter** discuss the Appellate Body (AB) report in *EC – Bananas III (Article 21.5 – Second Recourse)*. The trade dispute over the European Union's (EU)[1] banana-importation regime is one of the longest-standing cases in the history of the WTO. This particular report concerned the second compliance Panel under Art. 21.5 DSU (Dispute Settlement Understanding). The AB was summoned by the EC to assess substantial findings made by the compliance Panel under Arts. II and XIII of the GATT, as well as a

---

1 As of 1 December 2009, with the passage of the Lisbon Treaty, the European Community is now called European Union. We refer to its historic name only when necessary (because, for example, it participated in a dispute under the name 'European Communities').

host of procedural issues. For the most part, the AB upheld the Panel's findings against the EC. Overall, the authors find little reason to criticize the findings of the AB. The outcome of the dispute is hardly surprising, given that the contested measure only marginally differed from the measure at issue in the first recourse to a compliance Panel. But the authors still find some facets of the dispute interesting. For practitioners, the role of *estoppel* in WTO litigation, the legal effect of Panel suggestions, and the relevance of Uruguay Round Modalities Papers as interpretative tools should be of interest. The case also raised some more systemic issues concerning, for instance, the economics of tariff quotas, the inherently discriminatory nature of tariff-quota allocation in the WTO, the lack of temporary opt-outs in the WTO legal framework, and the relevance of compliance proceedings for the damage calculation under Art. 22.6 DSU.

Prusa and **Vermulst** examine two closely related disputes, *United States–Measures Relating to Shrimp from Thailand* and *United States–Customs Bond Directive*, both of which concerned the United States' enhanced continuous bond requirement for goods subject to antidumping and countervailing duties. Because of perceived problems with its ability to collect antidumping duties, the US amended its bonding requirements in 2004. Under the new rules, importers were required to secure a bond for an amount equal to the cash-deposit rate in effect on the date of entry of the merchandise, multiplied by the importer's value of imports from the previous year, as well as to pay cash deposits equal to the amount of antidumping duties per entry. The US claimed that the additional deposit was reasonable and necessary to guarantee duty payment in case the antidumping duty increased during the administrative review. Thailand and India claimed that the additional deposit was unreasonable and an additional action against dumping, and was therefore impermissible under GATT 1994 and the Anti-Dumping Agreement (AD). The AB upheld the Panel's findings that, while the Ad Note to Arts. VI:2 and VI:3 GATT authorizes the imposition of security requirements during the period following the imposition of an antidumping duty order, the additional security requirement resulting from the application of the bond requirement to shrimp was not 'reasonable' within the meaning of the Ad Note. The AB reversed the legal interpretation by the Panel that there is no obligation under the Ad Note to assess the risk of default by individual importers; however, the AB upheld the Panel's finding that the bond requirement is not 'necessary' within the meaning of Art. XX(d) GATT. As a result, the AB upheld the Panel's conclusion that the application of the bond requirement to shrimp was inconsistent with Art. 18(1) AD because it was inconsistent with the Ad Note to Arts. VI:2 and VI:3 GATT and not justified by Art.XX(d) GATT. The authors consider the AB's legal and economic reasoning to be largely correct. In their view, the US employed a sledgehammer to kill a mosquito, and the AB used the concepts of 'reasonableness' in the Ad Note and 'necessity' in Art. XX(d) GATT to reject what fundamentally was a lack of proportionality, while leaving the door open for more reasonable application of bonding requirements.

The next paper in the volume, written by **Bown** and **Meagher**, analyzes the Panel Report in *Mexico–Olive Oil*, a report that was not appealed. The case involved a countervailing-duty measure imposed by Mexico on imports of olive oil from the EU (in particular, Spain and Italy). In the authors' view, while the *Mexico–Olive Oil* dispute was neither particularly complicated nor very controversial, the decision raised several issues that gave rise to new interpretations of the relevant agreements or that illustrated some of the recurring problems in challenging anti-dumping or countervailing-duty measures in WTO dispute-settlement proceedings. In the case at hand, the Panel did not give much credence to evidence that the main complaint of the domestic industry was the loss of a distribution agreement and brand-name rights with a Spanish exporter. The authors first analyze as potentially problematic the manner in which the Panel addressed the question of whether Mexico sufficiently ruled out 'any known factors' aside from the impact of the subsidy on the injury suffered by its domestic olive-oil industry. Second, the authors describe the quandary of how to implement findings of procedural violations associated with the Agreement on Subsidies and Countervailing Measures (SCM) and the AD. Finally, they discuss some examples of important 'nonissues' that were present in the dispute but were surprisingly noncontentious. They emphasize in particular how an issue such as 'pass-through' – one that has proven to be quite divisive in earlier WTO jurisprudence on subsidies and countervailing measures – was not controversial in this dispute, given the context of the market and policies at issue in the case.

Crowley and **Howse** discuss the *US–Stainless Steel* (*Mexico*) dispute. It concerned a Mexican complaint that the US method of calculating dumping margins by using 'zeroing procedures' leads to calculated margins that do not fully reflect export prices above normal value. The authors see two interesting issues being addressed in the dispute. First, what role does and should *stare decisis* (precedent) play in the WTO dispute-resolution system? Here the authors agree with the US that there is no formal *stare decisis* in the WTO. But they nevertheless argue that, overall, the institutional structure and foundational norms of the WTO imply the need for panels to be bound by the prior decisions of the AB. Their economic analysis describes the costs and benefits of legal systems with and without precedent. The second interesting issue in the case is the circumstances under which exceptional methodologies, i.e. 'zeroing', can better achieve the stated objectives of the agreement than the standard methodologies explicitly stated in the agreement. Regarding methodology, it is argued that any analysis of the suitability of a methodology (i.e. 'zeroing') must be undertaken jointly with an analysis of the underlying objective of the agreement (i.e. remedying injury). The authors consider a simple example of 'ordinary dumping' and a simple example of 'targeted dumping'. Both examples involve at least one episode of dumping in which the export price is below normal value and there is evidence that the domestic industry is injured by dumping in the sense that it receives a level of producer's surplus that is lower than it would have been if the exporter had not dumped. The targeted-dumping example is constructed so that the legal requirements of the exceptional method of Art. 2.4.2 AD, the weighted-average-to-transaction method (W-T), are satisfied. It is shown that zeroed antidumping duties are excessive under ordinary dumping, but they are necessary to fully remedy the injury caused by a stylized, yet highly plausible, case of targeted dumping. However, in the example of the latter type of dumping, the foreign pricing strategy of the new-customer discount is a practice that economists widely regard as a normal and fair aspect of market competition. Normative welfare economics recognizes this more intense competition as the source of improved aggregate welfare in the importing country. Economically speaking, the concern thus lies not in the application of the law, but in the law itself. As the example illustrates, the AD could be construed to deter pro-competitive pricing. A normative analysis of economic welfare would find that the use of the exceptional method in the targeted-dumping example presented here reduces the welfare of both the importing country and the world.

In their analysis of the Appellate Body determination in *Canada/United States – Continued Suspension of Obligations in the EC – Hormones Dispute* ('*Continued Suspension*'), **Hoekman** and **Trachtman** discuss the relationship between the National Treatment obligation in Article III GATT, and the requirement under the Agreement on Sanitary and Phytosanitary (SPS) Measures that such measures be based on a risk assessment that takes into account available scientific evidence. In their view, the AB's reasoning makes it clear that the primary purpose of the SPS Agreement is to discipline discriminatory regulation, and not the level of protection. The case also clarifies in their view the fact that *de facto* protection created by an SPS measure must be motivated by demonstrating that the measure is addressing a market failure that stems from the existence of a scientifically based health or safety concern. The latter requirement is effectively a means for determining the intent of an SPS measure. But while intent is a factor that is ostensibly not relevant in Art. III GATT cases, the emphasis on intent still does not constitute a deviation from the basic concern with preventing illegitimate discrimination against imported products.

Davey and **Sapir** address the AB determination in the *US–Upland Cotton (Article 21.5–Brazil)* dispute. Two of the four issues in this AB report concerned the proper scope of Art. 21.5 DSU compliance panel proceedings; the other two issues concerned the AB's review of the Panel's use of evidence. On the Art. 21.5 DSU issues, the AB essentially ruled that a compliance panel could evaluate the WTO consistency of (i) the entirety of an implementation measure (including parts of the measure that did not specifically implement DSB recommendations and rulings) and (ii) new subsidy grants made under a program in respect of which prior subsidy grants had been found to cause serious prejudice so as to determine whether the new grants also resulted in serious prejudice. On the evidentiary issues, the AB upheld the Panel's conclusions, although it modified certain parts of the Panel's reasoning. The authors find that the most interesting aspect of the case was the substantial deference showed by the AB to the Panel's consideration of causation and nonattribution issues. This deference was striking compared to the lack of deference that the AB has given to national authorities on those issues. But the authors also welcome what they interpret as an interest on behalf of the AB to require the use of analytical tools on the part of panels evaluating serious-prejudice cases.

Wauters and **Vandenbussche** review the AB report on *China–Auto Parts*. This dispute concerned a set of regulatory measures imposing a 25% 'charge' on imported automobile parts used in the manufacture of motor vehicles in China. The main legal question in this case concerned the nature of this charge: should it be viewed as a border charge (tariff concession) or an internal charge, and then be subjected to the nondiscrimination requirement of Art. III GATT? The authors examine the reasoning of the AB relating to the difference between these two types of charges. They discuss the role and relevance of this distinction in the GATT/ WTO legal system in general, and for the purposes of resolving this dispute in particular. They also address the important systemic question relating to the review of a WTO Member's domestic laws for purposes of determining their GATT/WTO consistency. This was an important issue in this case, as China claimed that the Panel misunderstood the meaning of the relevant (Chinese) Decree and requested the AB to review the Panel's erroneous reading of this Decree. The authors express concern over the distinction drawn by the AB between legal and factual elements of relevance in the interpretation of domestic laws. The 'economic bone' in this case is less straightforward: it is not clear if the AB's decision is desirable from a welfare point of view. The main reason is that many questions relevant to the case were left unaddressed by the AB. Due to the lack of factual evidence to substantiate its findings, the Panel's ruling remains rather speculative on certain accounts. For this purpose the authors engage in their own examination of the facts, using mainly a unique dataset of Chinese firm-level data. Among other things, the authors interpret the data to suggest that the import duties on complete car vehicles or car parts would mainly affect Chinese customers, given that domestic sales are more important than exports. On the other hand, the data suggests that an import-competing industry for car parts existed at the time of the measure, and also that it seems to have grown substantially over time at a higher pace than the car-assembly industry during the period the circumvention duty applied; these latter facts tend to substantiate the claim made by the Panel that the local industry was favored by China's trade policy, and that the policy could probably better be seen as an industrial policy than as an intentional circumvention of China's trade liberalization commitments.

Finally, **Conconi** and **Wouters** critically review the main findings of the AB in the case *India–Additional Import Duties*. This ruling sheds light on the interplay between two core provisions of the GATT, namely Art. II (Schedules of Concessions) and Art. III GATT. The question on the allocation of the burden of proof was central in this dispute. In its ruling, the AB considered that charges inconsistent with Art. II:2(a) GATT fall within the scope of Art. II:1(b) GATT, and hereby underscored the distinction between 'border charges', covered under Art. II GATT, and 'internal charges', covered under Art. III GATT. In the authors' view, it was unfortunate that the AB failed to reveal the substantive obligation imposed on these charges under Art. II:1(b) GATT. In their opinion, such charges should be covered under 'ODCs' (other duties and charges) and therefore only be deemed consistent with Art. II:1(b) GATT in the unlikely case that they were explicitly recorded. The AB also held that the burden of formulating a *prima facie* case under Art. II:2(a) GATT rests on the complainant where the potential for application of Art. II:2(a) GATT is clear from the face of the challenged measure. At the same time, the AB also stressed the respondent's responsibility of underpinning any alleged justification under Art. II:2(a) GATT. This could also be induced from the AB's strong criticism of India's refusal to answer the Panel's written question regarding the operation of the internal charges. The authors are less critical of the AB decision from an economic point of view. What its ruling on *India–Additional Duties* clearly establishes is that Art. II:2(a) GATT can be used as an exception to Art. II:1(b) GATT, implying that WTO Members can impose border taxes above their market-access commitments. However, they can only do so in a way that is consistent with Art. III GATT, implying that border taxes cannot be in excess of domestic taxes. The authors maintain that these rules may help to internalize both terms of trade and domestic externalities and to increase global efficiency.

Commentary on the Appellate Body Report in *EC–Bananas III (Article 21.5)*: waiver-thin, or lock, stock, and metric ton?

SIMON A. B. SCHROPP

International Analyst, Sidley Austin LLP

DAVID PALMETER

Sidley Austin LLP (retired)

Abstract: At first glance, the Appellate Body Report in *Bananas III (Article 21.5; Second Recourse)* does not seem to be a case for the *Guinness Book*.
The AB upheld most of the Panel's findings, and the EC lost big. This was hardly surprising, given that the contested measure only marginally differed from the measure at issue in the first recourse to a compliance Panel. It is at second sight that this AB Report reveals its interesting facets. We highlight a few remarkable legal and economics aspects, some of a more systemic nature, some offering practical insights: For practitioners, the role of *estoppel* in WTO litigation, the legal effect of Panel suggestions, and the relevance of Uruguay Round Modalities Papers as interpretative tools may be of interest. Readers more concerned with systemic aspects of the WTO may take interest in the economics of tariff quotas, the inherently discriminatory nature of tariff-quota allocation in the WTO, and the relevance of compliance proceedings for the damage calculation under Article 22.6 of the DSU.

1. Introduction

The trade dispute over the European Community's banana importation regime is one of the longest-standing cases in the history of the WTO.[1] The fact-load of this case is mind-boggling, and through the years *Bananas* has left a long trail of panels, arbitrations, and procedural battles. The Appellate Body (AB) Report on the second compliance Panel under Article 21.5 of the Dispute Settlement Understanding (DSU) is the presently last stage in the *Bananas* saga.

The AB was summoned by the EC to assess substantial findings made by the compliance Panel under Articles II and XIII of the GATT, as well as a host of

The authors would like to thank Chad Bown, Alexander Keck, Hunter Nottage, and Nadia Rocha for valuable input. All opinions should be attributed to the authors and neither to the institution they are affiliated with, nor to its clients. It goes without saying that the authors assume full responsibility for all errors, flaws, and lapses.

1 See exemplarily Jackson and Grané (2001).

procedural issues. Sadly for the researcher charged with commenting on this case (but fortunate for the practitioner), there is little scope for criticism against the findings of the AB. Nevertheless, the compliance proceedings in *Bananas III* offer some interesting general legal and economic aspects, for example on the legal nature of Panel suggestions, the economics of tariff quotas, and the relationship between Article 21.5 Panels and arbitrations under Article 22.6 of the DSU.

This paper proceeds as follows: Section 2 gives a brief overview of the rich factual and legal background of *Bananas III*. In Section 3, we summarize the claims on appeal and the AB's findings, and offer a few observations. Section 4 provides a richer discussion of the legal and economic aspects in connection with the *Bananas III* dispute. Section 5 concludes.

2. Factual background and original compliance Panel findings

In this section of the paper, we present a brief overview of the order of events, cite the relevant documents, and provide a summary of the claims in the Article 21.5 proceedings, as well as of the findings of the Panel Report.

2.1 Order of events[2]

As a result of the Single European Act of 1993, the European Union (EU) initiated the so-called 'Common Market Organization for Bananas' (CMOB). Important for the case at hand, CMOB was characterized by a preferential zero-tariff quota of 857,700 metric tons (mt), dedicated uniquely to bananas originating in African, Caribbean, and Pacific State (ACP) countries, as well as by a global quota of 2 million mt for bananas imported from either third countries or non-traditional imports from ACP countries (MFN suppliers).[3] In-quota MFN tariff rates were 75 €/mt; out-of-quota imports were possible, albeit at a virtually prohibitive rate of 680 €/mt.[4]

The CMOB was contentious from the beginning, with a GATT Panel in 1993 and one in 1994 concluding that it was inconsistent with various GATT rules.[5] In an effort to address the rulings of the GATT panel, the European Communities (EC) signed the 'Framework Agreement on Bananas' (Bananas Framework Agreement or BFA) in October 1994 with four of the five countries that had initiated the original GATT panel. Among other things, the BFA introduced

---

2 The authors of this text appreciate that the factual situation of the *Bananas* saga is rather convoluted. A timeline of events in chronological order, accompanied by short explanations, is annexed at the end of this paper for the reader's convenience.

3 The preferential ACP tariff quota was an atavism from Europe's not-so-splendid colonial past. It was carved out in the context of the Lomé Convention.

4 See IATRC (2001: 163).

5 GATT DS/32R (*Bananas I*) and GATT DS/38R (*Bananas II*), respectively.

country-specific quota allocations under the EC's global MFN tariff quota for Venezuela, Costa Rica, Colombia, and Nicaragua.[6] At the creation of the WTO in 1994, the BFA was annexed to the European Communities' tariff schedule.

Ecuador and the United States, among others, challenged the CMOB under the newly created WTO dispute-settlement body (DSB) in September 1995. In particular, the complainants alleged that EC Regulation 404/93, from 1993 (the Original Banana Import Regime) was inconsistent with WTO rules and was justified neither by the BFA, nor the Agreement on Agriculture, nor was it covered by the Lomé Article I Waiver. The EC lost both in front of the original panel and the Appellate Body.[7] After this defeat, the EC amended its banana import regime by enacting EC Regulation 2362/98 in combination with Council Regulation 1637/98 (the Compliance Banana Import Regime). As the first compliance Panel confirmed, this Compliance Banana Import Regime was an unsuccessful attempt to comply with the original DSB rulings and recommendations.[8]

As a response to the DSU Article 22.6 arbitration, which granted both the United States and Ecuador the authorization to suspend concessions and other obligations, the EC concluded two (nearly identical) 'Understandings on Bananas' with Ecuador and the US in 2001. In both Understandings, whose pertinent parts are replicated below, the EC promised to introduce a *tariff-only* regime for banana imports *no later than* 1 January 2006. In the interim, the EC was obligated to implement a tariff-quota import regime on the basis of historical licensing effective as of 1 July 2001 (para. C). While the EC notified both Understandings to the DSB as 'mutually agreed solutions', the US and Ecuador, in separate communications, stated that the Understanding did not constitute a mutually agreed solution pursuant to DSU Article 3.6; rather, the Understandings identified the *means* by which a long-standing dispute could be solved.[9]

On 14 November 2001, the Ministerial Conference adopted two waivers concerning the EC banana import regime. The Doha Article I Waiver (Article I Waiver), which includes an Annex on Bananas (Bananas Annex), granted ACP countries

---

6 The pertinent parts of the BFA are replicated below.

7 On 25 September 1997, the DSB adopted the AB Report as well as four separate Panel Reports in the original *EC–Bananas III* case (WT/DS27/AB/R, WT/DS27/R/ECU, WT/DS27/R/GTM, WT/DS27/R/HND, WT/DS27/R/MEX, WT/DS27/R/USA). The AB found that EC Regulation 404/93, from 1993 ('the Original Banana Import Regime') was inconsistent with WTO rules and was not justified by either the BFA or the Lomé Article I Waiver. The Original Bananas Import Regime constituted a violation of GATT Articles I:1, II, III:4, and XIII, as well as GATS Article XVII.

8 The Compliance Banana Regime foresaw a duty-free tariff quota of 857,000 mt for banana suppliers originating in ACP countries, a tariff quota of 2,553,000 mt with a tariff of €75/mt for all MFN suppliers, as well as a €200 tariff preference on out-of-quota imports for ACP countries. Predictably, the compliance Panel ('the first compliance panel') found that the Compliance Banana Import Regime taken by the EC to implement the DSB's rulings and recommendations were inconsistent with GATT Articles I and XIII, as well as GATS Articles II and XVII and made suggestions pursuant to DSU Article 19.1 how the EC could bring its measures into conformity. The Panel report was not appealed and was adopted on 6 May 1999.

9 AB Report, paras. 8, 207, 208.

preferential tariff access to the market of the EC.[10] The Doha Article XIII Waiver (Article XIII Waiver) concerned the EC's separate autonomous tariff quota of 750,000 mt for bananas of ACP origin and was intended to expire on 31 December 2005, thus covering the entire period until the entry into force of the EC's tariff-only regime on 1 January 2006, as promised in the Understanding on Bananas.

On 29 January 2001, the EC adopted yet another banana import regime, which shall be called the 'Interim Banana Import Regime'. This import regime was in place between 2001 and the end of 2005.[11] It is worthy of note that the EC's Interim Banana Regime was never challenged by any WTO Member.

In view of the enlargement of the EU, the EC informed the WTO of its intention to rebind its bananas tariff schedule under GATT Article XXVIII on 31 January 2005. Pursuant to the earlier agreement under the Bananas Annex attached to the Article I Waiver of 2001, a two-stage arbitration process set in, in which the arbitrator assessed whether the EC's rebinding proposal would result in at least maintaining total market access for MFN banana suppliers. Two consecutive arbitrations in August and October of 2005 rejected the EC's final proposal.[12]

On 1 January 2006, instead of enacting a tariff-only regime (as promised in the 2001 Understanding on Bananas), EC Regulation 1964/2005 entered into force, which established a tariff rate of €176/mt on all banana imports, as well as a special zero-tariff quota of 775,000 mt set aside for bananas of ACP origin. This is the measure at issue for the purposes of these proceedings. As a response, Ecuador, for the second time, requested the establishment of a compliance Panel pursuant to DSU Article 21.5. In its request, Ecuador claimed inconstancy of the EC Banana Import regime adopted by the EC, inter alia, under EC Regulation 1964/2005. The United States followed suit soon thereafter.[13]

---

10 The Bananas Annex set out a special two-stage arbitration process, in case the EC was planning on rebinding its tariff on bananas. Subject to the fulfillment of the rebinding requirements, it was agreed that the Article I Waiver applied until 31 December 2007, or until after the second rebinding arbitration was concluded and the 'new regime' had entered into force, whichever applied first.

11 Based on EC Regulations 216/2001 and 2587/2001 this Interim Banana Import Regime comprised a tariff quota 'A' of 2,200,000 mt for all suppliers at a tariff of 75€/mt for MFN suppliers and a zero tariff for ACP exporters; a tariff quota 'B' of 453,000 mt for MFN suppliers at 75 €/mt for MFN suppliers and a zero tariff for ACP; and a tariff quota 'C' of 750,000 mt reserved exclusively for ACP suppliers at a tariff rate of zero. The out-of-quota tariff gave a tariff preference of €300/mt to ACP countries.

12 The EC's final tariff modification proposal consisted of an MFN tariff rate for bananas of €187/mt and a 775,000 mt duty-free quota import of ACP bananas. The arbitrators concluded that the EC had failed to rectify the matter in accordance with the Annex on Bananas, which caused the Article I Waiver to legally expire on 1 January 2006 (see Annex on Bananas, fifth tiret; reproduced in footnote 481 of the AB Report).

13 It is noteworthy that this Bananas Import Regime only marginally differs from the Compliance Banana Regime of 1998 (cf. footnote 8 above). This was acknowledged by the AB in its Report (para. 352), when stating: 'We agree with the Panel that the main difference between the tariff quota regime examined by the first Ecuador Article 21.5 panel [the Compliance Banana Regime] and the EC Bananas Import Regime at issue in these proceedings is the level of the quantitative limit (857,700 versus 775,000 mt of duty-free imports) [footnote omitted]. However, that difference is of no relevance [for the questions at issue].'

While the compliance proceedings were underway, but before the issuance of the interim report in the US Panel, the EC adopted Council Regulation 1528/2007, as a latest reform in its long lists of banana import regimes. This 'Novel Banana Import Regime' repealed all earlier banana import regulations and eliminated the contentious preferential tariff-free quota of 775,000 mt for ACP countries, and thus finally instituted a pure tariff-only import regime.

2.2 Relevant documents

Three documents are particularly pertinent for understanding the background of this case. These are: (i) relevant parts of the EC Tariff Schedule annexed to the GATT; (ii) passages from the Banana Framework Agreement, which is annexed under 'Other terms and conditions' to the EC Tariff Schedule in column 7; and (iii) pertinent passages from the 2001 Understanding on Bananas that the EC concluded with the United States and Ecuador after having lost the Article 22.6 arbitration.

Part I, Section I-B (Tariff Quotas) of the European Communities' Schedule reads:

Description of product	Tariff item number(s)	Initial quota quantity and in-quota tariff rate	Final quota quantity and in-quota tariff rate	Implemen-tation period from/to	Initial negotiating right	Other terms and conditions
1	2	3	4	5	6	7
Fresh bananas, other than plantains	0803 00 12	2,200,000 t 75 ECU/t	2,200,000 t 75 ECU/t			As indicated in the Annex

The 'Annex' contains the text of the Bananas Framework Agreement, which reads in relevant parts:

1. The global basic tariff quota is fixed at 2,100,000 t for 1994 and at 2,200,000 t for 1995 and the following years, subject to any increase resulting from the enlargement of the Community.
2. This quota is divided up into specific quotas allocated to the following countries:

Country	Percentage of the global quota
Costa Rica	23.4
Colombia	21.0
Nicaragua	3.0
Venezuela	2.0
Dominican Republic and other ACP concerning non-traditional quantities	90.000 t.
Others	46.32 % (1994)–46 % (1995)

7. The in-quota tariff rate shall be 75 Ecus/tonne.

8. The agreed system will be operational by 1 October 1994 at the latest, without prejudice to any provisional or transitional measures to be examined for the year 1994.

9. This agreement shall apply until 31 December 2002. Full consultations with the Latin American suppliers that are GATT Members should start no later than in year 2001.

 The functioning of the agreement will be reviewed before the end of the third year, with full consultation of GATT Member Latin American suppliers.

10. This agreement will be incorporated into the Community's Uruguay Round Schedule.

11. This agreement represents a settlement of the dispute between Colombia, Costa Rica, Venezuela, Nicaragua and the Community on the Community's banana regime. The parties to this agreement will not pursue the adoption of the GATT panel report on this issue.

The two Understandings on Bananas, concluded pursuant to the original *Bananas III* dispute between the EC and Ecuador and US, respectively, provide in paras. B and C (Ecuador and United States) and G (Ecuador):

B. In accordance with Article 16(1) of Regulation No. (EEC) 404/93 (as amended by Regulation No. (EC) 216/2001), the European Communities (EC) will introduce a Tariff Only regime for imports of bananas no later than 1 January 2006 ...

C. In the interim, the EC will implement an import regime on the basis of historical licensing as follows:

 1. Effective 1 July 2001, the EC will implement an import regime on the basis of historical licensing as set out in Annex 1.

 2. Effective as soon as possible thereafter, subject to Council and European Parliament approval and to adoption of the Article XIII waiver referred to in paragraph F, the EC will implement an import regime on the basis of historical licensing as set out in Annex 2. The Commission will seek to obtain the implementation of such an import regime as soon as possible.

G. The EC and Ecuador consider that this Understanding constitutes a mutually agreed solution to the bananas dispute.

2.3 Arguments by the complainants and findings by the compliance Panel

Both Ecuador and the United States initiated Article 21.5 proceedings claiming continued WTO inconsistency of EC Regulation 1964/2005 and related measures (the Bananas Import Regime). Ecuador – for the second time – claimed that the EC had 'failed to implement the rulings and recommendations of the DSB in the original dispute and continues to be in breach of its obligations as a WTO Member'. In particular, Ecuador requested that the Panel find that the EC measures are inconsistent with: (i) GATT Article I, 'because the European Communities applies different and more favourable duties to bananas originating in ACP countries than those applied to bananas originating in Ecuador and most or all other WTO members'; (ii) GATT Article II, 'because the European Communities applies a tariff (currently €176/mt) on the import of bananas originating in Ecuador (and other WTO Members) that is above the EC bound rate of duty under Article II, which is €75/mt'; and (iii) GATT Articles XIII:1 and 2, 'because the European Communities continues to provide a tariff rate quota system reserved exclusively for bananas of ACP origin, while Ecuador is denied any share of the preferential quota, let alone the share to which it is entitled under Article XIII'.[14]

The US also claimed that the EC had 'failed to implement the rulings and recommendations of the DSB in the original dispute and continues to be in breach of its obligations as a WTO Member'. Specifically, the United States requested that the Panel find that the EC measures are inconsistent with: (i) GATT Article I, 'because the European Communities applies a zero tariff rate to imports of bananas originating in ACP countries in a quantity up to 775,000 mt, but does not accord the same duty-free treatment to imports of bananas originating in all other WTO Members'; and (ii) GATT Articles XIII:1 and 2, 'because the European Communities reserves the 775,000 mt zero-duty tariff quota for imports of bananas originating in ACP countries and provides no access to this preferential tariff quota to imports of bananas originating in non-ACP substantial or non-substantial supplying countries'.[15]

The compliance Panel rejected various procedural arguments and preliminary issues brought forth by the EC and found violations of GATT Articles I, II, and XIII. It recommended that the DSB request the EC to bring its inconsistent measures into conformity with its obligations under the GATT 1994.[16]

3. Claims on appeal, findings of the AB, and some observations

In this section, we summarize the claims on appeal and the AB's findings and offer a few observations. We start with procedural issues (subsection 3.1) and then discuss substantive questions before the AB (subsection 3.2).

3.1 *Procedural issues*

3.1.1 *Article 9.3 DSU and Rule 20(2)(d)(i) of AB Working Procedures*

Two preliminary procedural issues were raised on appeal and both were rejected by the AB. The EC alleged that the Panel acted inconsistently with DSU Article 9.3 by failing to harmonize the timetables of the proceedings in the Ecuador and

---

14 Compliance Panel Report, *EC–Bananas III* (*Ecuador*) (*21.5, Second Recourse*), para. 3.1.
15 Compliance Panel Report, *EC–Bananas III* (*United States*) (*21.5, Second Recourse*), para. 3.1.
16 Compliance Panel Report, *EC–Bananas III* (*Ecuador/United States*) (*21.5, Second Recourse*), paras. 8.1–8.5.

US cases. The EC requested that the Panel's failure to harmonize the timetables 'be reversed'.[17] The United States, on the other hand, as an appellee, contended that the EC's Notice of Appeal did not satisfy the requirements of Rule 20(2)(d)(i) of AB Working Procedures because the EC allegedly had failed to identify just which findings it deemed to be erroneous because it failed to mention the paragraph numbers of the US Panel Report to which the issues appealed related. The US requested that the AB dismiss the EC's appeal entirely.

In both cases, the AB continued its practice of rejecting procedural claims that are not supported by a showing of actual denial of due process. In the case of the EC's Article 9.3 claim, the AB held that 'the mere possibility that due process rights of the European Communities could have been adversely affected by the Panel's decision to maintain separate timetables in these proceedings is not sufficient to establish that the due process rights of the European Communities have indeed been compromised'.[18] Similarly, in the United States's appeal, the AB ruled that 'the deficiencies in the European Communities' Notice of Appeal do not lead to dismissal of the European Communities' appeal', since even the US in the oral hearing had acknowledged that it had not been 'prejudiced by the absence of paragraph numbers'.[19]

3.1.2   The legal effect of the Understandings on Bananas and the use of estoppel in the WTO

The AB affirmed, for different reasons, the Panel's rejection of the EC's argument that the legal effect of the Understandings on Bananas was to preclude the complainants from initiating compliance proceedings. The dispute centered on the question whether the Understandings amounted to a 'solution mutually acceptable to the parties to the dispute and consistent with the covered agreements' within the meaning of Article 3.7 of the DSU, and, if so, whether such agreed solution could preclude the complainants from bringing their claims under Article 21.5 DSU.

The Panel had found that the complainants could be barred from initiating compliance proceedings only if the Understandings constituted a 'positive solution and effective settlement of the dispute'. The AB disagreed with this legal test, but agreed with the Panel that the complainants were not barred from initiating compliance review.

Nothing in Article 3.7, the AB noted, 'establishes a condition under which a party would be prevented from initiating compliance proceedings'.[20] Members do not waive recourse to Article 21.5 review simply by entering into a mutually agreed solution absent 'a clear indication in the agreement between the parties of a relinquishment of the right to have recourse to Article 21.5'.[21]

---

17 AB Report, para. 30.
18 AB Report, para. 197.
19 AB Report, para. 283.
20 AB Report, para. 211.
21 AB Report, para. 212.

In the course of its analysis, the AB expressed its disagreement with two inter-mediate conclusions of the Panel. The first was the Panel's reasoning that the conclusion of the Understandings *after* adoption of the original rulings and rec-ommendations by the DSB was relevant to the question whether complainants were barred from bringing 21.5 review proceedings. 'We see nothing in Article 3.7 or elsewhere in the DSU ... that would preclude recourse to Article 21.5 proceed-ings after the adoption of recommendations and rulings by the DSB', the AB said.[22] It went on to note that 'the DSU itself clearly envisages the possibility of entering into mutually agreed solutions after recommendations and rulings are made by the DSB'.[23] In addition, the AB disagreed with the Panel's reliance on ostensibly conflicting statements as to the legal nature of the Understandings made at the DSB after they were signed.[24] Such statements, the AB said, may be taken into account where the interpretation of a document is not clear, but they have limited relevance when documents are unambiguous. '[E]x *post* communications of the parties concerning the Understandings have, at best, slight evidentiary value.'[25]

While the AB used several paragraphs[26] to discuss the text of the two Understandings, its main point was that, in order for a party to be barred from recourse to Article 21.5, the mutually agreed solution must explicitly state that the complainant relinquishes that right.[27] Thus, even though the Understanding in-volving Ecuador declared in paragraph G that '[t]he EC and Ecuador consider that this Understanding constitutes a mutually agreed solution to the banana dispute', this statement did not entail a waiver of its Article 21.5 review rights by Ecuador.[28]

Finally, the AB agreed with the EC that the Panel had erred in its interpretation and application of the 'good faith' requirement of Article 3.10 DSU, but upheld the Panel's conclusion that Ecuador and the US had acted in good faith in bringing the review proceeding. According to the AB, its Report in *US–Offset Act (Byrd Amendment)* was misread by the Panel.[29] In *US–Byrd*, the AB noted, it had ad-dressed the principle of good faith as it relates to a substantive provision. In *Bananas III*, the case before it now, on the other hand, the Panel and the AB had to consider the principle as a procedural impediment for a Member to initiate review proceedings.[30]

In the course of its discussion on this point, the AB stated that, while the EC did not use the term, it was in fact advancing an *estoppel* argument.[31] It quoted from its

22 AB Report, para. 215.
23 Ibid.
24 See footnote 9 and accompanying text.
25 AB Report, para. 216.
26 AB Report, paras. 217–222.
27 AB Report, para. 221.
28 Ibid.
29 AB Report, para. 227.
30 Ibid.
31 Ibid.

Report in *EC–Export Subsidies on Sugar*,[32] that 'even assuming *arguendo* that the principle of estoppel could apply in the WTO, its application would fall within these narrow parameters set out in the DSU'.[33] The 'narrow parameters' referred to are those of DSU Article 3.10 regarding good faith in deciding to have recourse to dispute settlement.

The estoppel allegations in both *EC–Sugar* and *Bananas III* involved the question of whether a complaining Member should be barred from proceeding with its complaint. However, in the context of working procedures for a dispute-settlement proceeding, the two Panels and the AB have employed the estoppel principle, but – as with the EC in *Bananas III* – without using the term.[34] Thus, for example, in *US–Steel Plate*, the Panel denied India the right to pursue a claim that it had explicitly abandoned in its first written submission.[35] Similarly, in *Mexico–Corn Syrup (Article 21.5 – US)*, the AB held that failure to pursue an objection to the absence of consultations before the DSB prevents a Member from arguing that the Panel was improperly established. 'A Member that fails to raise its objections in a timely manner, notwithstanding one or more opportunities to do so, may be deemed to have waived its right to have a panel consider such objections.'[36] Even though words such as 'waiver' are used instead of 'estoppel', decisions of this kind amount to estoppel within the conduct of a case. This, of course, is a very different matter from holding that a Member is estopped from even initiating a proceeding in the first place.

3.1.3 'Repeal' of the challenged measures

In the case of the United States's Report, the EC argued that the Panel was wrong in making findings with respect to a measure that had ceased to exist.[37] The EC contended that the Panel had acted inconsistently with its obligation under Articles 3.4 and 3.7 of the DSU, which instruct panels to secure a positive solution to the dispute. In addition, the EC alleged that the Panel had provided a 'concealed' recommendation by stating that the original DSB recommendations and rulings 'remained operative'.[38]

With respect to the Panel having made *findings* on an expired measure, the AB cited its earlier ruling in *US–Upland Cotton*, where it had held that 'whether or not a measure is still in force is not dispositive of whether that measure is currently

---

32 Appellate Body Report, *European Communities – Export Subsidies on Sugar*, WT/DS265/AB/R, WT/DS266/AB/R, WT/DS283/AB/R, adopted 19 May 2005.

33 AB Report, para. 227, quoting *EC–Export Subsidies on Sugar*, para. 312.

34 See Palmeter and Mavroidis (2004: 43–45, 78).

35 DS206/R, 29 July 2002, para. 7.29.

36 AB Report, *Mexico–Corn Syrup* (WT/DS132/AB/RW), at para. 50.

37 The reader is reminded that in 2007, the EC enacted the 'Novel Bananas Import Regime' (EC Regulation 1528/2007) which replaced the zero-percent tariff quota afforded exclusively to ACP countries of the Bananas Import Regime under EC Regulation 1964/2005.

38 AB Report, paras. 45–48.

affecting the operation of any covered agreement'.[39] The AB reminded that the present case is different from *US–Upland Cotton* in that the measure on appeal in these proceedings was still in full force at the time the Panel was established and expired only towards the end of the Panel proceedings.[40] With respect to the EC's allegation that the Panel had made 'concealed' *recommendations*, the AB stated that it does 'not believe that the Panel made a specific recommendation', reminding that the Panel in its Report in the US 21.5 challenge (at para. 8.13) had stated that it '*makes no new recommendation*' and that the 'original DSB recommendations and rulings in this dispute remain operative'.[41] Consequently, the AB deemed it within the discretion of a panel to decide how it takes into account subsequent modifications or a repeal of the measures at issue.

The authors of this commentary believe that the AB was right in upholding Panel findings on the expired measure. If repealed policies could not be decided upon by WTO dispute panels, then Members would have an easy time engaging in strategic gamesmanship by entering into a repeal/amendment strategy, where the amended measure nominally replaces its ancestor yet shares most of its characteristics. A Member would never be able to challenge the measure at issue – simply because the respondent would make sure that it is not 'at issue' anymore, thanks to repeal and amendment. A decision with respect to an expired measure is also efficient, since it makes consecutive 'measures taken to comply' vulnerable in later 21.5 proceedings if it is too close to the original measure.

3.1.4   Legal effect of Panel suggestions and the relationship of Articles 19.1 and 21.5 of the DSU

In the Ecuador case, the EC requested that the AB dismiss Ecuador's claims under Article XIII, because the latter's 'claims are in reality a challenge on the measures *suggested* by the [first Ecuador Article 21.5] Panel, rather than on the measures *actually taken* by the European Communities'.[42] The EC maintained that, once a Panel or AB report, containing suggestions made pursuant to Article 19.1 DSU, has been adopted, 'the consistency of the *measures suggested* by the original panel with the covered agreement cannot be challenged by the complaining party before an Article 21.5 panel', because parties are obliged to 'unconditionally accept' the DSB's recommendations, rulings, and suggestions, by virtue of Article 17.14 read in combination with Article 16.4 DSU.[43] According to the EU, the compliance Panel should have first checked if the challenged measures were indeed the measures suggested by the original panel. And if the EC has effectively implemented any of the suggestions made by the first compliance Panel, the Panel

---

39 AB Report, para. 267.
40 AB Report, para. 269.
41 AB Report, paras. 272, 273.
42 AB Report, para. 317, emphasis in original.
43 AB Report, para. 317, emphasis in original.

should rule 'without any further analysis' that these measures are consistent with the covered agreements.

The AB assessed the legal nature of the Panel or AB suggestions pursuant to Article 19.1 DSU and found that suggestions, while potentially providing useful guidance, following a Panel suggestion does not guarantee substantive compliance with the rulings and recommendations by the DSB. Interpreting the language of Articles 19.1 and 21.5 of the DSU, the AB ruled that suggestions are not themselves the subject of review and a compliance Panel is limited to the assessment of the existence or consistency with the covered agreements of the *measures* taken to comply with the rulings and recommendations, but not of previous suggestions made. Hence, the AB upheld the Panel's finding that the adoption by a Member of a measure that directly implements a suggestion made by a Panel pursuant to Article 19.1 DSU does not prevent a complaining party from challenging the consistency of that measure with the covered agreements in an Article 21.5 proceeding.

Article 19.1 DSU authorizes Panels and the AB to 'suggest ways in which the Member concerned' may come into compliance. This rarely used authority was utilized by the first Article 21.5 Panel requested by Ecuador.[44] Based on this suggestion, the EC argued to the AB that Ecuador's claim under Article XIII GATT should be dismissed. According to the EC, the WTO consistency of measures suggested by a Panel cannot be challenged in a compliance review. The EC reasoned that adoption of reports under Articles 16.4 and 17.14 of the DSU covers all the recommendations and rulings in the report, including any suggestions as to compliance.[45]

The EC's argument was rejected by the AB. Article 19.1 DSU, it noted, neither directly addresses the legal status of suggestions, nor are they subject to review.[46] However, '"measures taken to comply *with the recommendations and rulings*", but not "measures taken to comply *with suggestions*"' are subject to Article 21.5 review, regardless of whether those measures were suggested.[47] 'The adoption of a panel or Appellate Body report by the DSB makes the recommendations and rulings therein binding upon the parties', the AB held. But 'adoption by the DSB does not make suggestions for implementation binding upon the parties'.[48] 'Even if the measure taken to comply conformed to a suggestion made, this would not bar [a Member] from bringing Article 21.5 proceedings to determine whether the implementing measure achieves full compliance with the DSB recommendations and rulings.'[49] Further, the Appellate Body noted that 'the fact that a Member has

---

44 Compliance Panel Report *EC–Bananas (Ecuador) (21.5, First Recourse)*, paras. 6.154–6.159.
45 AB Report, para. 317.
46 AB Report, para. 322.
47 Ibid. (emphasis added).
48 AB Report, para. 323.
49 AB Report, para. 324.

chosen to follow a suggestion *does not* create a presumption of compliance in Article 21.5 proceedings'.[50]

We believe the AB's reasoning is sound. Full compliance with DSB rulings cannot simply be presumed just because the respondent declares that its measure taken to comply conforms to the Panel's suggestions under Article 19.1 DSU.[51] This would unduly change the nature of the obligation from one of complying with the rulings and recommendations, based on certain WTO provision(s) to implementing compliance suggestions. Also, the parties see compliance suggestions for the first time when they receive the Panel's report. They have no opportunity to address – much less to challenge – a proposed suggestion. Yet, a suggestion that might seem to result in compliance may, upon further examination, fail to do so.[52] A complaining Member should not be denied 'its day in court' to challenge directly the question of whether a measure taken to comply in fact does so, whether or not that measure has been suggested.

Petros Mavroidis suggests that, irrespective of the legal force of a suggestion, a WTO Member that has accepted a suggestion should be presumed to be in compliance.[53] Provided this is a rebuttable presumption, we would agree. But such a presumption would seem to be of little, if any, benefit to the Member concerned, since a complaining Member challenging a measure taken to comply effectively already has the burden of proving non-compliance in any event. True, if a compliance Panel is composed of the same individuals who made the suggestion, a complaining Member might, as a practical matter, face an uphill challenge. At the AB stage, the complaining Member might face an even more difficult challenge because there is no further appeal. This suggests that the AB has been wise not to make suggestions, in part because of its short timetables, when it has not had the opportunity to benefit from briefings and arguments from the parties on any particular suggestion.

An irrebuttable presumption would deny complaining Members a fair opportunity to challenge the substance of a measure taken to comply that follows a suggestion and clearly does not seem to be justified by the terms of Article 19.1.

---

50 AB Report, para. 325 (emphasis added).

51 AB Report, para. 323.

52 As an example, the authors of this commentary are not certain whether the suggestions of the Article 21.5 Panel were entirely GATT conforming. The Panel suggested that the EC could bring its measures into conformity by, inter alia, 'maintaining its bound and autonomous MFN tariff quotas ... by allocating ... shares by agreement with all substantive suppliers consistently with Article XIII:2 of the GATT 1994. The MFN tariff quota could be combined with ... a preferential tariff quota for ACP countries, provided a waiver from Article XIII of the GATT 1994 was obtained' (Panel Report, *EC–Bananas III (Article 21.5 – Ecuador)*, paras. 6.156–6.158). However, such a tariff preference to ACP countries seems to nevertheless violate Article I:1 of the GATT.

53 See the contribution of Mavroidis in this volume. See also Mavroidis (2007: 416) and Mavroidis (2000).

3.1.5   Article 3.8 DSU and nullification or impairment suffered by the US and Ecuador

As a final procedural issue, the EC requested that the AB reverse the Panel's legal interpretations that the ACP preference in the Banana Import Regime had caused nullification or impairment (NoI) to Ecuador or the United States. In the case of Ecuador, the EC argued that the quantity limitation on ACP imports entering at zero-tariff was actually a 'benefit' to Ecuador, because it put a 'cap' on the preferential treatment of ACP countries and consequently limited the amount of duty-free ACP banana imports. In addition, the EC argued that the Panel had failed to explain how the measure at issue had caused NoI *over and above* that already found under GATT Article I (a finding that the EC had not appealed). According to the EC, the Panel engaged in 'double counting' of NoI by adding to the negative effects caused by the ACP preference under Article I GATT the 'limitation of these negative effects through the quantity limit'.[54]

The AB dismissed the EC's claims, stating that both infringements of Article I and Article XIII GATT trigger the presumption of NoI. Nullification or impairment resulting from inconsistencies with Articles I and XIII GATT may thereby 'coincide' or 'overlap'.[55] However, such coincidence and overlap is only relevant to the calculation of the total level of NoI suffered for the purposes of an arbitration pursuant to DSU Article 22.6. According to the AB, it is not for the AB to decide on the extent of such overlap, and a demonstration by the EC that NoI may overlap is not sufficient to rebut the presumption in Article 3.8 DSU that any of these infringements constitutes a *prima facie* case of NoI.

In the case of the United States, the EC claimed that the Panel had confused the notion of 'nullification or impairment' with that of 'legal standing' in that the US had never been deprived of any competitive opportunities to export bananas. The EC pointed out that the US had always been a net importer of bananas and had never exported bananas to any country in the world, let alone the EU.

The AB agreed with the EU that 'standing' is a broader concept than NoI, but concluded that the Panel did not confuse those two issues. It ruled that it was insufficient for the EC to allege that the Panel had failed to explain the effect on the US internal market, noting that the burden of rebutting the presumption resides with the EC. Citing *US–Superfund*, the AB supported the Panel's finding that 'the arguments advanced by the European Communities on the alleged lack of nullification or impairment have not rendered irrelevant the considerations made by the panel and by the Appellate Body in the course of the original proceedings, regarding the actual and potential trade interests of the United States in this dispute'. The AB agreed with the earlier panels that the US is a producer of bananas and that a potential export interest by the United States thus cannot be excluded. It also held that 'the internal market of the United States for bananas could be affected by

54 AB Report, para. 77.
55 AB Report, para. 360.

the EC bananas regime and by its effects on world supplies and world prices of bananas'.[56]

This conclusion is consistent with earlier jurisprudence of both the AB and Panels. In the initial *Bananas III* proceedings, for example, both the original panel and the AB had found that it is not necessary for a Member to have a 'legal interest' as a prerequisite to initiating dispute settlement.[57] The Panel in *Korea–Dairy* interpreted 'legal interest' to mean 'economic interest' and concluded that 'under the DSU there is no requirement that parties have an economic interest'.[58]

We end this section with a general observation from the AB's examination of procedural issues: at various instances, the AB digressed and examined issues that were not pertinent for reaching its conclusions.[59] The question whether a tribunal's ruling should be narrowly focused on the facts of the case before it, or whether it should be broader than the minimum necessary to decide the case, has long been a matter of jurisprudential dispute. There are advantages and disadvantages to each approach.

A judicially modest, narrow ruling has the advantage of not anticipating problems that have not yet arisen and not foreclosing argument that might arise when those problems are squarely presented. It allows fine distinctions to be drawn between different factual situations, and reduces risk of unintended and unanticipated consequences. On the other hand, it can lead to uncertainty by leaving parties in the dark as to how a tribunal might rule in future cases with slightly different factual situations. It therefore can result in further, extended, litigation to settle outstanding questions.

A broad ruling, on the other hand, has the advantage of providing guidance to interested parties, thus reducing the need for further litigation to resolve outstanding questions. But it risks making unanticipated errors as the tribunal moves into areas that were not thoroughly aired during the course of the dispute.

In *Bananas III*, the AB adopted both approaches. When considering whether the Understanding on Bananas was a 'measure taken to comply', the AB noted that 'strictly speaking, we would not be required to assess whether the EC Bananas Import Regime fell within the scope of Article 21.5 because of a "particularly close relationship" to the declared measure taken to comply'.[60] However, because the Panel made findings on this question, and because the parties argued it before the AB, the AB addressed the question and made additional findings.[61]

---

56 AB Report paras. 458 and 466.

57 Original Panel Report *EC–Bananas III*, para. 7.49 and original Appellate Body Report, para. 132, note 64.

58 Panel Report, *Korea – Definitive Safeguard Measure on Imports of Certain Dairy Products*, as modified by the Appellate Body, WT/DS98/AB/R, para. 7.13.

59 For example, AB Report at paras. 213–216, 252–255.

60 AB Report, para. 252.

61 Ibid.

At a later point in its opinion, discussed above, the AB found that it did not need to decide whether nullification and impairment resulting from an inconsistency in quota allocation under Article XIII may coincide or overlap with that resulting from an inconsistency of a tariff preference with Article I:1.[62]

The AB was probably correct in both instances. Rather than adopt an iron-clad rule, it seems wiser to approach this question as the AB did, with an eye to the specific situation it faces. When dealing with a question that had been dealt with by the Panel and argued by the parties on appeal, it went ahead and offered its views on the issue. But when dealing with an issue implicating aspects of Article I, Article XIII, and tariff preferences that it did not have to decide, it wisely took a narrow, cautious approach.

3.2   Substantive issues

3.2.1   Non-discriminatory administration of tariff quotas under Article XIII

On substance, the EC appealed the Panel's findings that the duty-free tariff quota reserved for ACP banana imports falls within the scope of Article XIII GATT and was inconsistent with Articles XIII:1, XIII:2, and XIII:2(d), which regulate the non-discriminatory application of quantitative restrictions and tariff quotas.

The EC essentially brought forth three arguments, all of which the AB rejected.

The first argument the EC made was that Article XIII does not apply at all in the case of tariff quotas, since Article I GATT prevailed over Article XIII in case of an overlap of the two provisions. The EC claimed that the Panel had developed a flawed theory pursuant to which a lower tariff offered to one Member automatically becomes a quantitative restriction on all other Members as soon as it was accompanied by a quantitative cap. According to the EC, such an interpretation would deprive the MFN principle of Article I:1 GATT of any value and would render WTO-inconsistent limitations on trade preferences offered by developed countries to developing countries under the 'Enabling Clause'.

In response to the EC's claim, the AB assessed the relationship between Articles I and XIII GATT. According to the AB, tariff quotas thus must comply with both Articles I:1 and XIII. This protects Members against differential in-quota duties (thanks to Article I GATT), against discriminatory access to quota shares (Article XIII:1), and against discriminatory administration of quota allocation (Article XIII:2). In the absence of Article XIII, Article I would not provide specific guidance on how to administer tariff quotas in a non-discriminatory fashion in the allocation of quota shares. Hence, the AB determined that with respect to tariff quotas the application of Article I does not prejudge the application of Article XIII.

As its second argument, the EC challenged the applicability of Article XIII:1 because of the identity of the party affected by the 'restriction' in place. According to the EU, the Panel had misinterpreted the notion of 'quantitative restriction'

---

62 AB Report, para. 361.

contained in Article XIII:1 because the limitation on the tariff preference for ACP suppliers did not constitute a restriction *imposed on the imports of the* '*aggrieved Member*' (i.e. on imports originating in the complainants' territory), but on imports from third countries (namely the ACP countries). As a consequence, the EC contended that there was 'no basis that would allow an examination of whether "similar" quantitative restrictions are also imposed on all other countries'.[63]

In addressing this question, the AB read Article XIII:1 with reference to a tariff quota and stated: 'Article XIII:1 is rendered thus: no *tariff quota* shall be applied by a Member on the importation of any product ... of any other Member, unless the importation of the like product of all third countries is similarly made subject to the *tariff quota*.' Taking a broad interpretation of the term 'restriction', the AB ruled that imports of like products of all third countries must have access to, and be given an opportunity for, participation.[64] Applying Article XIII:1 to the facts of the case, the AB ruled that since the zero-tariff quota reserved for ACP countries plainly excluded non-ACP countries, the tariff quota did not equally apply to, or similarly restrict imports of, like products from MFN countries, thus offending the principle of access to, and participation in, a tariff quota enshrined in Article XIII:1.[65]

The third argument brought by the EU was that Article XIII:2 on non-discriminatory distribution of tariff quotas did not apply to the EC import regime *vis-à-vis* Ecuador and the US, because both countries were not even subject to the Banana Import Regime in question. Since the contentious EC tariff quota only concerned imports from ACP countries, imports from the US and Ecuador were only subject to a simple tariff – an issue that should be dealt with under Article I of the GATT.

The AB explained that Article XIII:2 regulates the distribution of tariff quotas among Members. It noted that 'the chapeau of Article XIII:2 requires that the tariff quota be distributed so as to serve the aim of a distribution of trade approaching as closely as possible the shares that various Members may be expected to obtain in the absence of the tariff quota'.[66] The AB continued that Article XIII:2(d) on historical allocation of quota shares is a permissive safe haven: compliance with the requirements of Article XIII:2(d) is presumed to lead to a distribution of trade as foreseen in the chapeau of Article XIII:2. Examining the EU Banana Import Regime under these provisions, the AB stated that ACP preference failed to meet the requirements regarding the distribution and allocation of shares

---

63 AB Report, para. 70.

64 AB Report, para. 337 (emphases added). On this issue, the AB disagreed with a particular interpretation of the term 'restriction' in Article XIII:1 by the Panel as '[a]ny benefit accorded to fresh bananas of only some Members presumably affect[ing] the competitive opportunities of like bananas imported from other Members', stating that such overly broad interpretation would mean that even a simple tariff preference would be inconsistent with Article XIII (ibid., para. 346).

65 AB Report, para. 338.

66 Ibid.

in Article XIII:2. It noted that the exclusion of non-ACP suppliers from the tariff quota is not aimed 'at a distribution of trade ... approaching as closely as possible the shares which the various Members might be expected to obtain in the absence of restrictions', as required by Article XIII:2. It further ruled that 'the exclusion of non-ACP suppliers [does not] respect the "safe harbour" allocation requirements in Article XIII:2(d) based upon the representative proportions of Members having a substantial interest in the supply of bananas to the European Communities'.[67]

The authors of this paper have four brief comments on the AB's examination of Article XIII GATT. First, the AB was right in arguing that tariff quotas, being quotas and tariffs at the same time, must comply with the requirements of Article I:1, as well as with the non-discrimination obligation of Article XIII. Only if these provisions act in concert can abusive tariff quotas be effectively avoided: Article XIII:1 safeguards equal access to, or participation in, a certain tariff-quota regime. Once all MFN countries have equal access to a tariff quota, equal in-quota treatment must be ensured. This consists of uniform in-quota tariffs, and of equitable quota distribution among exporting countries. Article I:1 GATT safeguards the former; Article XIII:2 the latter. Hence, Articles I and XIII apply to different elements of an import measure.

Second, we believe that the AB was right in interpreting the non-discrimination tenet for quota allocation as a most-favored nation (MFN) treatment principle.[68] In the context of tariff quotas, non-discrimination could theoretically be interpreted as: (i) granting equitable shares to all (current and potential) exporters; (ii) allotting the global quota in proportion to current suppliers; (iii) first-come, first-served regime of quota filling; or (iv) as an MFN regime according to the free-trade counterfactual (see Skully, 2001).[69] However, we believe that only the MFN interpretation can satisfy the free-trade counterfactual enshrined in the chapeau of Article XIII:2, which states that '[i]n applying import restrictions ... contracting parties shall aim at a distribution of trade in such product approaching *as closely as possible* the shares which the various contracting parties might be expected to obtain *in the absence of such restrictions*'. Also, the language used in the Agreement on Safeguards, particularly in Article 5.2 on the application of

---

67 It elaborated: 'Allocating the entire tariff quota exclusively to ACP countries, and reserving no shares to non-ACP suppliers, cannot be considered to be based on the respective shares of ACP and non-ACP supplier countries in the European Communities' banana market' (ibid.).

68 'Article XIII adapts the MFN-treatment principle to specific types of measures, that is, quantitative restrictions, and, by virtue of Article XIII:5, tariff quotas' (AB Report, para. 342). 'Article XIII ensures that a Member applying a restriction or prohibition does not discriminate among *all other* Members' (ibid., para. 343). Per contra, see the comment to this paper by Prof. P. C. Mavroidis in this volume. The author points out that the position of Article XIII within the GATT may hint at the fact that it, just as Article XI on quantitative restrictions, was meant to be an exception to the MFN principle enshrined in Article I GATT.

69 As Hudec (1997: 178) reports, those different positions on the interpretations of non-discriminatory allocation of quantitative restrictions were prevalent already in the 1930s, when the League of Nations-sponsored World Economic Conferences were being held.

safeguard measures, is nearly identical to certain passages in Article XIII. As many authors have argued (e.g., Jackson, 1997), the Agreement on Safeguards mandates MFN treatment of all exporters.[70] Finally, if the wording of Article XIII was meant to be an explicit departure from the fundamental WTO (and economic) principle of non-discrimination among a Member's trading partners, the founding fathers of the WTO should have made such deviation more explicit. However, nothing in the preparatory work of the WTO is suggestive of that (Hudec, 1997).

Our third comment is that despite this *de jure* MFN obligation for quota allocation in Article XIII:2, Article XIII:2(d) allows for *de facto* discrimination of certain suppliers and therefore is in striking contrast to the principles laid out in the chapeau of Article XIII:2. From an economic perspective we have to state: an alleged MFN tenet under the chapeau of Article XIII:2 cannot be reconciled with the 'safe haven' of historical quota allocation of Article XIII:2(d). This will be shown in more detail below (Section 4.1.3).

Finally, the AB was correct in rebutting the EC's peculiar notion of 'discriminatory' vs. 'preferential' quantitative restrictions (QR), which implies that an import regime falls under the purview of Article XIII, only if the complainant is a direct subject of a QR and therefore 'aggrieved'. From a political-economic perspective, such view is baseless. Given that imports under any QR are a zero-sum game among competing exporters, it is obvious that a 'preferential' QR to one set of countries – here ACP suppliers – necessarily goes to the detriment of all other countries – here MFN suppliers. Members excluded from a preferential QR necessarily are 'restricted' and therefore suffer losses relative to a situation without QR.

3.2.2 Doha Article I Waiver as 'subsequent agreement'

The EC Banana Import Regime provided for an MFN tariff of €176/mt on all banana imports that did not fall under the ACP tariff quota of 775,000 mt at zero tariff. In the compliance proceedings, Ecuador had requested the Panel to find WTO-inconsistency with that provision. According to Ecuador, this provision was inconsistent with the EC's tariff schedule, that is its obligations under Article II GATT, which contained an MFN tariff quota of 2.2 million mt with an in-quota tariff rate of only €75/mt. The compliance Panel had found that while the MFN tariff quota and the accompanying tariff rate of €75 had undeniably expired on 31 December 2002 (under the terms of paragraph 9 of the Banana Framework Agreement; see above), the tariff quota nevertheless had been extended through 'common intention' of all WTO Members. According to the Panel, such common intension had manifested itself in the Article I Waiver. The Panel had held that the Article I Waiver modified the Schedule of the EC, and therefore was to be considered a 'subsequent agreement regarding the *interpretation* of the original treaty'

---

70 See Article 2.2 of the Safeguards Agreement (SGA): 'Safeguard measures shall be applied to a product being imported *irrespective of its source*' (emphasis added), but see Mavroidis (2007: 375).

as mentioned in Article 31(3)(a) of the Vienna Convention on the Law of Treaties (Vienna Convention).[71]

On appeal, the EC requested the AB to reverse this finding. It claimed that the Panel erred in determining that the Doha Article I Waiver was a subsequent agreement on the interpretation of the EC Tariff Schedule. The EC brought forth two arguments. First, even by the Panel's own standards, the Waiver did not *interpret*, but *modify* the EC Schedule by extending the tariff-quota concession beyond 31 December 2002. In addition, the Waiver did not contain any such 'common intent'.[72]

In examining this issue, the AB set off with a general discussion on the 'roles and functions' of four basic methods that Members may use to interpret or modify WTO law: (i) waivers (Article IX:3 of the WTO Agreement); (ii) multilateral interpretations (Article IX:2); (iii) multilateral amendments (Article XI); (iv) tariff renegotiations (Article XXVIII GATT).

The AB found that waivers are specific and exceptional instruments. Their purpose is not to modify existing provisions or to create new law or add or amend obligations under a covered agreement, but to relieve certain WTO Members from obligations temporarily, subject to very tight timelines and notification requirements. Thus, the AB concluded that the Panel had erred in finding that the Article I Waiver was a subsequent agreement to the EC schedule, especially because the WTO has in stock a particular instrument dealing with tariff modification in the form of Article XXVIII.

Although it was not necessary to do so, the AB went on to examine whether there really existed a 'common intent' among parties in extending the tariff-quota concession in the EC schedule by means of the Doha Waiver.[73] The AB did not see how the language of the Article I Waiver had expressly extended the MFN tariff quota of 2.2 million mt, the in-quota tariff rate of €75/mt, or the terms of the BFA. It noted that the 'Doha Article I Waiver is concerned with the zero-duty preference for ACP suppliers, not with the tariff quota concession for MFN suppliers specified in the European Communities' Schedule'.[74] On this basis, the AB reversed the Panel's findings that the Doha Article I Waiver constituted a subsequent agreement reflecting the common intention of WTO Members that the EC tariff-quota

71 The Panel held that the Doha Article I Waiver was an agreement reached between the same parties that agreed to incorporate the BFA as an annex to the EC Schedule of Concessions; that it was subsequent to the BFA; and that the Waiver, just like the BFA, dealt with, inter alia, the EC's WTO market-access commitments relating to bananas. In addition, the Panel concluded that the common intention of WTO Members as reflected in the text of the Article I Waiver was the following: pending the Article XXVIII GATT negotiations on the rebinding of the EC banana tariff, the EC's MFN tariff-quota concession continues to constitute the EC's bound commitments regarding bananas (AB Report, paras. 376–377).

72 AB Report, para. 386.

73 Such examination does not strike us as necessary, since the AB found the Doha Article I waiver not to be a subsequent agreement. Hence, the content of the Doha I waiver is irrelevant for this dispute.

74 AB Report, paras. 396–403.

concession would continue to constitute its scheduled commitments regarding bananas, pending the completion of the Article XXVIII negotiations.

We believe that the AB was right in finding that the Doha Article I Waiver was not a subsequent agreement on the interpretation of treaty provisions in the sense of Article 31(3) of the Vienna Convention. An extension of an MFN tariff quota clearly constitutes a temporary modification of the EC's Schedule of Concessions, and therewith by virtue of Article II:7 GATT, a modification of the covered agreements. However, this episode in *Bananas III* unveils a more systemic problem of the WTO, namely that temporary opt-out mechanisms are missing in the WTO (Schropp, 2009a).

The WTO is an incomplete contract among sovereign countries, where previously unforeseen contingencies or 'shocks' occur with a high probability (Horn *et al.*, 2009; Maggi and Staiger, 2008). Unforeseen shocks can give rise to 'regret contingencies' (Goetz and Scott, 1981), and all parties to the contract could benefit from letting the affected party temporarily 'escape', or 'opt out' of, the agreement, subject to an adequate compensation payment. The WTO knows several *de jure* emergency escape mechanisms, such as GATT Articles XVIII, XIX, and XX. However, enactment of those emergency relief mechanisms is exacerbated by significant levels of conditionality, which greatly reduces their usability.[75]

In *Bananas III*, the AB held the view that 'if the duration of the tariff quota concession in the European Communities' Schedule had to be modified or extended, negotiations under Article XXVIII would be the proper procedure to follow'.[76] However, given the elaborate and extensive procedure entailed in Article XXVIII, the tool of tariff renegotiation is evidently not designed for urgent *temporary*, but for *permanent* deviations:[77] first, the procedure is excruciatingly complicated and thus renders emergency and temporary protection virtually

---

75 The level of conditionality of an escape clause is composed of two elements: *Enactment thresholds* and *scope of application* (Schropp, 2009a). Enactment thresholds are contingency-related preconditions that the injurer has to surpass before making use of a flexibility mechanism. Enactment costs are sunk, and compensation payments do not form part of conditionality related costs. The second element of conditionality is the *scope of application*, the contractual deployment strings attached to the use of a trade-policy flexibility mechanism. The ease of use of a flexibility instrument is thus a function of the level of both conditionality and scope of application. As an example of how the level of conditionality can limit a trade flexibility tool, consider the safeguards clause under Article XIX GATT. For a safeguard measure to be imposed, an enacting country must show that 'i) as a result of *unforeseen development*; ii) imports in *increased quantities*; iii) have *caused* or threatened to cause; iv) *serious injury* to the domestic industry producing the v) *like product*' (see Mavroidis, 2007). Once the enacting country has jumped through that hoop, it can only invoke the safeguards measure exclusively in times of economic distress and apply such safeguard only once. Tariffs and QR are the only permissible trade instruments. The duration of safeguard measures is for a period of four years, although this can be extended up to eight years, subject to the findings of a mandated review panel (Article 7.1 SGA). In principle, safeguards cannot be directed at the country or set of countries that are the source of the injury (by virtue of Article 2.2 SGA). Instead, they have to be 'MFNed', that is applied on a non-discriminatory basis.

76 AB Report, para. 395.

77 Messerlin (2000: 162) contends that renegotiation under Article XXVIII is a disproportionate instrument for the aim of *temporary* protection.

impossible.[78] Second, tariff renegotiations are an untargeted, non-discriminatory measure. Tariff concessions must be offered by the demanding Member on an MFN basis, thus reducing its value as an efficient emergency relief. Third, strategic gamesmanship on the part of Members affected by the proposed tariff change make speedy conclusions rather unlikely. The affected Members hold a substantial bargaining power *vis-à-vis* the requesting Member, if they know that the latter is under a sizeable pressure to temporarily opt out of its previously made concessions.[79]

In sum, whenever Members strive for temporary, transient, deviations from previously agreed concessions, the WTO legal framework proves slack and burdensome. In order to avoid that, Members make use of various *de facto* opt-out mechanisms (anti-dumping, anti-subsidy measures, breach of the agreement, voluntary export restraints, etc.); more flexible and user-friendly ways of compensated contractual escape should be found (Mahlstein and Schropp, 2007; Schropp, 2009a).

3.2.3   Interpretation of the EC market-access commitments and expiry of the EC's 'MFN' tariff quota

Given that the AB reversed the Panel's findings on the interpretation of the legal nature of the Article I Waiver, the AB was asked to consider Ecuador's conditional appeal on the interpretation of the EC's market-access commitments and the expiry of its MFN tariff-quota concession beyond 31 December 2001. Ecuador submitted that the Panel had erred in finding that the expiry of the Bananas Framework Agreement had automatically implied the termination of the EC's tariff-quota concession *vis-à-vis* all MFN exporters under the terms of its Schedule. Ecuador held that paragraph 9 of the BFA ('This agreement shall apply until 31 December 2001') did not establish an expiration date for the entire concession with respect to bananas. According to Ecuador, paragraph 9 rather established

---

78 If the renegotiation request does not happen to fall into an official triennial renegotiation period of three months (laid out in GATT Article XXVIII.1), the injuring Member has to secure the prior authorization of *all* Members in order to enact its right to renegotiate (Article XXVIII.4). As per *Interpretative Note ad Article XXVIII GATT* (paras. 4.1, 4.4), the injurer must submit a written request to the Council of Trade in Goods, the relevant organ to decide. The requesting Member must supply comprehensive statistical and other information justifying its appeal and listing the effects of the envisaged measure. The Council will then give notice of its *consensus* decision within 30 days. *Interpretative Note ad Article XXVIII GATT* at para. 4.5 states that later on in the process the same Council determines – that is *all* WTO Members decide unanimously – whether the compensation offered by the injurer is sufficient. This sort of conditionality is certainly apt to slow down the process of reacting promptly to unforeseen contingencies and unanticipated shocks.

79 Members with 'substantial interest' in exporting into the renegotiating Member have an incentive to hold out their counterpart. Knowing that time is precious for the Member seeking emergency relief, the affected Members may engage in opportunistic procrastination (foot-dragging) with the aim of influencing the *ex post* distribution of the resulting non-performance gains in their favor (cf. Fearon, 1998). This may result in either hold-out welfare losses and a 'blackmail-premium' for the victim, or even lead to an outcome in which the affected Member appropriates all the *ex post* gains from seizing the regret contingency.

expiry only of those terms and conditions in the BFA related to the renegotiation of quota shares (as Article XIII:2 requests Members to conduct). It thus argued that the EC's MFN tariff-quota concession remained in effect, and requested the AB to uphold the Panel's ultimate conclusion that 'the tariff applied by the European Communities to MFN imports of bananas set at €176/mt … without consideration of the tariff quota for 2.2 million mt bound at an in-quota tariff rate of €75/mt, [is] in excess of that set forth … in the European Communities' Schedule' and thus inconsistent with Article II:1(b) of the GATT.[80]

In addressing Ecuador's appeal, the AB held as a preliminary issue that there are 'limits to the terms, conditions, or qualifications that may be incorporated in a Member's Schedule of concessions', but that the scheduling of temporal limitations to a tariff concession in the BFA was not incompatible with prior dispute-settlement findings. To determine whether the EC's tariff-quota concession *vis-à-vis* all non-ACP countries had really expired on 31 December 2001, the AB examined *all* relevant parts of the EC Schedule, including the column entries in Part I, Section I-B of the EU's Schedule and the BFA annexed to it under 'other terms and conditions'.

In Part I, Section I-B (entitled 'Tariff Quotas'), replicated above, the EC Schedule contains a tariff-quota concession of 2.2 million mt at €75 in Column 4 ('*final* quota quantity'). The BFA, referred to in Column 7 and annexed to the EC Schedule, repeats the in-quota amount and in-quota tariff (paragraphs 1 and 7), but states in paragraph 9: 'This agreement shall apply until 31 December 2002.' The AB claimed to give full meaning and effect to both the final tariff-quota concession in Column 4 and the temporary nature of the BFA referred to in paragraph 9, when it ruled that 'the Bananas Framework Agreement constitutes an agreement on the allocation, management and reallocation of country-specific shares within the "global basic tariff quota" referred to in paragraph 1. Therefore, we are of the view that the sentence "[t]his agreement shall apply until 31 December 2002" in paragraph 9 refers to an agreement on the allocation of shares.'[81]

The AB then turned to supplementary means of interpretation of the EC Schedule, specifically to the negotiating history of the EC tariff concessions and the BFA, the Uruguay Round 'Modalities Paper', the Doha Article I Waiver, and the EC request for tariff renegotiations under Article XXVIII. The AB largely found confirmation in its interpretation and concluded that the tariff-quota concession for 2.2 million mt bound at the in-quota rate of €75/mt remained in force beyond 31 December 2002 until the rebinding of the EC's Schedule of Concessions for bananas. Accordingly, the AB upheld the Panel's initial findings – albeit for different reasons – that the tariff applied by the EC to MFN imports on bananas, set at €176/mt, without consideration of the tariff quota of 2.2 million mt bound at an in-quota tariff of €75/mt was inconsistent with Article II:1(b) of the GATT.

---

80 AB Report, para. 412.
81 AB Report, para. 425.

The Modalities Papers used during the Uruguay Round negotiations expressly provide that they 'shall not be used as a basis for dispute settlement proceedings'.[82] The EC, accordingly, challenged the Panel's use of the Uruguay Round Modalities Paper for agricultural market access as a means of supplementary interpretation. The AB disagreed with the EC.

The prohibition on the use of the Modalities Paper simply means, the Appellate Body said, that 'it does not in itself confer on WTO Members' rights and obligations enforceable in dispute settlement. However, this does not preclude references to the Modalities Paper when interpreting the WTO agreements and Members' Schedules of Concessions that were prepared in accordance with these modalities.'[83]

This statement was consistent with the Panel's conclusion in *EC–Export Subsidies on Sugar* in which the EC had referred to that Modalities Paper as a supplementary means of interpretation.[84] However, in the *Sugar* dispute the AB had not found it necessary to rule on the relevance of the Modalities Paper.[85] In the present *Bananas III* dispute, however, the AB quoted with seeming approval the statement of the Panel in *Sugar*:

> Clearly, the so-called Modalities Paper is not a covered agreement and thus cannot provide for WTO rights and obligations to Members. Nonetheless, it could be relevant when interpreting the Agreement on Agriculture, including Members' Schedules.[86]

This decision seems correct, but it does raise an issue concerning its possible impact on the – already tedious – negotiating process. Now that it is clear that preparatory documents, such as the Uruguay Round Modalities Papers, may be used as supplementary means of interpretation, despite their 'shall not be used as a basis for dispute settlement proceedings' language, agreement on modalities in current and future negotiations might become even more difficult to achieve.

4. A law and economics perspective on certain aspects of the AB Report in *Bananas III (21.5)*

In this section, we will examine the basic economics of tariff quotas and how different methods of tariff-quota administration can influence the distribution of trade. This will be followed by a discussion of the interrelationship between compliance Panels and arbitrations under Article 22.6 DSU.

---

82 AB Report, para. 442.
83 Ibid.
84 Appellate Body Report, *EC–Export Subsidies on Sugar*, para. 198.
85 Ibid. para 199.
86 Panel Reports, *EC–Export Subsidies on Sugar*, para. 7.350 (footnotes omitted), quoted by the Appellate Body Report in *Bananas III (21.5)* at note 517.

4.1   Article XIII GATT and the economics of tariff quotas

The AB upheld the Panel's finding that the measure in question, the ACP preference, violates GATT Articles XIII:1 (on non-discriminatory *access* to tariff
quotas), the chapeau of Article XIII:2 (non-discriminatory *administration* of tariff
quotas), and Article XIII:2(d) (the 'safe haven' for tariff-quota administration
based on historical quota allocation). Examining the economics of tariff quotas,
we have three broader comments to make: first, given that tariff quotas in practice
operate exactly like quantitative restrictions, their special status in the GATT is
economically dubitable and can only be explained by the politics of multilateral
negotiations. Second, the AB's examination of the chapeau of Article XIII:2 can be
seen as too cursory (and possibly flawed), depending on the interpretation of the
non-discrimination counterfactual construed in that Article. Third, Article
XIII:2(d) on historical quota allocation is an evident violation of the non-discrimination obligation in the chapeau of Article XIII:2. To wit, historical allocation of quota rights discriminates against the most efficient exporters and grants
economic rents to less competitive producers. Such an outcome is in contradiction
to the non-discrimination mandate enshrined in the chapeau of Article XIII:2.
Even worse, nearly all quota-allocation mechanisms in practice today bear the
inherent risk of discriminatory allocation of quota rights. Seen from an economic
perspective, quota-right auctions comply with the strict non-discrimination standard set out in the chapeau of Article XIII:2. Transferable quota rights are another
viable alternative of achieving a non-discriminatory distribution of trade.

4.1.1   A brief economic assessment of tariff quotas

A tariff-rate quota, or tariff quota, is a two-tiered tariff, consisting of a lower *in-
quota* tariff (t), applied to the first Q units of imports, and a higher over-quota
tariff (T).[87] Tariff quotas are not considered quantitative restrictions, because
technically they do not limit import quantities. Therefore, 'tariff quotas do not fall
under the prohibition of Article XI:1 and are in principle lawful under the GATT
1994',[88] since exporters may always import by paying the over-quota tariff. The
precondition, however, is that the tariff rates are applied consistently with the
MFN tenet of Article I GATT, that in-quota and out-of-quota tariffs do not exceed
bound tariff concessions (Article II GATT), and that the quota administration is in
accordance with the disciplines of Article XIII GATT.[89] Yet, if the over-quota tariff
makes it prohibitively expensive to import, the tariff quota yields the same import
volume as a traditional quota.

---

87 The terms 'tariff quota' and 'tariff-rate quota' are usually used interchangeably in the literature.
Technically, 'tariff quota' is a more accurate description, because it includes specific tariffs, while tariff-
rate quota excludes them.

88 Appellate Body Report, para. 335.

89 Article XIII applies to tariff quotas by virtue of Article XIII:5.

Figure 1. Tariff quotas and import demand

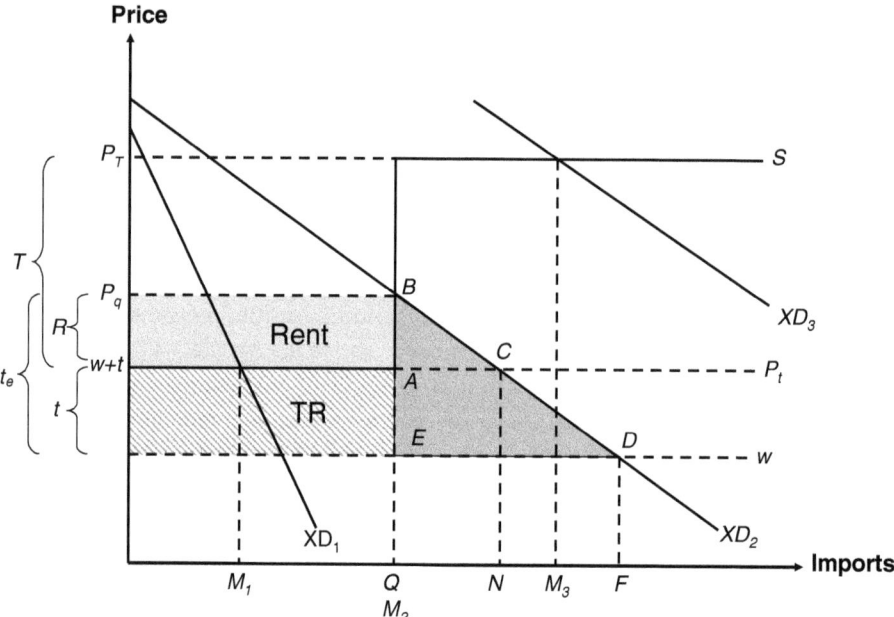

Source: Based on Skully (2001: Figure 5).

To see that, consider Figure 1, which illustrates the operation of a tariff quota. Imports are plotted on the *x*-axis, prices on the *y*-axis. For simplicity, the effective supply curve of exports (*S*) into the importing country consists of two horizontal lines. The lower line represents the in-quota imports and extends from zero to point *Q* at the price $P_t = w + t$, whereby *w* is the prevailing world price and *t* is the in-quota tariff rate. At *Q* the supply curve makes a vertical jump to connect in-quota with over-quota imports. The upper part of the supply curve represents the effective supply of over-quota imports at the price $P_T = w + T$, where *T* is the over-quota tariff.

The effect of a tariff quota on trade depends on the excess demand for imports. Figure 1 shows three possible excess-demand conditions (labeled XD_{1-3}). The intersections of XD_{1-3} with *S* fix three different import levels (points M_1, M_2, M_3). At XD_1, the quota *tariff* is binding, meaning that domestic excess demand is M_1, which is less than the quota volume *Q*. The tariff quota functions like an ordinary tariff applied at the in-quota rate. At M_2, the tariff *quota* is binding and *Q* limits the supply available in the domestic market at a price P_q. With a binding quota, both domestic quantity is less and prices are higher than what would prevail if the tariff quota did not exist and only a tariff were applied at the in-quota rate of *t* (point *N*). Without any tariff, quantities would be demanded at the free-trade level of *F*. Excess-demand curve XD_3, finally, represents a high level of demand, sufficient to sustain imports at the over-quota tariff T. With a prevailing demand curve of XD_3, T is binding, and M_3 units are imported.

Some observations about tariff quotas: first, tariff quotas are inefficient whenever the tariff quota is binding. At import quantity Q, less imports are available compared to a tariff-only regime (point N) and a free-trade regime (point F). This leads to economic deadweight loss compared to the tariff-only and free-trade scenarios (illustrated by the shaded triangles ABC and BED, respectively). Secondly, tariff quotas produce exporter rents, whenever the quota Q or the out-of-quota tariff T is binding. The economic rent is illustrated by the rectangle ABP_qP_t, denoted 'Rent'. Third, whenever there are rents to be seized, imports must be rationed.[90] Rationing is the essence of tariff-quota administration (more on that below). Rationing is also at the core of additional inefficiencies, because (i) it allows otherwise non-competitive suppliers to export at a higher price and (ii) suppliers competing for rents may engage in wasteful activities, such as bribery.[91]

As our final observation, to take up a point made above, depending on the out-of-quota tariff T, a tariff quota acts exactly like a quantitative restriction, with the only exception that at least parts of the economic rents accrue to the importing government in the form of tariff revenues (hatched rectangle AP_twE, denoted TR in Figure 1). In the original *Bananas III* dispute, the EC had an out-of-quota tariff of €680/mt of bananas. As was pointed out in footnote 4 above, this constituted a prohibitive tariff. Hence, the Original Banana Import Regime basically acted as a quantitative restriction, and therefore circumvented the obligations of Article XI GATT. The special status of tariff quotas is difficult to understand from a purely economic point of view, and is probably better explained by the political economy of the Uruguay Round negotiations.[92]

90 In case that excess demand XD_2 is prevailing, N units of potential supply must be rationed among Q units of demand.

91 We note that the WTO is not concerned with the volume and distribution of *rents*, but solely with the volume and distribution of *trade*. However, as will become clear in the next section, the distribution of rents has a significant impact on the distribution of trade, not least because the distribution of rents motivates the politics of tariff-quota administration.

92 Many pundits argue that the tariffication of existing quantitative restrictions and the 'minimum access' obligation pursuant to the Uruguay Round have not led to a noticeable increase in trade, because WTO Members used new tariff quotas to maintain traditional import flows. This can be explained by several factors. First, as mentioned, the Modalities Paper was not incorporated into the Single Undertaking. As a result, the Modalities disciplines were left to the discretion of individual countries and thus were not always followed in practice. Secondly, tariff quotas were often set for products characterized by tariff peaks, so the out-of-quota tariffs remain prohibitive. Third, the management of tariff quotas is incoherent among Members and highly intransparent. Fourth, countries employed various tricks to circumvent the tariffication obligation (for example, by allocating quotas to countries that are unlikely to export the relevant commodity). Finally, the way Members administer their tariff quotas has a large role on the so-called quota fill (IATRC, 2001: 2).

4.1.2 The distribution of trade under tariff quotas and the AB's test of Article XIII:2

The chapeau of Article XIII:2 of the GATT reads in pertinent parts:

> In applying import restrictions to any product, contracting parties shall aim at a distribution of trade in such product approaching as closely as possible the shares which the various contracting parties might be expected to obtain in the absence of such restrictions ...

This language implies the construction of the following counterfactual: how would the world look *in the absence of such restrictions* – in this case, in the absence of a *tariff quota*? The distribution of trade under this counterfactual shall then be used to compare the actual distribution of trade under the tariff quota to check for possible discrimination against exporting countries.[93] Yet, Article XIII:2 does not state which counterfactual is pertinent. There are potentially three plausible counterfactuals implied by Article XIII:2: (i) a free-trade counterfactual, that is a situation that would exist absent *any* import restrictions; (ii) a tariff-equivalent counterfactual, that is a situation in which the same quantities were imported as in the presence of an in-quota tariff only; and (iii) a quota-equivalent counterfactual in which the imported quantities were limited in the same way as under the quota at issue. As will be argued below, each of these three counterfactuals could potentially be compliant with the MFN principle.

To see how these three counterfactuals differ, consider Figure 2, which is a slight variant of Figure 1, this time with an upward-sloping excess-supply curve (XS). The world price w is fixed where excess-demand and excess-supply curves intersect, setting a free-trade quantity of F. If the in-quota tariff were applied in the absence of the quantitative restriction, domestic consumers would demand a quantity of N units. Under a quota-equivalent counterfactual, the importing government would import the same quantity as under the quote (Q).

Importantly for the *Bananas III* case at hand, those three counterfactual scenarios involve substantially different distributions of trade. If trade were completely unrestricted, suppliers inframarginal to world price w would be willing to export to the domestic market.[94] The composition of this group of suppliers, that is their export shares, would then be the basis for a non-discrimination test under Article XIII:2. In the tariff-equivalent counterfactual, where the imported quantity were limited to N units, only suppliers inframarginal to a fictitious price P_{te} would be willing to export their goods to the importing country. The composition of suppliers in this second scenario could potentially differ, because suppliers inframarginal to w, but extramarginal to P_{te}, would drop out of the relevant MFN supplier group. Even fewer suppliers, namely only the most competitive ones,

---

93 Basically, a pie chart of exporter market shares under a non-discriminatory tariff quota should look identical to the pie chart in the absence of such quota, just with the second pie being smaller (Skully, 2001).

94 The word *inframarginal to price x* essentially means 'fit to compete at a price x in market Y'.

Figure 2. Three interpretations of the counterfactual construed in Article XIII:2

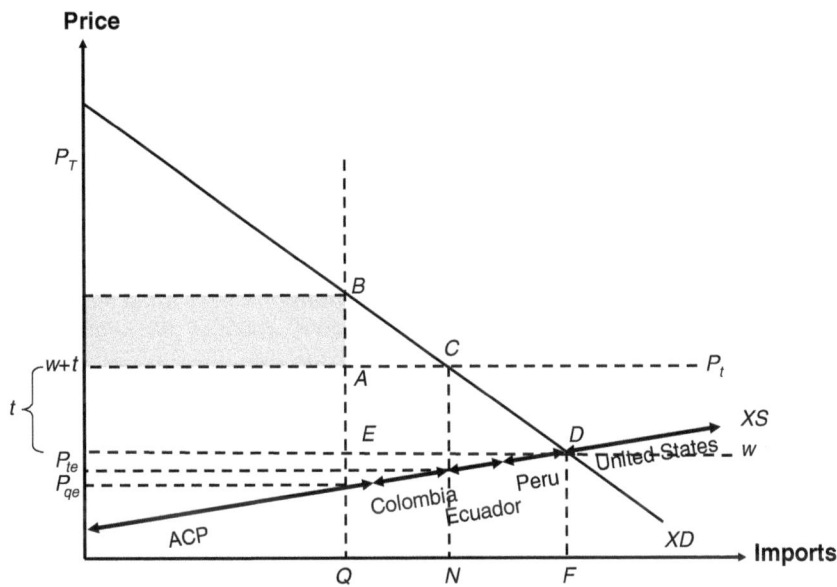

Source: Based on Skully (2001: Figure 5).

would manage to export, if quantity was limited according to the quota-equivalent counterfactual (quantity Q at a fictitious price P_{qe}). The group of suppliers and therewith counterfactual export shares will again differ from the other two scenarios.

Figure 2 lists a hypothetical group of competing importers of bananas and stacks them in their order of competitiveness, that is according to their (hypothetical) cost of production.[95] Imagine for the sake of argument that ACP countries were the most competitive suppliers, followed by Colombia, Ecuador, Peru, and the United States. Imagine now that the zero-tariff quota would be quite small, e.g. 10,000 mt of bananas.

Depending on the counterfactual chosen, a discrimination examination under Article XIII:2 yields strikingly different results. Under the free-trade scenario, all exporters except the United States would export to the country at issue. All those exporters should thus be granted a certain in-quota share. Under the tariff-equivalent counterfactual, Ecuador and Peru would drop out of consideration, and

---

95 The excess-supply curve in Figure 2 is the linear combination of excess-supply curves of exporting countries. More competitive suppliers (like Colombia) would thereby have steeper domestic excess-supply curves than would less competitive countries (such as the US in our fictitious example).

in-quota trade should be distributed among ACP members and Colombia only. Finally, taking the quota-equivalent counterfactual as the legal benchmark, a quota allocation to ACP countries would be fully justified.

The AB in its Report justified the EC's violation of Article XIII:2 with the following words:

> The tariff quota also fails to meet the requirements regarding distribution and allocation in Article XIII:2. The exclusion of non-ACP suppliers from the tariff quota is not aimed 'at a distribution of trade … approaching as closely as possible the shares which the various Members might be expected to obtain in the absence of [the] restrictions', as required by Article XIII:2. *On the contrary, the exclusion of non-ACP suppliers is not aimed at a distribution of trade that affords access to, and competitive opportunities under, the tariff quota to all supplying Members reflecting their comparative advantage … Allocating the entire tariff quota exclusively to ACP countries, and reserving no shares to non-ACP suppliers, cannot be considered to be based on the respective shares of ACP and non-ACP supplier countries in the European Communities' banana market.* As a result, the exclusion of non-ACP suppliers from the tariff quota of 775,000 mt reserved for ACP countries is inconsistent with the requirements … the chapeau of Article XIII:2.[96]

We submit that we believe the AB's finding to be correct in substance. However, in the light of the above, the AB's analysis could be seen as slightly too cursory, because the AB did not state which counterfactual it applied in reaching its finding, and what the competitive position of ACP suppliers really is, as compared to their competitors. The EU could have argued for the quota-equivalent counterfactual and asserted that ACP countries are the only banana suppliers inframarginal to a hypothetical price of P_{qe}.[97]

4.1.3 Quota-allocation methods, distribution of trade, and the inherent contradictions in Article XIII:2 GATT

As the title suggests, Article XIII regulates the non-discriminatory administration of, inter alia, tariff quotas. The AB has opined that Article XIII:2 extends the MFN principle to quota allocation, an interpretation to which the authors of this comment agree.[98] The principle of non-discrimination among all exporting Members asserts that trade shares should be determined by the relative efficiency of suppliers, but not by alternative, discriminatory criteria. The methods with which tariff quotas are allocated among different countries have a significant impact on

---

96 AB Report, para. 340 (emphasis added).

97 An interpretation of Article XIII:2 that champions a quota-equivalent counterfactual, however, is not watertight. After all, why should exporters offer their imports at price P_{qe} if they could receive a much higher price w on the world markets?

98 See footnote 68 and accompanying text.

the distribution of trade. WTO Members have notified at least six distinct allocation methods for their tariff quotas:[99]

- applied tariffs,
- auctions,
- license on demand (LoD),
- first-come, first-served (FCFS),
- historical allocation (HA), and
- discretionary allocation (either through state-trading enterprises or through producer groups),

whereby applied tariffs and auctions can be grouped together as 'market allocation' methods, while LoD, FCFS, and HA can be categorized into the broad group of 'quasi-market allocation' methods.

As will be argued below, only truly market-based allocation methods, namely applied tariffs, quota auctions, and markets for quota-rights resale satisfy the principle of distributive justice among WTO Members, while the design of all other methods is inherently discriminatory against the most competitive suppliers.[100] Notably, historical allocation, the so-called 'safe haven' mentioned in Article XIII:2(d), is inherently flawed and therewith contradicts the chapeau of Article XIII:2.

4.1.3.1   Market allocation methods

Notifying *applied tariffs* is just another way of saying that the tariff quota is not enforced, and that all imports are allowed at preferential in-quota tariff rates. The resulting distribution of trade is non-discriminatory, because the tariff quota acts just like a tariff (see demand curve XD_1 in Figure 1).[101] Applied tariffs do not address the problem of having to ration tariff-quota shares among competing exporting Members. We hence do not consider this method further.

The *auctioning of tariff-quota rights* is generally deemed to be an efficient way to allocate the right to export amongst competing exporters (Bergsten *et al.*, 1987; Skully, 2001; Skully, 1999). For the following elaborations, consider again Figure 1. Auctions neutralize quota rents (R), and mimic the allocative outcome of a tariff-only scenario, in which a tariff equivalent t_e would be applied. In the absence of the tariff quota, exporters inframarginal to the world price w would be willing to import. The presence of a binding quota invites less competitive suppliers, namely those that are extramarginal to w, but inframarginal to P_q, into the importing market, because the prevailing domestic price allows these higher-cost suppliers to stay in the market, and possibly to capture some of the rent R.

---

99 Members must notify the WTO about how they administer tariff quotas in their Tariff Schedules.

100 However, it is not certain whether quota auctions are GATT conforming. In addition, they are politically difficult to enact. These issues will be discussed in subsection 4.1.3.5 infra.

101 Over half of all notified tariff quotas are not enforced (Skully, 1999: 8). However, the over-quota tariff can be reapplied at will, which injects a certain level of incertitude for foreign exporters.

In an auction, suppliers have to bid for the right of supplying the importing market. The most competitive suppliers are willing to pay approximately $R = P_q - (w + t)$ for the opportunity to sell at the price of P_q and to make a riskless profit of R per unit sold. Exporters extramarginal to the world price w will be outbid by these inframarginal suppliers. The importing government realizes gains from trade equal to the auction revenue R plus the in-quota tariff t. This allocation is exactly identical to the one that would result from the tariff-equivalent of a tariff quota t_e.

4.1.3.2   Quasi-market allocation methods[102]

License on demand (LoD), first come, first served (FSFS), and historical allocation (HA) are a mix of market allocation and a random lottery among certain exporters. All three methods result in discriminatory allocation of quotas; in the best case, their results match that of an auction, but such an outcome would be purely coincidental.

Under *License on demand*, exporters are invited to apply for licenses at the beginning of a given quota period, specifying the quantity of imports they would like to carry out. If domestic demand is sufficient, the quota binds. The sum of all quota requests is denoted as Q^*. With $Q^* > Q$, the quota binds. To ration export licenses, every bidder's application quantities are reduced proportionally by factor λ, so that $Q = \lambda Q^*$, whereby λ is a rationing factor, and $0 < \lambda < 1$ holds.

This tariff-quota administration method is very likely to produce a biased distribution of trade that violates the non-discrimination tenet of Article XIII:2 GATT. Consider Figure 3, which shows the supply side of imports. The domestic price is P, the world price w, and the unit quota rent is $R = P - w$. S is an upward-sloping supply curve of imports into the country at issue.[103] The area under the supply curve represents payments to factors employed to the product at issue. Exporters extramarginal to w must spend resources in excess of w to produce a unit of output. Hence, extramarginal production destroys value; extramarginal suppliers would not be able to import under free-trade conditions.

LoD allocation is a form of lottery among all exporters inframarginal to the domestic price P (that is, inframarginal and extramarginal suppliers alike). They all have an incentive to enter into the quota lottery to capture some of the riskless quota rent R. Rational applicants, cognizant of the rationing, have an incentive to overstate their license requests. Thus, quantity applied for exceeds the in-quota supply: $Q^* = 1 > Q = \lambda$. To deal with quota oversubscription, each applicant is granted a pro rata share of the global quota. The effective supply curve under the tariff quota thus skews leftwards (S^0), to reflect the random draw among all

---

102 The following analysis of tariff-quota allocation methods borrows heavily from Skully (2000) and Skully (2001).
103 To reduce clutter, Figure 3 assumes an in-quota tariff of zero, a prohibitive out-of-quota tariff, and that the domestic market clears at P. Domestic price P and free-trade quantity I are normalized to 1.

Figure 3. Tariff-quota allocation methods

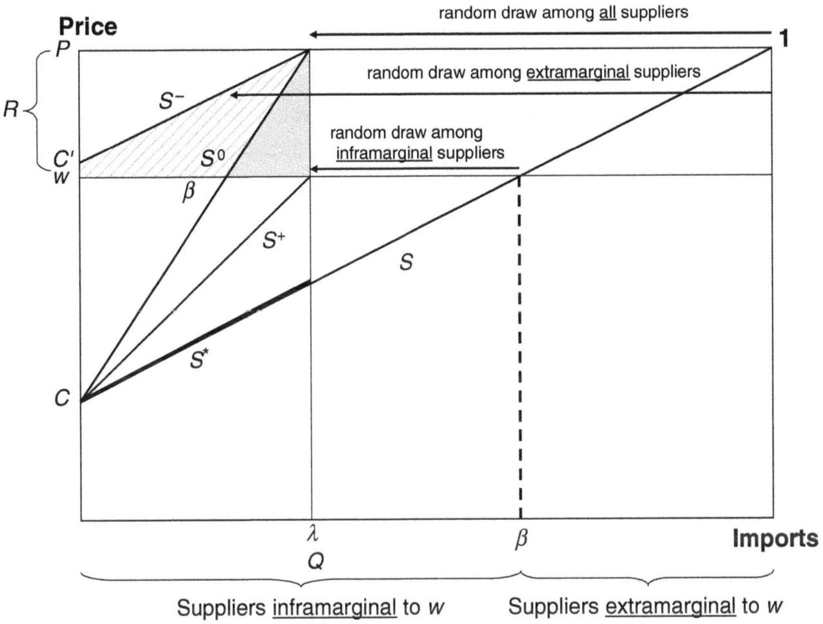

Source: Based on Skully (2001: Figure 5).

suppliers inframarginal to P. The proportion of quota rights granted to exporters inframarginal to w is β the proportion of competitive free-trade suppliers. LoD allocation causes the displacement of $\lambda(\Lambda - \beta)$ inframarginal suppliers by extra-marginal suppliers, *who would not have supplied the import market under free trade*. Hence, the expected distribution of trade differs from the free-trade counter-factual, which consists uniquely of inframarginal suppliers. The welfare loss from LoD allocation is shown by the shaded triangle to the right of S^0. The loss of welfare can be interpreted as an indicator of how the expected distribution of trade under LoD differs from the tariff-equivalent counterfactual distribution of trade.

First-come, first-served allocation allows importation at the in-quota tariff until the quota is filled. To analyze the distribution of trade under FCFS, some as-sumptions must be made about the correspondence between an exporter's will-ingness to supply and his place in the FCFS queue.[104] We examine four scenarios: (a) an optimistic scenario in which the lower-cost exporter is always placed ahead of the less competitive supplier; (b) a realistic scenario in which the otherwise uncompetitive higher-cost supplier queues before the competitive exporter; and

104 FCFS can lead to a 'run to the docks', which introduces a host of further inefficiencies that shall not be examined here, such as transaction costs from shipments waiting idly in front of the docks, pro-cessing bottlenecks, redundancy back-up shipments, etc.

two intermediate scenarios in which (c) there is a zero correlation between cost and place in the queue and (d) there is a positive, but imperfect relationship.

Consider first scenario (a): the lower-cost exporters are always placed ahead of less competitive exporters; then the effective quota supply curve is exactly the original supply curve S in the interval $(0, \lambda)$. Call this segment of the S-curve S^*. However, because competitive suppliers can easily sell on the world markets at w, the world price becomes the lower bound on their willingness to supply the import market. Assuming that each inframarginal supplier is equally likely to supply the import market, a random drawing from the set of inframarginal suppliers is the result, yielding the effective quota supply curve S^+. Under this allocation, efficient discrimination between inframarginal low-cost and extramarginal high-cost exporters is achieved and the tenet of non-discrimination is adhered to. Yet note well that this scenario presupposes a *perfect* correlation between competitive rank and place in the queue. Such an outcome, if it ever happens, is very unlikely.

Consider the opposite situation, scenario (b), in which the highest-cost suppliers undertake efforts – and succeed – in queuing before low-cost suppliers.[105] When low cost of production is inversely correlated with the position in the queue, the expected outcome may be represented by the supply curve termed S^-, in the far-left corner of Figure 3 (S^- is a leftward shift of the extramarginal segment of curve S). From a welfare perspective, but also from a non-discrimination point of view, such an outcome is unwelcome, since all those inframarginal suppliers, who would have supplied the import market in the absence of the tariff quota, are crowded out by high-cost exporters. A completely biased distribution of trade is the result.[106]

Next, consider scenario (c) a zero correlation between cost and rank in the queue. As was discussed previously under the LoD allocation method, a random selection of inframarginal (competitive) and extramarginal (non-competitive) suppliers from a population uniformly distributed over the interval (C, P) has the expected distribution represented by the supply curve S^0.

Finally, an FCFS process with a positive, but imperfect, correlation (scenario (d)), will yield an expected allocation of quota rights between S^0 and S^+ over the range $(0, \lambda)$. Hence, some expected inframarginal displacement will occur in this case of positive but imperfect correlation too, whereby the lower the correlation between low cost and rank in the queue, the greater the expected displacement (the closer the actual supply curve will be to S^0).

In sum, a tariff-quota allocation method of FCFS will lead to a displacement of between none and all inframarginal suppliers, depending on the correlation between comparative advantage and place in the queue. Even if there is a zero

---

105 Such scenario with a negative correlation between cost and place in the queue is not entirely unrealistic: Otherwise non-competitive exporters will make extra efforts to tap rent-laden markets; presumably, these are the only markets in which these extramarginal producers can sell at all. So, they specialize in securing pole position in the 'run for the docks' that the FCFS allocation triggers.

106 The area below S^- in the range $(0, \lambda)$ represents wasted resources and thus welfare loss (the sum of the hatched and shaded planes in Figure 3).

correlation (an unrealistically optimistic suggestion), a fraction of $\lambda(\Lambda - \beta)$ infra-marginal suppliers will get crowded out by otherwise uncompetitive producers.

Historical allocation finally can be viewed as an extreme variant of an FCFS or LoD allocation. Whereas FCFS and LoD are annual lotteries, historical allocation of quota shares is essentially a one-time-only draw. A particular realization is sustained for many years and remains invariant to changes in underlying market conditions. Examining the US sugar import regime ever since 1934, Skully (1998) shows that quota rights for US sugar imports have undergone major reallocations every 15 years only.[107]

Bown and McCulloch (2003), in an empirical study dealing with safeguard protection, show that (tariff) quotas preserving historical market shares discriminate among foreign suppliers, as compared to safeguards implemented by simple tariffs (a regime that maintains the comparative advantage of suppliers). The authors empirically prove that safeguards implemented through quantitative restrictions (HA) discriminated against suppliers whose market shares had been growing over the 'representative period' leading up to the quota, in favor of suppliers whose share had been declining.[108] They conclude that 'quota and [tariff quota] safeguards used to protect domestic suppliers may also provide some relief to established trading partners whose positions in the relevant import market have been adversely affected by increased competition from other import sources'.[109]

To sum up our findings on quasi-market allocation mechanisms for tariff quotas: Auctions, LoD, and HA are all special cases of a general FCFS process. An auction is equivalent to a FCFS allocation with *perfect* correlation between competitive situation and rank in the queue (curve S^+ in Figure 3), LoD is equivalent to a random FCFS process with a *zero* correlation between cost and place (supply curve S^0), and HA is a 'sticky' random FCFS allocation somewhere between the S^* and S^0 curves. All allocation methods, except tariff-quota auctions, inherently discriminate against those competitive (inframarginal) suppliers that would divide up the import market amongst themselves in the absence of a tariff quota.

---

107 Taiwan has a historical tariff quota share of 24,000 short tons of sugar into the United States. Taiwan always fills that quota. However, this is the only sugar Taiwan exports; the country's production does not satisfy domestic demand. The 24,000 short tons of domestic sugar exported to the US are sourced cheaply from Australia or Thailand (IATRC, 2001: 74).

108 The logic here is straightforward: 'Consider two exporting countries, A and B, with opposite trends in market share for the good whose domestic suppliers are about to be protected by a safeguard. In the three years prior to the year the [quota] is imposed (year t), country A's market share has fallen from 15 per cent in year $t-3$ to 10 per cent in year $t-2$ to 5 per cent in year $t-1$. Under a ... quota, allocation of market shares based on the average of historical levels would reward A with a 10 per cent market share in year $t+1$, twice its actual share in the year before the safeguard was imposed. On the other hand, B's market share has risen from 5 per cent in $t-3$ to 10 per cent in $t-2$ to 15 per cent in $t-1$. Under a safeguard quota with allocation of market shares based on average historical levels, B's market share would drop to 10 per cent in $t+1$, one-third less than it achieved in the final year before the safeguard was imposed' (Bown and McCulloch, 2003: 332).

109 Ibid., p. 337.

4.1.3.3   Discretionary allocation methods

Discretionary methods of tariff-quota allocation delegate quota administration and allocation processes to domestic groups or organizations, for example state-trading enterprises (STE) or certain organizations that represent producer interests. How STE or producer groups go about allocating the quota rights remains within their discretion. Usually, they fill quotas depending on domestic demand. It is difficult to generalize discretionary allocation methods, because they cannot be reduced to formal algorithms, but instead are subject to certain domestic decision processes. Anecdotal evidence from case studies leads to the conclusion that discretionary methods are often divorced from commercial considerations and open for political strategizing, personal enrichment, and nepotism.[110] The Panel report in *Turkey–Rice* has shown just how intransparent such discretionary quota-allocation methods can be.[111]

4.1.3.4   Article XIII:2(d) GATT and historical allocation

Article XIII:2(d) on HA of tariff quota states:

> In cases in which a quota is allocated among supplying countries the contracting party applying the restrictions may seek agreement with respect to the allocation of shares in the quota with all other contracting parties having a substantial interest in supplying the product concerned. In cases in which this method is not reasonably practicable, the contracting party concerned shall allot to contracting parties having a substantial interest in supplying the product shares based upon the proportions, supplied by such contracting parties during a previous *representative period*, of the total quantity or value of imports of the product, due account being taken of any *special factors* which may have affected or may be affecting the trade in the product. (emphasis added)[112]

Article XIII:2(d) nominally allows Members to transfer and reallocate tariff-quota rights among exporting countries, in line with changing economic and competitive conditions, according to the free-trade counterfactual during a 'representative period'. If countries actually made use of this possibility, this would greatly reduce the risk of a biased distribution of trade and substantially mitigate discriminatory allocation of tariff-quota shares. However, even after some careful study, the authors are unaware of a single case where uncompensated reallocation among quota holders occurred in accordance with Article XIII:2(d), first sentence.

---

110 See IATRC (2001: chapters 8 and 9); see also Skully (1999: 16–19).
111 See Gantz and Schropp (2009).
112 The two italicized terms have been subject to further definition in a series of Interpretative Notes to Article XII. With respect to *representative period*, the convention is to use a three-year period prior to the imposition of a restriction, where possible. Regarding *special factors*, it is noted that this term includes, among others, (i) changes in relative productive efficiency between foreign producers; (ii) the existence of new or additional ability to export; (iii) reduced ability to export.

The lack of such reallocations can be explained by the technical difficulties of constant reallocation of quota shares, and by the political economy of tariff quotas.

Under permanent reallocation of quota shares, the importing government reassesses on a rolling basis the competitiveness of all foreign exporters and accordingly reallocates shares at the beginning of every period. However, doing so presupposes quite a high level of sophistication and information on the part of the importing government. And there is no reason to believe that bureaucracies, even in the most advanced countries, have the means to constantly 'outsmart' the market. Abstracting from the significant costs of such endeavor, individual mistakes, slackness, corruption, and incompetence could potentially foil such government-induced constant allocation from the start.

Looking at the political economy of tariff-quota allocation, one primary reason why importing governments allocated exporter quotas in the first place was to appease suppliers harmed by the imposition of the quota.[113] Tariff quotas thus were used in a fashion very similar to voluntary export restraints (VER). Highly competitive countries 'voluntarily' reduce their exports in exchange for quota rents. What was initiated as compensation to otherwise competitive exporters over time turned into an entitlement. Once foreign exporters are vested with quota rights, a proposed (uncompensated) reallocation of shares will presumably upset them and spark vivid threats and politically harmful responses against the importing Member.

In summary, evidence shows that HA as an allocation method seriously biases the distribution of trade and discriminates against those exporters that would have seized large import shares in the absence of such tariff-quota allocation: First, unless historical shares were initially auctioned off, chances are high that their original allocation did not reflect the free-trade allocation of shares.[114] Second, unless HA is not continuously updated and redistributed, it will cement an outdated situation that does not reflect accurately the current competitive situation.[115]

Hence, HA as a distributive principle is very likely to discriminate against the most competitive suppliers and therefore, by nature of the political economy of its operation, violates the chapeau of Article XIII:2, which mandates a non-discriminatory allocation of tariff-quota shares. Hence, ironically, Article XIII advocates both non-discrimination *and* discrimination at the same time.[116]

---

113 Bown and McCulloch (2003, footnote 11) explain the political economy of quota allocation in cautious terms: 'A possible justification for the discriminatory treatment is that traditional suppliers have "paid" for their market access with their own earlier concessions, while newer entrants have not. In fact, newer entrants are often also new to the GATT/WTO system.'

114 As the analysis in the previous subsection showed, if historical shares were initially allocated according to a FCFS or LoD system, distribution was biased *ab initio*.

115 The IATRC (2001) report on tariff quotas, chapters 5–11, contains a number of case studies, including tariff quota regimes under HA.

116 See Hudec (1997: 178 *et seq.*).

Article XIII:2(d) in essence is not a 'safe haven', but a legally available tool of discrimination.

As was shown above, the same goes for almost all other allocation methods, namely license on demand, first come, first serve, and discretionary methods. They lead to a biased distribution of trade, displacing a good number of competitive (inframarginal) exporters that would have secured significantly bigger market shares under the free-trade counterfactual.

4.1.3.5   Ways of making quota allocation compatible to Article XIII:2 GATT

We now turn to three alternative methods of tariff-quota administration to see whether tariff allocation can be compatible with the chapeau of Article XIII:2 GATT at all. These three methods are: active government involvement, tradable quota rights, and quota auctions.

A first option of safeguarding a non-discriminatory quota-allocation regime is active government involvement, either in the form of a permanent reallocation of tariff-quota shares, or in the form of continuous tariff setting. We have discussed the logistical and technical problems of constant quota reallocation in section 4.1.3.4 above. As an alternative, tariff quotas can be actively administered by constantly setting import tariffs, and therewith domestic prices. As was discussed above, government action could bring about imports equal to the quota quantity Q by increasing the in-quota tariff such that the import tariff dissipates all economic rents to quota holders (that is, by having a quota-equivalent tariff equal to $t_e = P_q - w$ in Figure 1). However, such tariff management poses at least two problems: for one, exact knowledge of domestic excess-demand elasticity and other market information is indispensable for determining the correct tariff rate. Also, market conditions can change quickly, so that tariff rates need to be updated continually. Both factors most probably overburden any – even highly developed – bureaucracy.

A second option for achieving an unbiased distribution of trade under a tariff quota is to establish a resale market for tariff-quota rights. When tariff-quota rights are non-transferable, the entitled country must produce and export the good to realize the quota rent. This will motivate extramarginal producers to export, even though under a free-trade scenario they would not do so.[117] Hence, non-transferability of quota rights ties the distribution of *rents* to the distribution of *trade*. Allowing quota rights to be traded unties this connection between rents and actual trade patterns. Resale of tariff-quota rights can help avoid the incidence of deadweight loss caused when extramarginal suppliers are displacing competitive inframarginal producers. Neglecting information gathering and transaction costs for a moment (and assuming economic agents are rational), extramarginal quota

---

117 As was shown in footnote 107, some quota holders produce and export only to fill their quota and pocket the quota rents, but then end up importing from cheaper sources. Such an outcome is economically wasteful.

holders should be willing to sell their quota rights to those exporters that are competitive on the world markets. Such trades should be expected to occur at a price R per unit, the amount equal to the quota rent or the marginal auction bid. Since extramarginal quota holders value the quota rent at R or less (depending on their own cost structure), while inframarginal suppliers value the right to export at R or more (depending on their level of competitiveness), a liquid market for quota rights should be easily established.

From the point of view of the WTO, the only relevant consideration is the distribution of *trade*; the allocation of *rents* is irrelevant per se. With quota resale allowed, the final distribution of trade is equivalent to that under free trade, under accurate yearly reallocation, under quota-equivalent tariffs, and under auctions. The only difference is that quota rents are captured by the initial quota holders, not by the importing government.

Markets are the most efficient way of rationing scarce supplies and demands. The third option of tariff-quota allocation is to directly use the market mechanism, and to auction off quota rights. Tariff-quota auctions should be the most favorite option to economists, because the allocation mechanism is swift and efficient. In addition, auctions cannot be rigged easily; the most competitive producer gets rewarded, thus stimulating suppliers to become ever-more efficient.

Yet, tariff auctions are rarely applied.[118] If tariff-quota auctions are so perfect, why are they in such little use? We find economic, political, and WTO legal reasons.

Economically, tariff-quota auctions require markets that are sufficiently liquid, that is possess a large volume of trade and a high number of competing bidders. If this is not the case, auctions can lose some of their appeal to policymakers. Another concern is monopolization: it is possible for one exporter or group to purchase the entire portion of the right to import, and then withhold part of the licensed-import quantity to maximize revenues.[119]

There is also a *political explanation* for the low number of tariff-quota auctions in use today. Auctions are markets and as such hard to control. If the administering government prefers to transfer quota rents to certain countries (VER-style) rather than collecting rents as auction revenue, it will decide not to auction off the quota rights. Presumably, such zeal was guiding the EC in its Banana Import Regime.

Finally, there may be *WTO-legal* reservations against utilizing tariff-quota auctions.[120] One argument against auctioning import rights runs as follows: under Article II GATT, countries schedule their maximum tariffs. By auctioning off

---

118 According to Skully (1999: 8), only 4% of all tariff quotas notified in 1999 came out of auctions. More up-to-date information on tariff quotas can be obtained on the WTO website (http://docsonline.wto.org/gen_home.asp?language=1&_=1) (last visited 19 November 2009). Most tariff quotas bear the code G/AG/N/member.

119 However, Bergsten *et al.* (1987) argue that simple procedures can be designed to guard against this monopolization of quota rights.

120 This section draws on insights gathered from Skully (1999).

quota rights, exporting countries may bid in excess of the tariff ceiling, thus potentially violating the tenets of Article II:1(b) and affording a greater protection than previously afforded.

A Member could argue that auctioned importing rights effectively paid by its exporters, *de facto* amount to an increase in the importing Member's bound rate. As an important preliminary issue: who is granted the quota – the importer or the exporter? If a quota-imposing Member grants an export quota to other Members, then the exporters seize the economic rent and there would likely be less of a legal problem. With import quotas, however, the importers are entitled to the quota rents. A tariff-quota auction paid for by exporters could then, arguably, be considered an increase in the level of protection. This interesting legal issue is left to future research.

From an economic perspective, however, a violation of Article II:1(b) seems less problematic and easily deflated. Auctions only change the allocation of quota *rents* (a circumstance to which the WTO should be indifferent), but not the *volume* of trade, which essentially remains the same. The unit rent is simply absorbed as auction revenue instead of being captured by quota holders.

Another argument against quota auctions is that auctions may constitute an extra fee on imports in violation of Article VIII:1(a).[121] Again, from an economic point of view, no additional protection is afforded to domestic products. Also, one may argue that the importing government, as the creator of the initial restriction to trade, may have a prior claim to the rents thereof. It may *choose* to transfer these rents to foreign suppliers for free (e.g. under a FCFS allocation method), but exporting countries have no actionable *right* to such rents. Since the WTO has nothing to say about the entitlement to economic rents, auctioning quota rights could thus be interpreted simply as a tool for the importing country to change the market value of the financial asset transferred.

From a legal point of view, things may seem less straightforward. It could be argued that, by auctioning quota rights, foreign producers who have invested heavily in building up an export market and created tangible goodwill, *de facto* get expropriated if their auction bid is not successful.[122]

A final concern about quota auctions we can think of could be that auction revenue constitutes taxation for fiscal purposes. Most tariff quotas were constructed in the aftermath of the Uruguay Round to replace import quotas. True,

---

121 Article VIII:1(a) reads: 'All fees and charges of whatever character (other than import and export duties and other than taxes within the purview of Article III) imposed by contracting parties on or in connection with importation or exportation shall be limited in amount to the *approximate cost of services rendered and shall not represent an indirect protection to domestic products or a taxation of imports or exports for fiscal purposes*' (emphasis added).

122 Palmeter (2003: 100–103) argues that the introduction of certain US quota-auction schemes discussed in the United States would effectively have expropriated exporters, destroying their prior investments in marketing and customer relations, while depriving them of their right to choose their customers (the license holder).

these former quotas did not generate revenue; they simply provided domestic protection and transferred rents to select participants. However, since the motivation for tariff quotas was to replace harmful quantitative restrictions, neither the objective, nor the effect of original quotas (and their tariff-quota equivalents) was the generation of tax revenue for fiscal purposes. In addition, the auctioning of tariff-quota rights, albeit creating revenues, is requited by the transfer of rights to riskless rent in an amount largely equivalent to the auction price.[123]

To summarize, nearly all conventional methods of tariff-quota allocation are inherently discriminatory, and are thus in violation of the chapeau of the MFN principle articulated in the chapeau of Article XIII:2 GATT. To mimic the non-discriminatory free-trade equivalent distribution of trade under a tariff-quota regime, we offered three potential avenues, all of which have their own flaws. Economists would concur that auctions are the most efficient quota-allocation method. Yet we have to remark that exporter rents are dissipated in the bidding process and will end up going to the importing government – a situation that may be politically contentious. New forms of auctions should be assessed that allow inframarginal exporters to participate in the quota rents, so as to encourage their participation in the quota auction.

4.2   Looking forward: the relationship between compliance Panels and Article 22.6 arbitrations

An appeal of an Article 21.5 proceeding is the last hurdle faced by a successful complainant before an Article 22.6 arbitration can take place. By virtue of Article 22.7 DSU, the arbitrator is tasked with quantifying the amount of suspensions of concessions or other obligations to which the complainant is entitled.[124] Looking at the *Bananas III* appeal of the US and Ecuador's compliance challenge, we find it surprising that the AB did not seize the opportunity to indicate more clearly how its findings will affect and color an arbitrator's calculation of countermeasures under Article 22.4 DSU.[125]

Surely, the AB Members understand the salience of Article 22.6 arbitrations. Even if they do not take place with high frequency, the type and amount of trade sanctions awarded to the complainant may well have a significant impact on how frequently the dispute-settlement system is used in the first place, and even on the size of *ex ante* trade-liberalization commitments by WTO Members.[126]

---

123 Governments should be careful with how the auction revenues are being used. Handing them over to domestic import-competing firms à la *US–Byrd* and *US–FSC* is potentially WTO inconsistent.

124 Article 22.7 DSU reads in pertinent parts: 'The arbitrator acting pursuant to paragraph 6 ... shall determine whether the level of such suspension is equivalent to the level of nullification or impairment. The arbitrator may also determine if the proposed suspension of concessions or other obligations is allowed under the covered agreement.'

125 Article 22.4 DSU reads: 'The level of the suspension of concessions or other obligations authorized by the DSB shall be equivalent to the level of the nullification or impairment.'

126 If WTO dispute settlement systematically *under*-compensated successful complainants, Members anticipating ever to be in that situation will react in several ways, all of which seriously impair the

We note three issue areas in which the AB could have shed more light on how its rulings in the Article 21.5 appeal affect the subsequent Article 22.6 proceedings, but decided not to do so. These issues are: (i) the implication of 'overlap and coincidence' of nullification or impairment (NoI); (ii) the starting date of retaliation and how to deal with repealed measures; (iii) how different definitions of NoI influence the calculation methodology.

4.2.1 The implication of 'overlap and coincidence' of NoI

In connection with its Article XIII appeal, the EC claimed that the compliance Panel had failed to explain how the EC's violation of Article XIII 'caused any *new* or *additional* nullification or impairment to Ecuador ... beyond the nullification under Article I',[127] which the EC had conceded to by not appealing it. According to the EC, the Panel had 'double-counted' the trade damage accruing to Ecuador.[128] The AB responded that nullification or impairment (NoI) resulting from inconsistencies with Article I:1 and XIII may 'coincide or overlap, and that any such overlap is relevant only to the calculation of the total level of nullification or impairment'. It concluded that it does 'not need to pronounce on such questions in these Article 21.5 proceedings'.[129]

In the case of NoI experienced by the US, the EC held that the arbitrators in the original Article 22.6 proceedings in 1999 had found that the *sources* of NoI of benefits accruing to the US had uniquely been claims under the GATS and that no GATS obligations were at issue in the present 21.5 dispute.[130] The AB replied that it had not held in the original proceeding that the United States had suffered NoI exclusively as a result of violations of the GATS and that the GATS was not the only source of trade damage.[131] Hence, it established an overlap of NoI under different agreements. The AB concluded:

> We agree with the arbitrators that the question whether nullification or impairment exists within the meaning of Article 3.8 of the DSU, and the question of what level of suspension of concessions is equivalent to the level of nullification or impairment under Article 22.6, are distinct. [footnote omitted] *Therefore, the*

---

functioning of the multilateral trading system. Members may decide to refrain from litigating and instead resort to *extra*-contractual means of retribution and/or aggressive self-help behavior. They may opt for bilateral resolution outside the WTO forum, seek retaliation outside the trade realm (e.g. by political coercion), engage in unilateral retaliation (e.g. Section 301 of the *US Trade Act of 1974*), enact retaliatory AD action, enter into retaliatory litigation, or design strategic retaliation tactics (e.g. 'carousel' retaliation). In anticipation of a low retaliation amount, disgruntled Members may also decide to partially exit the WTO system by engaging in preferential trading agreements, by withdrawing from plurilateral agreements and protocols, or by refraining from participating in trade talks. Finally, disappointed Members may decide to liberalize less in future trade rounds (or to block a successful conclusion), in the hope of suffering less nullification or impairment in future disputes (Schropp, 2009a).

127 AB Report, para. 77 (emphasis in original).
128 AB Report, para. 358.
129 AB Report, para. 360.
130 AB Report, paras. 82, 474.
131 AB Report, paras. 473–474.

question how the arbitrators calculated the level of nullification or impairment under Article 22.6 arises in a different procedural context in WTO dispute settlement.[132]

We submit that we would have liked to see more guidance from the AB in the issue of sources, overlap and coincidence of NoI. True, the task of quantification of trade damages is conducted uniquely by the arbitrator and not by the dispute Panel or AB,[133] but is it also the arbitrator's task to decide on the *sources* of NoI, and whether overlap and coincidence of NoI has occurred – and what the concept of 'overlap and coincidence' of NoI means in the first place?

First, it seems cursory by the AB simply to state that questions of the *sources* and *level* of NoI are 'different', that is distinct from questions of *existence* of NoI, and that it is only concerned with the latter, leaving the former questions in the hands of the arbitrator. This is not helpful, given that the reason why damage exists should bear some connection to how large it is. Hence, there is considerable overlap between the concept of *existence* and *sources*. We will deal with this relationship in subsection 4.2.3.

Next, on the issue of coincidence and overlap, the AB pronounced that overlap and coincidence of NoI exists, but shied away from discussing the implications of that finding. What is the arbitrator to do, if the same measure causes NoI under, say, Article XI GATT, and adverse effects in the form of serious prejudice under Article 5(c) of the *SCM Agreement*? Should he calculate one or two damage numbers? Should he then use the higher number? Or should he add both calculations and then determine and factor out areas of overlap? Generally, what *is* the overlap of serious prejudice and NoI? In addition, how can NoI caused by breach of two distinct GATT rules overlap? Are Members harmed more – or differently – under a violation of, say, Article III.2 than under Article XI GATT? The authors of this comment fail to see any systemic reasons why this would be the case. Yet, after the AB's pronouncement in *Bananas III*, arbitrators will have to start thinking about issues of overlap and coincidence, not least, since complainants may try to boost the numbers by claiming overlap instead of coincidence, whenever possible. In so doing, the arbitrator will have numerous question marks but no clarification from the AB.

4.2.2 Expired measures and the starting date for retaliation

With respect to the EC's repeal of the ACP tariff preference, the AB ruled that it 'consider[s] it to be within the discretion of the panel to decide how it takes into account subsequent modifications or a repeal of the measure at issue'.[134] The AB also referred to a remark made in its report in *US–Upland Cotton*, stating that

---

132 AB Report, para. 475 (emphasis added).
133 In that respect, the EC is wrong in reproaching the AB with 'double-counting'. The AB does not 'count' NoI at all.
134 AB Report, para. 270.

'whether or not a measure is still in force is not dispositive of whether that measure is currently affecting the operation of any covered agreement'.[135]

These statements hardly give any guidance to the arbitrator, who is supposed to deal with the quantification of NoI caused by a measure that is no longer in existence. Who decides whether a repealed measure should be included in the calculation of NoI, the dispute Panel/AB, or the arbitrator? If a Panel or the AB decides to take into account the repeal of the measure, that is rules against the existence of NoI, yet the arbitrator finds that the repealed measure has persistent effects, may the arbitrator calculate trade damages of the withdrawn measure nevertheless?

If a repealed measure is to be included, what is the cut-off date for such in-clusion? In the present case, the repeal happened long after the original reasonable period of time (RPT), but before the end of the Article 21.5 proceedings. May the complainant ask for retaliation rights amounting to the damage suffered until the measure was repealed (or its effects subsided)? A similar issue came up in the Article 22.6 proceedings in the *US–Upland Cotton* case,[136] when the US repealed a prohibited cotton export subsidy (the so-called Step 2 payments) one full calendar year after the end of the RPT.[137] Brazil as the complainant demanded retaliation rights for a one-time countermeasure, while the US argued that the program was terminated and that Brazil was hence seeking authorization for *retroactive* remedies not permitted by the DSU. The United States essentially argued that countermeasures may only be authorized as long as a Member has not come into compliance with the DSB's rulings and recommendations. According to the US, if there is no longer a measure, there is no more WTO inconsistency to be dealt with. Brazil opposed this view, arguing that retaliation rights begin with the end of the original RPT, and that Article 21.5 proceedings are a mere 'sus-pension in time'. Thus, Brazil claimed, Article 21.5 proceedings are irrelevant for the sake of quantification of countermeasures (provided that the complainant wins the compliance proceedings).[138] Hence, according to Brazil, a one-time retaliation award compensating for the year after the RPT but before the repeal of Step 2 payments does not constitute retroactive damages, but is faithful to Article 4.9 of the *SCM Agreement*, which obliges the DSB to 'grant authorization to the complaining Member to take appropriate [and not disproportionate] counter-measures'.[139]

---

135 AB Report, para. 267.

136 *United States – Subsidies on Upland Cotton* (WT/DS267).

137 See the contribution of Bill Davey and André Sapir in this volume.

138 Brazil cited to the arbitrator in *US–FSC* and *US–Gambling* who held that countermeasures should be assessed as of the date of expiry of the implementation period.

139 For details of the *US–Upland Cotton* Article 22.6 arbitration, see http://www.ustr.gov/trade-topics/enforcement/dispute-settlement-proceedings/wto-dispute-settlement/subsidies-upland-cott (USsubmissions) and http://www.mre.gov.br (last visited 19 November 2009) (Brazil's submissions).

Pending circulation of the arbitrator's report in *US–Upland Cotton*, this issue is currently unresolved. It could, however, have been resolved by the AB long before at the opportunity of these *Bananas* proceedings, if the AB had been more explicit about how to deal with expired measures, and, more generally, whether counter-measures are measured starting from the original RPT or only after the Article 21.5 proceedings.[140]

4.2.3 The nature of nullification or impairment

In its report, the AB made a series of statements about how to determine the existence of nullification or impairment. At various instances, the AB held that in order to assess whether the complainants had suffered any NoI, not only actual trade effects suffered were important. According to the AB, also '"competitive opportunities" and, in particular, any potential trade interest' by the complainant matter.[141] The AB also referred to a statement it had made in the original proceedings, opining that if the United States did not even have a potential export interest, '[t]he internal market of the United States for bananas could be affected by the EC bananas regime by its effects on world supplies and world prices for bananas'.[142]

The AB's three-pronged definition of NoI (actual trade damages; competitive opportunities; internal market of the complainant) should be given meaning in the subsequent arbitration process, even though its statements were made in the context of establishing the *existence* of NoI, and not the *level* of NoI, and even though compliance proceedings are procedurally different from Article 22.6 arbitrations.[143] *Existence* of NoI predisposes its level.[144] In other words, we believe that in *Bananas III* the AB has defined the *nature* of NoI, and proclamation on the nature should logically be the basis for any calculation or quantification exercise.

If our interpretation is correct, according to which the AB's definition of the nature of NoI cannot be logically detached from its quantification, then arbitrators will face new challenges in the quantification of NoI. The integration of *potential trade interests* and *competitive opportunities*, as well as damage suffered in the *internal market* of the complainant, is quite a departure from

---

140 We note here that if the United States's interpretation were right and NoI were calculated as of the end of the 21.5 proceedings only, this would clearly impact on the substance, or even put an end to, future sequencing agreements between Members, because it would put complainants at a serious disadvantage.

141 AB Report, para. 469, citing the *US–Superfund* case. See also para. 466. By 'competitive opportunities', the AB apparently meant the United States's opportunities to export bananas into the EC, but also its 'competitive relationship' with any banana exporting country in the world (see ibid. paras. 80, 81).

142 AB Report, para. 466. See also paras. 128, 175, 458, 470, 476.

143 AB Report, para. 475.

144 If the issues of *level* and *existence* of NoI were decoupled, that is if the level of NoI bore no relationship with trade damages suffered by the complainants, then the level could potentially be zero. But at a level of zero, NoI would not exist.

the way NoI has been interpreted (and calculated) so far, namely as actual trade damages, or 'exports foregone' suffered after the RPT (see Bown and Ruta, 2009; Schropp, 2009b). If we are right in believing that the definition of NoI must determine, or at least have an impact on, the methodology used for calculating the level of NoI, new ways of quantifying trade damages may become necessary.[145]

To be clear, the authors believe that the question of *existence* of NoI is different from that of the *level* – but not independent of it. It is the responsibility of Panels and the AB to determine whether NoI exists and the separate responsibility of Article 22.6 arbitrators to then quantify it. Nevertheless, to guide arbitrators in their already difficult job, WTO Panels or the AB should be more precise about what they believe the nature of NoI to be, and in what ways this could affect or determine the damage calculation. This, we believe, will greatly support arbitrators in their work.

To summarize, although there is no doubt that the framers of the DSU entrusted the 22.6 arbitrator with the ultimate calculation of the amount of NoI, the authors believe that it is the Panel's or the AB's obligation to make clear the nature and duration of the NoI it finds, so that arbitrators need not wonder which elements they should evaluate. In the present *Bananas III (21.5)* report by the AB, just as in many other reports, the AB has left too many issues for the arbitrator to deal with. In particular, the AB was slightly remiss in giving too little indication and guidance as to how the arbitrator shall deal with the issues of (i) overlap and coincidence of NoI, (ii) previously repealed measures, and (iii) the relevant definition of NoI.

Some authors have rightly argued that Article 22.6 arbitrations could benefit from Appellate Body review (e.g. Lockhart, 2009), and arbitrators on occasion have lamented over the lack of guidance that the DSU holds in stock for the calculation of NoI. This should encourage the AB to spend more time and thought on the consequences that their statements (or the omission thereof) will have on this last step of WTO litigations.

---

145 If NoI is defined as *impairment of competitive opportunities*, a quantification methodology based on discounted cash flows, or option-pricing models is pertinent. If NoI is defined as damage suffered in the *internal* market of the complaining party as a result of the respondent's measure in question, another calculation methodology may be needed: to quantify damages based on factors *intrinsic* to the complaining country's domestic markets, a calculation akin to those required by Article 6.3 of the *SCM Agreement* may be applied. To recall, Article 6.3 of the *SCM Agreement* defines trade damage (serious prejudice) inter alia as price undercutting in the market of another Member, significant price suppression and depression, lost sales, or increase in the world market share of the subsidizing Member. The calculatory benchmark for these damages is quite different from the 'exports foregone' standard so far applied in Article 22.4 DSU cases.

5. Conclusion

At first glance, the Appellate Body Report in *Bananas III* (*Article 21.5; Second Recourse*) does not seem to be a case for the *Guinness Book*. The EC should not have appealed the Panel Report, and the AB did a good job upholding most of the Panel's findings. It is at second sight that the AB Report reveals its interesting facets. Practitioners may be interested in the role of *estoppel* in WTO litigation, the legal effect of Panel suggestions, the relevance of modalities papers as interpretative tools, and other legal aspects we discussed. Readers more interested in law and economics theory may find food for thought in our examination of the economics of tariff quotas and the inherently discriminatory nature of Article XIII:2, our assessment of temporary opt-outs in the WTO, or our discussion of the relevance of compliance proceedings for the damage calculation under Article 22.6 of the DSU.

References

Bergsten, C. Fred, Kimberly Ann Elliott, Jeffrey J. Schott, and Wendy E. Takacs (1987), *Auction Quotas and United States Trade Policy*, Washington, DC: Institute for International Economics.

Bown, Chad P. and Rachel McCulloch (2003), 'Non-discrimination and the WTO Agreement on Safeguards', *World Trade Review*, 2(3): 327–348.

Bown, Chad P. and Michele Ruta (2009), 'The Economics of Permissible WTO Retaliation', forthcoming in Chad P. Bown and Joost Pauwelyn (eds.), *The Law, Economics and Politics of Retaliation in WTO Dispute Settlement*, Cambridge: Cambridge University Press.

de Gorter, Harry and Ian Sheldon (eds.) (2001), 'Agriculture in the WTO: Issues in Reforming Tariff-Rate Import Quotas in the Agreement on Agriculture in the WTO', Department of Applied Economics, International Agricultural Trade Research Consortium, University of Minnesota, St Paul, Minnesota.

Fearon, James D. (1998), 'Bargaining, Enforcement, and International Cooperation', *International Organization*, 52(2): 269–305.

Gantz, David A. and Simon A. B. Schropp (2009), 'Rice Age: Comments on the Panel Report in *Turkey – Measures Affecting the Importation of Rice*', *World Trade Review*, 8(1): 145–177, and in Henrik Horn and Petros C. Mavroidis (eds.), *The American Law Institute – The WTO Case Law of 2006–2007: Legal and Economic Analysis*, Cambridge: Cambridge University Press.

Goetz, Charles J. and Robert E. Scott (1981), 'Principles of Relational Contracts', *Virginia Law Review*, 67(2): 1089–1150.

Horn, Henrik, Giovanni Maggi, and Robert W. Staiger (2009), 'Trade Agreements as Endogenously Incomplete Contracts', *American Economic Review*, forthcoming.

Hudec, Robert E. (1997), 'Tiger, Tiger in the House: A Critical Appraisal of the Case Against Discriminatory Trade Measures', in John H. Jackson and Alan O. Sykes (eds.), *Implementing the Uruguay Round*, Oxford: Clarendon Press, pp. 167–212.

Jackson, John H. (1997), *The World Trading System: Law and Policy of International Economic Relations*, 2nd edn, Cambridge, MA: MIT Press.

Jackson, John H. and Patricio Grané (2001), 'The Saga Continues: An Update on the Banana Dispute and Its Procedural Offspring', *Journal of International Economic Law*, 4(3): 581–595.

Lockhart, Nicolas (2009), 'A commentary to Thomas Sebastian's contribution entitled "The Law of Permissible WTO Retaliation"', forthcoming in Chad P. Bown and Joost Pauwelyn (eds.),

    The Law, Economics and Politics of Retaliation in WTO Dispute Settlement, Cambridge: Cambridge University Press.

Maggi, Giovanni and Robert W. Staiger (2008), 'On the Role and Design of Dispute Settlement Procedures in International Trade Agreements', NBER Working Paper 14067.

Mahlstein, Kornel and Simon A. B. Schropp (2007), 'The Optimal Design of Trade Policy Flexibility in the WTO', HEI Working Paper 27-2007 (available at www.hei.unige.ch).

Mavroidis, Petros C. (2007), *Trade in Goods*, Oxford: Oxford University Press.

Mavroidis, Petros C. (2000), 'Remedies in the WTO Legal System: Between a Rock and a Hard Place', *European Journal of International Law*, 11(4): 763–813.

Messerlin, Patrick A. (2000), 'Antidumping and Safeguards', in Jeffrey J. Schott, *The WTO After Seattle*, Washington, DC: Institute for International Economics, pp. 159–183.

Palmeter, David (2003), *The WTO as a Legal System: Essays on International Trade Law and Policy*, London: Cameron May.

Palmeter, David and Petros C. Mavroidis (2004), *Dispute Settlement in the World Trade Organization: Practice and Procedure*, 2nd edn, Cambridge: Cambridge University Press.

Schropp, Simon A. B. (2009a), *Trade Policy Flexibility and Enforcement in the WTO: A Law and Economics Analysis*, Cambridge: Cambridge University Press.

Schropp, Simon A. B. (2009b), 'The Equivalence Standard Under Article 22.4 DSU: A "Tariffic" Misunderstanding?', forthcoming in Chad P. Bown and Joost Pauwelyn (eds.), *The Law, Economics and Politics of Retaliation in WTO Dispute Settlement*, Cambridge: Cambridge University Press.

Skully, David W. (2001), 'Economics of Tariff-Rate Quota Administration', Technical Bulletin No. 1893, Economic Research Service, US Department of Agriculture.

Skully, David W. (2000), 'US Tariff-Rate Quotas: Historical Allocation and Non-discrimination', *Agricultural and Resource Economics Review*, 29(1): 81–90.

Skully, David W. (1999), 'The Economics of TRQ Administration', International Agricultural Trade Research Consortium, Working Paper #99-6.

Skully, David W. (1998), 'Auctioning the Tariff Quota for US Sugar Imports', in *Sugar and Sweetener: Situation and Outlook Report*, US Department of Agriculture, Economic Research Service, Market and Trade Economics Division, May (SSS-223): 17–22.

Appendix I: Order of events in Banana III

Date	Measure/event	Annotations
1993/02/13	EC Regulation 404/93 enters into force **'Original Banana Import Regime'** (the 'Common Market Organization for Bananas')	Measure at issue in original *Bananas III* litigation – Deficiency payment system for EU banana importers – Special distribution of import licenses depending on the origin of traders – Preferential tariff quota of 857,700 mt for ACP countries at zero tariff – MFN tariff quota of 2 million mt – Prohibitive out-of-quota tariff rate of €680/mt
1994/10/01	EC Tariff Schedule on bananas, incl. **Bananas Framework Agreement** (Annex to EC's GATT Schedule)	Annex indicates 'terms, conditions or qualifications' of tariff schedule – Introduction of a global basic tariff quota fixed at 2,200,000 mt for 1995, subject to enlargement of the European Union – Introduction of country-specific allocations of quota rights to Venezuela, Costa Rica, Colombia, and Nicaragua taken from the global MFN quota – In-quota tariff of 75 €/mt – Para. 9 states that the Agreement shall apply until 31 Dec. 2002
1997/09/25	DSB adopts Panel and AB reports in original *EC–Bananas III* case	– Original Banana Import Regime not justified by Banana Framework Agreement, Agreement on Agriculture, Lomé Article I Waiver – Violation of Arts XIII, I:1, and III:4 GATT and Arts. II and XVII GATS
1998/12/18	Request for first 21.5 Panel by Ecuador	
1999/01/01	EC Regulation 2362/98 in combination with Council Regulation 1637/98 (adopted 1998/10/28, effective 1999/01/01) **'Compliance Banana Import Regime'**	Unsuccessful attempt to comply with original DSB rulings and recommendations (R&R) EC Regulation 2362/98 replaces earlier regime in response to R&R in original *EC–Bananas III* Report: – Duty-free TRQ of 857,000 mt for ACP – TRQ of 2,553,000 mt with tariff of 75€/mt for MFN suppliers – Out-of-quota imports: ACP are granted €200 preference

Appendix I (*Cont.*)

Date	Measure/event	Annotations
1999/04/09	Decision by 22.6 Arbitrator in US case	Arbitrator awards level of suspension of concessions and other obligations up to an amount of US$191.4 m/year (United States) and US$201.6 m/year (Ecuador). The US suspends tariff concessions; Ecuador does not exercise its righs to suspend concessions under GATT, GATS, and TRIPS
1999/05/06	DSB adopts first 21.5 Report (not appealed)	Measures taken by EC (under Regulation 2362/98) inconsistent with Arts. I and XIII GATT – Panel made suggestions pursuant to Art. 19.1 DSU how EC could bring its measures into conformity
2000/03/24	Decision by 22.6 Arbitrator in Ecuador case	
2001/01/29	EC Regulations 216/2001 and 2587/2001: Amended EC Reg 404/93 **'Interim Banana Import Regime'**	EC Banana Regime 2002–2005 was never challenged – TRQ A of 2,200,000 mt for all suppliers at 75€/mt for MFN suppliers and zero tariff for ACP – TRQ B of 453,000 mt for MFN suppliers at 75€/mt for MFN suppliers and zero tariff for ACP – TRQ C of 750,000 mt at zero tariff for ACP – Out-of-quota tariff: tariff preference of €300 for ACP countries
2001/04/11	**Understanding on Bananas** with US	(see p. 81 of AB report) – EC promises to introduce a tariff-only regime for banana imports **no later than Jan. 1, 2006** – in the interim EC will implement an import regime on the basis of historical licensing effective as of July 1, 2001 – EC considers Understanding a mutually agreed solution – Ecuador and US consider Understanding a means by which dispute can be solved
2001/04/30	**Understanding on Bananas** with Ecuador	See p. 5 of AB Report
2001/11/14	**Doha Article I Waiver** including **Annex on Bananas**	– Waiver grants preferential tariff treatment for ACP countries – Annex sets out special two-stage arbitration process for re-binding on EC tariff schedule – Subject to fulfillment of rebinding requirements, Waiver applies until 31 Dec. 2007

Appendix I (*Cont.*)

Date	Measure/event	Annotations
2001/11/14	**Doha Article XIII Waiver**	Waiver grants TRA of 775,000 mt at zero tariff to ACP countries
2005/01/01	EU enlargement from 'EU 15' to 'EU 25'	Enlargement of customs union forces EC to rebind its banana tariff in accordance with Art. XXVIII GATT
2005/01/31	EC informs WTO of intension of rebinding bananas tariff schedule under Art. XXVIII	2-stage Arbitration process according to Doha Article I Waiver is kicked off
2005/08/01	1st Rebinding Arbitration report against EC following '**Modified Offer (I) on Banana Import Regime**'	EC's offer of an MFN tariff of 230€/mt is rejected
2005/10/27	2nd Rebinding arbitration report against EC following '**Modified Offer (II) on Banana Import Regime**'	EC's offer of a tariff of €187/mt and 775,000 mt duty-free TRQ for ACP is rejected
2006/01/01	EC Regulation 1964/2005 (adopted 2005/11/29) enters into force '**Bananas Import Regime**'	Measure at issue: – Single tariff rate of €176/mt for all MFN suppliers – TRQ of 775,000 mt for ACP countries with zero tariff
2006/01/01	Deadline for EC introduction of tariff-only regime according to Understanding on Bananas	EC did not enact a tariff-only regime; instead, it introduced Regulation 1964/2005
2007/03/20	Establishment of Ecuador 21.5 Panel	
2007/07/12	Establishment of US 21.5 Panel	
2007/12/20	EC Regulation 1528/2007 '**Novel Banana Import Regime**'	– Repeals EC Regulation 404/93 – Modifies Regulation 1964/2005 – Eliminates preferential TRQ for ACP – Establishes a tariff-only import regime for bananas
2008/04/07	Circulation of Ecuador 21.5 Report	
2008/05/19	Circulation of US 21.5 Report	
2008/08/28	EC informs WTO of Appeal	
2008/08/29	Adoption of US and Ecuador 21.5 report	
2008/11/26	AB Report on *Bananas III* (21.5) is issued	

Guilt by association:
US – Measures Relating to Shrimp from Thailand
and
US – Customs Bond Directive for Merchandise Subject to Anti-Dumping/Countervailing Duties

THOMAS J. PRUSA

Rutgers University and NBER

EDWIN VERMULST

Vermulst, Verhaeghe & Graafsma

Abstract: The United States's enhanced continuous bond requirement [EBR] for goods subject to anti-dumping and countervailing duties was the focus of this dispute. Because of perceived problems with its ability to collect anti-dumping duties, the US amended its bonding requirements in 2004. Under the new rules, importers were required to secure a bond for an amount equal to the cash-deposit rate in effect on the date of entry of the merchandise multiplied by the importer's value of imports from the previous year, as well as pay cash deposits equal to the amount of anti-dumping duties per entry. The US claimed the additional deposit was reasonable and necessary to guarantee duty payment in case the anti-dumping duty increased during the administrative review. Thailand and India claimed that the additional deposit was unreasonable and an additional action against dumping and was therefore impermissible under GATT 1994 and the Anti-Dumping Agreement. The Appellate Body upheld the Panel's findings that while the Ad Note to Article VI : 2 and 3 GATT 1994 authorizes the imposition of security requirements during the period following the imposition of an anti-dumping duty order, the additional security requirement resulting from the application of the EBR to shrimp was not 'reasonable' within the meaning of the Ad Note. The Appellate Body reversed the legal interpretation by the Panel that there is no obligation under the Ad Note to assess the risk of default by individual importers; however, the AB upheld the Panel's finding that the EBR is not 'necessary' within the meaning of Article XX(d) of the GATT 1994. As a result, the AB upheld the Panel's conclusion that the application of the EBR to

The views expressed in this paper are those of the authors and all omissions and errors are also of the authors. We would like to thank Ken Pierce and Daniel Porter for their very helpful comments and suggestions.

shrimp was inconsistent with Article 18(1) of the Anti-Dumping Agreement because it was inconsistent with the Ad Note to Article VI:2 and 3 of the GATT 1994 and not justified by Article XX(d). We consider the AB's legal and economic reasoning to be largely correct. The US employed a sledgehammer to kill a mosquito and the AB used the concepts of 'reasonableness' in the Ad Note and 'necessity' in Article XX(d) to reject what fundamentally was a lack of proportionality, while leaving the door open for more reasonable application of bonding requirements.

1. Introduction

In February 2005, the United States imposed definitive anti-dumping duties on imports of certain frozen warmwater shrimp from a half-dozen countries, including Thailand and India. This dispute concerns measures related to this anti-dumping order. The focus of the dispute was a US bonding requirement that was imposed for the first time in this case.

Under US law, after the Department of Commerce makes its preliminary dumping determination, cash deposits will be collected or bonds may be posted by the importer on entries of merchandise being investigated. After the initial investigation is complete and an anti-dumping duty order is issued, importers are required to pay cash deposits on entries. Technically, because the US has a retrospective system for assessing anti-dumping duties (ADD) and countervailing duties (CVD) saying that deposits are paid is not the same as saying duties are assessed. To the contrary, ADD and CVD are assessed only after the conclusion of an administrative review by the Department of Commerce.[1] If the dumping margin decreases, importers receive (some portion of) their deposits back plus interest. If the dumping margin increases in the administrative review, importers have to pay additional duties (e.g., the value of subject imports times the increase in margin).

The US's combination of prospective deposits and retrospective assessment significantly complicates the collection issue. On the one hand, cash deposits are collected on new import entries at each *exporter*'s assigned rate; therefore, all importers purchasing from a given exporter will pay the same cash-deposit rate regardless of the actual transaction price. On the other hand, each *importer* can be assessed a different amount for its ultimate ADD liability for past entries. It is possible, for instance, that even though a dumping margin for a certain exporter increases, not all importers will necessarily need to pay additional duties. For example, suppose importer A buys from exporter X at $60, while importer B buys from exporter X at $100. During an administrative review, importer B might find

---

[1] If no review is requested, the entries are liquidated at the rate in effect at the time of entry.

all of its cash deposits refunded, while importer A might be required to pay an additional duty beyond the cash deposit.[2]

Throughout 2002 and 2003, there were growing concerns in the US about un-collected ADD/CVD.[3] In an attempt to reduce the risk that assessed duties would not be collected, the US adopted new rules – referred to as the 'enhanced continuous bond requirement' (EBR). The new policy was imposed for the first time in February 2005. The maiden application involved imports of warmwater shrimp. Under the new rules, importers of shrimp from India and Thailand (and the other subject countries) had to secure a bond for an amount equal to the cash-deposit rate in effect on the date of entry of the merchandise multiplied by the importer's value of imports from the previous year, as well as pay cash deposits equal to the amount of the ADD per entry.[4] India and Thailand complained that the new bonding requirement violated WTO rules. In addition to making cash deposits at the ADD rate, the new rules required importers to tie up hundreds of millions of dollars of capital (to cover the bond), thereby greatly limiting their ability to finance other business operations. India and Thailand also objected because these rules were imposed even though there had not been *any* defaults of warmwater shrimp anti-dumping duties by India or Thailand (or, for that matter, by any subject country); moreover, the US's own studies indicated that there had been no significant defaults on any imported products from India or Thailand. While other agriculture/aquaculture products had defaulted on anti-dumping duties, Thailand and India believed warmwater shrimp exporters had done nothing to warrant being subjected to the EBR – that they had been found guilty by association rather than by action.

The Appellate Body (AB) found that the enhanced continuous bond requirement 'as applied' by the United States in Shrimp was not 'reasonable' within the meaning of the Ad Note to GATT Article VI:2 and 3. This Ad Note provides in relevant part that a contracting party may require reasonable security (bond or cash deposit) for the payment of anti-dumping or countervailing duty pending final determination of the facts in any case of suspected dumping or subsidization. However, the AB rejected India's claim that the Amended Customs Bond Directive, by virtue of which the enhanced continuous bond requirement was imposed, was inconsistent 'as such' with the Anti-Dumping Agreement.

---

2 Notwithstanding that importer B did not owe any ADD for past entries, importer B will still have to pay the cash-deposit rate levied on exporter X for future entries. Importer B could then get a refund after conclusion of the next administrative review if the same pricing facts continue to exist.

3 *United States – Measures Relating to Shrimp from Thailand* [hereinafter: *US–Shrimp (Thailand)*] (WT/DS343/AB/R, 16 July 2008) AB, footnote 194. According to the United States, while historically annual uncollected anti-dumping duties from importers had been relatively low (rarely exceeding US$10 million a year), outstanding anti-dumping liability for 2004 alone reached an unprecedented US$225 million for agriculture and aquaculture cases, that is for merchandise similar to shrimp.

4 Importers also were required to post the standard continuous bond requirement. The standard continuous bond amount is $50,000 or 10% of the total taxes and fees paid in the previous 12-month period whichever is greater.

We consider the AB's legal and economic reasoning to be largely correct. The AB used the concepts of 'reasonableness' in the Ad Note and 'necessity' in Article XX(d) to reject what fundamentally was a lack of proportionality, while leaving the door open for more reasonable application of bonding requirements. In effect, the AB's decision suggests that had the US used a flyswatter rather than a sledge-hammer to mitigate the problem of defaults, the additional bonding requirement could have been WTO-consistent. Our main criticism of the AB is that it could have been much sharper in its critique of the US's justification for the EBR. From an economic perspective, the unreasonableness of the EBR with respect to shrimp goes well beyond the AB's critique.

The remainder of the paper is organized as follows. In Section 2, we provide some background to the dispute. In Section 3, we discuss the key claims of the parties and provide an overview of the AB's findings. In Section 4, we will discuss legal and economic aspects of the determinations. In Section 5, we offer some concluding comments and perspectives on possible alternative policies toward re-ducing default risk under the retrospective system.

2.   Background to the dispute

According to the United States General Accounting Office (GAO), shortfalls in collecting ADD/CVD did not exist or at least were not widely publicized until about 2000.[5] Around that time, inadequacies in the US's long-standing duty-collection procedures began to be exploited and the US experienced a significant increase in the amount of unpaid ADD/CVD.[6] US Customs and Border Protection ('Customs') reported that it was unable to collect $130 million in ADD/CVD in fiscal year 2003, $260 million in fiscal year 2004, and $93 million in fiscal year 2005.[7] In comparison, the United States reported to the WTO that prior to 2000 uncollected duties rarely exceeded $10 million annually.[8]

Awareness of and passions about the unpaid duties were stoked by the Continued Dumping and Subsidy Offset Act of 2000 (CDSOA) or, as it is more commonly known, the 'Byrd Amendment'.[9] CDSOA modified the Tariff Act of 1930 and instructed Customs to put all ADD/CVD into special accounts, one for each case. Previously, ADD and CVD revenue went directly into the general US

5 United States Government Accountability Office, *Antidumping and Countervailing Duties: Congress and Agencies Should Take Additional Steps to Reduce Substantial Shortfalls in Duty Collection*, GAO-08-391, March 2008 [hereinafter GAO (2008)], p. 9.

6 *US–Shrimp (Thailand)* AB, para. 190.

7 United States Government Accountability Office, *International Trade: Customs' Revised Bonding Policy Reduces Risk of Uncollected Duties, but Concerns about Uneven Implementation and Effects Remain*, GAO-07-50, October, 2006 [hereinafter GAO (2006)], p. 1.

8 *US – Shrimp (Thailand)* AB, footnote 194.

9 See Henrik Horn and Petros C. Mavroidis (2006), 'United States – Continued Dumping and Subsidy Offset Act of 2000', in Henrik Horn and Petros C. Mavroidis (eds.), *The WTO Case Law of 2003 – The American Law Institute Reporters' Studies*, Cambridge: Cambridge University Press.

Treasury. Under CDSOA, at the end of each fiscal year the money collected in each case-by-case account was paid out directly to the companies who participated in the original investigation.[10] The first CDSOA payouts were made late in 2001. The amount of money flowing to eligible domestic firms was quite large, with hundreds of millions of dollars of payments annually flowing to eligible domestic firms.[11] If the duties were not collected, however, Byrd payouts could not be made.

By 2003, the United States perceived it had an ADD/CVD collection problem, at least in part because some CDSOA eligible industries were not receiving the payment to which they were entitled. Under existing Customs rules importers needed to post a continuous customs bond equal to US$50,000 or 10% of the annual estimated duties, taxes, and fees paid during the preceding year, whichever is greater. Of course, the standard continuous customs bond was not designed with ADD/CVD in mind. Customs concluded that the standard bond did not provide sufficient protection in light of the retrospective system, which created a risk that Customs would not be able to collect the full amount of ADD/CVD owed. Customs' analysis revealed that the collection problem was particularly severe for agriculture/aquaculture products. Customs deduced that agriculture/aquaculture products had certain characteristics, such as low capitalization, that made them high risk for defaults on ADD/CVD owed. [12]

On 9 July 2004, Customs announced a revision to its standard bond policy for bonds covering certain imports subject to ADD/CVD orders. The revised policy – referred to as the enhanced continuous bond requirement – required importers to obtain a bond equal to 100% of the estimated ADD/CVD for items imported over the previous 12 months. The EBR was originally imposed pursuant to the Customs Bond Directive 99-3510-004 on Monetary Guidelines for Setting Bond Amounts issued on 23 July 1991 (the '1991 Customs Bond Directive'); it was later amended by a number of subsequent measures. Collectively, the EBR and its amendments are referred to as the 'Amended CBD'.[13]

Customs' internal analysis of the new requirement suggested the EBR would essentially double the amount of ADD/CVD revenue protected[14] and hence would reduce the amount of uncollected revenue. Customs recognized the extra funds would often not be required and believed that the posting of additional bonds would not be burdensome to importers. In particular, premiums required by surety companies for the standard continuous bond were generally small. Furthermore,

---

10 Details on the rules governing CDSOA duty disbursement can be found on the US Customs website, http://www.cbp.gov/xp/cgov/trade/priority_trade/add_cvd/cont_dump/.

11 According to GAO, more than $1 billion in CDSOA payments were made during the 2001–2004 period. See *United States Government Accountability Office, International Trade: Issues and Effects of Implementing the Continued Dumping and Subsidy Offset Act*, GAO-05-979, September 2005.

12 *US–Shrimp (Thailand)* AB, para. 59.

13 *United States – Customs Bond Directive for Merchandise Subject to Anti-Dumping/Countervailing Duties* [hereinafter: *US–Customs Bond (India)*] (WT/DS345/AB/R, 16 July 2008) Panel, para. 2.2.

14 GAO (2008), p. 27.

Customs did not design the EBR to apply to all existing ADD/CVD orders or even to all new orders. Rather, the new guidelines would apply only to 'covered cases' within 'special categories' of merchandise. The scope and applicability would be determined on a case-by-case basis.

In January 2004, an anti-dumping investigation involving warmwater shrimp from six countries (Brazil, China, Ecuador, India, Thailand, and Vietnam) was initiated.[15] According to the US government, imports of warmwater shrimp were a suitable test case for the revised bond policy, because:

(1) warmwater shrimp shared characteristics with other agriculture/aquaculture products that indicated a risk that Customs and Border Protection may not be able to collect the full amount of duties owed; (2) it represented a large volume of imports and faced potentially high anti-dumping duties; and (3) shrimp imports were duty-free, therefore, most shrimp importers had no history of normal duty payments and had minimum $50,000 bonds.[16]

Said differently, even though shrimp importers had never defaulted on any ADD/CVD payments, Customs believed they were at high risk of doing so because importers of similar products (e.g., crawfish tail meat) had defaulted in the past.

A final affirmative injury determination on warmwater shrimp was made in January 2005. On 1 February 2005, Customs applied the revised EBR policy to imports of shrimp from the six countries subject to ADD. To date, agriculture/ aquaculture merchandise remains the only merchandise designated as a 'special category' and shrimp is the only 'covered case' designated within the agriculture/ aquaculture category.

3. Claims

3.1 Panel stage

There were several substantive claims before the Panel. India and Thailand challenged the EBR 'as applied' in the shrimp anti-dumping investigation under a number of provisions of the Anti-Dumping Agreement [hereinafter: ADA], the Agreement on Subsidies and Countervailing Measures [hereinafter: SCM Agreement] and the GATT. India also challenged the EBR 'as such' under various GATT provisions. Thailand challenged the use of model zeroing in the original anti-dumping investigation under ADA Article 2.4.2.

The Panel found that the US Department of Commerce [USDOC] acted inconsistently with ADA Article 2.4.2 by using model zeroing when calculating dumping margins. The US did not appeal this decision to the AB. Given that the issue

---

15 US Department of Commerce investigations A-351-838, A-570-893, A-331-802, A-533-840, A-549-822, and A-552-802; US International Trade Commission investigations 731-TA-1063-731-TA-1068.

16 GAO (2006), p. 4.

was not appealed to the AB and given the large body of scholarship on zeroing, we will not discuss the issue in this paper.[17]

The heart of the dispute involves the Panel's determinations with respect to the EBR. First, and perhaps the most significant determination, the Panel concluded that the application of EBR 'constitutes "specific action against dumping"' and is not in 'accordance with the provisions of the GATT 1994 as interpreted by the ADA'.[18] Therefore, the Panel concluded the application of the EBR is inconsistent with ADA Article 18.1.

Second, the Panel concluded that the 'additional security requirements resulting from the application of the EBR were not "reasonable" within the meaning of the Ad Note' and found that 'the application of the EBR was not "in accordance with the provisions of the GATT 1994, as interpreted by" the Anti-Dumping Agreement'.[19]

Third, the Panel found that the application of the EBR, prior to imposition of the anti-dumping order, in conjunction with the initial provisional measures resulted in the imposition of provisional measures 'in excess of "the amount of the anti-dumping duty provisionally estimated", contrary to Article 7.2 of the Anti-Dumping Agreement'.[20]

Fourth, the Panel found that the Amended Customs Bond Directive allows US Customs to exercise discretion to designate 'covered cases' and 'special category' merchandise in order to impose the EBR, and is thus not mandatory in nature and hence rejected all of India's 'as such' claims.[21]

3.2 Key issues analyzed by the Appellate Body

India and Thailand appealed a number of the Panel's findings and legal interpretations, including those related to the meaning of the Article VI:2 and 3 Ad Note and the standard for determining 'reasonableness' under the Ad Note. India also appealed issues related to its 'as such' claims and the consistency of the

---

17 See Edwin Vermulst (2005), 'The WTO Anti-Dumping Agreement', *Oxford Commentaries on International Law: Oxford Commentaries on the GATT/WTO Agreements*, Oxford: Oxford University Press, pp. 51–62; Edwin Vermulst and Daniel Ikenson (2007), 'Zeroing under the WTO Anti-Dumping Agreement: Where Do We Stand?', *Global Trade and Customs Journal*, 2(6): 231–242; Merit E. Janow and Robert W. Staiger (2003), 'European Communities – Anti-Dumping Duties on Imports of Cotton-Type Bed Linen from India', in Henrik Horn and Petros C. Mavroidis (eds.), *The WTO Case Law of 2001 – The American Law Institute Reporters' Studies*, Cambridge: Cambridge University Press; Chad Bown and Alan Sykes (2008), 'The Zeroing Issue: A Critical Analysis of Softwood V', *World Trade Review*, 7(1): 121–142; Thomas J. Prusa and Edwin Vermulst, 'United States – Laws, Regulations and Methodology for Calculating Dumping Margins (Zeroing) and United States – Measures Relating to Zeroing and Sunset Reviews?', forthcoming *World Trade Review*, 2009.

18 *US–Shrimp (Thailand)* Panel, paras. 7.77–7.79; *US–Customs Bond (India)* Panel, paras. 7.51–7.53.

19 *US–Shrimp (Thailand)* Panel, paras. 7.150–7.151; *US–Customs Bond (India)* Panel, paras. 7.128–7.129.

20 *US–Customs Bond (India)* Panel, paras. 7.143–7.146.

21 *US–Customs Bond (India)* Panel, para. 7.227.

Amended CBD with ADA Article 9 and SCM Agreement Article 19; the United States raised issues regarding the Panel's findings on the 'reasonableness' of the EBR and also its findings under GATT Article XX(d).

We note that the same panelists examined the complaint by Thailand (*US–Shrimp (Thailand)*) and the complaint by India (*US – Customs Bond Directive*); the Panel determined the two complaints covered 'substantially … the same matter'.[22] The WTO issued separate Panel reports;[23] however, given the considerable overlap, the two disputes were consolidated into a single Appellate Body report.

3.2.1 'As applied' claims

3.2.1.1 Temporal scope of GATT Article VI:2 and 3 Ad Note

Thailand and India argued that the EBR was a 'specific action against dumping' pursuant to ADA Article 18.1. Per the jurisprudence of the AB, three conditions must be met to prove a violation of Article 18.1: (1) the measure must be specific to dumping; (2) the measure acts against dumping; and (3) the measure has not been taken in accordance with the provisions of the GATT as interpreted by the ADA.[24]

The Panel had found that the first two conditions were demonstrated by Thailand and India, and these findings were not appealed by either party.[25] A key issue for condition 3 is the relationship between the Ad Note to GATT Article VI:2 and 3 and the ADA. The Ad Note provides that:

> As in many other cases in customs administration, a Member may require reasonable security (bond or cash deposit) for the payment of anti-dumping or countervailing duty pending final determination of the facts in any case of suspected dumping or subsidization.

Thailand and India argued that the Ad Note is inapplicable once an action is found to be a specific action against dumping because the Ad Note cannot be applied independently of the ADA and the Ad Note cannot provide an independent basis to create a fourth permissible response to dumping. Thailand and India further argued that the 'temporal scope of the Ad Note is restricted to securities taken as provisional measures' and that, consequently, the Ad Note did not apply once final measures were imposed.[26]

---

22 *US–Customs Bond (India)* and *US–Shrimp (Thailand)* Panel, para. 1.5.
23 *US–Customs Bond (India)*, Panel Report, WT/DS345/R, 29 February 2008 and *US–Shrimp (Thailand)*, Panel Report, WT/DS343/R, 29 February 2008.
24 *US–Shrimp (Thailand)* Panel, para. 7.41.
25 *US–Shrimp (Thailand)* AB, paras. 196–201.
26 Ibid., paras. 203–204.

3.2.1.1.1 Interpretation of the phrase 'pending final determination of the facts in any case of suspected dumping'

The AB began by analyzing 'whether the Ad Note authorizes security requirements after the imposition of an anti-dumping duty order and, accordingly, whether the application of the EBR falls within the temporal scope of the Ad Note'.[27] In making its determination, the AB first examined the meaning of the phrase 'final determination of the facts'. The AB pointed out that at issue was which final determination is being referred to in the Ad Note in the case of a retrospective duty-assessment system: 'the determination pursuant to which an anti-dumping duty order is imposed at the end of an original investigation; or the determination of the final liability for payment of anti-dumping duties pursuant to an assessment review under a retrospective duty assessment system'.[28] The AB concluded that the Ad Note's reference to 'the payment of a duty is key to ascertaining the temporal scope of the Ad Note because it reveals the nature of the obligation whose performance the security seeks to guarantee'.[29] The AB also stated that in 'a retrospective duty assessment system, this risk might also exist after the anti-dumping duty order has been imposed, arising from the difference between the amount collected at the time of import entry and the final liability assessed in an assessment review'. The AB therefore determined that 'the term "final determination" in the Ad Note includes the determination that is made to assess the final liability for payment of anti-dumping duties under Article 9.3.1 in a retrospective duty assessment system'.[30]

Next, the AB pondered the ordinary meaning of the terms 'suspected dumping'. Is dumping 'suspected' only up to the imposition of the ADD order, or does it continue to remain suspected until the final liability is determined in successive assessment reviews? Regarding this issue, the Panel had concluded that 'under the retrospective duty assessment system of the United States, dumping remains suspected even after the issuance of an anti-dumping duty order',[31] because the existence of dumping is established only after an assessment review is undertaken. The AB disagreed with the Panel's legal reasoning, noting that the existence of dumping is determined in an original investigation under Article 5; the subsequent uncertainty pertains only to the *amount* of dumping liability. However, the AB argued that the term 'dumping' in the Ad Note covers both the existence of dumping and the amount or margin of dumping. The AB concluded that the Ad Note 'authorizes the taking of a reasonable security after the imposition of an anti-dumping duty order, pending the determination of the final liability for payment of the anti-dumping duty'.

---

27 Ibid., para. 219.
28 Ibid., para. 220.
29 Ibid., para. 221.
30 Ibid., para. 221.
31 Ibid., para. 225.

3.2.1.1.2   EBR constitutes an additional response to dumping

Thailand and India also claimed that the security required under the EBR constitutes a fourth permissible response to dumping. However, the AB ruled that any security taken for guaranteeing the payment of a lawfully established duty liability would not *necessarily* constitute a 'specific action against dumping'. Rather, the security 'should be evaluated in the light of the nature and characteristics of the security and the particular circumstances in which it is applied'.[32] Because a security is generally 'ancillary to the principal obligation that it guarantees',[33] the AB concluded that 'a reasonable security taken in accordance with the Ad Note for potential additional anti-dumping duty liability does not necessarily, in and of itself, constitute a fourth autonomous category of response to dumping'.[34]

3.2.1.1.3   Relationship between EBR and ADA Article 7

Thailand and India argued that ADA Article 7, on provisional measures, 'interprets, governs, and implements the Ad Note to Article VI:2 and 3 of the GATT 1994, and that, therefore, a security cannot be justified under the Ad Note independently of Article 7'.[35] This implies that 'the scope of the Ad Note should therefore be limited to securities taken as a provisional measure in accordance with Article 7'.[36]

While acknowledging the overlap between the Ad Note and Article 7, the AB considered that the Ad Note 'allows the taking of a reasonable security for payment of the final liability of anti-dumping duties after an anti-dumping duty order has been imposed where such security may be needed to ensure that the difference between the duty collected on import entries and the final duty liability is collected'.[37] The AB therefore rejected Thailand and India's claim that the Ad Note 'is completely subsumed under Article 7 so that the taking of a reasonable security is not allowed after a definitive anti-dumping duty is imposed'.[38]

3.2.1.2   Reasonableness of the bond requirement

On the question of whether the EBR as applied to shrimp was 'reasonable' under the Article VI Ad Note, the Panel had found that the US 'could not properly have found, on the basis of the evidence relied on by the United States at the time it applied the EBR, that the rates of dumping established in the subject shrimp order were likely to increase'.[39] As a result, the Panel had concluded that the additional

---

32 Ibid., para. 230.
33 Ibid., para. 231.
34 Ibid., para. 231.
35 Ibid., para. 232.
36 Ibid., para. 232.
37 Ibid., para. 233.
38 Ibid., para. 233.
39 Ibid., para. 249.

security requirements resulting from the application of the EBR are not 'reasonable' within the meaning of the Ad Note.

Two aspects of the Panel's decision were appealed. First, the United States appealed the 'not reasonable' finding. In addition, Thailand and India questioned the Panel statement that 'in the context of the application of the EBR, there is no additional obligation under the Ad Note to assess the risk of default of individual importers'.[40]

3.2.1.2.1   Obligation to assess risk of individual importers

The AB set out a two-step approach to the issue of how 'reasonableness' under the Ad Note is to be assessed. The first step, it explained, 'involves a determination of the "likelihood" of an increase in the margin of dumping of an exporter as a result of which there will be a significant additional liability to be secured. This determination should have a rational basis and be supported by sufficient evidence.'[41] The second step 'involves a determination of the "likelihood of default" on the part of importers in respect of whom such additional liability is likely to arise'.[42]

The AB added three clarifying comments: (i) the 'evaluation of the reasonableness of the amount of security demanded would depend on the magnitude of the likely additional liability and the risk of default by importers'; (ii) the required 'security must obviously reflect and be commensurate with the likely magnitude of the non-payment or non-collection risk that has been established on a proper basis'; and (iii) 'security requirements that impose excessive additional costs on the importers may convert the security into an impermissible specific action against dumping'.[43] The AB then stated that additional security could be taken only:

> if a Member properly determined that the rates of dumping provided for in the anti-dumping order were likely to increase (such that the cash deposits provided for in the anti-dumping order would not provide sufficient security for the relevant case of suspected dumping).[44]

The AB went further and stated that the 'Member would also need to determine the likely amount of the additional liability arising from such increase in order to ensure that the amount of the security requirement is commensurate with that additional liability'; and it agreed with the Panel that 'it would not be reasonable to require additional security simply because of the possibility of rates of dumping increasing', since 'a mere possibility is not sufficient to establish likelihood of increase'.[45]

40 Ibid., para. 253.
41 Ibid., para. 258.
42 Ibid., para. 258.
43 Ibid., para. 258.
44 Ibid., para. 259.
45 Ibid., para. 260.

The AB disagreed with the Panel's suggestion that risk of default of individual importers need not be assessed. To the contrary, the AB considered 'the risk of default of individual importers ... an important factor in an analysis of the reasonableness of a security'.[46]

3.2.1.2.2 Reasonableness of the likelihood rates would increase

According to the US submissions, the decision by Customs 'to apply the EBR to subject shrimp was mainly based on the following elements, namely, that: (i) in agriculture and aquaculture sectors, the margin of dumping increased in about one third of cases, and such increase was significant; (ii) importers of agriculture and aquaculture merchandise were the source of the bulk of defaults on the payment of anti-dumping duties; and (iii) the potential additional liability was significant because of the heavy volume of shipments subject to the anti-dumping duty orders'.[47]

Because the US had not demonstrated any likelihood of an increase in the margin of dumping at the time the EBR was applied, the AB rejected the US argument that the EBR was 'reasonable'. In particular, the AB said that the US's statement that margins of dumping had increased in 38% of cases in the agriculture and aquaculture sectors as a whole did not constitute sufficient evidence to conclude that margins of dumping were likely to increase for subject shrimp.

Moreover, the AB considered that the EBR assumes that the final liability for payment of ADD will approximately double in each assessment review compared to the previously established margin. The AB saw 'no credible basis for this assumption underlying the EBR'.[48]

Finally, the AB noted that it did not 'see how the total value of subject shrimp shipments (US$2.5 billion, according to the United States) is, in and of itself, a relevant factor for determining whether there is significant additional liability, unless there is a significant increase in the margin of dumping of an exporter as well, because the cash deposits capture the liability on the total value of the shipments at the level of the existing estimated anti-dumping rates'.[49]

On this basis, the AB agreed with the Panel's conclusion that the United States 'could not have properly found, on the basis of the evidence relied upon by it, that the margins of dumping in respect of subject shrimp were likely to increase'. As a result, it upheld the finding of the Panel that the application of the EBR to subject shrimp is inconsistent with Article 18.1 of the Anti-Dumping Agreement.[50]

---

46 Ibid., para. 263.
47 Ibid., para. 264.
48 Ibid., para. 266.
49 Ibid., para. 267.
50 Ibid., para. 269.

3.2.2 '*As such*' claims

3.2.2.1 Amended CBD is inconsistent with Articles 1 and 18.1 of the ADA and Articles 10 and 32.1 of the SCM Agreement

India appealed the Panel's finding that the Amended CBD is not inconsistent 'as such' with ADA Articles 1 and 18.1 and SCM Agreement Articles 10 and 32.1.

The AB reasserted the Panel's mandatory vs. discretionary distinction as crucial for evaluating India's 'as such' claims. The AB confirmed the Panel's determination that the Amended CBD provisions were not a mandatory part of US practice, but rather just provided criteria for identifying 'covered cases' or 'special categories', and did not require US customs to designate 'covered cases' or 'special category' merchandise. The AB also rejected India's claim that the Amended CBD is 'as such' inconsistent because it imposes the EBR in every case in which the United States concludes that there is a likelihood of increase in margins because of the AB's earlier determination that the imposition of additional security is authorized under the Ad Note, provided it is reasonable.

3.2.2.2 ADA Article 9 and SCM Agreement Article 19

India appealed the Panel's finding that the Amended CBD is not inconsistent 'as such' and 'as applied' with ADA Articles 9.1, 9.2, 9.3, and 9.3.1 and 'as such' with SCM Agreement Articles 19.2, 19.3, and 19.4.

With respect to ADA Article 9, the Panel had concluded that the EBR falls outside the scope of this provision because Article 9 is concerned with the 'imposition and collection of anti-dumping duties'.[51] By contrast, the Panel asserted that 'a bond is not a "duty" and the term "duty" does not encompass bonds, because a bond does not yield public revenue at the time it is provided'.[52] The same logic applies to the SCM Agreement Article 19, 'the enhanced bond is not a countervailing duty', which means the EBR also falls outside the scope of Article 19.

The AB considered that 'the EBR imposed pursuant to the Amended CBD cannot be characterized as a "duty" within the meaning of the relevant provisions', and therefore it agreed with the Panel that bonds provided under the Amended CBD 'are not anti-dumping duties or countervailing duties', so that they 'fall outside' the scope of Articles 9 and 19.[53]

3.2.3 *US claim – the Panel's analysis of the term '*necessary*' in Article XX(d) of the GATT 1994*

The United States requested that, 'if the Appellate Body does not reverse the Panel's finding that the EBR is not a "reasonable security" within the meaning of the Ad

---

51 Ibid., para. 276.
52 Ibid., para. 276.
53 Ibid., para. 281.

Note, it should reverse the Panel's finding that, unless a Member demonstrates that the rates established in the anti-dumping duty order "are likely to increase", an additional security requirement cannot be considered to be "necessary" within the meaning of Article XX(d) of the GATT 1994'.[54]

India challenged 'the Panel's decision not to address "as a threshold question" whether Article XX(d) remains available to justify a "specific action against dumping or subsidization"'. India argued that if a measure is found to be a 'specific action against dumping' in violation of ADA Article 18.1, then a defense under Article XX(d) is not available.

The AB tackled the claim in two steps. First, the AB assumed, *arguendo*, that an Article XX(d) defense is available to the United States and would, therefore, proceed to consider the US appeal of the Panel's finding that the EBR is not 'necessary' to secure compliance with certain US laws and regulations within the meaning of Article XX(d). Second, assuming the answer to the first step is in the affirmative, it would then return to the question of the availability of an Article XX(d) defense.

As to the necessity issue, the AB recalled the Panel's finding that the EBR, as applied to subject shrimp, is not 'necessary' within the meaning of Article XX(d), given the Panel's earlier finding that the United States had failed to establish that rates of dumping in the anti-dumping duty order were likely to increase, such that it had also failed to demonstrate that additional security provided by the EBR reasonably correlated to any case of suspected dumping in excess of the dumping margin established in the anti-dumping duty order.[55] On appeal, the United States asserted that the Panel's necessity test 'was the same flawed test that it used to find that the EBR is not a "reasonable security" under the Ad Note' and, similar to arguments it advanced against the 'reasonableness' test adopted by the Panel in that context, the United States contended that 'a security may be "necessary" where there is a "likelihood" that the liability will accrue, but it is not "likely" (in the sense of substantial certainty) that this will occur'.[56]

The AB considered that 'the "necessity" test under Article XX(d) is different from the "reasonableness" test under the Ad Note'.[57] Past AB precedent established the following factors to be relevant in determining whether a measure is 'necessary':

> (i) the relative importance of the values or objectives the law or regulation is intended to protect; (ii) the extent to which the measure contributes to the realization of the end pursued – the securing of compliance with the law or regulation at issue; and (iii) the restrictive impact of the measure at issue on imports.[58]

---

54 Ibid., para. 304.
55 Ibid., para. 313.
56 Ibid., para. 314.
57 Ibid., para. 316.
58 Ibid., para. 316.

The AB then stated the 'United States has not demonstrated that the margins of dumping for subject shrimp were likely to increase significantly so as to result in significant additional liability over and above the cash deposit rates'.[59] It concluded, 'we do not, therefore, see how taking security, such as the EBR, can be viewed as being "necessary" in the sense of it contributing to the realization of the objective of ensuring the final collection of anti-dumping or countervailing duties in the event of default by importers'.[60]

In light of this conclusion, the AB found it unnecessary to express a view on the second step of the analysis.

4.   Legal and economic analysis

4.1   *Legal issues*

4.1.1   *Background discussion*

4.1.1.1   Retrospective vs. prospective collection of ADD/CVD

Most users of the anti-dumping instrument use a prospective duty-collection system, supposedly because it is administratively more convenient. Indeed, to the best of our knowledge, the United States is the only user that collects anti-dumping duties retrospectively.

Under a prospective duty-collection system, the duty rate is fixed at the end of the initial investigation and laid down in the final determination. This rate will then be imposed for the next five years, whether or not subsequent export transactions are actually dumped. Indeed, under a prospective system, an importer ironically will pay a higher amount of anti-dumping duties in cases where the exporter raises his export prices following the imposition of the duty, in other words, dumps less.[61] As a result, it may happen in prospective systems that, following the imposition of definitive duties, export prices decrease further because exporters and importers decide to share the burden of the payment of the duty.[62] Furthermore, as there is normally at least a 15-month gap between the initiation of

59 Ibid., para. 317.
60 Ibid., para. 317.
61 Anti-dumping duties are typically imposed in the form of ad valorem – percentage – duties. If, for example, in the original investigation period the normal value was $100, while the export price was $80, the dumping duty normally imposed would be [($100-$80)/$80 =] 25 %. Suppose that the exporter raises his export price to the non-dumped level of $100, the importer will have to pay a deposit of $25. If, on the other hand, the exporter continues to sell at $80, the importer will have to pay a deposit of only $20. Suppose that the exporter decides to sell at an export price of $60, e.g. dump even more, the importer would pay a deposit of only $15.
62 Some users with a prospective system, such as the EU, have enacted special provisions in their anti-dumping law to act against 'absorption' of anti-dumping duties by the exporter. However, empirical evidence indicates that anti-absorption investigations are relatively rare.

an investigation and the final determination, and the investigation period used to determine dumping (and injury) margins tend to end at the last full quarter of the calendar year preceding the month of initiation of the investigation, the duties collected are by definition based on 'stale' data.[63] Thus, under a prospective system, the rates are in principle set for five-year periods.[64] Furthermore, in a prospective system, both the calculation of the duty level and the payment of the duties are essentially exporter-specific. Suppose that the duty rate imposed on exporter X is 25%; all importers purchasing from exporter X will have to pay the 25% duty, regardless of the prices they pay. Thus, if importer A pays $60, while importer B pays $100, importer A will have to pay $15 while importer B will have to pay $25.

The US retrospective duty-assessment system, on the other hand, is a two-step system.[65] The first stage is the original investigation, culminating in a notice of anti-dumping duty order and imposition of an estimated anti-dumping duty deposit rate for each individually examined exporter and an 'all others' rate for all others. Importers subsequently purchasing from an exporter will then either pay the cash-deposit rate set for an individually examined exporter or the 'all others' cash-deposit rate, depending on their supplier. The second stage is the assessment of the final liability for payment of anti-dumping duties. Once a year, during the anniversary month of the order, interested parties may request the USDOC to conduct an assessment or periodic review to determine the final liability for payment of the ADD owed on entries that occurred during the previous year. If such a request is made, the USDOC will calculate a duty-assessment rate for each *importer* that sources from the exporters concerned and determine the final liability for the payment of the anti-dumping duties by that importer. The actual assessment of the ADD is therefore importer-specific. At the same time, the USDOC will then calculate a new cash-deposit rate for the *exporters* concerned, which will apply to all importers sourcing from such exporters. If no request is made, the cash deposits made on entries during the previous year are automatically assessed as the final duties. Thus, the advantage of the retrospective system is that it is very accurate and stimulates exporters to dump less because then the importers will get (part of) their cash deposits back. The disadvantage of the system is that it is costly because in principle there is a periodic review every year. Thus, it seems likely that multinationals with vertically integrated operations can use a retrospective system to their benefit by avoiding or minimizing dumping margins, while smaller exporters (and importers) may not find it worthwhile to go through the process every year.

---

63 Suppose, for example, that an investigation is initiated on 14 March 2009; the investigation period would then typically be the calendar year 2008. The final results of the investigation would probably be published around 13 June 2010. Thus, by that time, the original dumping findings would be based on data of a year and a half ago.

64 Unless interested parties request an interim review.

65 *US–Shrimp (Thailand)* AB, paras. 184–185.

4.1.1.2 Customs bonds in the US

All regular US importers are obliged to post a basic customs bond, equal to the greater of US$50,000 or 10% of the duties, taxes, and fees paid by the importer during the prior calendar year. The purpose of such bonds is to secure liabilities that may arise out of failure to perform various obligations imposed on importers under US laws or regulations. Importers subject to an anti-dumping duty order must also post such a bond in addition to the applicable cash-deposit rate.[66]

The EBR operates in addition to the basic bond rules and, as we have seen in Section 2 *supra*, requires importers in a 'covered case' (shrimp) within a 'special category' (agriculture and aquaculture) to post an enhanced continuous bond equal to 100% of the anti-dumping duty rate multiplied by the value of imports of the product concerned in the previous 12 months. The objective of the EBR is to ensure that in cases where the level of the anti-dumping duties owed turns out to be higher than the cash-deposit rate, there will be sufficient guarantees that the importers will pay the higher duties. Although parties disagreed before the Panel on the impact of the EBR in the shrimp case,[67] it seems relatively clear that there is a substantial impact, both because the posting of additional bonds costs money and because such posting may have a deterrent effect on importers, particularly in cases where there are many alternative sources of supply available, as was the case for shrimp.

Thus, it seems to us that, while the EBR in itself seems to pursue an acceptable objective, the basic issue is whether the EBR, as applied in the shrimp case, is a reasonable means to achieve that objective.[68] The Panel and the AB clearly found this not to be the case.

4.1.2 *The Ad Note Article VI:2 and 3 GATT 1994*

In order to determine whether the EBR, as applied in the shrimp case, constituted a 'specific action against dumping' not authorized within the meaning of Article 18(1) ADA, the Panel had followed the three-prong test set out by the AB in *US-1916 Act* and *US-Offset Act (Byrd Amendment)*. The Panel's findings that the application of the EBR was 'specific' to dumping and acted 'against' dumping were not appealed. However, part of the Panel's analysis that the EBR was not in accordance with the provisions of the GATT 1994, as interpreted by the ADA, more particularly the Ad Note, was appealed by India and Thailand. India and Thailand claimed both before the Panel and before the AB that the temporal scope of the Ad Note was restricted to securities taken as provisional measures and could therefore not be used as a justification for the EBR which, by definition, applied

---

66 Ibid., paras. 186–189.

67 Ibid., para. 195.

68 Although WTO law does not recognize the principle of proportionality as such, it seems to us that certain concepts implicitly incorporate this principle.

only during the second stage of the US retrospective system. However, the Panel and the AB disagreed, albeit it on different grounds, with the AB, emphasizing the phrase '*payment* of anti-dumping duty' and considering that in the retrospective US system the factual determination of the amounts of ADD payable takes place only in the duty-assessment review.[69] Although the AB did not agree with the Panel's view that the existence of dumping remains suspected even after the anti-dumping duty order has been imposed, it considered that the term 'dumping' in the Ad Note covers both the existence of dumping and the dumping amount/margin (the latter of which is only fixed in the course of the assessment review).

As regards the reasonableness of the application of the EBR to shrimp, the Panel had considered that it might be appropriate to apply an increased security such as the EBR if the authorities had properly determined that the rates of ADD established in the anti-dumping duty order were 'likely to increase' to the effect that the cash deposits would not provide sufficient security for the final liability, *quod non*. On the other hand, the Panel had also held that it was not necessary under the Ad Note to assess the risk of default of individual importers. The US appealed the former finding, while the latter was challenged by India and Thailand.

On appeal, the AB noted that the EBR applied to all importers of shrimp from the targeted countries. Yet, there were various scenarios possible under which an increased liability might not occur; for example, if no assessment review is requested, if the rate for an exporter goes down or – even if the dumping margin of an exporter were to go up – specific importers might still benefit from a lower assessment rate, in which case the cash deposits would have to be refunded. The AB considered a two-step approach necessary to assess the reasonableness of a security such as the EBR. First of all, there should be a determination of a likelihood of an increase in the dumping margin of an exporter as a result of which there would be a significant additional liability to be secured. Second, there should be a determination of a likelihood of default on the part of the (individual) importers in respect of whom the additional liability would be likely to arise. The AB therefore upheld the 'likely' standard applied by the Panel, but rejected the Panel finding that importer-specific analysis of the default risk was not necessary. The AB further agreed with the Panel's assessment that the US could not have properly found that the dumping margins for shrimp were likely to increase on the basis of the evidence before it. As the first step of the analysis was not satisfied, the AB upheld the Panel's findings that the EBR as applied to shrimp was not reasonable within the meaning of the Ad Note and therefore violated Article 18.1 of the ADA.

Thus, while the AB rejected the EBR, as applied to shrimp, it seems clear that the door is open for the US to come up with a more polished version of the EBR that would allow a more targeted use of additional bonding requirements.

---

69 *US – Shrimp (Thailand)* AB, paras. 221–222.

4.1.3   Article XX(d) GATT 1994

With regard to the United States affirmative Article XX(d) defense, the Panel had found that, unless a Member demonstrates that the rates established in the anti-dumping duty order are likely to increase, an additional security requirement cannot be considered as 'necessary' within the meaning of Article XX(d). The United States appealed this finding. India, in turn, appealed the finding on the ground that, if a measure is found to be a specific action against dumping not authorized under Article 18.1 ADA, an Article XX(d) defense is not available.

The AB considered the US appeal first on the assumption that an Article XX(d) defense would not be precluded by a finding of inconsistency with Article 18.1 ADA. It considered that the 'necessity' test of Article XX(d) was different from the 'reasonableness' test of the Ad Note and that the factors relied upon by the Panel to evaluate 'necessity' were correct. These were (i) the relative importance of the values or objectives the law or regulation is intended to protect; (ii) the extent to which the EBR contributes to the realization of the end pursued; and (iii) the restrictive impact of the EBR on imports. Like the Panel, the AB did not consider the second condition satisfied in light of the US failure to demonstrate that the margins of dumping for shrimp were likely to increase significantly so as to result in significant additional liability. As a result, the AB did not consider the EBR as being 'necessary' as it did not contribute to the end pursued, and declined to rule on India's claim.

One may wonder whether this analysis is correct. The purported objective of the EBR is to secure potential additional liability that might arise from significant increases in the amount of dumping after the imposition of an anti-dumping duty order.[70] The AB accepts the legitimacy of this objective. Supposedly, the EBR does contribute to achieving this objective because it limits the risk of default and therefore it would appear to meet the second prong, too. The problem with the EBR, as applied in shrimp, is that it overshoots and therefore constitutes a disproportionate tool to achieve the stated objective. However, it seems to us that this would have been tackled more appropriately under the third prong of the test.

4.2   Economic issues

There are two areas of the AB's decision that require further discussion: the risk of default and the reasonableness of the EBR.

4.2.1   Risk of default for shrimp

We agree with the Panel and AB's finding that (i) the US must demonstrate that the rates of dumping established in the subject shrimp order were likely to increase and (ii) that such a determination was not possible on the basis of the evidence relied on by the US at the time it applied the EBR. The first point is self-evident. On the

---

70 Ibid., para. 317.

second point, however, we think the AB could have commented more forcefully regarding the evidence provided by the US.

In its submissions, the United States 'CBP's analysis at the time indicated that with respect to agriculture/aquaculture cases, rates increased 33% of the time, did not change 11% of the time, and decreased 56% of the time'.[71] The US also submitted that '[w]hen rates increased, they increased by, on average, 285%'.[72] The Panel did not find the US submission probative because the US did not provide any break-out as to the causes for the rate increases, the sizes of the rate increases, and whether defaults were associated. This final point is particularly crucial as rate increases are a necessary but not sufficient condition for payment default. The Panel also noted that US submissions made it impossible to know what fraction was a result of error on the part of Customs, or error or fraud on the part of other parties.[73] Furthermore, the United States had provided no explanation as to how any alleged historical trend in respect of dumping rates for agriculture/aquaculture cases generally might justify conclusions regarding the likelihood of dumping rates for subject shrimp.[74] The AB affirmed the Panel's views.

From what we have been able to ascertain, the US provided no information that directly demonstrated that warmwater shrimp exporters and importers (i) had defaulted or (ii) were likely to default. With respect to (i), given that the EBR was imposed coincidental with the final ADD order, there was no history of defaults to justify the decision to impose the EBR. With respect to (ii), the US's justification for the EBR was the following: other agriculture/aquaculture products had defaulted; therefore, shrimp was likely to default. Said differently, shrimp was guilty by association.

We believe the AB was correct in challenging the value of the US statistics for determining the risk of default, but could have made its critique much more forcefully. If nothing else, given the skewed nature of defaults, other summary statistics may have been more probative. Whether the mean or median is the preferred measure of 'typical' significantly depends on the distribution. For example, according to GAO (2008) most unpaid ADD/CVD bills are quite small, less than $300; a few large unpaid bills result in the mean being over 80 times larger than the median.[75] The US's reliance on mean values hides the fact that very few exporters and importers were involved in large defaults. In fact, the US knew that just four importers were responsible for over one-third of the defaults.[76] We note that the US's main point – that a small identifiable set of exporters and importers account for a large amount of defaults – may still be valid. The more problematic

---

71 *US–Shrimp (Thailand)* Panel, para. 7.143; *US–Customs Bond (India)* Panel, para. 7.120.
72 *US–Shrimp (Thailand)* Panel, para. 6.40.
73 *US–Shrimp (Thailand)* Panel, para. 7.143; *US–Customs Bond (India)* Panel, para. 7.121.
74 *US–Shrimp (Thailand)* Panel, para. 7.144; *US–Customs Bond (India)* Panel, para. 7.122.
75 GAO (2008), p. 17.
76 Ibid., p. 16.

aspect of the case is that the US did not present compelling evidence that shrimp exporters/importers would be large defaulters.

Specifically, the AB should have made it clear that the US needed to clearly distinguish the risk for default in shrimp as an agriculture/aquaculture case from the other characteristics that might lead to default. There are a number of other factors that contribute to the risk of default, most of which suggest warmwater shrimp was not like the other products with large defaults.

4.2.1.1   What was known about defaulters?

A US study performed at the same time as the WTO AB hearings revealed far more information about the risk of default than apparently was shared with the Panel or AB. GAO (2008) found the uncollected duties were highly concentrated in five key ways:[77]

1. **Industry:** The agriculture/aquaculture industry represented 87% of the total amount of uncollected ADD/CVD.
2. **Product:** Four products were responsible for about 85% of the total amount of uncollected ADD/CVD. These four products are crawfish tail meat ($354 million), garlic ($75 million), honey ($43 million), and mushrooms ($41 million).
3. **Country of Origin:** Importers purchasing products from China are associated with 90% of the total amount of uncollected duties.
4. **Importers:** A single importer accounted for 20% of the total amount of uncollected ADD/CVD. Four importing companies (out of the 27,000 subject to ADD/CVD duties) accounted for more than one-third of the total, and 20 companies accounted for 63% of the total.
5. **Shipper Status:** Importers purchasing from companies undergoing a special 'new shipper' review accounted for about 40% of uncollected ADD/CVD.

Of the five characteristics, Customs appears to have focused on just one – industry. The US knew at the time it imposed the EBR that neither India nor Thailand had defaulted on ADD/CVD payments and that an astonishing 90% of the defaults were associated with Chinese products; the US also knew that a small number of importers were responsible for the majority of defaults.

The fact that new shippers account for such a large fraction of payment defaults is problematic because the EBR does not discourage new shippers from 'dumping and running'. Under the new-shipper bonding option, which has now been suspended, an exporter that did not have its own deposit rate under an ADD or CVD order – and that did not ship to the US during the period covered by the original investigation – could obtain its own rate by undergoing a 'new shipper' administrative review. Importers could satisfy the duty deposit requirement on imports shipped by an exporter undergoing a new-shipper review by posting a bond. Cash deposits were not required for new shippers. Moreover, the EBR would not result

---

77 Ibid., pp. 13–16.

in any additional bonding requirement. Whether the EBR is 'reasonable' should depend in part on the extent to which it mitigates the default problem; the fact that new shippers are a major loophole in the EBR challenges the notion that it is reasonable.[78]

4.2.1.2 Is shrimp like other defaulters?

Shrimp had never been subject to a US ADD order and so had never been the source of any uncollected ADD/CVD. Nor was there any evidence that imports from Thailand or India had resulted in significant defaults.[79] Even though the US appears to have ignored other attributes associated with default, it is possible that the one factor the US focused on – industry – trumps the other factors. Specifically:

> United States Customs concluded that: agriculture/aquaculture industries were characterized by low capitalization and high debt-to-equity ratios; importers of this type of merchandise had been responsible for significant defaults in the past; and shrimp importers of merchandise were therefore likely to have a heightened risk of default due to similarities with these other agriculture/aquaculture importers.[80]

Even if the AB accepted the US's argument on the relationship between capitalization and default, the AB should have demanded the US demonstrate that the shrimp market is 'like' the other cases with significant default.

It is well known that the trade effects of ADD/CVD vary by the size of the margin, the number of subject countries, and the total import market share under order.[81] A case with plentiful non-subject (unrestrained) suppliers might provide importers little incentive to purchase from subject exporters; likewise, all else equal, a case with lower margins will likely lead to less default as there will be less incentive to significantly change pricing and sourcing in response to the duties.

To get a sense of the risk of how the shrimp case compared with the other cases with large payment defaults, we compiled some easily available public information on the cases – information to which the US government undoubtedly had access.[82]

---

78 Legislation was put forth in July 2005 to close the 'new shipper' loophole. See Vivian C. Jones, 'New Shipper Reviews', *CRS Report for Congress*, 5 October 2005.

79 Only three countries were mentioned in GAO (2008) as being major exporters with significant payment default, China ($550 m), Argentina ($11 m), and Vietnam ($12 m). All other countries accounted for just $40 m in defaults (page 15).

80 *US–Shrimp (Thailand)* AB, para. 59.

81 See Thomas J. Prusa (1997), 'The trade effects of US antidumping actions', in Robert C. Feenstra (ed.), *Effects of US Trade Protection and Promotion Policies*, Chicago: University of Chicago Press; Thomas J. Prusa (2001), 'On the Spread and Impact of Antidumping', *Canadian Journal of Economics* 34(3): 591–611. For an analysis focusing solely on agricultural products, see Colin A. Carter and Caroline Gunning-Trant (2009), 'US Trade Remedy Law and Agriculture: Trade Diversion and Investigation Effects', University of California, Davis Agricultural & Resource Economics working paper, January 2009.

82 Chad P. Bown (2007) 'Global Antidumping Database' (Version 3.0), June, available online at www.brandeis.edu/~cbown/global_ad/.

Table 1. Cases with significant ADD/CVD payment defaults

Product	Subject countries	Original invest. final dumping margin (%)	Import market share (%)
Fresh garlic (1994)	China	376.67	65.4
Honey (2000)	Argentina	30.24	50.1
	China	183.80	29.6
Crawfish (1996)	China	201.63	99.8
Certain preserved mushrooms (1998)	Chile	142.43	4.2
	China	198.63	54.7
	India	9.97	7.7
	Indonesia	15.35	24.4
Warmwater shrimp (2004)	Brazil	7.05	1.9
	China	112.81	11.4
	Ecuador	3.58	7.2
	India	10.17	8.2
	Thailand	5.95	25.5
	Vietnam	25.76	7.3

We begin by reporting some basic case information, including margins (Table 1). We note that China is subject to orders in each case. In addition, in each case the duties on China are quite large, over 100%.

In most other respects, the cases differ. Garlic and crawfish only involve a single subject country, while honey involved two countries and mushrooms involved four. Shrimp involve six countries. In all of the cases (except shrimp), China was the single largest subject supplier. The two cases with the largest defaults (crawfish and garlic) both had just a single country subject to ADD and the final original margins were extraordinarily large (201% and 377%, respectively). In crawfish, China accounted for essentially all imports. In garlic, China sourced almost two-thirds of imports. Hence, the incentive to avoid the ADD/CVD margin was particularly acute in those cases. By contrast, the margins in the shrimp case were modest and there appear to be many alternative suppliers.

The difference between shrimp and the other four cases with large defaults can also be seen if we plot the import market shares and the ADD margins (Figure 1). All else equal, the larger a single country's market share, the less viable are the alternative subject and non-subject suppliers. All else equal, the larger the ADD, the greater the incentive to avoid paying the duty. Taken together, we expect cases closer to the origin (i.e., lower market share and lower margin) to be less likely to default. As seen in the scatter plot, the countries involved in the shrimp case (depicted by a hollow square marker) lie far closer to the origin than the countries in the other cases (depicted by the solid diamonds). At face value, the incentive to default on payments in the shrimp case appears to be far less than in the other cases.

Figure 1. ADD margin and import market share

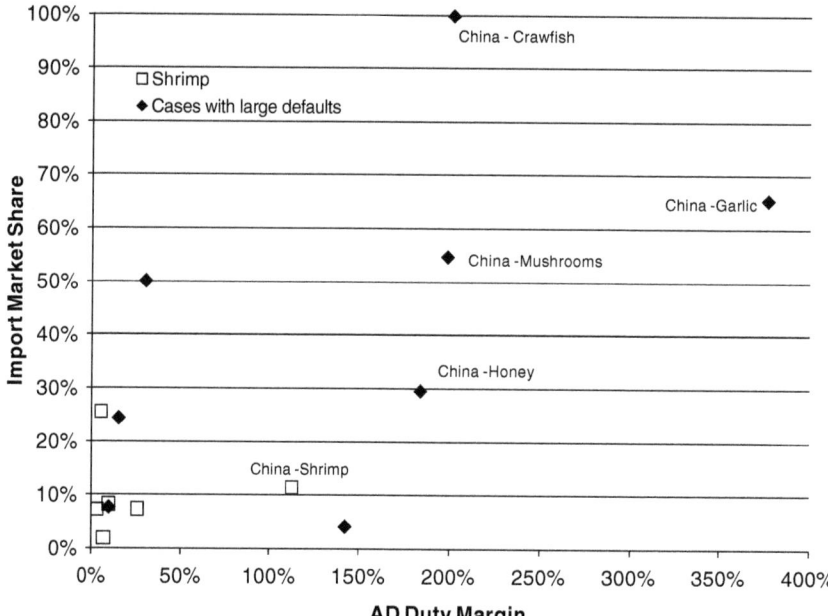

Easily identifiable differences between the shrimp case and the other cases with large default make it difficult to assume that the risk of default was inordinately high in the shrimp case, especially for the Thai and Indian shippers.

4.2.2 *The need to evaluate exporter and importer risk*

The US argued that in the context of the application of the EBR, there is no additional obligation under the Ad Note to assess the risk of default of individual importers. The US argued that only the risk of exporter default needed to be considered. The AB disagreed and stated 'the risk of default of individual importers is an important factor in an analysis of the reasonableness of a security'.[83]

We do not see how it is possible to assess risk of default without examining importer risk. Under the US system, an exporter will be assigned an ADD rate but importers must post the bond and/or pay the cash deposit. Even if an exporter is willing to adjust pricing in such a way that will result in larger final duties, the importer will determine whether default occurs. If the US had knowledge, for instance, that the same importers who defaulted on catfish ADD were ready to import shrimp, it would be reasonable to assume there was a high risk of default. On the other hand, if the US had knowledge that large, long-time established

---

83 *US–Shrimp (Thailand)* AB, para. 263.

importers were ready to import shrimp, it would not necessarily be reasonable to assume there was a high risk of default. The US not only presented no evidence that it considered the importer risk, but in fact rejected the notion that importer risk mattered. This ignores the behavior of the agent primarily responsible for the defaults.

4.2.3   Cost of EBR

The EBR imposed higher costs on exporters than Customs analysis predicted. Customs analysis prior to the enactment of the EBR apparently was limited to the possible bond premium increases that shrimp importers might incur. However, the premium increases are arguably the least significant cost imposed by the EBR. For example, suppose US$1 million of shrimp product is imported and the dumping margin is 15 %. An importer would have to pay $150,000 cash deposit and pur-chase another $150,000 bond. Historically, a surety company charges about 5 % premium for the bond, which implies an additional cost of $7,500. Customs ap-pears to have anticipated an increase in the premium and that is indeed what occurred. The EBR resulted in a doubling of the premium, meaning the cost of the above hypothetical bond might rise to $15,000.[84] Relative to the dollar value of imports, the bond premium is small in either case (0.75 % and 1.5 % in the two scenarios). To the extent that this would have been the full cost, we agree that the EBR would not be inordinately burdensome.

Customs overlooked, however, two other costs associated with the EBR. First, sureties began to require 100 % collateral to secure the EBR.[85] Thus, in addition to the $150,000 cash deposit and $15,000 bond payment the importer also needed to set aside $150,000 in assets; these assets were held by the sureties to protect them in case of a major increase in ADD liability and could not be used by the importer to back other types of investments.[86] Second, the lengthy delays as-sociated with the retrospective system meant that the costs of the bonds were 'stacked' over several years. That is, even though the administrative review might be initiated after 12 months, the review takes at least 12 months to complete; if either party appeals the determination, then several years can easily pass before the deposits are liquidated – and the whole time the surety will be imposing on-going payments for the bond and will be holding the full amount in collateral. On average, the lag between entry of the merchandise and liquidation was about 3.3 years.[87] Hence, what at first glance appears to be a policy that imposes a small additional cost but yields huge benefits to US Customs turns out in fact to impose significant costs and cash constraints on exporters and importers. The process repeats each subsequent year. When one considers that Thailand exports about

---

84 See Annex C, Executive Summaries of the First Written Submission of the Third Parties, WT/DS345/R, (18 May 2007), p. C-21.
  85 GAO (2006), p. 6.
  86 Ibid., p. 6.
  87 GAO (2008), p. 23.

US$1 billion of warmwater shrimp to the US every year, the 100% collateral charge will mean that hundreds of millions of dollars were held as collateral during the review process.

5. Concluding comments

The Appellate Body found that the EBR, as applied in the shrimp case, was neither a reasonable security within the meaning of the GATT 1994 Note Ad Article VI : 2 and 3, nor was it a 'necessary' enforcement mechanism within the meaning of Article XX(d) GATT 1994. It therefore constituted an additional action against dumping not authorized under Article 18(1) ADA. As explained in detail above, we consider the AB's findings and reasoning largely correct.

The AB report does not preclude an authority from imposing additional bonding requirements to cover the risk of default by importers. However, in a retrospective system, such as the one employed by the United States, such bonding requirements probably could only be imposed on the basis of an importer-specific assessment of its default risk. Thus, designation of categories of merchandise and covered cases will almost certainly not be sufficient, no matter the motivation.

New shippers accounted for about 40% of the unpaid ADD. Given that the EBR did not address the new-shipper issue, the US amended its new-shipper policy. Previously, an importer purchasing from a new shipper could satisfy the duty deposit requirement on imports shipped by an exporter undergoing a new-shipper review by posting a bond. In 2006, the US Congress amended the new-shipper rules and now requires importers to submit a cash deposit to cover the entire estimated ADD/CVD for the subject merchandise. By doing this the new shippers were put on a level playing field with existing shippers. This policy strikes us as a much more proportionate response and targeted to the problem of unpaid duties.

Mexico–Olive Oil: Remedy without a cause?

CHAD P. BOWN

Department of Economics and International Business School, Brandeis University, Waltham, MA, USA

NIALL MEAGHER

Advisory Centre on WTO Law

Abstract: This paper provides a legal-economic analysis of the unappealed WTO Panel Report in *Mexico–Olive Oil*. The case involved a countervailing-duty measure imposed by Mexico on imports of olive oil from the European Communities (in particular, Spain and Italy). The dispute raised important issues regarding the determination of causation of injury, as neither the Panel nor the investigating authority gave much credence to evidence that the main complaint of the domestic industry was the loss of a distribution agreement and brand-name rights with a Spanish exporter. The dispute also raised interesting concerns regarding the remedies for violations of procedural obligations in the conduct of anti-dumping/ countervailing-duty investigations and the right of a domestic producer that has ceased production to seek protection under the trade-remedy laws.

1. Introduction

Approximately half of the jurisprudence of the WTO dispute-settlement system consists of disputes arising out of trade-remedy or contingent-protection measures imposed by WTO Members. Given this fact, it might be expected that the jurisprudence on the WTO *Anti-Dumping* and *Subsidy and Countervailing Measure (SCM) Agreements* would be relatively settled. Not so. Each new WTO dispute under these agreements, including the recent unappealed WTO Panel Report in *Mexico–Olive Oil*, throws up both new issues that have yet to be resolved and recurring issues where the jurisprudence continues to evolve.

While the *Mexico–Olive Oil* dispute was neither particularly complicated nor very controversial, the decision raised several issues that gave rise to new interpretations of the relevant agreements or that illustrated some of the recurring problems in challenging anti-dumping or countervailing-duty measures in WTO

The authors thank our discussant, Kamal Saggi, as well as Thomas Prusa, Meredith Crowley, Petros Mavroidis, Jorge Huerta Goldman, and the participants at the ALI Review of WTO Case Law 2008 Conference in Geneva for helpful comments. Shranutha Reddy provided outstanding research assistance. All remaining errors are our own.

85

dispute-settlement proceedings. First, we analyse as potentially problematic the manner in which the Panel addressed the question of whether Mexico sufficiently ruled out 'any known factors' aside from the impact of the subsidy on the injury suffered by its domestic olive-oil growing industry. Second, we describe the quandary of how to implement findings of procedural violations associated with the *SCM* and *Anti-Dumping Agreements*. Finally, we discuss some examples of important 'non-issues' that arose in the dispute. In particular, we point out how an issue such as 'pass-through' – one that has proven to be quite divisive in earlier WTO jurisprudence on subsidies and countervailing measures – was not controversial in this dispute given the context of the market and policies at issue in the case.

The rest of this paper proceeds as follows. In Section 2, we introduce the legal facts of the dispute as well as political-economic history of events surrounding the WTO case. Section 3 describes the legal findings of the WTO Panel Report, and Section 4 provides our legal-economic analysis of the dispute. Finally, Section 5 concludes.

2. Background

In this section of the paper, we first establish the legal and factual background of the case before turning to the underlying political-economy 'facts' to understand better the market environment and incentives at stake in the both the underlying Mexican countervailing-duty (CVD) investigation and the subsequent WTO dispute-settlement proceedings.

2.1 Legal and factual background

This dispute arose out of a CVD measure imposed by Mexico on imports of olive oil from the European Communities (EC). The matter began in March 2003, when a Mexican company, Fortuny, submitted an application to the Mexican investigating authority, Economía, for the imposition of CVDs on imports of olive oil from the EC. The application alleged that during the period April–December 2002, subsidized imports of olive oil from the EC materially retarded the establishment of an olive-oil industry in Mexico. Economía published a notice of initiation of the investigation on 16 July 2003. A preliminary resolution imposing provisional CVDs was published on 10 June 2004. A final resolution imposing definitive CVDs was published on 1 August 2005 – almost 25 months after the investigation was initiated. The EC requested consultations under the WTO *Understanding on Rules and Procedures Governing the Settlement of Disputes* (the DSU) on 31 March 2006 and requested the establishment of a Panel on 7 December 2006. The Panel's Report was circulated to the membership of the WTO on 4 September 2008 – in less time (21 months), ironically, than Economía took to complete the investigation. The Panel Report was not appealed.

Table 1. Mexico's 2001 tariff rates on imports of olive-oil products, in percent

Tariff category	Harmonized system product at the 8-digit level				
	15091001	15091099	15099001	15099002	15099099
MFN bound rate	45.0	45.0	45.0	45.0	45.0
MFN applied rate	10.0	10.0	20.0	20.0	20.0
Preferential rates:					
NAFTA countries (US, Canada)	0.0	0.0	0.0	0.0	0.0
Chile, Costa Rica, Uruguay	0.0	0.0	0.0	0.0	0.0
Colombia, Venezuela	2.8	2.8	5.7	5.7	5.7
Nicaragua	7.0	7.0	14.0	14.0	14.0
El Salvador, Guatemala, Honduras	8.8	8.8	17.5	17.5	17.5
European Community	9.0	9.0	18.0	18.0	18.0

Source: Data collected by authors from the WTO's Integrated Database via WITS. The MFN applied tariff rates are the same as the 2001 rates reported in the table for years 1999–2003.

There was little dispute in either the investigation or the WTO dispute that the EC had in fact provided the subsidies in question. The EC had, after all, notified the measures at issue as subsidies to the WTO. Instead, the investigation and, later, the WTO dispute, turned on other issues, including the following two questions in particular: (i) as the EC paid the subsidy to the olive growers, rather than the olive-oil producers, whether Economía could treat the subsidy as having been provided to the olive-oil exports without conducting a 'pass-through' analysis, and (ii) whether the fact that the Mexican producer had ceased production affected either the producer's standing to seek relief or the injury analysis. While the facts are not fully clear, it appears that the Mexican producer, Fortuny, may have ceased production after it lost the right to use a Spanish brand name, Ybarra, to market its domestically produced olive oil in the Mexican market. As we will discuss, the commercial relevance of the loss of the right to this brand name is a key issue in the economic analysis of the case.

2.2 The trade, policies, political-economy facts, and background of the case

Before turning to a discussion of the legal findings in the dispute and our legal-economic analysis, we first establish a basic understanding of the political economy of the markets and policies involved in the case. Understanding these features is critical to help inform our later analysis and choice of how to model the issues that arise.

First, as Table 1 indicates, Mexico's WTO tariff binding during this time for the olive-oil imports involved in the dispute was 45 %, and its MFN applied tariff rate

Figure 1. Mexico's imports of olive oil by foreign source, 1996–2007

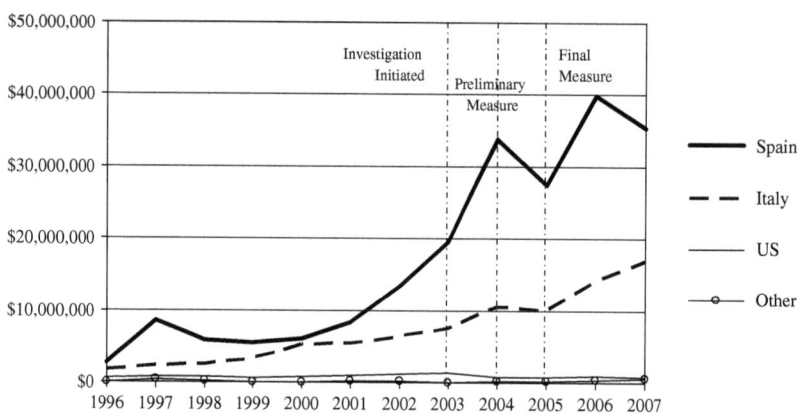

Source: Data collected by authors. Mexico's imports under HS (1996) categories 150910 (Virgin olive oil) and 150990 (Other olive oil), data taken from the UN Comtrade via WITS.

during this time period ranged from 10% to 20%, depending on the olive-oil sub-product. According to its tariff schedule, Mexico apparently offered many different preferential rates to different trading partners. These included free trade in olive-oil products to its trade-agreement partners under NAFTA, as well as separate arrangements with Chile, Costa Rica, and Uruguay. Interestingly, and notwithstanding the countervailing-duty order, even the EC received a small Mexican tariff preference in these products below Mexico's MFN applied rate.

As Figure 1 illustrates, the deep tariff preferences that Mexico offered to other countries (listed in Table 1) beyond what it granted to exporters from the EC apparently had very little effect on Mexico's import sourcing during this time period. More than 90% of Mexican imports of these olive-oil products derived from Spain or Italy alone. The only other single foreign source with more than 1% of Mexico's olive-oil imports during this time period was the United States, and the level of the value of US exports to Mexico during this time period is relatively flat at roughly $1 million per year.[1]

As Figure 1 also documents, the value of the combined EC exports to Mexico at stake is relatively small. We understand that this is much less than the value of the trade at stake in a number of other WTO disputes, including several initiated by the EC on behalf of its exporters' foreign-market-access interests, which frequently run into the hundreds of millions and even billions of dollars worth of annual exports. Before the initiation of the countervailing-duty investigation in 2003,

---

1 Since the value of Mexico's olive-oil imports from the US during this time period is relatively constant at roughly $1 million per year, in the face of growing Mexican imports from the EC the US share of the Mexican import market steadily declined from a high of 11.4% in 1996 to 1.6% in 2007.

Figure 2. The importance of the Mexican market to Spain's and Italy's
olive-oil exporters, 1996–2007

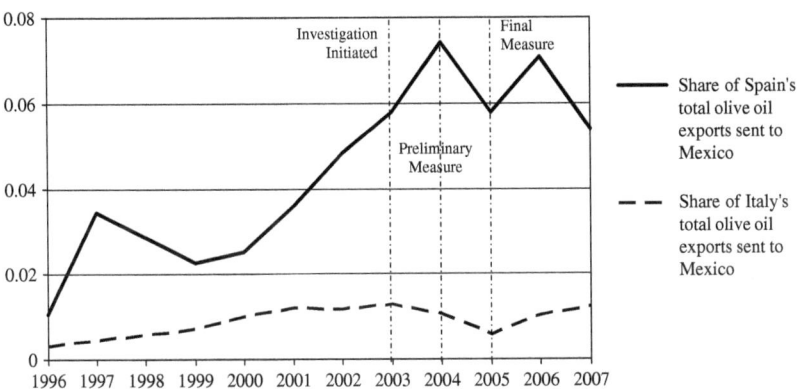

Source: Data collected by authors. Spain and Italy exports under HS (1996) categories 150910 (Virgin olive oil)
and 150990 (other olive oil), data taken from the UN Comtrade via WITS. Exports are 'extra-EC-15' for all
years in the sample.

Mexican combined imports from Spain and Italy had never been more than $30
million per year. Nevertheless, as Figure 1 also illustrates, Mexico was a growth
market for Spanish and Italian exporters of olive oil. Even after the initiation of the
CVD investigation in 2003 and the imposition of the preliminary CVD in 2004,
Spain (and to a lesser extent Italy) continued to expand its exports to Mexico.
There was slight growth between 2004 and 2007, with combined Spanish and
Italian sales of over $50 million in both 2006 and 2007, even *after* imposition of
the final CVD order. As we describe in more detail below, the Spanish firm
Ybarra's 2002 decision to halt its brand-licensing arrangement with (what would
become) the Mexican olive-oil firm Fortuny is consistent with what is suggested
by a simple analysis of the time path of the trade data; i.e., that the Spanish firm
may have ended the licensing arrangement in which it sourced olive oil locally
(from growers and processors within Mexico) in order to switch to supplying
the Mexican market under the Ybarra brand with an increase in *exports* of olive oil
from Spain. Indeed, the Panel noted that the loss of this arrangement led to a
decline in Fortuny's sales to the Ybarra distribution network in 2001–2002.[2]

While Spanish and Italian olive-oil exports to Mexico during this time period
are relatively small in dollar terms (Figure 1), as Figure 2 indicates, Mexico has
become an increasingly important export market for Spanish olive-oil producers,
comprising 5–7% of its total (extra-EC) olive-oil exports during 2003–2007,

2 Panel Report, *Mexico – Definitive Countervailing Measures on Olive Oil from the European
Communities* (Panel Report hereinafter), at para. 7.315.

compared to a 2–4% share during 1996–2001. While not pictured, the dominant export market for Spanish firms is the United States (23–28% of total extra-EC exports). Other important markets include Japan, Australia, and to a lesser extent Brazil and Korea. The Mexican market is relatively less important for Italian olive-oil exporters, as also indicated by Figure 2, as it accounts for only roughly 1% of Italy's total (extra-EC) olive-oil exports. The most important export markets for Italy for olive oil are the United States (55–60% of total extra-EC exports), Japan, Australia, and Canada.[3]

The EC's subsidy programme for olive oil was originally established pursuant to Regulation No. 136/66 of September 1966, which was subsequently modified to regulate further the modalities for and amount of the olive-oil subsidy. Economía cited Regulation No. 1638/98 (20 July 1998), Regulation No. 1794/2002 (9 October 2002), and Regulation 1221/2003 (8 July 2003) as the other EC measures by which the subsidy was provided during the period under investigation. Economía found that pursuant to these measures, subsidies were provided to olive-oil growers based on the subsequent quantity of olive *oil* actually produced. At the EC level, the maximal per-unit subsidy was based on an overall community-wide production quota that was then divided among the five olive-growing EC states (France, Greece, Italy, Portugal, and Spain). Spain, Italy, and Greece received the vast majority of the quota. If any of these states exceeded their production quota, the per-kilogram amount of the subsidy was reduced proportionately based on the amount by which actual production in each country exceeded the quota. In the year 2001/2002, the subsidies to producers in Spain and Italy amounted to €0.64/kg and €1.01/kg respectively.[4] The regulations governing the subsidy contained no conditions as to whether the olive oil was to be sold in domestic or export markets.

3 Given that the United States is such an important export market for both Spanish and Italian olive-oil producers, it is worth investigating whether the EC's primary political-economy motive in filing a WTO dispute against Mexico is concern that Mexican development of a domestic olive-oil-producing industry might lead to a formidable competitor entering the more important US market. One potential reason for such a concern would be if Mexican olive-oil firms were advantaged relative to EC firms in the US market through a substantial tariff preference granted under NAFTA. According to the WTO's Integrated Database (obtained via WITS), this motive can be ruled out as the size of the US tariff preference to Mexico granted under NAFTA is only 5 cents per kilogram of olive oil (*vis-à-vis* the US MFN applied rate to which EC firms are subject), which is extremely small given the world price of olive oil.

4 See Economía's Resolución final de la investigación por subvención de precios sobre las importaciones de aceite de oliva virgen, originarias de la Unión Europea (Comunidad Europea), principalmente del Reino de España y la República Italiana, independientemente del país de procedencia, 1 August 2005, para. 22.89. Using Spain as an example, the amount of the subsidy was derived as follows: Spain's national production quota was 760,027 tons, while actual production was 1,562,531 tons. The normal subsidy for production that came in at or under the national quota level was €1.3225/kg. The actual per-unit subsidy was calculated by multiplying the normal subsidy by the ratio of the quota level to actual production: €1.3225/kg × (760,027/1,562,531) = €0.64/kg.

3. Discussion of legal findings

In this section, we discuss the WTO Panel's findings on the claims brought by the EC challenging Economía's final determination to impose countervailing duties.

3.1 'Peace Clause' claims

The EC challenged several aspects of Economía's investigation and determination. While most of the EC's claims arose under the *SCM Agreement* and Article VI of the *General Agreement on Tariffs and Trade 1994* (the 'GATT 1994'), the EC also claimed that Mexico had failed to exercise 'due restraint' in initiating a CVD investigation under Article 13(b)(i) of the WTO *Agreement on Agriculture* – the so-called 'Peace Clause'. Since the Peace Clause applied only during the period of implementation of the *Agreement on Agriculture*, which expired at the latest in 2004, this issue is now largely of historical interest and merits only brief discussion. The Panel began by holding that because Article 13 of the *Agreement on Agriculture* was in force on the date on which Economía initiated the investigation, it applied to Economía's initiation of the investigation. The Panel also noted, however, that because Economía conducted the investigation as if Article 13 applied, it would proceed on the same basis.[5]

The EC's first claim was that Economía acted inconsistently with Article 13(b)(i) of the *Agreement on Agriculture* by accepting an application for an investigation on the basis of an allegation of material retardation of a domestic industry, rather than on the basis of an allegation of 'injury' as expressly referred to in Article 13(b)(i). The Panel rejected this claim, noting that 'injury' is defined in footnote 45 of the *SCM Agreement* to include 'material retardation'.[6] The Panel also noted that, in fact, Economía had initiated the investigation on the basis of injury, in this broader sense, and imposed both the provisional and definitive duties on the basis of 'material injury' rather than 'material retardation'.[7]

Next, the EC argued that Mexico acted inconsistently with Article 13(b)(i) of the *Agreement on Agriculture* by failing to show 'due restraint' in initiating the investigation. The Panel interpreted 'due restraint' to refer to a 'proper, regular, and reasonable demonstration of self-control, caution, prudence and reserve'.[8] The Panel then rejected all three grounds on which the EC alleged that Economía had failed to exercise due restraint. First, the Panel found that a failure to hold consultations with the EC prior to initiating the investigation was not a lack of due restraint. Second, the Panel rejected the claim that Economía did not spend enough effort investigating the issue of whether there were domestic producers other than Fortuny before initiating the investigation, noting that Economía had conducted a four-month investigative process on this issue before initiating the investigation.

---

5 Panel Report, paras. 7.54, 7.59.
6 Ibid., para. 7.61.
7 Ibid., para. 7.63.
8 Ibid., para. 7.67.

Finally, the Panel rejected the EC's claim that Economía failed to show due restraint by allegedly converting an application based on an allegation of 'material retardation' into an investigation of 'material injury'. In conclusion, the Panel noted that Economía appeared to have 'proceeded with prudence and caution, indicating self-restraint rather than a lack thereof'.[9]

3.2   Initiation of the investigation

The EC's next set of claims related to the initiation of the investigation. The EC claimed that Economía acted inconsistently with Article 13.1 of the *SCM Agreement* by failing to invite the EC for consultations, or by failing to provide an appropriate time interval for consultations to take place, prior to the initiation of the investigation. Article 13.1 provides that 'as soon as possible after an application [for a CVD investigation] is accepted, and in any event before *the initiation of any investigation*, the [exporting] Members ... shall be invited for consultations with the aim of clarifying the situation ... ' (emphasis added). The EC argued that the investigation was 'initiated' on 2 July 2003, the date on which the Minister signed the initiation resolution, while Mexico argued that the initiation took place on 16 July 2003, the date on which the resolution was published in Mexico's Official Journal. Since Mexico invited the EC for consultations on 4 July 2003 and the consultations took place on 17 July, the Panel had to resolve the issue of when the investigation was 'initiated' for the purposes of the SCM Agreement.

The Panel noted that resolution of this issue involved questions of both law and fact: the legal question of what constituted 'initiation' within the meaning of the SCM Agreement and the factual question of when this 'initiation' took place in the Mexican investigation. With respect to the former question, the Panel noted that footnote 37 of the *SCM Agreement* defines 'initiated' to mean the 'action by which a Member formally commences an investigation'.[10] The Panel considered that this definition left it up to Members to determine the date on which it would 'formally commence' investigations and, therefore, that what constitutes 'initiation' may vary based on the procedural rules in each Member's CVD law.[11] Examining Mexican law, the Panel concluded that, as a factual matter, the date of initiation under Mexican law was the date on which the notice takes legal effect, which is the day after the date of publication in the Official Journal, not the date on which the Minister signed the resolution.[12] Accordingly, the Panel rejected the EC's claim that the invitation for consultations was made only after the initiation of the investigation.

The Panel also rejected the EC's claim that Mexico acted inconsistently with Article 13.1 by failing to hold consultations, or to provide sufficient time for

---

9 Ibid., para. 7.80.
10 Ibid., para. 7.24.
11 Ibid., paras. 7.27–7.28.
12 Ibid., para. 7.30.

consultations to take place, before the initiation of the investigation. The Panel interpreted the obligation in Article 13.1 as being limited to an obligation to invite the responding Member for consultations and did not imply an obligation to *hold* consultations before initiating the investigation.[13]

3.3 Procedural claims regarding the conduct of the investigation

The EC made three claims regarding the conduct of the investigation by Economía. First, the EC claimed that the investigation took too long: Mexico acted inconsistently with Article 11.11 of the *SCM Agreement* by failing to complete the investigation within one year and in no case more than 18 months after the date of initiation. As noted above, the investigation took more than 24 months from the date of initiation (17 July 2003) to the date of the final resolution (1 August 2005). The Panel found that Article 11.11 imposes a clear and unequivocal rule that no investigation may exceed 18 months and, therefore, that Mexico had acted inconsistently with Article 11.11.[14]

Second, the EC claimed that Mexico acted inconsistently with Article 12.8 of the *SCM Agreement* by failing to provide the interested Members and parties with the 'essential facts under consideration which form the basis for the decision whether to apply definitive measures'. Mexico argued that the preliminary resolution constituted the disclosure of the essential facts on which the final decision was to be made. The EC responded that a preliminary resolution was not a suitable vehicle to disclose 'essential facts' because company-specific information could not be provided in a public resolution and, in any event, additional 'essential facts' could come to light in further investigations following the preliminary determination. The Panel interpreted the term 'essential facts' to refer to 'the specific facts that underlie the investigating authority's final findings and conclusions in respect of the three essential elements – subsidization, injury and causation – that must be present for application of definitive measures'.[15] The preliminary resolution could serve to disclose these facts only if new 'essential facts' were not incorporated into the record following the issuance of the preliminary resolution. In this case, the Panel found that Economía did not appear to rely in the final determination on any facts that had not been disclosed in the preliminary resolution.[16] Moreover, the EC failed to establish that it was denied an opportunity to defend its interests following the publication of the preliminary resolution.[17] Accordingly, the Panel found that the EC had failed to establish that Mexico had acted inconsistently with Article 12.8.

Finally, the EC argued that Mexico acted inconsistently with Article 12.4.1 of the *SCM Agreement* by failing to require interested parties to provide

---

13 Ibid., para. 7.35.
14 Ibid., paras. 7.120–7.123.
15 Ibid., para. 7.110.
16 Ibid., para. 7.115.
17 Ibid., paras. 7.112–7.113.

nonconfidential summaries of confidential information. The Panel noted that merely providing a public version of a confidential document, from which the confidential information has been deleted, may not be sufficient to satisfy Article 12.4.1, because the public version may not 'permit a reasonable understanding of the substance of the information submitted in confidence' within the meaning of Article 12.4.1.[18] The Panel also noted that a statement of reasons why summarization of the information is not permitted may be provided only in 'exceptional circumstances'.[19] The Panel disagreed with the reasoning of the Panel in *Mexico–Steel Pipes and Tubes* with respect to the corresponding obligation in Article 6.5.1 of the *Anti-Dumping Agreement* that the investigating authority was not required to examine the reasons why summarization of the confidential information would not be possible.[20] However, the Panel agreed with the *Mexico–Steel Pipes and Tubes* Panel that merely providing access to the confidential version of the document constituted an alternative to compliance with the requirements of Article 12.4.1 of the *SCM Agreement* (and Article 6.5 of the *Anti-Dumping Agreement*) regarding the provision of public summaries of confidential information.

Turning to the case before it, the Panel found that while Economía required public versions of confidential documents, it did not require summarization of the confidential information and it was not possible to obtain a reasonable understanding of the deleted information from the public versions.[21] In addition, while some parties asserted in general statements that summarization was not possible because of exceptional circumstances, these statements were unsupported assertions. Economía could not have assessed, therefore, whether such 'exceptional circumstances' existed.[22] Accordingly, the Panel concluded that Mexico acted inconsistently with its obligations under Article 12.4.1 by failing to require nonconfidential summaries of confidential information or a statement of why, due to exceptional circumstances, such summarization was not possible.

3.4   'Pass-through' of subsidy benefits

The first substantive issue addressed by the Panel was the EC's claim that Mexico acted inconsistently with Articles 1 and 14 of the *SCM Agreement* by failing to calculate properly the benefit conferred on the recipient of the subsidies at issue pursuant to Article 1.1 of the *SCM Agreement* and by failing to explain adequately its calculation pursuant to Article 14 of the *SCM Agreement*. The EC argued that Mexico should have conducted a 'pass-through' analysis to determine the extent to which any benefits received from the subsidies by olive growers were passed through to exporters of olive oil to Mexico. The EC argued that the olives were an

18 Ibid., paras. 7.87–7.88.
19 Ibid., paras. 7.89–7.90.
20 Ibid., para. 7.92.
21 Ibid., paras. 7.96–7.98.
22 Ibid., paras. 7.99–7.101.

input into the product actually exported and subject to the investigation and that the exporters of olive oil were not related to the olive growers, who actually received the subsidies at issue.[23] Mexico argued that the subsidies at issue were direct subsidies on the production of olive oil and had been notified as such to the WTO. Accordingly, no pass-through analysis was required.[24]

As the Panel noted at the start of its analysis, there has been considerable discussion of 'pass-through' issues in WTO law.[25] The Panel noted that in *US–Softwood Lumber IV*, the Appellate Body found that where a subsidy is conferred on the production of an input product used to produce the imported product under investigation, and the producer of the input product is unrelated to the producer of the importer product, a pass-through analysis must be conducted to determine the extent to which the subsidy on the input product was transferred to the imported product. This is necessary to ensure that the amount of any CVD imposed is not in excess of the amount of the subsidy on the imported product in accordance with GATT Article VI:3.[26] The Panel noted the pass-through analysis is required only where the producer of the input product and the producer of the imported product are not related.[27] Also, a pass-through analysis is not necessary where both the input product and the finished product fall within the definition of the product under investigation.[28] Finally, the Panel noted that the extensive jurisprudence on whether benefits from nonrecurring subsidies continued to exist and could be deemed to be transferred to a producer's new owners following the privatization of state-owned producers was not relevant to the case at hand.[29]

The Panel began its analysis of the EC's pass-through claims by noting that while the previous jurisprudence found the legal basis for the obligation to conduct a pass-through analysis in GATT Article VI:3, the EC did not bring a claim under that Article and, instead, based its pass-through claims on Articles 1 and 14 of the *SCM Agreement*.[30] The Panel understood the EC's claim with respect to Article 1 of the *SCM Agreement* to be that the failure to conduct a pass-through analysis was inconsistent with the aspect of the definition of a subsidy under Article 1.1(b) that 'a benefit is thereby conferred'.[31] The Panel also noted that, in response to questioning, the EC had suggested that the obligation to conduct a pass-through analysis was 'implicit' in Articles 1 and 14.[32]

The Panel found that Article 1.1(b) contains a definition of the term 'subsidy'. Thus, the provision addresses only the question of whether a benefit *existed* and,

23 Ibid., para. 7.125.
24 Ibid., para. 7.128.
25 Ibid., para. 7.130 et seq.
26 Ibid., para. 7.139, citing Appellate Body Report, *US–Softwood Lumber IV*, paras. 140–147.
27 Panel Report, para. 7.140.
28 Ibid., para. 7.143.
29 Ibid., para. 7.141.
30 Ibid., para. 7.145.
31 Ibid., para. 7.147.
32 Ibid., para. 7.148.

therefore, whether or not there was a subsidy.[33] However, the Panel found, Article 1.1(b) does not establish a requirement to calculate precisely the amount of any benefit accruing.[34] The Panel's total separation of the question of the existence of a subsidy and the amount of the subsidy is a little discordant, especially in light of the *de minimis* provision of Article 11.9 of the *SCM Agreement*, under which CVD investigations must be terminated when the amount of a subsidy is *de minimis* (less than 1 %). It should be noted, however, that the EC expressly told the Panel that its argument was *not* that a benefit was not provided or that a subsidy did not exist, but simply that Economía had failed to determine the *amount* of the subsidy under Article 1.1.[35] Since the Panel concluded that Article 1.1 does not impose a requirement to determine the amount of the benefit, it concluded that Mexico did not act inconsistently with that provision by failing to conduct a pass-through analysis.

With respect to the EC's pass-through claim under Article 14 of the *SCM Agreement*, the Panel understood the EC's claim to be that because Economía failed to conduct a pass-through analysis where one was required, its explanation of how it calculated the amount of subsidization was not reasoned and adequate and, therefore, inconsistent with Article 14.[36] Article 14 provides, *inter alia*, that the method used to calculate the benefit 'shall be transparent and adequately explained'. The Panel saw nothing in this language to suggest that Economía was required to conduct a pass-through analysis or that the failure to do so meant that Economía's analysis was not transparent or adequately explained.[37] To the contrary, the Panel failed to see 'how the Final Resolution either lacks transparency as to the method used to calculate the benefit to the recipient or fails to adequately explain that method'.[38]

The Panel went on to conclude that even if Article 14 could be construed to contain an obligation to conduct a pass-through analysis, it would find no basis to conclude that Economía had acted inconsistently with that obligation.[39] In the Panel's view, the evidence supported Economía's view that the subsidy in question consisted of aid to olive growers *for the production of olive oil*.[40] Thus, the olive grower received aid only to the extent that it could prove that it has converted olives into olive oil and was paid only on the basis of actual kilograms of olive oil produced.[41] In other words, the subsidy was not a subsidy for an input product (olives) that may have been passed through to the imported product (olive oil) but

---

33 Ibid., para. 7.151.
34 Ibid., para. 7.152.
35 Ibid., para. 7.150.
36 Ibid., para. 7.154.
37 Ibid., para. 7.159 et seq.
38 Ibid., para. 7.168.
39 Ibid.
40 Ibid.
41 Ibid.

was a subsidy provided for the production of the imported product (olive oil) itself.[42] Accordingly, the Panel found that the EC had failed to establish that Mexico acted inconsistently with Article 14 of the *SCM Agreement* by failing to conduct a pass-through analysis.

In addition to the pass-through claims, the EC also made three additional claims with respect to how Economía calculated the benefit under Article 14 of the *SCM Agreement*. The EC argued that (i) Economía failed to adjust its calculation for a portion of the EC's olive-oil exports that were not subject to the subsidy; (ii) Economía failed to make adjustments for certain costs incurred by exporting companies; and (iii) Economía's calculation of the subsidy margin was inflated because Economía compared the amount of the subsidy with the exporter's sales prices at the ex-factory level rather than at the CIF level. The Panel rejected all of these claims.[43]

3.5 Definition of 'domestic industry'

The EC claimed that the applicant, Fortuny, did not produce the like product either at the time of the application or during the period of the injury investigation. Consequently, Mexico acted inconsistently with Article 16 of the *SCM Agreement* by initiating the investigation on the basis that Fortuny's application was made 'by or on behalf of the domestic industry' within the meaning of that Article.

The Panel noted that the definition of the domestic industry in Article 16.1 of the *SCM Agreement* refers to 'producers'. The Panel then found that to 'produce' refers to the nature of the activity of bringing something into existence.[44] The Panel noted that the precise issue of whether a company that did not actually produce at a given time could be considered as a producer, and hence part of the 'domestic industry' for the purposes of Article 16 had not previously been addressed in the jurisprudence.[45] However, the Panel endorsed the approach taken in the *US–Lamb* dispute of focusing on the essential nature of the business activities of a given enterprise as determinative of whether the enterprise could be included in the domestic industry for the product.[46] Based on this approach, the Panel found no basis to exclude from the domestic industry companies whose essential nature included production of the like product but who simply did not do so at a given point in time.[47]

---

42 Ibid.
43 Ibid., paras. 7.170–7.176.
44 Ibid., para. 7.192.
45 Ibid., para. 7.193.
46 Ibid., para. 7.196. The issue in *US–Lamb* was whether enterprises that did not actually produce the like product itself (i.e., growers of live lambs) could be considered as producers of the like product (i.e., processed lamb meat). The Panel and the Appellate Body concluded that because the lamb growers did not themselves process lamb meat, they could not be considered as part of the domestic industry producing lamb meat. Ibid., para. 7.195.
47 Ibid., para. 7.196.

The Panel found contextual support for its interpretation in several other provisions of the *SCM Agreement*, including Article 15.2, which provides that a determination of the volume and effects of subsidized imports on domestic prices for the like product can be made by reference to either 'production' or 'consumption'. The Panel interpreted this reference to consumption to mean that an injury determination could properly be made even in the absence of actual production at a given time.[48] The Panel also noted that the list of injury factors to be considered under Article 15.4 of the *SCM Agreement* reflected a 'multifaceted approach' to determining the condition of the enterprises involved and that actual and potential declines in output constituted only one element of this analysis. In these circumstances, the Panel considered that actual output at a given point in time was not necessarily to fall within the definition of a producer of the like product.[49] The Panel also observed that there may be several commonplace reasons why producers might routinely not produce at a given point in time, including seasonality, technology innovations, distribution cycles, and *force majeure*.[50]

Finally, the Panel turned to the object and purpose of the countervail provisions of the *SCM Agreement*. Since the object and purpose was to provide for the application of trade remedies in circumstances where subsidized imports cause material injury or a threat thereof, or material retardation, of a domestic industry, it would make no sense to exclude companies that were not actually producing at a given point in time from those remedies.[51] Otherwise, an industry that was 'so badly injured as to be forced to cease production for some period ... would be disqualified from obtaining the very remedy aimed at addressing such injury'.[52] Accordingly, the Panel found that Article 16.1 does not require that an enterprise or group of enterprises seeking CVD relief must actually produce the like product, either around the date of filing of their application or during the injury period of investigation, in order to be considered 'producers' and, therefore, part of the 'domestic industry' within the meaning of Article 16.1.[53]

The Panel then turned to the question of whether Fortuny was a 'producer' of the like product. The Panel noted that Economía relied on extensive factual information in determining that Fortuny was a 'producer' of olive oil, including its (and its predecessor's) history of production, monthly business data for three previous years, information regarding the state of its facilities, and its business plan to resume production. Economía also conducted verification at Fortuny's premises, which established that production actually resumed after the preliminary resolution. Economía also tested the viability of Fortuny's business plan.[54] Based

48 Ibid., para. 7.198.
49 Ibid., paras. 7.200–7.201.
50 Ibid., para. 7.202.
51 Ibid.
52 Ibid., para. 7.203.
53 Ibid., para. 7.204.
54 Ibid., paras. 7.209–7.212.

on these facts, the Panel concluded that Economía made a reasoned and adequate determination, supported by positive evidence, that Fortuny was in fact a producer of the like product.[55] Accordingly, the Panel rejected the EC's claims that Mexico improperly treated Fortuny as a producer and, consequently, improperly treated Fortuny as part of the domestic industry within the meaning of Article 16.1 of the *SCM Agreement*.

The EC also claimed that Economía failed to examine adequately whether there were producers of olive oil other than Fortuny and whether there was sufficient support for the application among the domestic industry within the meaning of Article 11.4 of the *SCM Agreement*. The Panel rejected this claim, noting that Article 11.4 did not preclude the investigating authority from making this determination solely on the basis of information provided by the applicant.[56] In the Panel's view, whether the investigating authority needs further information to make this determination must be decided on a case-by-case basis.[57]

In the present case, the Panel found that Economía reviewed detailed evidence, from both Fortuny and other sources, as to whether there were other producers of olive oil, and concluded there was no evidence before Economía of the existence of any other producers.[58] Accordingly, the Panel rejected the EC's claim that Mexico acted inconsistently with Article 11.4 of the *SCM Agreement* in determining whether there was support for the application.

The Panel also rejected a claim by the EC under Article 16.1 of the *SCM Agreement* and Article VI:6(a) of the GATT 1994 that Economía failed to determine properly whether Fortuny constituted the entire domestic industry. Again, the Panel rejected this claim, setting out over the course of three pages of its report the steps taken and evidence assembled by Economía as to the possible existence of other producers.[59] The Panel also noted that no other companies came forward during the course of the investigation.[60]

3.6 Claims relating to the injury analysis

The EC's final set of claims related to Economía's injury analysis. First, the EC argued that it was not clear whether Economía's final determination was one of material retardation or material injury and that it would be inconsistent with Article VI:6 to make simultaneous findings of both. The Panel rejected this claim, finding as a matter of fact that Economía made a finding of material injury, not material retardation, in both its preliminary and final resolutions.[61]

---

55 Ibid., para. 7.214.
56 Ibid., para. 7.225.
57 Ibid., para. 7.228.
58 Ibid., paras. 7.230–7.237.
59 Ibid., para. 7.245.
60 Ibid., para. 7.247.
61 Ibid., para. 7.279.

Next, the EC claimed that Economía's injury analysis was inconsistent with Article 15.4 because Economía used data from nine-month periods in each year of the injury period of investigation (April–December 2000, 2001, and 2002), rather than full-year data for those years, as the basis of its injury determination. Citing the Panel Report in *Mexico–Steel Tubes and Pipes*, the Panel noted that the use of partial-year periods could be accepted only if the investigating authority could explain how developments within the partial period were reflective of the period as a whole and whether the partial periods were justified and not anomalous in the particular case.[62] The Panel rejected Mexico's explanations that the use of the nine-month periods may avoid distortions in the data and found that Mexico had acted inconsistently with Article 15.4 of the *SCM Agreement* in using these partial periods.[63] Based on this finding, the Panel decided to exercise judicial economy with respect to the EC's other claims under Articles 15.1 and 15.4, including the claims that Economía acted inconsistently with Article 15.1(a) by basing its analysis of the volume and price effects of the subsidized imports on data from Fortuny's business plan rather than 'actual' price data for part of the period of investigation.[64]

The EC also argued that Economía did not properly examine any known factors other than the subsidized imports that may have caused injury to the domestic industry within the meaning of Article 15.5 of the *SCM Agreement*. The EC referred to six other factors in particular, including *inter alia*, Fortuny's loss of its distribution network, its loss of the right to use a Spanish brand name (Ybarra), and its high costs.[65] The Panel interpreted the obligation to examine other known factors in Article 15.5 as consisting of two parts. First, the investigating authority is required to consider other factors known to it either as a result of its own investigation or because they were raised by the interested parties. Second, the investigating authority is required to analyse each of those factors separately and to explain the nature and extent of the injurious effects of these other factors, separating and distinguishing them from the injurious effects of the subsidized imports.[66] Because the Panel found that Economía had addressed each of the six factors identified by the EC in its preliminary and final resolutions, concluding that none of them caused injury to the domestic industry, the Panel focused its analysis on the adequacy of Economía's analysis.

The Panel conducted a detailed review of Economía's analysis of each of the factors referred to by the EC.[67] Based on this analysis, the Panel concluded that Economía had not 'dismiss[ed] these factors with qualitative assertions. Rather, it carefully examined, separated and distinguished the effects of each factor from the

---

62 Ibid., para. 7.286.
63 Ibid., para. 7.290.
64 Ibid., paras. 7.252, 7.291.
65 Ibid., para. 7.294.
66 Ibid., para. 7.305.
67 Ibid., paras. 7.309–7.316.

effects of the subsidized imports, and reasonably concluded that these factors were not contributing to the injury suffered by Fortuny.'[68] The Panel also found that while there might be factual circumstances in which it would be necessary to examine the *collective* impact of the other known factors, it was not necessary in this case, where Economía reasonably concluded that none of the other factors caused injury.[69] Accordingly, the Panel found that the EC had failed to establish that Mexico had acted inconsistently with Article 15.5 of the *SCM Agreement*.

3.7 Summary of the Panel's findings

To summarize, the Panel rejected most of the EC's claims, finding that Mexico acted inconsistently only with: (i) Article 11.11 of the *SCM Agreement*, by failing to conclude the investigation within 18 months; (ii) Article 12.4.1, by failing to require nonconfidential summaries of confidential information or an explanation of the reasons why summarization was not possible; and (iii) Article 15.1, by limiting the injury analysis to nine-month periods in each year of the injury period of investigation.[70] The Panel rejected the rest of the EC's claims and, not surprisingly, declined to make a suggestion, pursuant to the second sentence of Article 19.1 of the DSU, that repeal of the measure would be the most appropriate means of bringing the measure into conformity with Mexico's obligations.

This may not seem like a very successful outcome for the EC. Nevertheless, at the DSB meeting of 11 December 2008, Mexico notified the DSB that it had withdrawn the measure effective 18 November 2008. However, it is not clear that Mexico's withdrawal of the measure was directly in response to the Panel Report or the nature of the Panel's rulings and recommendations – Mexico's statement to the DSB referred to a domestic-court decision ordering Economía to terminate the measure.

4. Legal-economic analysis

In this section, we discuss in more detail the following issues raised by the WTO Panel Report in this case: (i) Economía's and the Panel's analysis of 'any [other] known factors' in the causation analysis under Article 15.5 of the *SCM Agreement*, including both the legal standard of review applicable to the Panel's analysis and the economic issues arising out of the analysis; and (ii) the nature of Members' obligations to implement rulings and recommendations regarding 'procedural' violations of WTO contingent-protection laws, including, in this case, the time limit on the completion of an investigation under Article 11.11 of the *SCM Agreement*. We will also discuss briefly some other issues arising out of the

---

68 Ibid., para. 7.317.
69 Ibid., para. 7.318.
70 Ibid., para. 8.1.

case, including the pass-through issue and the Panel's reliance on Fortuny's business plan as evidence of injury.

4.1 Injury by subsidy and Mexican examination of 'any known factors'

4.1.1 Legal aspects of the findings on 'any known factors': standard of review

Before discussing the economic aspects of the case, a brief discussion of the legal aspects of the Panel's findings on 'any known factors' under Article 15.5 of the *SCM Agreement* is merited. At the beginning of its Report, the Panel discussed at length the standard of review it was required to apply to Economía's determination. The Panel noted the Appellate Body's statement that a Panel's role was to 'inquire whether the evidence and explanation relied on by the investigation authority reasonably supports [the investigating authority's] conclusions'.[71] The Panel also quoted at length from the Appellate Body Report in *US–Softwood Lumber VI (Article 21.5–Canada)*, in which the Appellate Body stated, *inter alia*, that:

> The panel must examine whether the explanations provided demonstrate that the investigating authority took proper account of the complexities of the data before it, and that it explained why it rejected or discounted alternative explanations and interpretations of the record evidence. A panel must be open to the possibility that the explanations given by the authority are not reasoned or adequate in the light of other plausible alternative explanations, and must take care not to assume itself the role of initial trier of facts, nor to be passive by 'simply *accept[ing]* the conclusions of the competent authorities'.[72]

At the outset of its analysis of the Article 15.5 claims, the Panel quoted the Appellate Body's statement in *US–Hot-Rolled Steel* that this analysis (actually, its analog in the *Anti-Dumping Agreement*) required that:

> Investigating authorities must make an appropriate assessment of the injury caused to the domestic industry by other known factors, and they must separate and distinguish the injurious effects of the dumped imports from the injurious effects of those other factors. This requires a satisfactory explanation of the nature and extent of the injurious effects of the other factors, as distinguished from the injurious effects of the dumped imports.[73]

Like all attempts to articulate precise standards by which tribunals must review determinations of lower authorities, this standard of review is problematic. The line between making a careful examination of whether the investigating authority did its job properly, on the one hand, and not becoming a *de novo* trier of the facts,

---

71 Ibid., para. 7.3, quoting Appellate Body Report, *US–Countervailing Duty Investigation on DRAMS*, para. 187.

72 Appellate Body Report, *US–Softwood Lumber VI (Article 21.5–Canada)*, para. 93, quoting Appellate Body Report, *US–Lamb*, para. 106.

73 Panel Report, para. 7.301, quoting Appellate Body Report, *US–Hot-Rolled Steel*, para. 226.

on the other hand, is very fine. It is particularly problematic with respect to the review of determinations such as material injury and causation determinations, where there are standards as to *how* the investigating authority is to make its determination but no objective definitions of what constitutes sufficient injury or causal link. These problems are clearly displayed in this Panel Report.

In its review of Economía's 'any known factors' analysis, the Panel stated that it would first factually analyse Economía's causation analysis and then consider whether it was consistent with Article 15.5.[74] The Panel went on to recite, in some detail, how Economía addressed each of the other factors at issue. It must be acknowledged that Economía's analysis was more detailed than is often the case. However, the second part of the Panel's analysis is less clear. After reciting how Economía analysed each factor, the Panel either offered no review of Economía's analysis[75] or, at the end of its recapitulation of the analysis, merely asserted that Economía 'reasonably found'[76] that the factor was not a cause of injury to Fortuny. In a brief conclusory paragraph, the Panel stated that Economía 'carefully examined, separated, and distinguished the effects of each factor from the effects of the subsidized imports, and reasonably concluded that these factors were not contributing to the injury suffered by Fortuny'.[77] Since the Panel merely summarized Economía's analysis, however, it is difficult to discern how or where the Panel determined that Economía's analysis and conclusions were 'reasonable'.

The systemic concern here is that Panels might perceive *any* independent review of the evidence on their part as involving them impermissibly as *de novo* triers of fact, with the danger that the obligation on the investigating authority would be reduced simply to an obligation to provide a lengthy explanation of its determination. The obligation may become an obligation to provide a 'reasoned' determination rather than a 'reasonable' one. As noted, this concern is more acute with respect to inherently subjective determinations such as those of injury and causation, where reviewing Panels are likely to be especially careful to avoid a *de novo* review. For the purpose of the present paper, we draw attention to this issue simply to illustrate why Panels tend to avoid the sort of analysis contained in the following subsections.

4.1.2 *Economic purpose of CVD provisions of the SCM Agreement*

In order to make a legal-economic assessment of the Panel's logic and decisions, it is necessary to understand the main objective of the *SCM Agreement* that allows importing countries to respond with countervailing duties when a trading partner imposes subsidies that affect exported products. We follow the logic, coherently presented in Grossman and Mavroidis (2003) as well as many other contributions

---

74 Panel Report, para. 7.308.
75 Ibid., paras. 7.311, 7.312, 7.315, and 7.316.
76 Ibid., paras. 7.313, 7.314.
77 Ibid., para. 7.317.

to the ALI series, that the objective of the *SCM Agreement* is to discourage subsidies that harm the import-competing interests of domestic producers.[78] We follow the specific approach of Grossman and Mavroidis (2003: 186) who state 'Articles 14 and 19 [of the *SCM Agreement*] require the size of the countervailing duty to be set so as to just offset the adverse effects of the subsidy on conditions in the domestic industry. This latter provision can only be understood as an attempt to restore competitive conditions in the industry to what they would have been had the subsidy been absent.'

From this perspective, one fundamental question in this dispute is whether the 'benefit' to EC exporters of olive oil had an effect on the conditions of competition between EC firms and domestic Mexican producers of olive oil. Essentially, the issue is whether the Mexican firms were injured by the benefit conferred to the subsidy-receiving EC firms. We examine this possibility within the context of a more formal economic model that we present below.

However, before turning to the analysis, it is necessary to identify the second important issue highlighted by Grossman and Mavroidis; i.e., that the relevant counterfactual to examine is the 'competitive conditions in the industry … had the subsidy been absent'. More concretely, in particular, Article 15.5 of the *SCM Agreement* states that in a CVD investigation '[t]he authorities shall also examine any known factors other than the subsidized imports which at the same time are injuring the domestic industry, and the injuries caused by these other factors must not be attributed to the subsidized imports'. In this particular dispute, the Panel was satisfied that Mexico had met the burden of examining 'any known factors' that might be the alternative cause of injury to the domestic olive-oil industry. Our analysis is not as charitable, as the simple economic model that we analyse below suggests a number of important questions that the Panel might have more fully addressed.

Consider Figure 3, which presents a simple illustrative model describing the Mexican and EC market for olive oil that is broadly consistent with the underlying events at issue in this case. We assume there are two countries (the EC and Mexico) that trade only this one good under competitive conditions that we model with simple linear supply and demand curves. The three panels combine to illustrate: Figure 3(a) the Mexican domestic market for olive oil, Figure 3(c) the EC's domestic market for olive oil, and Figure 3(b) the 'international' market for olive oil in which the countries' import demand and export supply curves determine the equilibrium level of international trade. From Figure 3(a), it is apparent that Mexico is a relatively costly supplier of olive oil (S_{MEX}^0). Thus, for a range of world prices that are sufficiently low, the difference between Mexico's domestic demand for olive oil (D_{MEX}^0) and its domestic supply will be given by its import demand curve for olive oil, given by MD_{MEX}^0, in Figure 3(b). On the other hand, Figure 3(c)

---

78 See, for example, Grossman and Mavroidis (2005a), Grossman and Mavroidis (2005b), and Horn and Mavroidis (2006).

Figure 3. The initial equilibrium and olive-oil trade before the 'shocks'

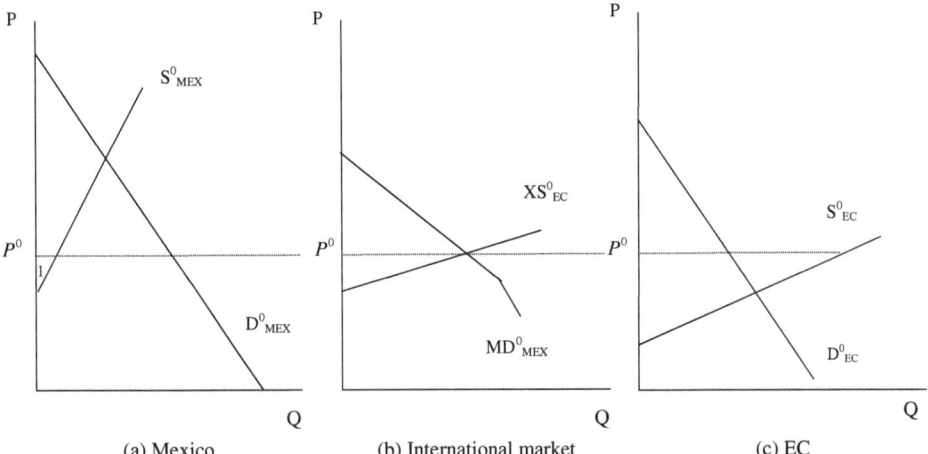

(a) Mexico   (b) International market   (c) EC

illustrates the EC as apparently a lower-cost supplier of olive oil (S^0_{EC}). Thus, at relatively low world prices, the difference between the EC's domestic demand for olive oil (D^0_{EC}) and its domestic supply will be given by its export supply curve for olive oil, given by XS^0_{EC}, in Figure 3(b).

We begin with an initial equilibrium outcome of liberal trade and before the occurrence of any shocks that we will introduce momentarily.[79] The intersection of the Mexican import demand and EC export supply curves in Figure 3(b) determines the initial equilibrium price, P^0, and at this world price the EC exports olive oil to Mexico. At this initial equilibrium price, Mexico has a small domestic industry whose level of production is given by the intersection of the price, P^0, with its domestic supply curve, S^0_{MEX}. The Mexican industry's economic welfare under this initial outcome, which will be the benchmark by which we measure 'injury' in the analysis that follows, is given by the triangular area '1' in Figure 3(a).

The information presented in the Panel Report identifies at least two potentially important 'shocks' to the determinants of supply and demand in this economic system that could substantially disturb the equilibrium in a way that causes injury to the Mexican industry. We will present an analysis of each in turn. The first 'shock' is the subsidy granted to EC producers of olive oil. The second 'shock' is the severance of a relationship between the Mexican firm Fortuny and the Spanish firm Ybarra in 2002, which prevented Fortuny (the legal Mexican business successor in 2002 to the former firm Formex-Ybarra) from carrying the Ybarra brand or of having access to the Ybarra distribution network within Mexico.

---

79 The analysis would not materially change if we were to start from an initial equilibrium in which Mexico imposed a small tariff on EC exporters of olive oil, as was the case in this dispute.

Figure 4. The isolated effect of a production subsidy to EC olive-oil producers

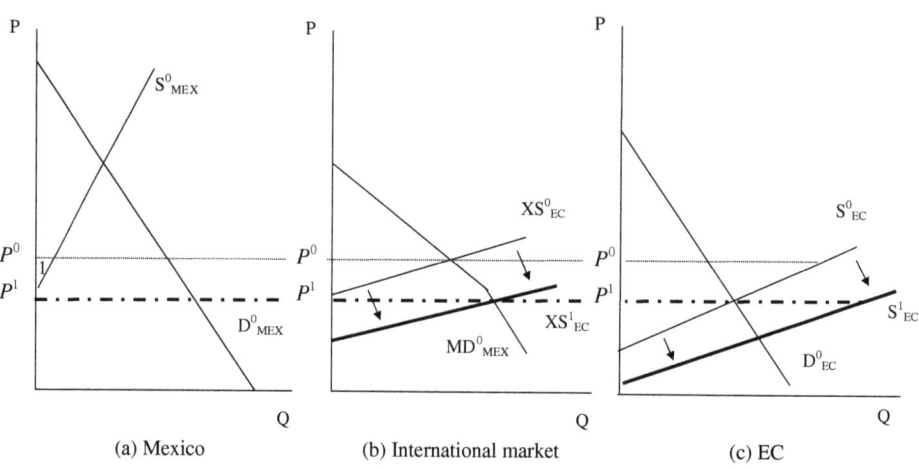

(a) Mexico   (b) International market   (c) EC

4.1.3 The isolated effect of an EC olive-oil-production subsidy on the market

In Figure 4, we first examine the implications of a production subsidy to the EC firms that produce olive oil. As we argue elsewhere in more detail, we find little to suggest that the subsidies were not received by olive-oil-producing firms and that they were not also contingent on their level of production. The effect of such a subsidy can be analysed by tracing through the impact beginning in Figure 4(c). A production subsidy to the EC industry lowers the marginal cost to producing each additional unit of olive oil and is represented by an outward shift in the EC's domestic supply curve from S_{EC}^0 to S_{EC}^1. Because the domestic supply curve has changed, for any given price, the EC's industry's willingness to export (i.e., the difference between the domestic supply curve and the domestic demand curve) also changes. Thus, in Figure 4(b), the EC's export supply curve shifts in response to the domestic subsidy from X_{EC}^0 to XS_{EC}^1. The intersection of Mexico's (unchanged) import demand curve MD_{MEX}^0 with the new EC export supply curve XS_{EC}^1 occurs at a slightly lower equilibrium price, P^1. As is consistent with the facts of this case, the new price P^1 is lower than the point at which the Mexican industry's supply curve intersects the price axis; i.e., the lowest price it is willing to receive to produce a positive level of output before shutting down.

If this were the only 'shock' taking place in this market during this time period, the analysis would be very straightforward. Since the EC subsidy reduces the equilibrium price of olive oil, it is the cause of injury to the Mexican olive-oil industry, which would be represented in Figure 4(a) as the loss of producer surplus associated with the initial price P^0, given by the area '1'. However, as we illustrate next, there is reason to suspect that this was not the only 'shock' taking place

Figure 5. The isolated effect of the loss of the Ybarra brand and distribution network to Mexican olive-oil producers

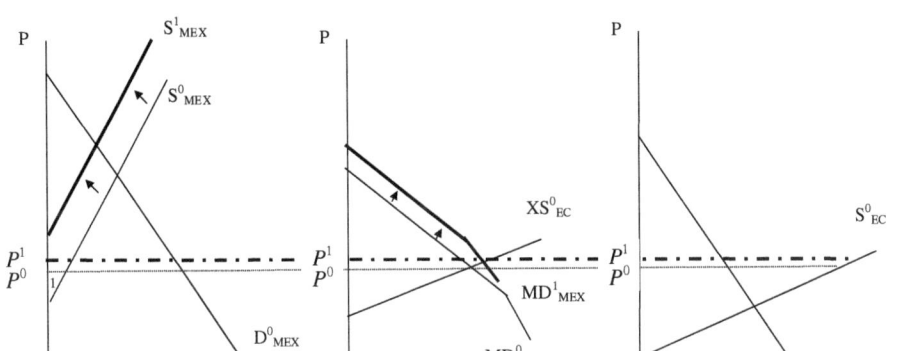

(a) Mexico   (b) International market   (c) EC

during this time period. This complicates the issue of causation in the injury-determination analysis.

4.1.4   *The isolated effect of the loss of the Ybarra brand and distribution network to Mexican olive-oil producers*

We next examine the potential implications of the severance of a relationship between the Mexican firm Fortuny and the foreign firm Ybarra in 2002, which meant that Fortuny could no longer carry the Ybarra brand or have access to the Ybarra distribution network in Mexico. Begin again with the initial equilibrium outcome described in Figure 3, which is the benchmark illustrated in Figure 5. The need for Fortuny to create a *new* distribution network and to do *new* marketing to establish its new brand after 2002 suggests a sudden increase in its costs, which is represented on the figure as an inward shift in the Mexican supply curve from S^0_{MEX} to S^1_{MEX}; i.e., the marginal cost to Fortuny to produce the same quantity of olive oil has increased.[80]

Since Mexico's import demand curve is determined by the difference between its domestic demand and domestic supply, an inward shift of the domestic supply

---

80 An alternative to modeling this as a negative cost shock facing the Mexican industry would be to model it as a negative demand shock. For example, if the loss of the Ybarra brand caused Mexican consumers to switch their demand for olive oil away from Mexican-produced olive oil toward an alternative product, this would cause the domestic demand curve (D^0_{MEX}) in Figure 5(a) to shift in. While not pictured in Figure 5, this would cause Mexico's import demand schedule (MD^0_{MEX}) to shift in, resulting in a lower equilibrium price of olive oil. This would also lead to injury to the Mexican olive-oil producers through a loss of producer surplus (area '1').

curve (Figure 5(a)) corresponds with an outward shift of Mexico's import demand curve from MD^0_{MEX} to MD^1_{MEX} in Figure 5(b). The new, post-'shock' equilibrium price for olives is at P^1. As we have illustrated it, so as to be consistent with one possible interpretation of the economic facts of the case, this slightly higher price of olive oil in this instance is too low for the Mexican domestic industry to produce any olive oil (Figure 5(a)) under its new cost structure reflecting both its 'old costs' plus the new expenditures necessary for distribution and marketing. Thus, we have documented one situation in which it is possible that the negative shock to Fortuny of the additional costs to branding/distribution associated with the severed relationship with Ybarra is itself a sufficient cause of injury to the firm to cause the firm to shut down (produce zero units of olive oil domestically).

Indeed, the injury suffered by the domestic industry in both Figure 4 (the EC subsidy) and Figure 5 (the severance of the Ybarra relationship) of these scenarios is the same. In both 'pre-shock' scenarios, the industry received a producer surplus of area '1'. In both 'post-shock' scenarios, the Mexican firms shut down, so its producer surplus is zero. Thus, the two instances have an identical loss of producer surplus.

The Panel accepted Mexico's argument that Economía had examined the brand and distribution network issues as potential 'factors' and properly ruled them out as causes of injury to Fortuny. In the case of the brand issue, the Panel accepted Economía's reasoning that 'other unknown brands had been successful in penetrating the Mexican market. For those reasons, Economía did not accept the argument by the exporters that Fortuny's inability to use the Ybarra brand was causing it injury in the sense of preventing Fortuny from resuming operations.'[81] From an economic perspective, the fact that other brands had penetrated the Mexican market fails to address the issue that Fortuny's need to establish a new brand is a new cost that it will have to incur (that it did not have to face before 2002) and thus will 'cause' its supply curve to shift upward (see again Figure 5(a)).

Furthermore, with respect to the issue of the distribution network, the Panel also accepted the Mexican argument that 'Economía noted that Fortuny had indicated that it had access to a distribution network, which it planned to use when it resumed operations'.[82] From an economic perspective, the Panel failed to address the issue that there needs to be an assessment of how costly it was for Fortuny to develop this new distribution network (a cost to its production that it also did not have to face before 2002). If this was costly, it was therefore also a cause of Fortuny's upward shift of its supply curve (see again Figure 5(a)), resulting in the new equilibrium price and the possibility that it may be at a level sufficiently low for Fortuny to have to shut down production.

81 Panel Report, para. 7.311.
82 Panel Report, para. 7.312.

4.1.5 The combined effects of the EC subsidy and the severance with Ybarra

In reality, both the elements of Figure 4 (the EC subsidy) and Figure 5 (the do-mestic cost shock associated with the severance of the relationship with Ybarra) are likely to have been at play in injuring the Mexican industry in this instance. Potentially, the investigating authority could have done more to disentangle em-pirically the relative importance of the competing explanations for the injury to the domestic industry. For example, if the loss of the Ybarra brand and distribution network were the dominant cause of the injury to the domestic industry, the model in Figure 5 predicts that the equilibrium price of olive oil consumed in Mexico would *increase* compared to the pre-shock level, holding other factors constant. On the other hand, if the EC subsidy were the dominant cause of the injury to the domestic industry, the model in Figure 5 predicts the equilibrium price of olive oil consumed in Mexico would *decrease* compared to the pre-shock level. Therefore, without a more *empirically* based assessment of the relative sizes of the two con-tributing causes of the injury to Fortuny that would control for other factors, Economía's reasoning (and the Panel's acceptance of this reasoning) is not suf-ficient to rule out convincingly the importance of other known causes of injury to Mexican industry aside from the subsidy.

To conclude this section, consider again the Grossman and Mavroidis insight that the size of the CVD should be determined so as to restore the industry's conditions of competition to what they would have been in the counterfactual situation of the EC subsidy being absent. In this instance, the subsequent fact that the imposed Mexican CVD did not result in a high enough increase in the equi-librium price to induce the Mexican producer to reenter into the production of olive oil suggests it was not able to overcome the other causes of injury (spending resources on a new distribution network and advertising/marketing to establish a new brand name) to the Mexican producers that caused the upward shift in the domestic supply curve illustrated in Figure 5(a). Indeed, the lack of reentry into this market by the domestic firm following the imposition of an actual counter-vailing duty provides anecdotal evidence that these 'other' causes of injury that Economía convinced the Panel it had adequately considered, but which it deter-mined were not important, may have actually been quite sizable.

4.2 Implementation of 'procedural' violations of the SCM and Anti-Dumping Agreements

The Panel's finding that Mexico acted inconsistently with Article 11.11 of the *SCM Agreement* by failing to conclude the investigation within 18 months raises the question of how Members that are found to have acted inconsistently with the 'procedural' requirements of the *SCM* and *Anti-Dumping Agreements* in their conduct of countervailing-duty and anti-dumping investigations must implement the Panel findings in those cases.

Article 19.1 of the DSU provides that when a measure is found to be inconsistent with a provision of the WTO agreements, the Member concerned is recommended to 'bring the measure into conformity' with the relevant legal obligations. Put simply, the Member must fix the problem. But, while it may be simple to fix an improperly calculated anti-dumping or CVD duty rate by recalculating it, how is a Member to fix, *post hoc*, a problem such as a failure to complete an investigation within the deadline specified in the *SCM Agreement*? There seem to be only two possibilities – one would be to conclude that the failure led to a fatally flawed measure and, therefore, to terminate the measure; the other would be to redo the investigation completely within the proper time limit. The former might seem an unduly harsh remedy for the implementing Member, the latter would certainly be an unduly severe remedy for the successful complaining Member!

This issue has not arisen clearly in previous Panel proceedings. Given the tendency in trade-remedy disputes for complainants to make a wide variety of claims, the defending Members generally must implement with respect to several claims, including both 'procedural' and 'substantive' claims. In such cases, in implementing with respect to 'substantive' claims (such as the recalculation of a dumping margin), the implementing Member normally 'fixes' the procedural violation by, for example, in the case of an infringement of an exporter's right to comment, allowing the exporter that right in the implementation proceedings. Because the exporting Member is generally more concerned with fixing the substantive violations, which may lead directly to reduced anti-dumping or CVD rates, than with the ephemeral benefits of remedying the procedural violations, this *modus operandi* is more or less accepted. In proceedings under Article 21.5 of the DSU, moreover, complaining Members have focused on the 'substantive' violations that are more likely to affect the existence of the measure or the amount of the applicable anti-dumping or countervailing duty than the 'procedural' violations, which are perceived as being unlikely to affect either the existence or the amount of the measure.

Similarly, Panels have exercised their right under Article 19.1 of the DSU to make suggestions as to how the defending Member could implement the recommendations only in situations where the Panel has considered the violations of the *Anti-Dumping Agreement*[83] to be 'fundamental and pervasive'.[84] The only violations that Panels have emphasized over others as grounds for suggesting that a measure be terminated are those relating to the initiation of the investigation.[85]

In contrast, there does not appear to have been a case in which the *only* issues for implementation related to what would normally be considered as 'procedural' claims in which the due-process rights of the exporter or exporting Member were found not to have been properly respected.

---

83 No Panel has exercised its discretion under Article 19.1 with respect to a countervailing-duty measure challenged under the *SCM Agreement*.

84 See Panel Report, *Mexico–Steel Pipes and Tubes*, para. 8.9.

85 Ibid., para. 8.12. See also Panel Report, *Guatemala–Cement I*, para. 8.6.

Thus, it remains unclear how a Member must bring a measure that is founded on a 'procedural' violation of WTO rules into compliance. A senior lawyer in the WTO secretariat has suggested that Members may not be required to do *anything* in these circumstances:

> The issue of implementation may be even more problematic where the fault is purely one of process … Indeed, how does a Member in fact bring an anti-dumping measure 'into conformity' when the flaw is a failure to consult before initiating the investigation? Unless one accepts the proposition that a procedural flaw invalidates a resulting measure and that the whole proceeding must therefore always be redone – an approach that would seem draconian and which would encourage Members to seek out the most minor procedural flaws – it may well be that in such a case no concrete steps are required for implementation.[86]

It is not clear what support there is in the text of the *Anti-Dumping* or *SCM Agreements*, or indeed the DSU for this fairly extreme view, which runs counter to the principle of *ubi jus, ibi remedium*. The only basis for this view would appear to be the pragmatic view that Members, or at least those that frequently use contingent-protection measures, are reluctant to accept that measures would have to be terminated based on what are perceived as technical errors in the investigation leading to the imposition of the measure. It could also be argued that since it is impossible to know how the investigation might have unfolded had the procedural violation not occurred, it is not reasonable to assume that the measure would not have been imposed in the same manner even if all procedural requirements had been respected.[87]

Perhaps there is no single answer to this problem. With respect to some 'procedural' violations, such as the delay in completing the investigation in this case, the question is stark: either the measure must be terminated or there is no remedy at all. With respect to other violations, such as a failure to afford an opportunity to exporters to defend their interests under Article 6.2 of the *Anti-Dumping Agreement* or Article 12.3 of the *SCM Agreement*, a defending Member could, in theory, remedy the violation by affording the exporters an opportunity to defend their interests by submitting comments in an implementation proceeding. It would be naïve, however, to assume that an opportunity to submit comments in an implementation proceeding a couple of years after the measure has already been imposed will have the same impact as the same opportunity *might* have had during the original investigation. With respect to other 'procedural' violations, such as the Panel's finding in this case that Economía acted inconsistently with Article 12.4.1

---

86 Kreier (2005: 60–61).

87 See Panel Report, *Guatemala–Cement I*, para. 7.42 ('while it is possible that the investigation would have proceeded in the same manner had Guatemala timely notified Mexico before proceeding to initiate the investigation, we cannot say that the course of the investigation would not have been different').

of the *SCM Agreement* by failing to require nonconfidential summaries of confidential information, it is even more difficult to speculate whether compliance with the obligation initially would have changed the outcome of the initial investigation.

A further complication of this problem arises out of the Panel and Appellate Body rulings in the *Mexico–Anti-Dumping Measures on Rice* dispute. In that dispute, the Appellate Body upheld the Panel's finding that a determination of injury in an anti-dumping investigation was not based on positive evidence of actual injury where there was a 15-month gap between the end of the period of investigation and the initiation of the investigation, and a gap of almost three years between the end of the period of investigation and the imposition of final anti-dumping duties.[88] This requirement of proximity in time between the period of investigation and the imposition of trade-remedy measures raises the question of whether it is *ever* possible to 'fix' a flawed trade-remedy measure.

For example, if, in the present case, Mexico had initiated implementation proceedings to bring its olive-oil CVD measure into compliance with the Panel's rulings and recommendations, those proceedings would have been initiated in late 2008 and likely not initiated until early 2009. However, the period of investigation used by Economía was April to December 2000, 2001, and 2002. Thus, an implementation proceeding may have resulted in the imposition of WTO-consistent CVDs (for the first time) in 2009, based on data that would be almost seven years old. This would presumptively be inconsistent with the Appellate Body and Panel rulings in *Mexico–Anti-Dumping Measures on Rice*. However, it is unlikely that Panels in future Article 21.5 proceedings would take the position that anti-dumping or CVD measures that are found to be inconsistent with the *Anti-Dumping* or *SCM Agreements* cannot subsequently be brought into compliance in implementation proceedings because the investigation period would be so outdated (arguably, it would be improper for the implementing Member to use a new and updated period of investigation in the implementation proceedings without initiating an entirely new investigation).

As noted, there is little guidance in the jurisprudence to date on what, if anything, is the implementation obligation with respect to 'procedural' rights and obligations under the *Anti-Dumping* or *SCM Agreements*. The issue is likely to remain unclear until a Panel is confronted squarely with the question of what an investigating authority must do to implement with respect to purely 'procedural' violations. In the meantime, however, the lack of clarity as to how findings with respect to 'procedural' issues must be implemented may serve to discourage potential complainant Members, especially developing countries with lesser resources, from pursuing these claims in dispute-settlement proceedings.

---

88 Appellate Body Report, *Mexico–Anti-Dumping Measures on Rice*, paras. 158–172.

4.3 Other issues in the Panel Report

The Panel Report raises some other issues that might be more interesting in a different context. For the reasons described below, however, they merit only brief mention here.

4.3.1 The 'pass-through' issue

The issue of whether a 'pass-through' analysis is required has been controversial in WTO jurisprudence, especially in the context of the privatization of manufacturers benefiting from the subsidies. In this case, however, the pass-through issue was ultimately not controversial from a legal or economic point of view. As a legal matter, the Panel found that the EC had raised its claims under the wrong provisions of the GATT 1994 and the *SCM Agreement* (Articles 1 and 14 of the *SCM Agreement* rather than Article 10 of the *SCM Agreement* and Article VI:3 of the GATT 1994). It is unclear why the EC proceeded as it did.[89] In any event, in its consideration of the EC's claims under Articles 1 and 14, the Panel indicated that even if the obligation to conduct a pass-through analysis in appropriate circumstances could be found in the provisions cited by the EC, the Panel would not have found a pass-through analysis to be necessary in this case. The Panel cited the fact that the olive growers received aid only to the extent that the olives grown were actually converted into olive oil.[90] In effect, the Panel found that where the subsidy was actually provided on the basis of the finished product that was subject to the investigation and not on the basis of the input product, a pass-through analysis would be redundant. It is hard to disagree with this commonsensical conclusion from either economic or legal standpoints.

4.3.2 Is a producer that has ceased to produce entitled to seek trade-remedy relief?

As explained above, the EC made much of its claims that Fortuny could not constitute a 'domestic industry' for the purposes of and entitlement to relief under the CVD laws because it had ceased production. We have no quarrel with how the Panel addressed this issue: as the Panel noted, there are many 'normal' business or commercial situations in which companies may cease production and these should not disqualify such companies from recourse to the trade-remedy laws. In addition, the availability of trade-remedy relief in cases of the material retardation of the establishment of a domestic industry supports, rather than undermines, the notion that relief should be available in cases of material retardation of the *re*-establishment of a domestic industry. Finally, as the Panel noted, a domestic industry could have ceased production because it was so badly injured by the very

---

89 See Panel Report, para. 7.145, n.185.
90 Ibid., para. 7.168.

imports against which it then sought relief: as the Panel stated, to deny such an industry recourse to the trade-remedy laws would be 'absurd'.[91]

The more interesting question may be how to identify the point at which a domestic industry that has ceased production is *no longer* entitled to the relief of the trade-remedy laws: at what point can the patient be said to be beyond resuscitation by means of anti-dumping or CVD duties? In the language of economic analysis, the key question is when the firm's situation converts from being temporarily 'shut down' – a short-run phenomenon in which it decides not to produce in the current period because prices are not high enough to cover its variable costs – to a permanent decision to 'exit' the industry. The Panel did not fully resolve this issue. However, it noted that Fortuny had maintained its olive groves and production facilities and had created a new brand and label and, of course, its business plan.[92] In the circumstances, the Panel considered that the patient was not beyond resuscitation. A more definitive answer to this question, however, will have to wait for another day.

4.3.3 Reliance on the domestic producer's business plan as evidence of injury

As noted above, the Panel exercised judicial economy with respect to the EC's claims under Articles 15.1 and 15.4 of the *SCM Agreement* that raised the issue of Economía's reliance on Fortuny's business plan in its analysis of the volume and price impact of the subsidized imports on the domestic industry. It would have been interesting to have a more detailed discussion by the Panel of whether, and in what circumstances, evidence of domestic-industry factors, including prices, can be based on such 'non-actual' sources as a business plan. Article 15.1 of the *SCM Agreement* requires that a determination of injury be based on 'positive evidence' and an 'objective examination' of the impact of the imports.

Generally, the evidence in question would be actual prices and performance of the domestic industry. In cases of material retardation of the establishment of a domestic industry, there would quite likely not be 'actual' evidence of the performance or prices of the domestic industry and the investigating authority would have to rely on projections. Interestingly, in this case, the Panel found that Economía's determination was based on a finding of material injury, not on material retardation.[93] However, it makes sense also to permit investigating authorities to rely on evidence such as business plans in appropriate situations. In this case, the Panel considered the fact that Fortuny did not actually produce was sufficient grounds to allow Economía to rely on the business plan. However, the Panel did not address the issue of whether investigating authorities were required to approach evidence such as business plans with greater skepticism than ordinary price or financial data. Given the potential for gaming the system in preparing

---

91 Ibid., para. 7.203.
92 Ibid., para. 7.213.
93 Ibid., para. 7.279.

such evidence, a degree of caution in approaching such evidence would seem appropriate.

5. Conclusions

The *Mexico–Olive Oil* dispute was neither as complicated nor as controversial as some WTO trade-remedy cases. By the first measure of any judicial decision, the Panel's Report was a success: it was not appealed. By another measure of WTO dispute-settlement proceedings, it was also successful: Mexico implemented the Panel's rulings and recommendations promptly and, from the point of view of the EC, effectively by terminating the measure. Nevertheless, as we hope the above discussion explains, the case illustrates some of the problems that arise in even the less controversial trade-remedy dispute-settlement proceedings. In the respects we highlighted, the Panel's approach to these problems suggests that the review by WTO Panels of trade-remedy measures remains an art in need of more science.

References

Appellate Body Report, *United States – Safeguard Measures on Imports of Fresh, Chilled or Frozen Lamb Meat from New Zealand and Australia*, WT/DS177/AB/R, WT/DS178/AB/R, adopted 16 May 2001, DSR 2001:IX, 4051.

Appellate Body Report, *United States – Anti-Dumping Measures on Certain Hot-Rolled Steel Products from Japan*, WT/DS184/AB/R, adopted 23 August 2001, DSR 2001:X, 4697.

Appellate Body Report, *United States – Countervailing Duty Investigation on Dynamic Random Access Memory Semiconductors (DRAMS) from Korea*, WT/DS296/AB/R, adopted 20 July 2005, DSR 2005:XVI, 8131.

Appellate Body Report, *Mexico – Definitive Anti-Dumping Measures on Beef and Rice, Complaint with Respect to Rice*, WT/DS295/AB/R, adopted 20 December 2005, DSR 2005:XXII, 10853.

Appellate Body Report, *United States – Investigation of the International Trade Commission in Softwood Lumber from Canada – Recourse to Article 21.5 of the DSU by Canada*, WT/DS277/AB/RW, adopted 9 May 2006, and Corr.1, DSR 2006:XI, 4761.

Economía, 'Resolución final de la investigación por subvención de precios sobre las importaciones de aceite de oliva virgen, originarias de la Unión Europea (Comunidad Europea), principalmente del Reino de España y la República Italiana, independientemente del país de procedencia', 1 August 2005, para. 22.89; available at http://www.pymes.gob.mx/upci/paginas/dofsc908.pdf (last accessed 22 October 2009).

Grossman, Gene M. and Petros C. Mavroidis (2003), '*United States – Imposition of Countervailing Duties on Certain Hot-Rolled Lead and Bismuth Carbon Steel Products Originating in the United Kingdom*: here today, gone tomorrow? privatization and the injury caused by non-recurring subsidies', in Henrik Horn and Petros C. Mavroidis (eds.), *The WTO Case Law of 2001*, Cambridge: Cambridge University Press.

Grossman, Gene M. and Petros C. Mavroidis (2005a), '*United States – Countervailing Duties on Certain Corrosion-Resistant Carbon Steel Flat Products from Germany*: the sounds of silence', in Henrik Horn and Petros C. Mavroidis (eds.), *The WTO Case Law of 2002*, Cambridge: Cambridge University Press.

Grossman, Gene M. and Petros C. Mavroidis (2005b), '*United States – Countervailing Measures Concerning Certain Products from the European Communities*: recurring misunderstanding of non-recurring subsidies', in Henrik Horn and Petros C. Mavroidis (eds.), *The WTO Case Law of 2002*, Cambridge: Cambridge University Press.

Horn, Henrik and Petros C. Mavroidis (2006), *United States – Final Determination with Respect to Certain Softwood Lumber from Canada* (AB-2003-6, WT/DS257/AB/R), in Henrik Horn and Petros C. Mavroidis (eds.), *The WTO Case Law of 2003*, Cambridge: Cambridge University Press.

Kreier, Jesse (2005), 'Contingent trade remedies and WTO dispute settlement: some particularities', in Rufus Yerxa and Bruce Wilson (eds.), *Key Issues in WTO Dispute Settlement: The First Ten Years*, Cambridge: Cambridge University Press.

Panel Report, *Guatemala – Anti-Dumping Investigation Regarding Portland Cement from Mexico*, WT/DS60/R, adopted 25 November 1998, as modified by Appellate Body Report WT/DS60/AB/R, DSR 1998:IX, 3797.

Panel Report, *United States – Safeguard Measures on Imports of Fresh, Chilled or Frozen Lamb Meat from New Zealand and Australia*, WT/DS177/R, WT/DS178/R, adopted 16 May 2001, as modified by Appellate Body Report WT/DS177/AB/R, WT/DS178/AB/R, DSR 2001:IX, 4107.

Panel Report, *Mexico – Anti-Dumping Duties on Steel Pipes and Tubes from Guatemala*, WT/DS331/R, adopted 24 July 2007.

Panel Report, *Mexico – Definitive Countervailing Measures on Olive Oil from the European Communities*, WT/DS341/R, adopted 21 October 2008.

US–Stainless Steel (Mexico)

MEREDITH CROWLEY

Federal Reserve Bank of Chicago, 230 S. LaSalle, Chicago IL 60604

ROBERT HOWSE

New York University School of Law

Abstract: The *US–Mexico Stainless-Steel* dispute presents two interesting questions. First, what role does and should stare decisis (precedent) play in the WTO dispute-resolution system? Second, are there circumstances under which exceptional methodologies, i.e. 'zeroing', can better achieve the stated objectives of the agreement than the standard methodologies explicitly stated in the agreement? We argue that the institutional structure and foundational norms of the WTO imply the need for Panels to be bound by the prior decisions of the Appellate Body. Our economic analysis describes the costs and benefits of legal systems with and without precedent. Regarding methodology, we argue that any analysis of the suitability of a methodology (i.e. 'zeroing') must be undertaken jointly with an analysis of the underlying objective of the agreement (i.e. remedying injury). We conclude that, under limited circumstances, the 'zeroing' methodology is more effective at remedying injury than the ordinary methodology outlined in the Anti-Dumping Agreement.

1. Introduction

Background

On 26 May 2006, Mexico requested consultations with the United States (US) regarding how the US was calculating dumping margins.[1] The parties held consultations on 15 June 2006, but the dispute could not be resolved. On 12 October 2006, Mexico requested the Dispute Settlement Body (DSB) to establish a Panel to examine the matter.[2] The Panel was established on 26 October 2006. Several

The opinions expressed in this paper are those of the authors and not necessarily those of the Federal Reserve Bank of Chicago or the Federal Reserve System. We thank Marco Bronckers, Jorge Huerta Goldman, Petros Mavroidis, David Palmeter, Kamal Saggi, and participants at the 2009 American Law Institute meeting on the WTO Case Law of 2008 for thoughtful comments and suggestions. Robert Howse is grateful to Ruti Teitel and Lewis Kornhauser for helpful discussions and suggestions. Joanna Langille, 2L NYU, provided excellent research assistance.

1 Consultations were requested pursuant to Article 4 of the Understanding on Rules and Procedures Governing the Settlement of Dispute (DSU), Article XXII of the GATT 1994, and Article 17 of the Agreement on Implementation of Article VI of the GATT 1994 (Anti-Dumping Agreement).

2 Pursuant to Articles 4 and 6 of the DSU, Article XXIII of the GATT 1994, and Article 17 of the Anti-Dumping Agreement.

countries retained their rights to participate in the Panel as third parties.[3] The Panel met with the parties in May and July of 2007.

Issues

Mexico argued that the US was using an incorrect method of calculating margins of dumping. US law requires the Department of Commerce (USDOC) to use so-called 'Zeroing Procedures', which, Mexico claimed, meant that they were calculating margins that did not fully reflect export prices above normal value. This was because, Mexico argued, of 'the non-inclusion in the numerator of the weighted average dumping margin calculations of the results of comparisons where the export price exceeds the normal value, when such results are aggregated in the calculation of the margins of dumping for the product under consideration as a whole'.[4] In essence, the US is treating negative results as zero, which conflicts with a number of the US's WTO obligations.

This argument focused on two specific complaints (their 'as such' claims). First, Mexico disagreed with how zeroing procedures were used in 'model zeroing in investigations' – where the weighted-average normal value is compared with the weighted-average export price. Mexico argued that this method is inconsistent with Articles VI:1 and VI:2 of the GATT 1994, Articles 2.1, 2.4, 2.4.2, and 18.4 of the Anti-Dumping Agreement, and XVI:4 of the WTO Agreement. Second, Mexico also disagreed with the use of the procedures in 'simple zeroing in periodic reviews' – periodic reviews where the weighted-average normal value is compared with individual export transactions. Mexico argued this was in conflict with Articles VI:1 and VI:2 of the GATT 1994, Articles 2.1, 2.4, 9.3, and 18.4 of the Anti-Dumping Agreement, and Article XVI:4 of the WTO Agreement.

In addition to these two 'as such' claims, Mexico also challenged how the USDOC was using zeroing procedures in the investigation and five periodic reviews on 'Stainless Steel Sheet and Strip in Coils from Mexico'[5] (their 'as applied' claim). It claims that this method was inconsistent with Articles VI:1 and VI:2 of GATT 1994, Articles 2.1, 2.4, 2.4.2, and 18.4 of the Anti-Dumping Agreement, and Article XVI:4 of the WTO Agreement.

The US responded by arguing that the 'as such' claims should be dismissed because zeroing procedures are not mandatory under US law. Further, even if zeroing procedures were being used, they were not prohibited in periodic reviews by the Anti-Dumping Agreement. This argument also applies to the 'as applied' claim, although the US did acknowledge that model zeroing took place in the *Stainless Steel Sheet* investigation.

---

3 Chile, China, the European Communities, Japan, and Thailand.

4 Panel Report, WT/DS344/R, page 2.

5 *Stainless Steel Sheet and Strip in Coils from Mexico*, 64 FR 30790 (USDOC) (8 June 1999), subsequently amended as *Stainless Steel Sheet and Strip in Coils from Mexico*, 64 FR 40560 (USDOC) (27 July 1999). See Panel Report, WT/DS344/R, page 2.

The third parties also contributed submissions. There was generally a consensus regarding model zeroing in investigations. Chile argued that the zeroing methodology was already found to be inconsistent with the WTO in previous Appellate Body decisions, and that therefore the Anti-Dumping Agreement should be amended to reflect this so future adjudication could be avoided. China argued that the use of zeroing is inconsistent with Articles 2.1, 2.4.2, and 2.4 of the Anti-Dumping Agreement, and that the Panel should follow the line of precedent and accept Mexico's claims. The EC submission argued that previous Panel and Appellate Body decisions had already produced a clear line of jurisprudence prohibiting zeroing. Even though stare decisis did not in principle apply to international tribunals, and there is no rule requiring WTO Panels to follow previous AB decisions, the EC argued that precedent should be given significant weight, because this provides 'security and predictability to the multilateral trading system'. Japan echoed these concerns, and argued that zeroing is prohibited. Thailand also argued that zeroing is inconsistent with GATT 1994 and the Anti-Dumping Agreement.

The third parties were also in substantial agreement that simple zeroing in periodic reviews was not permitted, and the arguments they made above largely apply in the simple-zeroing case as well.

Key findings of the Panel

The Panel issued its Report on 20 December 2007.[6] They issued a number of key findings.

Model zeroing in investigations

The Panel looked at the model-zeroing and simple-zeroing claims in turn. They began with the model-zeroing claim. First, they concluded that Mexico presented sufficient evidence to demonstrate 'the existence of the *Model Zeroing Procedures* under US law as of the date of establishment of this Panel'.[7]

Second, in response to the American argument that they had ceased using model zeroing, the Panel concluded that the US had, in fact, ceased to use the procedures.[8] Third, the Panel considered whether they should make recommendations on an expired measure, and concluded that there would be no point in making a recommendation relating to a measure that no longer exists.[9]

---

6 WT/DS 344/R. The *standard of review* used is set out in Article 11 of the DSU (the standard of review for WTO panels in general). Article 17.6 of the Anti-Dumping Agreement sets out the special standard applicable to disputes under the Anti-Dumping Agreement. In terms of the *rules of treaty interpretation* employed, Article 3.2 of the DSU incorporates Articles 31–32 of the Vienna Convention. The *burden of proof* is on the party making the complaint to establish a prima facie case, and the respondent must prove any evidence they are using in response.

7 Panel Report, WT/DS 344/R, page 17.

8 Panel Report, WT/DS 344/R, page 18.

9 Panel Report, WT/DS 344/R, page 19.

Fourth, the Panel considered whether model zeroing is WTO-inconsistent. They concluded that model zeroing in investigations is inconsistent 'as such' with Article 2.4.2 of the Anti-Dumping Agreement, and therefore it is inconsistent 'as applied' in the *Steel* case.[10]

Simple zeroing in periodic reviews

Next, the Panel considered the claims regarding simple zeroing in periodic reviews. First, they concluded that Mexico presented sufficient evidence to demonstrate the existence of the simple-zeroing procedures under US law.[11] Second, and crucially, the Panel concluded that simple-zeroing procedures 'as such' are *not* inconsistent with the WTO.[12] This is in spite of previous Appellate Body cases that had found the practice WTO-inconsistent.[13] The Panel justified this move by interpreting the relevant treaty provisions[14] and an examination of the potential consequences of a general prohibition on zeroing.[15]

Issues on appeal

Mexico appealed the Panel's decision. They argued that the Panel erred in finding that simple zeroing in periodic reviews is not, as such, WTO-inconsistent, and requested a reversal of the Panel's decision by the Appellate Body and a finding that the practice was prohibited. Mexico supported this claim by arguing that (a) dumping cannot be defined in terms of a specific product/category, as it was here;[16] (b) the Panel erred by concluding that anti-dumping measures are concerned with the pricing behaviour of importers in relation to individual import transactions;[17] (c) the Panel erred in concluding that the existence of a 'prospective normal value' system supports the view that anti-dumping duties can be calculated on a transaction-specific basis;[18] (d) the Panel's findings that the results are supposedly mathematically equivalent are irrelevant;[19] and (e) the Panel improperly justified its conclusions on the grounds of 'undesirable results'.[20] The US argued in response that, for five reasons, Mexico's interpretation contradicts the plain text of the agreements.[21]

Second, Mexico argued that the Panel erred in finding that simple zeroing in periodic reviews is not, as such, inconsistent with Article 2.4 of the Anti-Dumping Agreement, because of the arguments made in *US–Zeroing (Japan)* – that the

---

10 Panel Report, WT/DS 344/R, page 23.
11 Panel Report, WT/DS 344/R, page 29.
12 Panel Report, WT/DS 344/R, page 45.
13 Panel Report, WT/DS 344/R, page 32.
14 Panel Report, WT/DS 344/R, pages 32–44.
15 Panel Report, WT/DS 344/R, pages 44–45.
16 AB Report, WT/DS 344/AB/R, page 5.
17 AB Report, WT/DS 344/AB/R, page 6.
18 AB Report, WT/DS 344/AB/R, pages 6–7.
19 AB Report, WT/DS 344/AB/R, page 7.
20 AB Report, WT/DS 344/AB/R, page 8.
21 AB Report, WT/DS 344/AB/R, pages 11–15.

procedure is inherently biased.[22] The US responded by challenging Mexico's interpretation of 'fair comparison'.[23]

Third, Mexico argued that simple zeroing as applied in periodic reviews should be found inconsistent with the WTO as well, because of the arguments set out above.[24] The US argued in response that the Panel's initial reasoning was correct.[25]

Fourth, Mexico argued that the Panel acted inconsistently with Article 11 of the DSU by refusing to follow AB precedent, particularly given that one party (the US) remained the same.[26] The US contended that prior cases aren't binding.[27]

Appellate Body disposition

i. Did the Panel err in finding that 'simple zeroing in periodic reviews' is not, as such, inconsistent with Articles VI:1 and VI:2 of the GATT 1994 and Articles 2.1 and 9.3 of the Anti-Dumping Agreement?

The AB concluded that simple zeroing is, as such, inconsistent with Article VI:2 of the GATT 1994 and Article 9.3 of the Anti-Dumping Agreement, because simple zeroing results in an anti-dumping duty that exceeds an exporter's margin of dumping which operates as the ceiling for the amount of anti-dumping duty that can be levied in respect of the sales made by an exporter.[28]

ii. Did the Panel err in finding that the USDOC did not act inconsistently with Articles VI:1 and VI:2 by using simple zeroing in the five periodic reviews?

The AB concluded, again, that simple zeroing in periodic reviews is, as such, inconsistent with Article VI:2 of the GATT 1994 and Article 9.3 of the Anti-Dumping Agreement, for the same reasons, and therefore reversed the Panel on this issue.[29]

iii. Did the Panel err in finding that 'simple zeroing in periodic reviews' is not, as such, inconsistent with Article 2.4 of the Anti-Dumping Agreement and, consequently, in finding that the USDOC did not act inconsistently with that provision in the five periodic reviews at issue in this dispute?

Since the Panel's finding that simple zeroing was not inconsistent with Article 2.4 was based on the same erroneous findings that their other conclusions were based on, the AB reversed these findings of the Panel as well.[30]

---

22 AB Report, WT/DS 344/AB/R, page 9.
23 AB Report, WT/DS 344/AB/R, pages 15–16.
24 AB Report, WT/DS 344/AB/R, page 9.
25 AB Report, WT/DS 344/AB/R, page 16.
26 AB Report, WT/DS 344/AB/R, page 10.
27 AB Report, WT/DS 344/AB/R, page 17.
28 AB Report, WT/DS 344/AB/R, page 58.
29 AB Report, WT/DS 344/AB/R, page 59.
30 AB Report, WT/DS 344/AB/R, pages 60–61.

iv. Did the Panel fail to fulfill its obligations under Article 11 of the DSU by making findings that contradict those in previous Appellate Body reports adopted by the DSB?

The AB noted that '[t]he Panel's failure to follow previously adopted Appellate Body reports addressing the same issues undermines the development of a coherent and predictable body of jurisprudence'.[31] Further, the AB noted that it was 'deeply concerned about the Panel's decision to depart from well-established Appellate Body jurisprudence clarifying the interpretation of the same legal issues. The Panel's approach has serious implications for the proper functioning of the WTO dispute settlement system.'[32] However, the AB did not find a violation of Article 11, since the underlying defect of the Panel's approach was its erroneous interpretations of the law, which the AB had already reversed, thereby adequately remedying this defect.

2. Legal issues in the appeal

Are Panels bound by Appellate Body rulings?

The Panel below in this dispute had explicitly rejected the prior jurisprudence of the Appellate Body on zeroing. This explicit refusal to follow the approach of prior adopted AB rulings raised in a particularly direct and acute way the issue of 'vertical' stare decisis in the WTO dispute settlement system.

The AB first opined on 'vertical' stare decisis in its *Shrimp/Turtle* 21.5 ruling. There the AB noted:

> Malaysia [the Appellant] also objects to the frequent references made by the Panel to our reasoning in our Report in *United States – Shrimp*. The reasoning in our Report in *United States – Shrimp* on which the Panel relied was not *dicta*; it was essential to our ruling. The Panel was right to use it, and right to rely on it. Nor are we surprised that the Panel made frequent references to our Report in *United States – Shrimp*. Indeed, we would have expected the Panel to do so. The Panel had, necessarily, to consider our views on this subject, as we had overruled certain aspects of the findings of the original panel on this issue and, more important, had provided interpretative guidance for future panels, such as the Panel in this case … (para. 108). In this respect, we note that in our Report in *Japan–Taxes on Alcoholic Beverages*, we stated that:

> Adopted panel reports are an important part of the GATT *acquis*. They are often considered by subsequent panels. They create legitimate expectations among WTO Members, and, therefore, should be taken into account where they are relevant to any dispute.

---

31 AB Report, WT/DS 344/AB/R, page 67.
32 AB Report, WT/DS 344/AB/R, page 68.

This reasoning applies to adopted Appellate Body Reports as well. Thus, in taking into account the reasoning in an adopted Appellate Body Report – a Report, moreover, that was directly relevant to the Panel's disposition of the issues before it – the Panel did not err. The Panel was correct in using our findings as a tool for its own reasoning. (paras. 108–109)

Later, in *US–Oil Country Tubular Goods Sunset Reviews*, the Appellate Body held that 'following the Appellate Body's conclusions in earlier disputes is not only appropriate, but is what would be expected from panels, especially where the issues are the same' (para. 188).

In the present dispute, the AB reaffirmed its approach to 'vertical' stare decisis in these rulings. The AB held:

Dispute settlement practice demonstrates that WTO Members attach significance to reasoning provided in previous panel and Appellate Body reports. Adopted panel and Appellate Body reports are often cited by parties in support of legal arguments in dispute settlement proceedings, and are relied upon by panels and the Appellate Body in subsequent disputes. In addition, when enacting or modifying laws and national regulations pertaining to international trade matters, WTO Members take into account the legal interpretation of the covered agreements developed in adopted panel and Appellate Body reports. Thus, the legal interpretation embodied in adopted panel and Appellate Body reports becomes part and parcel of the *acquis* of the WTO dispute settlement system. Ensuring 'security and predictability' in the dispute settlement system, as contemplated in Article 3.2 of the DSU, implies that, absent cogent reasons, an adjudicatory body will resolve the same legal question in the same way in a subsequent case. (para. 160)

In the hierarchical structure contemplated in the DSU, panels and the Appellate Body have distinct roles to play. In order to strengthen dispute settlement in the multilateral trading system, the Uruguay Round established the Appellate Body as a standing body. Pursuant to Article 17.6 of the DSU, the Appellate Body is vested with the authority to review 'issues of law covered in the panel report and legal interpretations developed by the panel'. Accordingly, Article 17.13 provides that the Appellate Body may 'uphold, modify or reverse' the legal findings and conclusions of panels. The creation of the Appellate Body by WTO Members to review legal interpretations developed by panels shows that Members recognized the importance of consistency and stability in the interpretation of their rights and obligations under the covered agreements. This is essential to promote 'security and predictability' in the dispute settlement system, and to ensure the 'prompt settlement' of disputes. The panel's failure to follow previously adopted Appellate Body reports addressing the same issues undermines the development of a coherent and predictable body of jurisprudence clarifying Members' rights and obligations under the covered agreements as contemplated under the DSU. Clarification, as envisaged in Article 3.2 of the DSU, elucidates the scope and meaning of the provisions of the covered agreements in accordance with customary rules of interpretation of public international law. While the application of a provision may be regarded as confined to the context in which it takes place, the relevance of clarification contained in adopted Appellate Body reports is not limited to the application of a particular provision in a specific case. (para. 161)

We are deeply concerned about the Panel's decision to depart from well-established Appellate Body jurisprudence clarifying the interpretation of the same legal issues. The Panel's approach has serious implications for the proper functioning of the WTO dispute settlement system, as explained above. Nevertheless, we consider that the Panel's failure flowed, in essence, from its misguided understanding of the legal provisions at issue. Since we have corrected the Panel's erroneous legal interpretation and have reversed all of the Panel's findings and conclusions that have been appealed, we do not, in this case, make an additional finding that the Panel also failed to discharge its duties under Article 11 of the DSU. (para. 162)

In a subsequent case, *US–Continued Zeroing*, a Panel had occasion to interpret and apply the above holding of the AB. The Panel first of all said that it found the previous Panel rulings that had differed from the AB analysis of the same issues to be 'persuasive'. However, it was now, however reluctantly, required to follow the approach of the AB. The Panel considered that, while it was required, due to the considerations regarding 'expectations' and the stability and predictability of the system, to give weight to prior AB rulings, nevertheless that 'we do not consider that the development of binding jurisprudence is a contemplated element to enable the dispute settlement system to provide security and predictability to the multilateral trading system' (para. 7.179). The Panel went on to formulate its own test for the precedential weight of AB rulings: 'a panel cannot simply follow the adopted report of another panel, or of the Appellate Body, without careful consideration of the facts and arguments made by the parties in the dispute before it. To do so would be to abdicate its responsibilities under Article 11. By the same token, however, neither should a panel make a finding different from that in an adopted earlier panel or Appellate Body report on similar facts and arguments without careful consideration and explanation of why a different result is warranted, and assuring itself that its finding does not undermine the goals of the system' (para. 7.180). Applying its own test, the Panel held that, even if there were good reasons to deviate from the AB jurisprudence on the substance, the systemic goal of 'prompt settlement of disputes' would be undermined by doing so. The Panel observed that the AB had repeatedly reversed the Panels on these issues. The implication was that it would be perfectly legitimate for the Panel to deviate from the AB's jurisprudence, but that, since the AB would simply overrule the Panel once again, as a practical matter, the only result of such a deviation would be to delay a final settlement of the particular dispute, thus frustrating the 'prompt settlement' goal. In other words, the Panel obstinately could not accept that the AB is a genuine higher court, with superior legitimacy as such to the Panel in its role as interpreter of the law. Nor that the AB has *Competenz-Competenz* to decisively rule on systemic issues such as the relationship of the AB to other WTO institutions, such as Panels.

Analysis

In *Shrimp/Turtle 21.5*, the AB arguably avoided the distinctive issue of 'vertical' stare decisis by relying on its discussion of 'horizontal' stare decisis in *Japan–Alcohol*. Thus, the AB considered the basis for giving precedential weight to prior AB rulings as the same as that with respect to prior adopted GATT and WTO Panel rulings, namely 'legitimate expectations'. Perhaps because it was not faced with a direct affront to its authority by a Panel in that case, the AB did not expound on the distinctive role of the Appellate Body in the dispute settlement system, i.e. as a body that has the power definitely to reverse or modify any Panel ruling that is appealed to it. In the present dispute, we find for the first time an explicit treatment of the 'hierarchical' character of the dispute settlement system and the consciousness that the Panels and the AB perform 'distinct roles' in that system. The AB expresses, albeit in a very terse way, the notion that appellate review in the WTO was intended not only as a means of correcting error, or a 'second opinion', but at achieving a unified jurisprudence. Besides referring to the AB's power to reverse or modify Panel rulings, and the general notion that the purpose of the dispute settlement system includes the clarification of the law, the AB said little if anything about other features that point to its function as a 'high court' for the WTO. This especially goes to the question of *Competenz-Competenz*, i.e. to why the AB should be able to *decide* matters that go to the relationship of the AB to other institutions in the WTO. As with other cases that pose this kind of question, such as *India–BOP* and *Turkey–Textiles* (where the issue was justiciability of matters where a WTO committee has a decision-making role), the AB displays little awareness of the *Competenz-Competenz* character of the issue. Here one might contrast the approach of the Appeals Chamber of the ICTY in the case of *Tadic v. Prosecutor*, for example, which considered at some length the significance of a *judicial* function having been conferred on the tribunal, and the notion that there are powers 'incidental' to such a function.

Unlike the Panel in *US–Continued Zeroing*, one should not misrepresent the issue at stake as whether there is *de jure* stare decisis, i.e. binding jurisprudence, in the WTO system. Even in systems that are characterized as having such jurisprudence, it is recognized that the values that support stare decisis must be balanced with other values that may, on occasion, dictate the overruling of a previous decision, e.g. manifest injustice or a fundamental shift of social values, or decisive changes in underlying facts or realities presupposed by the ruling in question (see the US Supreme Court ruling in *Planned Parenthood* v. *Casey*). Conversely, in legal systems where there is no de jure stare decisis a rigid conception of the rule of law may lead to slavish following of past decisions, with indifference to countervailing values. What is really at stake in the stand off between the Panels and the

Appellate Body is the stature and authority of the AB as the judicial organ or judicial function of the WTO.

It is probably correct for several reasons to conclude that there is no de jure stare decisis in the WTO system; thus the AB's reluctance to insist on such a proposition is understandable. First of all, it is traditionally understood that, in international law, the rulings of courts and tribunals are only supplementary or secondary sources of international law (see ICJ Statute Article 38). This may be shifting with the increasing judicialization of international law and politics, for example, the now pervasive resort to prior decisions of courts and tribunals to prove, or even evolve, custom, and also with the functioning of appellate review itself in regimes such as the ICTY and ICTR as well as the WTO.

In fact, the Appeals Chamber of the ICTY has a well-developed doctrine of stare decisis (horizontal and vertical), despite the constitutive instrument of the tribunal being silent on stare decisis. In *Aleksovski*, where the ICTY first considered the issue of stare decisis,[33] the Appeals Chamber emphasized the importance of vertical stare decisis as an essential aspect of assuring the predictability and certainty of the application of the law, and as necessary to achieving fair treatment where like cases are treated alike.[34] It is also a basic feature of common-law systems and, while not a formal principle of civil-law systems, a functional one, and therefore should be applied.[35] At the same time, the Appeals Chamber stated that, in exceptional circumstances, the first instance could depart from precedent when there are 'cogent reasons in the interests of justice' and when the case is not similar.[36] These *exceptions* or *limits* on stare decisis are broadly consistent with the way it is practiced in domestic legal systems; this is to be contrasted with the Panel approach in *US–Continued Zeroing*, which suggests that the first instance should *routinely* consider whether or not appellate precedent is to be followed, and that not following such precedent only requires 'careful consideration and explanation of why a different result is warranted' – i.e. any reason will do, 'cogent reasons *in the interests of justice*' (emphasis added) are not required.

In the case of the WTO system, the WTO Agreement provides a political mechanism for authoritative interpretations of the covered Agreements and thus suggests that, as a matter of institutional separation of powers, even Appellate Body interpretations are not binding jurisprudence in a 'constitutional' sense.

But even in a system without such a formally binding jurisprudence, the reasons for a tribunal of first instance routinely deferring to the interpretative authority of the system's high court may be compelling.

---

33 *Prosecutor* v. *Zlatko Aleksovski*, Opinion and Judgement, Case No. IT-95-14/1-A (24 March 2000), available at http://www.icty.org/x/cases/aleksovski/acjug/en/ale-asj000324e.pdf (last visited 27 October 2009). This was the first case of the ICTY to consider the stare decisis issue. Tyner (2006) at 860.

34 *Prosecutor* v. *Zlatko Aleksovski*, Opinion and Judgement, Case No. IT-95-14/1-A at 47–48.

35 *Prosecutor* v. *Zlatko Aleksovski*, Opinion and Judgement, Case No. IT-95-14/1-A at 47.

36 Geert-Jan Alexander Knoops (2005).

To see this is the case in the WTO, we need to consider more institutional features of the system and the Panels and the AB specifically than the AB has been prepared to discuss. The AB represents and expresses the rule of law as a core value of the WTO system in a way that the Panel process does not, and cannot as currently constituted. The Panel process manifestly lacks, at least in practice, the rule-of-law quality of independence from political influence, including perceived influence. The parties to a particular dispute still retain in practice considerable influence over who are the panelists in that dispute. The panelists in turn typically remain government functionaries during their tenure as panelists, even if they are supposed to decide independently. Furthermore, it is widely known that the WTO Secretariat itself plays a major, behind-the-scenes role in shaping Panel rulings – a role quite different from the transparent, institutionally distinct, advisory role of the Advocate-General in ECJ proceedings for instance. Panelists are appointed *ad hoc*, dispute by dispute; dissatisfying a state that is a major user of the WTO dispute settlement system, or the Secretariat, may well lead to an individual never again being considered as a panelist in a future dispute. This provides a further avenue for political pressure on panelists.

Unlike the case of panelists, with respect to the Appellate Body, the credentials required for Members by the DSU itself seem designed specifically to facilitate the creation of a genuine jurisprudence, not merely satisfactory settlements of individual disputes. These are: 'The Appellate Body shall comprise persons of recognized authority, with demonstrated expertise in law, international trade and the subject matter of the covered agreements generally. They shall be unaffiliated with any government' (Art. 17.3). The requirement of 'recognized authority' is in itself significant: it suggests that the architects of the system were intending to ensure the kind of legitimacy that a high court demands. 'Demonstrated expertise in law' reminds us that *panelists* are often not jurists at all, let alone legal 'experts'. Finally, the stipulation that the Appellate Body members be 'unaffiliated with any government' indicates awareness that the judicial function demands a distance from interested politics that goes significantly beyond what is asked of panelists. In sum, the qualifications for AB Members differ from those for panelists significantly, and indicate the difference between what is required for dispute resolution on the one hand and what is expected of a high court on the other. There are further institutional features of appellate review at the WTO that should also be considered. First of all, appeal is of right. No leave is required and no vetting process is entailed. In such a system, there is an automatic and effective remedy for the failure of a Panel to follow previous AB decisions – appeal to the AB itself. It is difficult to imagine that the architects of such a system could have believed other than that AB jurisprudence would be controlling. Consider by contrast a different sort of 'second instance' – annulment proceedings in ICSID investor-state arbitration. There, the jurisdiction of the 'second instance' is limited to controlling certain kinds of abuses or dysfunctions of the 'first instance' – excess of jurisdiction, absence of reasons, bias. Provided an Annulment Committee remains within such a constrained jurisdiction, one would not expect a unified substantive juris-prudence as an intended outcome from a review procedure of this nature.

The collegiality practices of the AB – all cases are discussed among all the seven Members – further reinforce the sense that the AB has a systemic jurisprudential role distinct from that of Panels. The AB is able to see the implications of a legal interpretation in one case and in one context for many other situations and con-texts.

Since, as already noted, there is an effective remedy where a Panel fails to follow the AB, namely an appeal as of right to the AB, what is one to make of the defiant attitude of the Panels in the zeroing cases? Is this high-minded civil disobedience or quixotic tilting at windmills? Perhaps it is neither. Instead, it may well be a subtle and corrosive attempt to undermine the distinctive judicial stature of the AB. Why, in the presence of such defiance, would the AB do anything but reaffirm its pre-vious holdings? This would only happen if the AB understood the defiance as an intimidating message from powerful quarters within the WTO of dissatisfaction with its operations, and were capable of being influenced by such intimidation.

This is actually consistent with the explanation of the Panel in *US–Continued Zeroing* as to why it was going to give up and follow the AB. Perhaps revealing too much of its motivations for its own good, the Panel noted the failure of previous Panels to get the AB to back down: '7.181 As discussed above, we share a number of concerns raised by the panel in *US–Stainless Steel (Mexico)*, particularly with regard to the US mathematical equivalence argument. We recognize, however, that the Appellate Body in its report reversed the panel's findings and this report gained legal effect through adoption by the DSB. We note that this continues a series of consistent recommendations made by the DSB over the past several years follow-ing reports that addressed the same issues based largely on the same arguments.'

A major lesson here for the Appellate Body is that, if it is to preserve its own legitimacy, it must never change its mind, for such a change of mind will almost automatically be viewed as a concession to pressure from elsewhere in the system. In the *EC–Asbestos* case, the AB established a procedure for the submission of amicus briefs that caused considerable discontent among many WTO Members. When, in the end, the AB decided not to grant leave to file to any of the applicants, it was widely interpreted as having given in to such pressure, and here the AB did not reverse itself on any finding of law – arguably, it was simply reaction to a situation where none of the applications suggested the brief in question would offer new arguments beyond what the parties had pleaded. This has implications for *horizontal* stare decisis. By not reversing itself, the AB enhances or protects its own legitimacy as an independent judicial body. There is a downside here in the kind of challenge to its authority that the AB has faced in the zeroing cases. It would be good if the AB had the space to be able, in some instances, to reconsider and even reverse its prior jurisprudence, without thereby risking a loss of legit-imacy. Sometimes jurisprudence needs to evolve by such a transparent break with the acquis – the US Supreme Court case of *Lawrence* v. *Texas* is perhaps a case in point (the Court had to recognize explicitly that criminalization of sodomy could not be reconciled with the values of a fully evolved liberal democracy).

3. Economic issues

Dumping, injury, and zeroing in the Anti-Dumping Agreement

The Anti-Dumping Agreement does not prohibit dumping, i.e. selling at a price, Px, that is less than a good's normal value (NV). It prohibits dumping *if dumping causes injury to the domestic import-competing sector*.[37] The agreement allows the imposition of an anti-dumping duty that *just remedies any injury* and specifies that anti-dumping duties should be no higher than the minimum necessary to offset injury.[38] An important economic issue in the *US–Mexico Stainless Steel* case was: does zeroing help a country fulfill the intent of the Anti-Dumping Agreement, to offset injury to the domestic import-competing industry caused by dumping?

Previous economic analyses of zeroing cases have explained why various methodologies that incorporate zeroing in the calculation of the dumping margin are unreasonable, unfair, and/or inconsistent with normal practices in econometrics. Prusa and Vermulst (2009) offer an excellent assessment of the ways in which methodologies that utilize zeroing result in anti-dumping duties that are too high. However, this literature has largely ignored the relationship between the extent of dumping and the extent of injury. Given that the stated purpose of the agreement is to offset injurious dumping, it seems logical that an economic assessment of methods for calculating dumping margins should include an analysis of how much injury the duty determined under each method is able to remedy.[39] If a method employed in the dumping determination is systematically associated with anti-dumping duties that *more than compensate injury* and that create super-normal gains for the domestic industry, this calls into question the suitability of that methodology as a remedy for injurious dumping.

We consider a simple example of 'ordinary dumping' and a simple example of 'targeted dumping'. Both examples involve at least one episode of dumping in which the export price is below normal value and evidence that the domestic industry is injured by dumping in the sense that it receives a level of producer's surplus that is lower than it would have been if the exporter had not dumped.

The ordinary dumping example satisfies the legal requirements for margin calculation under the standard methods of Article 2.4.2, commonly referred to as the weighted-average-to-weighted-average (W-W) and the transaction-to-transaction (T-T) methods. The targeted-dumping example is constructed so that the legal

37 Article VI:I of the GATT 1994. Articles 5.2 and 5.6 of the Anti-Dumping Agreement.

38 The AB notes this in paragraph 93 of the Appellate Report WT/DS 334/AB/R. Article 11.1 sets out the overarching principle that '[a]n anti-dumping duty shall remain in force only as long as and to the extent necessary to counteract dumping which is causing injury'.

39 The standard practice in the US is to conduct dumping and injury analyses separately. The argument presented here does not challenge the practice of a bifurcated analysis.

requirements of the exceptional method of Article 2.4.2, the weighted-average-to-transaction method (W-T), are satisfied.

The analysis of these two stylized examples illustrates the extent to which weighted-average anti-dumping duties and 'zeroed' anti-dumping duties remedy injury to domestic producers caused by dumping. We show that zeroed anti-dumping duties are excessive under ordinary dumping; they overcompensate the domestic industry. Interestingly, zeroed anti-dumping duties are necessary to fully remedy the injury caused by a stylized, yet highly plausible, case of targeted dumping.

This positive economic analysis of Article 2.4.2 (on the calculation of dumping margins) and Article 11.1 (on the remedy of injury) demonstrates that the exceptional method for the calculation of dumping margins under Article 2.4.2 (the weighted-average-to-transaction method) is not *inutile* in the legal sense. The analysis shows that forcing mathematical equivalence between the ordinary methods (W-W or T-T) and the exceptional method (W-T) could undermine the intent of the agreement – to remedy injury caused by dumping – by under-compensating a domestic industry injured by targeted dumping.

In the examples presented, different remedies are necessary to offset injury under ordinary and targeted dumping.[40] This occurs because ordinary dumping is modeled as having only a transitory effect on the welfare of the domestic industry. Targeted dumping, in contrast, is a response by a foreign firm to an information problem. The act of targeted dumping permanently changes the nature of competition in the domestic market and leads to a persistent loss of welfare for the domestic industry.

The Appellate Body's report in *US–Mexico Stainless Steel*, paragraphs 92–96, touches on the idea that a legal review of methodologies specified in Articles 2.4.2 should be informed by and integrated with a review of the agreement's intent, to remedy injury. In a series of disputes over zeroing, the US has repeatedly put forward legal arguments that when a methodology is not explicitly prohibited by the agreement, deference should be given to national authorities. However, the legal-economic argument developed here counters that. If an economic analysis can show that a particular methodology systematically violates the agreement's intent, it seems reasonable to disallow that particular methodology. To clarify, the point is not that the Anti-Dumping Agreement prohibits zeroing. Rather, for cases in which zeroing (or any methodology) fulfills the intent of the agreement, it should be allowed. However, a methodology should not be utilized as a standard practice if it systematically undermines the intent of the agreement. This suggests

---

40 To be precise, a normative welfare analysis of each example, ordinary and targeted dumping, would find that an anti-dumping duty reduces welfare relative to free trade. Thus, the optimal policy in both cases is no duty. However, a positive analysis of the Anti-Dumping Agreement, which is only concerned with the welfare of import-competing producers, finds that different methodologies for calculating dumping margins are required to remedy injury under the two different cases.

Figure 1. Industry Supply, Consumer Demand and Export Supply in Country A

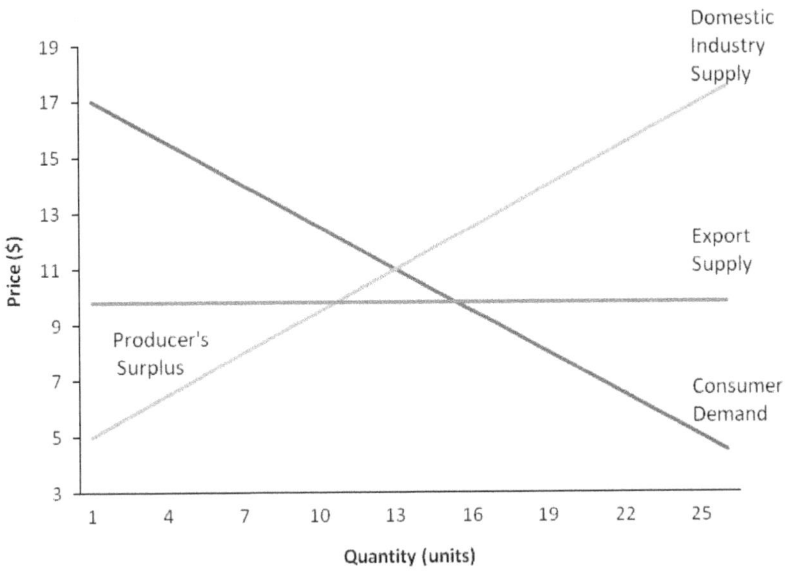

that the use of zeroing by the US might be reasonable in exceptional cases of targeted dumping, but not as a normal practice for cases of ordinary dumping.

Ordinary dumping

Consider an exporter who produces a good which is a perfect substitute for the domestically produced good of Country A. The domestic industry is competitive and industry supply is upward-sloping with data on quarterly domestic-industry output given by Figure 1. The product under question is a normal good with downward-sloping consumer demand in each quarter given in Figure 1. The exporter offers as many units of the good as consumers will demand at some price, P_x, which can change in each quarter of the year.[41] That is, export supply is perfectly elastic at the exporter's offered price.

In the first year that the exporter sells its good in Country A, it offers a different price in each quarter and supplies as many units as consumers demand at the

---

41 In this simple example, we abstract away from the reason for the price variation but assume that the exporter is not varying the price for reasons related to strategic competition. The underlying assumption is that the export price is changing in response to changes in a stochastic variable. For example, the export-pricing rule could be to charge a constant mark-up over marginal cost. If marginal cost varies over time, so will the export price. Alternatively, export-price variation might arise in response to changes in economic conditions in the foreign firm's own market as in papers by Staiger and Wolak (1992 and 1994) and Crowley (2008 and 2009).

Table 1. Export prices and sales volumes in year 1

Transaction date	Exporter's offered price (Px)	Exporter's normal value (NV)	Total quantity demanded (Qd)	Quantity supplied by domestic industry (Qs)	Imports (M)	Surplus of the domestic industry (PS)
Year 1 Q1	$8/unit	$10/unit	18	6	12	$9
Year 1 Q2	$11/unit	$10/unit	12	12	0	$36
Year 1 Q3	$6/unit	$10/unit	22	2	20	$1
Year 1 Q4	$10/unit	$10/unit	14	10	4	$25

offered price. For simplicity, we assume that the exporter's home market price (normal value) is $10/unit throughout the year.[42] Table 1 summarizes the total quantity sold to consumers in Country A, the quantity sold by the domestic industry in Country A, and the quantity sold by the exporter (imports) in each quarter. The producer's surplus of the domestic industry is total revenues in the industry, less the cost of production. This 'producer's surplus' is the economist's standard measure of economic welfare in an industry.[43]

Dumping margins and injury under ordinary dumping

The concept of 'injury' to an industry is difficult for economists to precisely define and measure. Legally, injury comprises multiple factors that describe an industry. Typically, injury is regarded as increasing with reductions in profits, sales, and employment.[44] Theoretically, we can define injury as the loss of producer's surplus, or economic welfare, in the domestic industry, relative to what it would have been if dumping had not occurred. In this example, the domestic industry would receive producer's surplus of $25 if the exporter sets its export price equal to normal value. Thus, the injury to the domestic industry from any dumped sale by the

42 This simplifying assumption implies that normal value and dumping margins will be the same under the W-W and the T-T methodologies and allows us to focus on the relationship between dumping and injury.

43 If input prices are constant, producer's surplus is equivalent to economic profits. If not, it includes gains to factors of production (Deardorff, 2005).

44 In this example, any reduction in the export price, fair or unfair, will result in fewer sales by the domestic producer and a lower level of producer's surplus. This simply means that both fair market competition with a low-priced foreign competitor and dumping by a foreign competitor will result in injury. What distinguishes 'injurious dumping' from injury under fair market competition is normal value, the level of the exporter's price in its own market. The arbitrariness of 'normal value', a concept that does not derive from normative welfare analysis, has been addressed in previous ALI case studies of zeroing (Janow and Staiger, 2003; Bown and Sykes, 2008; Prusa and Vermulst, 2009). This paper conducts a positive analysis of producer's surplus and injurious dumping given the arbitrarily derived legal definition of normal value.

Table 2. Export prices, dumping margins, and injury to the domestic
industry in year 1

Transaction date	Exporter's offered price (Px)	Exporter's normal value (NV)	Dumping margin (DM)	Imports (M)	Injury to the domestic industry
Year 1 Q1	$8/unit	$10/unit	$2	12	$16
Year 1 Q2	$11/unit	$10/unit	−$1	0	$0
Year 1 Q3	$6/unit	$10/unit	$4	20	$24
Year 1 Q4	$10/unit	$10/unit	$0	4	$0

exporter is $25 (the surplus it would have received at the lowest non-dumped price) less the producer surplus received when dumping occurs. If the exporter's price is above normal value and producer's surplus is above the minimal level of $25, then no injurious dumping has occurred. Table 2 summarizes the extent of domestic injury associated with dumping. The key point of the table is that with downward-sloping demand and upward-sloping industry supply, the extent of domestic injury increases as the margin of dumping increases.

What is the extent of injury when the dumping margin is negative? When the exporter offers a price of $11 in Country A, the domestic industry receives $36 of producer's surplus or $11 more than it would have received under the tougher level of fair competition implied by the lowest possible fair export price (i.e. $10). As there is no concept of negative injury in the GATT, we assign an injury level of $0 when the export price is $11. As a final observation on Table 1, we note that the average level of producer's surplus is $17.75 per quarter in the absence of any government response to dumping. Although the Anti-Dumping Agreement does not refer to an industry's average level of welfare over time, this measure is sometimes relevant for economic assessment. If the economic welfare of an industry is highly volatile, but the average level of welfare is high, this is of less concern to an economist than a situation in which the average level of economic welfare of an industry falls dramatically and irreversibly in response to an episode of dumping.

The ideal anti-dumping duty for remedying injury under ordinary dumping
Next, suppose that in year 2, the government of Country A could impose a unique anti-dumping duty on each transaction that was just sufficient to eliminate injury. What would this ideal transaction-specific anti-dumping duty be? Conceptually, the intent of the Anti-Dumping Agreement implies that we would set the duty on each dumped transaction to just offset injurious dumping. The ideal transaction-specific duty should ensure that the exporter's duty-inclusive price in Country A be at least normal value and that domestic producer's surplus be at least the level

Table 3. Imports and producer's surplus under an ideal transaction-specific
anti-dumping duty

Trans. date	Exporter's offered price (Px)	Dumping margin (DM)	Trans-specific AD duty (TSADD)	Price incl. of TSADD (Pd)	Total quantity demanded (Qd)	Quantity supplied by domestic industry (Qs)	Imports (M)	Surplus of the domestic industry (PS)
Year 2 Q1	$8	$2	$2	$10	14	10	4	$25
Year 2 Q2	$11	$–1	$0	$11	12	12	0	$36
Year 2 Q3	$6	$4	$4	$10	14	10	4	$25
Year 2 Q4	$10	$0	$0	$10	14	10	4	$25

obtained when the export price is equal to normal value.[45] Table 3 presents a
baseline ideal anti-dumping policy that fully achieves the Anti-Dumping
Agreement's intent of just eliminating injurious dumping and providing a level of
welfare to producers that is exactly what they would have received if the exporter
had charged a price equal to normal value.

Under this ideal policy, domestic producers receive a minimum level of surplus,
$25, in all quarters. The average level of producer's surplus is $27.75 per quarter,
dramatically larger than the $17.75 per quarter that is received under intermittent
dumping in year 1.

The weighted-average anti-dumping duty and injury under ordinary dumping
Consider next what happens to sales and domestic producer's surplus if an anti-
dumping duty equivalent to the weighted-average dumping margin obtained from
year 1 data were applied to every transaction in year 2 regardless of the actual
extent of dumping. This is a feasible, implementable anti-dumping policy available
to a government that does not have sufficient data in real time to impose the ideal
transaction specific anti-dumping duty from Table 3. The weighted-average
dumping margin based on data from year 1 is $2.89 for each imported unit. The
sales and producer's surplus obtained if the exporter offers the same prices in each
quarter of year 2 as it did in year 1 are reported in Table 4.[46]

45 Economists' objections to anti-dumping policy in general is based on the policy's failure to consider
consumer's welfare. In this example, consumer welfare is harmed in quarters 1 and 4 when the anti-
dumping duty is imposed relative to what it would have been under free trade.

46 Observe that when the exporter persists in offering its year 1 prices in year 2, it sells only 0.44 units
at the duty-inclusive price of $10.89 in quarter 1 and 8.44 units at the duty-inclusive price of $8.89 in
quarter 3. If the Country A government recalculated the dumping margin in year 2, it would obtain a
weighted-average dumping margin of $3.90/unit to impose on imports in year 3. This example clearly
highlights how the use of the W-W method with historical data can generate a dumping margin that drifts
up over time under normal downward-sloping import demand. Eventually, the exporter will be priced out
of the Country A market.

An alternative pricing scheme by the exporter is relevant to consider. Suppose the exporter raised its
export price to $10 in all quarters of year 2. Under this pricing scheme, the exporter's price inclusive of the

Table 4. Imports and producer's surplus under a weighted-average anti-dumping duty

Trans.date	Exporter's offered price (Px)	Wtd-avg. dumping margin (WDM)	Exporter's price incl. of WDM (Px + WDM)	Dom. price (Pd)	Total quantity demanded (Qd)	Quantity supplied by dom industry (Qs)	Imports (M)	Surplus of the domestic industry (PS)
Year 2 Q1	$8	$2.89	$10.89	$10.89	12.22	11.78	0.44	$34.69
Year 2 Q2	$11	$2.89	$13.89	$11	12	12	0	$36
Year 2 Q3	$6	$2.89	$8.89	$8.89	16.22	7.78	8.44	$15.13
Year 2 Q4	$10	$2.89	$12.89	$11	12	12	0	$36

Under the weighted-average anti-dumping duty, the domestic industry receives windfall gains to welfare in quarters 1 and 4. The table reports that the level of producer's surplus in quarters 1 and 4 is considerably greater than the baseline non-injured level of welfare of $25/quarter. Moreover, the average level of surplus over all four quarters is $30.45, greater than the average level of surplus of $27.75 obtained under the ideal transaction-specific duty.

The 'zeroed' anti-dumping duty and injury under ordinary dumping
How does zeroing affect sales and domestic producer's surplus? Under a rule to throw out transactions in which the export price is above normal value, only the transactions from quarter 1 and quarter 3 of year 1 are used to construct the weighted-average dumping margin. This implies an anti-dumping duty of $3.25/unit on all imports in year 2. Table 5 presents the consequences of a dumping margin with zeroing.

In Table 5, the weighted-average anti-dumping duty under zeroing creates levels of producer's surplus in quarters 1 and 4 that are excessive relative to the ideal transaction-specific anti-dumping duty that would just offset injury. Moreover, the level of producer's surplus in the first quarter is excessive relative to that under the implementable weighted-average anti-dumping duty. The average level of

duty would be $12.89 and its sales in Country A would fall to zero. The firm is immediately and forever shut out of the Country A market at a price equal to normal value under the weighted-average anti-dumping duty. If the exporter offers a price equal to normal value, no sales will occur. Thus, once the weighted-average anti-dumping duty is imposed, the government will never observe sales occurring at non-dumped prices. The Country A government can make a reasonable argument during sunset reviews that the threat of dumping persists. This illustrates one of the concerns that Blonigen and Park (2004) discuss in their study of the dynamic pricing behavior of foreign firms under the US system of administered review. Under a broad set of import demand functions, it might be impossible for a foreign exporter found guilty of dumping to ever see its duty reduced, even if it makes a good-faith effort to raise its export price to normal value.

Table 5. Imports and producer's surplus under a 'zeroed' anti-dumping duty

Trans.date	Exporter's offered price (Px)	Zeroed dumping margin (ZDM)	Exporter's price incl. of ZDM (Px + ZDM)	Dom. price (Pd)	Total quantity demanded (Qd)	Quantity supplied by dom. industry (Qs)	Imports (M)	Surplus of the domestic industry (PS)
Year 2 Q1	$8	$3.25	$11.25	$11	12	12	0	$36
Year 2 Q2	$11	$3.25	$14.25	$11	12	12	0	$36
Year 2 Q3	$6	$3.25	$9.25	$9.25	15.5	8.5	7	$18.06
Year 2 Q4	$10	$3.25	$13.25	$11	12	12	0	$36

welfare over four quarters is $31.52, the highest yet relative to the non-injured level of welfare of $25.

Dumping margins and injury under ordinary dumping: conclusions
Thus far, two concerns have been expressed. First, with downward-sloping demand and perfectly elastic export supply, any method of calculating a dumping margin that involves an averaging on historical data is biased toward excessive injury remediation relative to the injury remediation obtained under an ideal policy in which the anti-dumping duty raises the consumer price of an imported good to the exporter's normal value. Second and more importantly for the case under consideration, the use of zeroing in the calculation of the dumping margin exacerbates this problem.

In summary, the first point is that, under ordinary dumping, the use of zeroing in the construction of a dumping margin is objectionable on the grounds that it more than offsets injury. Given that the intent of the Anti-Dumping Agreement is to permit anti-dumping duties that just offset injury, a methodology that systematically creates super-normal gains for the industry seems to be fundamentally at odds with the agreement.

The Appellate Body Report is to be commended for its discussion and analysis in paragraphs 92–96 in which it argues that the economic intent of the agreement, to remedy 'injurious dumping', cannot be ignored in a review of the methodology employed by a member country.

Targeted dumping
Does allowing for zeroing in the construction of a dumping margin fulfill the intent of the Anti-Dumping Agreement to remedy the injury caused by targeted dumping? Or is it excessive?

Some arguments in favor of zeroing draw an analogy to speeding or shoplifting. A man caught driving 20 miles per hour above the speed limit or with $20 of stolen merchandise in his bag cannot point to the previous occasions on which he drove five miles per hour under the speed limit or paid top dollar for a purchase to absolve himself of a punishment. Why should episodes of dumping be treated differently?

The economist's objection to zeroing is that it creates a punishment that is excessive relative to the harm created by the episode of dumping. As the examples in the previous section illustrated, with downward-sloping demand, a weighted-average dumping margin will result in an anti-dumping duty that is most heavily weighted by the most egregious episodes of dumping. With margins based on historic, rather than real-time data, the policy is biased toward overcompensating the domestic industry for any injurious dumping. In these situations, the practice of zeroing exacerbates this bias.

Are there circumstances in which zeroing or a similar practice would be justified? The language of the exceptional method of Article 2.4.2 provides a hint. Exceptional methods for calculating dumping margins are permitted: 'if the authorities find a pattern of export prices which differ significantly among different purchasers, regions, or time periods, and if an explanation is provided as to why such differences cannot be taken into account appropriately by the use of a weighted-average-to-weighted-average or transaction-to-transaction comparison'.

In international trade, targeted dumping can occur when a foreign producer offers a generous new-customer-discount in an export market. Discounts offered to the new customers of a foreign producer would seem to satisfy the legal requirements for targeted dumping. Suppose a foreign producer targets new customers as the recipients of dumped merchandise. Repeat customers, who have bought the foreign-produced item on at least one previous occasion, are offered and purchase the foreign-produced good at the normal price that prevails in the exporter's own market. This pattern of pricing, discounts for new customers and no-discounts for repeat customers, would be apparent in any review of the exporter's sales records.

This type of pricing strategy, the new-customer-discount, is a normal practice for any producer that needs to address a particular information problem – its potential customers do not have sufficient information about the quality (or some other attribute) of its good to actually buy the good at its non-discounted price.[47]

---

47 The problem of asymmetric information between producers and consumers regarding product quality plagues many markets; used cars and mortgage-backed securities are famous examples. However, even products like cellphones or sneakers can embody an informational asymmetry. For these goods, the customer learns about the product's quality (or the match of the product's attributes to those desired by the consumer) only through the use of the product. In this context, incentives like new-customer price discounts or money-back guarantees can be highly effective at expanding a producer's market share.

A market with an information problem: product quality is difficult to observe
For concreteness, consider the market for widgets in Country B. Consumers have normal downward-sloping demand for two varieties of widgets: high quality and low quality. A consumer cannot substitute the low-quality widget for the high-quality widget, but the reverse is possible. The problem a consumer faces in purchasing a widget is that the widget's quality is difficult to verify *ex ante*. Quality can only be observed if the consumer purchases and uses the good. We assume that each producer completely specializes in the production of high- or low-quality widgets. Thus, once a consumer has purchased one widget from a particular producer and observed the quality of that purchase, she correctly infers the quality of all future purchases from that producer. We consider an extreme case of information-sharing: no consumer who purchases the good from a specific producer is able to share with other consumers any information about the quality of that producer's widget.[48]

On the production side, each producer of widgets chooses a production technology, high or low quality, and produces only widgets of that quality. Although the technology to produce the low-quality widget exists in Country B, domestic producers have some cost (e.g. labor) that is too high to profitably produce and sell the low-quality variety. Thus, all domestic producers specialize in high-quality widgets and consumers correctly perceive that any domestically produced widget is high quality. The quarterly domestic industry supply of high-quality widgets is upward sloping and is graphed in Figure 2.

Historically, the technology for high-quality widget production was not available outside Country B and foreign producers specialized in low-quality widget production. Consumers in Country B correctly inferred that all foreign-produced widgets were low quality. The production of low-quality widgets was (and is) highly competitive so that supply of low-quality widgets was (and still is) perfectly elastic at $9.00/unit.

Before the dissemination of the high-quality production technology to foreign countries, the equilibrium in Country B's high-quality widget market was given by Figure 2.

In the absence of any sales by a high-quality foreign producer, domestic consumers demand and domestic producers sell 12 units of high-quality widgets per quarter at a price of $11/unit. From this we can calculate that domestic producer's surplus is $36 per quarter in the absence of foreign competition (see Table 6, row 1).

In the low-quality widget market, demand is such that domestic consumers purchase four widgets per quarter from low-quality foreign producers for

---

48 An alternative extreme case of complete information sharing in which a single sale to a single consumer informs all market participants about a product's quality would yield similar qualitative results. A weighted-average dumping margin would be too small to remedy injury effectively while a 'zeroed' anti-dumping duty could.

Figure 2. Industry Supply and Consumer Demand for the high-quality good in Country B

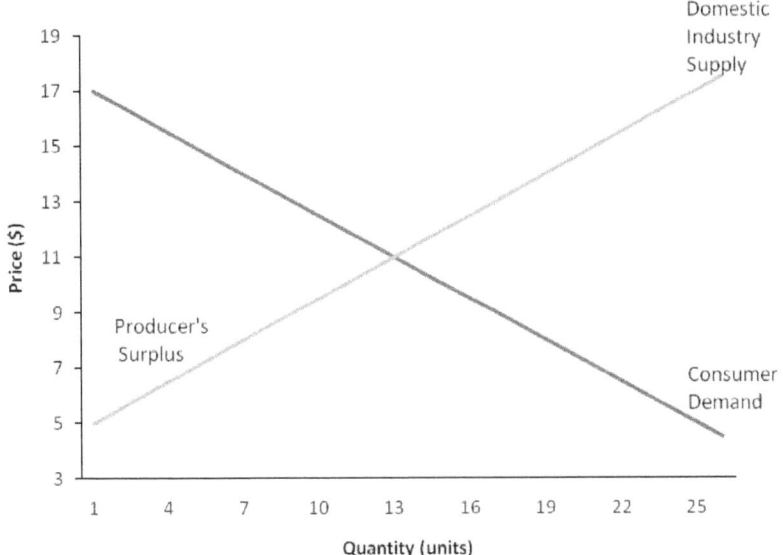

$9.00/widget. As there are no domestic producers of low-quality widgets, domestic producer's surplus in this market is always zero and we can dispense with any concerns of injury in this market under dumping.

A foreign producer targets new customers to receive dumped merchandise
In this environment, what happens when a foreign producer acquires the technology for producing high-quality widgets?[49] Suppose a new foreign producer, *High Quality Inc.*, completely specializes in the production of high-quality widgets and sells these widgets in its own market for $10/unit. When *High Quality Inc.* tries to enter the high-quality widget market in Country B, it confronts a dominant stereotype held by Country B consumers that foreign-produced widgets are low quality. The asymmetric information problem means that a potential customer must buy at least one *High Quality Inc.* widget before it recognizes it as a high-quality widget and values it accordingly. Thus, if *High Quality Inc.* offers its widgets for sale in Country B at $10/unit, no potential customer will purchase it. With low-quality widgets available at $9.00/unit and customer perceptions that all

49 Schott (2008) provides a detailed empirical analysis of changes in the variety and quality of goods imported into the US from China and a number of developed countries over a long time horizon. He finds that countries at lower stages of development export a wide variety of goods that are similar, but lower in quality than those exported by more developed countries. Moreover, he finds evidence that the developing countries export higher quality goods over time.

Table 6. Sales volumes and producer's surplus in high-quality widgets under different scenarios

Scenario	Exporter's offered price (Px)	Exporter's normal value (NV)	Total quantity demanded (Qd)	Quantity supplied by domestic industry (Qs)	Imports (M)	Surplus of the domestic industry (PS)
Prior to foreign entry	N.A.	N.A.	12	12	0	$36
Attempted foreign entry with info prob.	$10/unit	$10/unit	12	12	0	$36
Foreign entry if no info problem	$10/unit	$10/unit	14	10	4	$25
After targeted dumping ceases	$10/unit	$10/unit	14	10	4	$25

foreign-produced widgets are low quality, there is no demand for the output of *High Quality Inc.* in Country B at $10/unit. (See Table 6, row 2).

In the absence of an information problem, if *High Quality Inc.* offered unlimited quantities of its widgets at a fair, non-dumped price of $10/unit, the equilibrium in Country B in each quarter would be characterized by a domestic price of $10/unit, domestic consumption of 14 units, domestic industry sales of 10 units, imports from *High Quality Inc.* of 4 units, and $25 of producer's surplus for the domestic industry (see Table 6, row 3). Although the information problem precludes this outcome, it provides one benchmark against which we could judge policy responses.

As a solution to its information problem, *High Quality, Inc.* could offer a new-customer discount in which any Country B consumer who has never purchased a good from *High Quality Inc.* would be offered 1 unit at a price of $9. If that customer wanted to make additional purchases, *High Quality Inc.* would offer an unlimited quantity at $10/unit. In the short run, this discount creates a bifurcation in the market for high-quality widgets between 'informed' and 'uninformed' consumers. Once a consumer in Country B has bought a *High Quality Inc.* widget, he would be unwilling to pay more than $10 for a high-quality widget made by any producer. Table 7 presents a possible evolution of prices and sales of high-quality widgets by *High Quality Inc.*[50]

50 In this table, the assumption is that each consumer who buys a *High Quality Inc.* widget at the low-quality price of $9 in quarter *t*, demands one high-quality widget at a price of $10 in each subsequent quarter. Over the course of four quarters, every potential Country B consumer (of a high-quality widget at a price of $10) has attempted the purchase of a low-quality widget, but received a *High Quality Inc.* widget under the discount program instead. With the discount program beginning in the first quarter of year 1, all potential consumers of high-quality widgets are fully informed about the quality of *High Quality Inc.* by the first quarter of year 2.

Table 7. Export prices, dumping margins, and sales to the domestic industry under targeted dumping

Transaction date	Exporter's discount price (Pdisc)	Exporter's repeat customer price (Px)	Exporter's normal value (NV)	Dumping margin (DM) for dumped imports	Dumped Imports (Mdump)	Fairly priced imports (Mfair)
Year 1 Q1	$9	$10	$10	$1	4	0
Year 1 Q2	$9	$10	$10	$1	4	4
Year 1 Q3	$9	$10	$10	$1	4	4
Year 1 Q4	$9	$10	$10	$1	2	4
Year 2 Q1	N.A.	$10	$10	$0	0	4
All future dates	N.A.	$10	$10	$0	0	4

Under this strategy, *High Quality Inc.* is engaging in targeted dumping to new customers, but is charging the legally 'fair' normal value to repeat customers. By the first quarter of year 2, each of the 14 potential customers of high-quality widgets at the price of $10 will know that the desired product can be obtained from *High Quality Inc.* for $10. Thus, Country B consumers will refuse to pay the domestic producers' higher price of $11 for a high-quality widget. In order to survive, domestic producers will lower their prices to $10. Those that cannot profitably sell at $10 will exit the market. The long-run equilibrium in the high-quality widget market, after dumping by *High Quality Inc.* has ceased, is reported in row 4 of Table 6.

Importantly, the four episodes of dumping, in quarters one through four of year 1, have permanent effects. Because the targeted dumping informed customers about an identical, but cheaper product, the Country B high-quality widget market became more competitive. Essentially, the episodes of dumping that facilitated *High Quality Inc.*'s entry into the Country B market caused a permanent reduction in the economic welfare of domestic producers from $36 per quarter to $25 per quarter.

Should this reduction in the welfare of domestic producers be considered 'injury caused by dumping'? Or is it reasonable to attribute this injury to another cause? One view would hold that the cause of the welfare loss is the higher level of competition in the Country B market that exists in the wake of the new-customer discount. This view would hold that competition, not dumping, is the cause of the injury. However, others could reasonably counter that *but for* the targeted dumping, the baseline level of welfare in the industry would have been $36 per quarter forever. Under this criterion, it seems reasonable to conclude that the injury is caused by the targeted dumping.

The weighted-average anti-dumping duty and injury under targeted dumping
Suppose that at the beginning of year 2, the Country B government decided to impose an anti-dumping duty on imports from *High Quality Inc.* If they calculated

Table 8. Imports and producer's surplus under weighted-average anti-dumping duties

Trans. date	Exporter's offered price (Px)	Dumping margin (DM)	Exporter's price incl. of DM (Px + DM)	Dom. price (Pd)	Total quantity demanded (Qd)	Quantity supplied by dom. industry (Qs)	Imports (M)	Surplus of the domestic industry (PS)
Year 2 Q1	$10	$0.54	$10.54	$10.54	12.92	11.08	1.84	$30.69
Year 2 Q2	$10	$0.54	$10.54	$10.54	12.92	11.08	1.84	$30.69
Year 2 Q3	$10	$0.54	$10.54	$10.54	12.92	11.08	1.84	$30.69
Year 2 Q4	$10	$0.54	$10.54	$10.54	12.92	11.08	1.84	$30.69
Year 3 Q1	$10	$0	$10	$10	14	10	4	$25
Year 3 Q2	$10	$0	$10	$10	14	10	4	$25
Year 3 Q3	$10	$0	$10	$10	14	10	4	$25
Year 3 Q4	$10	$0	$10	$10	14	10	4	$25

the dumping margin by applying the weighted-average-to-weighted-average methodology on data from year 1, the anti-dumping duty for year 2 would be $0.54 on each imported unit. If *High Quality Inc.* continues to offer a price of $10 to all repeat customers in year 2, the domestic price under the anti-dumping duty would rise to $10.54 in all quarters. Producer's surplus in all quarters of year 2 would be only $30.69, considerably lower than the $36 per quarter that the industry would have received *but for* the targeted dumping by *High Quality Inc.* (See Table 8).

Let's assume that the Country B government conducts an annual review and uses transactions data from year 2 to construct the weighted-average dumping margin for year 3. Under this common scenario, the anti-dumping duty would fall to $0 per unit by year 3 because *High Quality Inc.* offered no discounts to new customers in year 2. The welfare of the domestic industry would be further reduced to $25 per quarter. Although there was no dumping by *High Quality Inc.* in year 2, the effects of its entry persist into all future periods as a permanent reduction in industry welfare.

The 'zeroed' anti-dumping duty and injury under targeted dumping
If the Country B government interpreted *High Quality Inc.*'s new-customer discount as a pricing pattern that warranted the use of the exceptional method under Article 2.4.2, it could calculate the dumping margin under a rule to 'zero out' all non-dumped transactions from year 1. This would yield an anti-dumping duty of $1 for each imported unit in year 2. Given the conditions of supply and demand in Country B's market for high-quality widgets, this is a prohibitive tariff that would restore to Country B the competitive conditions that would have ensued *but for* *High Quality Inc.*'s targeted dumping. Producer's surplus would return to its baseline 'non-injured' level. See Table 9.

Table 9. Imports and producer's surplus under 'zeroed' anti-dumping duties

Trans. date	Exporter's offered price (Px)	Dumping margin (DM)	Exporter's price incl. of DM (Px+DM)	Dom. price (Pd)	Total quantity demanded (Qd)	Quantity supplied by dom. industry (Qs)	Imports (M)	Surplus of the domestic industry (PS)
Year 2 Q 1–Q 4	$10	$1.00	$11.00	$11	12	12	0	$36

The evolution of the dumping margin and industry welfare in year 3 would depend on two factors: (1) how the Country B government treated the threat of continued dumping and (2) the ability of Country B consumers to remember a producer's quality over long periods of time.

If *High Quality Inc.*'s absence from the Country B market leads consumers to forget that *High Quality Inc.* makes high-quality widgets, then the only way in which *High Quality Inc.* can reenter the Country B market is through a second round of targeted dumping. Then there would be a real threat of injurious dumping. The Country B government could prevent this injury by maintaining the duty of $1/unit in year 3. Alternatively, if Country B chose to not impose an anti-dumping duty in the face of this threat, the cycle of *High Quality Inc.*'s entry through targeted dumping followed by a duty to remedy injury could be repeated indefinitely.

If Country B consumers had long memories, then *High Quality Inc.* would not need to dump its product in order to reenter the market in year 3. In this case, there is no threat that dumping would recur. But, reentry at a fair market price of $10/unit would cause injury to domestic producers. It is not entirely clear what options are available to Country B's government in these circumstances. The use of an anti-dumping duty in the absence of any real threat of continued dumping seems questionable. However, because there is a real threat of injury that would be the direct result of dumping that occurred during year 1, one could argue that the continuation of the prohibitive anti-dumping duty is permitted under the Anti-Dumping Agreement.

Dumping margins and injury under targeted dumping: conclusions
Under the Anti-Dumping Agreement, the new-customer discount is a targeted dumping strategy that results in permanent injury to the domestic industry in Country B. In response to this, the use of zeroing in the calculation of the dumping margin is necessary to fully offset the injury to the domestic industry. In this example, it is the only method that generates a sufficiently large duty to remedy the injury suffered by domestic producers. Interestingly, given the parameters of supply and demand in this example, the presence of an information problem renders the ordinary anti-dumping duty (from the W-W or T-T methods) ineffective at

remedying injury. The analysis herein shows that the exceptional method is not *inutile*; its value derives from the fact that, by not being mathematically equivalent to the ordinary methods, it is the only method that can restore the domestic economy to the state it would have been in had the targeted dumping never occurred.

To the extent that a perception of low quality is a prototypical problem for a firm entering a high-income market from a low- or middle-income country, the stylized example presented here might be, rather than exceptional, a highly relevant empirical phenomenon.

As a final point, we offer some thoughts on the normative welfare consequences of zeroing in dumping cases. In the targeted-dumping example, the foreign pricing strategy of the new-customer discount is a practice that economists widely regard as a normal and fair aspect of market competition. Because this discount allowed consumers to learn about the quality of the foreign-produced variety, it created more intense market competition that permanently reduced the welfare of the domestic producers. Normative welfare economics does not prescribe any policy response to this situation. Rather, it recognizes this more intense competition as the source of improved aggregate welfare in Country B.

Economically speaking, the concern lies not in the application of the law, but with the law itself. As the example illustrates, the Anti-Dumping Agreement could be construed to prohibit the use of large price discounts by new market entrants. In other words, the Agreement deters pro-competitive pricing. A normative analysis of economic welfare would find that the use of the exceptional method in the targeted-dumping example presented here reduces both the national welfare of Country B (under which producers would gain at the expense of consumers) and of the world. While it might be possible to identify cases in which anti-dumping duties have a favorable effect on aggregate economic welfare, they fail to do so in the cases considered here.

The economics of stare decisis

The economics literature on the efficiency of stare decisis in a domestic setting is divided into two broad classes of models that emphasize different types of uncertainty. All papers begin with the premise that insufficient information at the time a statute or contract is written necessitates an incompleteness in the law or contract. The law cannot fully describe what action should be taken by agents or by the court in every possible state of the world. The role of the legal system is to fill these gaps in the law with rulings issued by judges. The problem of economic analysis is to determine the extent to which a legal system is able to achieve socially optimal outcomes that leave all parties with the highest possible level of welfare.

To evaluate the economic efficiency of stare decisis as part of a legal system, begin with a simple world in which a legislature enacts a law at time zero. For concreteness, following Gennaioli and Schleifer (2007a and 2007b), suppose the law is a simple tort regarding the liability of a dog biting a man. At time zero, the legislature cannot foresee every possible relevant empirical criteria in every possible future case, so the enacted law is vague on numerous empirical dimensions. After enactment of the vague law, in each subsequent period, a case may be brought before a judge who must assign blame.[51]

The socially optimal law involves balancing the costs to the owner of restraining the dog and the costs to others of being bitten. Ideally, the law should induce owners of more aggressive dogs to make greater efforts to restrain their dogs than owners of gentler dogs. Thus, the socially optimal law should condition on criteria that are relevant to aggressive behavior. However, at time zero, legislators may not know which empirical criteria determine aggressiveness (size of the dog, color of the dog, congestion of a locality, weather, etc.). Thus, the law is by necessity vague.

Gennaioli and Schleifer (2007a) analyze a legal system in which a judge creates law by conditioning his judgment on an empirical basis that is, until that point in time, vague and in which judges in all future cases are obligated to rule in the same way with respect to that empirical criterion. Any case that comes before a judge has several empirical dimensions along which the judge could potentially institute a bright-line rule. Gennaioli and Schleifer assume that in hearing a case, a judge has two options: he can abide by the criteria laid out in prior cases or he may issue a new ruling by 'distinguishing' the current case from prior cases along one relevant empirical dimension that prior cases have left vague. They find that this system can facilitate the evolution of the law toward a social optimum over time.

Gennaioli and Schleifer refer to the process of abiding by previously decided cases and issuing different rulings only when it is possible to introduce a new empirical criterion as the *ratio decidendi* in a case as 'distinguishing'. If other empirical dimensions are relevant to achieving a socially efficient outcome, then a process in which judges are bound by stare decisis and gradually complete the gaps in the law by distinguishing (that is, adding a new bright-line rule in each subsequent case that is heard), can never achieve full efficiency. They point out that when relevant empirical dimensions are added to the body of law sequentially through a series of cases, the ultimate 'evolved' law is likely to be inferior to the fully optimal law that would condition on every possible relevant criterion from time zero. However, the beauty of stare decisis is that it moves the law toward a social optimum precisely when the fully optimal law is not feasible.

Stare decisis is desirable from an efficiency perspective for a number of reasons. By clarifying the law over time, it induces welfare-enhancing behaviors from agents without imposing unnecessary costs. In the dog-biting-a-man example, owners of aggressive dogs will come to understand that they must use leashes or suffer penalties, while owners of dogs that are widely regarded as mild-mannered

---

51 The vague law described here embodies aspects of both the discretionary contract and the vague contract in Maggi and Staiger (2008) discussed below.

will not be excessively burdened by leash requirements. This process of judge-made law will likely take place more rapidly than any legislative refinement of the law and any gaps in the law will likely prioritize the most salient circumstances.

However, these benefits come at a cost – the loss of flexibility. A critical assumption in the Gennaioli and Schleifer model is that a judge cannot make a rule that is a function of all relevant empirical dimensions at one point in time. This proxies for the idea that initial cases may not have the same important aspects as those that arise in later cases. A judge deciding a case in period $t+1$ might face what she regards as a unique case – a confluence of factors lay the fault with one party, but applying previously decided rules would assign blame to the other party. Stare decisis imposes two restrictions – backward and forward inflexibility in the law's interpretation with regard to specific empirical criteria. A general economic principle is that multidimensional rules are more efficient than unidimensional rules. For a judge deciding a case in period $t+1$, backward inflexibility implies that she must apply all the unidimensional bright-line rules from prior decisions to her current case. The option of distinguishing the law along a new empirical dimension might be undesirable if the only reasonable criterion along which this case may be distinguished from previous cases introduces an efficiency-reducing constraint on future cases. Because of the forward inflexibility of stare decisis, the judge may foresee that future justice is impaired by replacing vagueness in the law with a bright-line rule that moves the law away from the social optimum. The sequential way in which the law develops brings with it constraints on judicial discretion that can put the law on a track that will never reach the social optimum.

The same model is used by Gennaioli and Schleifer (2007b) to show that overruling introduces volatility into the law and that in a system where overruling is common, the law rarely converges to the social optimum. An additional concern with excessive overruling that is not addressed by Gennaioli and Schleifer has to do with the overall validity of the legal system in the eyes of its participants. When judges are not bound by precedent and issue opposite rulings in similar cases, these conflicting decisions can undermine agents' confidence in the fairness of the legal system. This could potentially lead to the system's collapse.

Gennaioli and Schleifer do not simultaneously analyze the two practices of distinguishing and overruling so we do not know what interesting results might obtain when the two practices interact within a system of law.

A second vein in the literature that compares case- and statute-law systems focuses on the timing on information revelation and its relationship to *ex ante* and *ex post* efficient decisions by judges. Anderlini *et al.* (2008) compare the efficiency of statute law to case law. The key distinction they model is the extent of judicial discretion to respond to the specific facts of a case in issuing a ruling. In the statute-law system, judges have no discretion to create new law, but must rigidly implement what the statute says with respect to the facts of a case; that is, the judge enforces rules that are *ex ante* efficient. This system is inflexible, but the upside is that the law is time consistent. The economy is largely free of moral-hazard problems that could arise if agents think that the court will bail them out of sticky situations.

In contrast, in a case-law system, benevolent judges have the freedom to issue rulings that take into account information that was not available to the parties at the time they entered into a contract. In rendering his decision, the judge can myopically fine-tune the law to the realized state of the world. At first blush, this makes the case-law system appear more efficient. However, the ruling is only *ex post* efficient in that specific case. More generally, this fine-tuning of the law to information that was not initially available introduces a time-consistency problem. Actors in the economy come to understand that benevolent judges will help them out when they get themselves into trouble. This leads to an increase in moral-hazard problems in the future.

The time-consistency problem is mitigated by what Anderlini *et al.* call *the dynamics of precedents*. Essentially, if a judge in a case-law system is forward-looking and issues a 'tough' ruling, he can constrain other judges to do the same in future cases. Agents come to see that judges will enforce *ex ante* efficient contracts and the temptation to engage in reckless behaviors subsides. Interestingly, in a model that is starkly different from Gennaioli and Schleifer (2007a), Anderlini *et al.* obtain a similar result – the case-law system with binding precedents cannot achieve full efficiency. Despite this, they conclude that a case-law system with binding precedents yields higher levels of welfare than a statute-law system when the rate of legal innovation is sufficiently high.

In contrast to the economic analyses of stare decisis written by economists, an earlier economic analysis by Kornhauser (1989) uses three criteria of traditional concern to lawyers – fairness, competency, and predictability – to assess stare decisis in four simple models that emphasize different sources of judicial error.

Kornhauser concludes that stare decisis is desirable for a court system characterized by judges with different values (biases) because it promotes fairness. Interestingly, Gennaioli and Schleifer's (2007a) paper is simply a more formalized version of Kornhauser's model of legal errors via changing values. Whereas Kornhauser showed that stare decisis promotes fairness, Gennaioli and Schleifer show that social welfare is promoted via fairness when stare decisis in the legal system is characterized by distinguishing. However, when the level of judicial bias is sufficiently high and judges have the ability to overrule prior rulings that they dislike, Gennaioli and Schleifer (2007b) show that the system is unfair and in-efficient.

Kornhauser persuasively argues that predictability in the law generated by stare decisis is beneficial because under it agents can form correct expectations about future legal obligations. Indeed, this, as we have noted earlier in the paper, appears to be the principal rationale of the Appellate Body in its first attempt to articulate at least a *de facto* stare decisis practice in the WTO (*Japan–Alcohol*). In a similar manner, Anderlini *et al.* (2008) use what lawyers refer to as a unitary model to demonstrate that stare decisis promotes efficiency by correcting a time-consistency problem. In essence, these later papers in the economics literature use the basic ideas in Kornhauser. However, rather than focusing on Kornhauser's ultimate legal criteria for evaluating the principle, the economics papers show that Kornhauser's legal criteria of fairness and predictability are the paths through which social welfare is maximized.

Overall, the law-and-economics literature on binding precedents concludes that stare decisis is a desirable feature for a purely domestic legal system. The question that arises is: how applicable are these findings to international public law and, specifically, the functioning of international trade law and dispute resolution?

The problem of a domestic legal system – a statute and a court system – is to constrain the behaviors of private agents in a socially optimal way. Agents that wish to pursue their own narrow self-interest are constrained by a court system that seeks to facilitate private interactions that are mutually beneficial.

The problem of a trade agreement is different. The agents that wish to pursue their own self-interest are governments that recognize that by restricting their own discretion to pursue self-interested policies, they can improve the well-being of their neighbors and, through reciprocal treatment, improve their own lot. In all states of the world, governments have an incentive to pursue self-interested policies, but the gains from these policies can vary with the realized state. The mechanism design challenge is to construct a contract- and dispute-resolution system that generates the highest welfare for all contracting governments over the broadest possible set of states of the world. Two problems are present. First, it is costly to foresee and describe all possible states. Second, information about the realized state (or social welfare under the realized state) is difficult for all parties and any arbiter to observe and verify.

The first problem necessitates an incomplete contract. The second implies that the potential gains from cheating on the agreement will vary with the arbiter's ability to observe information. A recent important contribution by economists that specifically addresses the role of the Dispute Settlement Body (DSB) in adjudication at the WTO is Maggi and Staiger (2008). They argue that a trade agreement and its dispute settlement process should be analyzed as a unified system.[52]

They compare three types of incomplete trade agreements: (1) a discretionary contract, (2) a vague contract, and (3) a rigid contract. These different types of contracts imply different roles for an activist adjudicating body. It can (1) fill the gaps in a discretionary contract, (2) interpret a vague contract, or (3) modify a rigid contract.[53]

In a static analysis, Maggi and Staiger conclude that a discretionary contract with a gap-filling Dispute Settlement Body (DSB) is optimal when the DSB's

---

52 The alternative of a legal system in which a statute-creating legislature and an adjudicating court are independent of and distinct from the parties to a contract is considered by Anderlini *et al.* (2008).

53 Note that the first role is similar to the practice of distinguishing described by Gennaioli and Schliefer while the third role was found by Anderlini *et al.* to be undesirable in a dynamic model because of associated moral-hazard problems.

rulings are sufficiently accurate or well informed. When the accuracy of the DSB's rulings is low, the optimal system is a vague or rigid contract and a non-activist DSB. Finally, when the observability of information falls in an intermediate range, a vague contract and an interpretive DSB is best.

Maggi and Staiger's analysis is pessimistic about the merits of stare decisis in international trade law. This somewhat surprising result arises because the DSB, after observing the true state of the world, does not know what policy is globally optimal with perfect accuracy. This lack of accuracy induces perverse behavior. Self-interested governments have a greater incentive to try to game the system under a precedent-setting DSB; importers try to get away with protectionist policies that are not justified and exporters file disputes against protectionist policies that are merited. Maggi and Staiger observe that precedent will simultaneously create welfare gains by reducing duplicative litigation costs. The resolution of this empirical tradeoff depends on the quality of the information available to the DSB. Maggi and Staiger (2008) conclude that the costs of stare decisis outweigh the gains when the DSB has access to better information.

In summary, the economics literature on stare decisis is divided. The conclusions drawn from each analysis depend critically on the information problems present in the system under examination. The economic model that best fits the features of the WTO system, Maggi and Staiger (2008), concludes that binding precedent in the dispute-resolution system is likely welfare-reducing under a realistic assumption about the quality of available information. This surprising result obtains because precedent induces socially undesirable and inefficient behavior on the part of contracting parties. Interestingly, the inclusion of binding precedent in court systems modeled by Gennaioli and Schleifer (2007a), Anderlini *et al.* (2008), and Kornhauser (1989) induces more socially desirable behaviors and leads to better outcomes. This suggests that the empirical question to address in evaluating legal systems is how binding precedent affects the behavior of agents over time.

References

Anderlini, Luca, Leonardo Felli, and Alessandro Riboni (2008), 'Statute Law or Case Law?', August, Georgetown University mimeo.

Blonigen, Bruce A. and Park Jee-Hyeong (2004), 'Dynamic Pricing in the Presence of Antidumping Policy: Theory and Evidence', *American Economic Review*, 94: 134–154.

Bown, Chad P. and Alan O. Sykes (2008), 'The Zeroing Issue: A Critical Analysis of *Softwood V*', *World Trade Review*, 7(1): 121–142.

Crowley, Meredith A. (2008), 'Split Decisions in Antidumping Cases', February, Federal Reserve Bank of Chicago mimeo.

Crowley, Meredith A. (2009), 'Cyclical Dumping and US Antidumping Protection: 1980–2001', Federal Reserve Bank of Chicago Working Paper (WP-2007-21), March.

Deardorff, Alan V. (2005), 'Glossary of International Economics', available at http://www-personal. umich.edu/~alandear/glossary (last visited 4 January 2010).

Gennaioli, Nicola and Andrei Shleifer (2007a), 'The Evolution of Common Law', *Journal of Political Economy*, **115**: 43–68.

Gennaioli, Nicola and Andrei Shleifer (2007b), 'Overruling and the Instability of Law', *Journal of Comparative Economics*, **35**: 309–328.

Janow, Merit E. and Robert W. Staiger (2003), 'EC–Bed Linen', in Henrik Horn and Petros C. Mavroidis (eds.), *The WTO Case Law of 2001: The American Law Institute Reporters' Studies*, Cambridge: Cambridge University Press, pp. 115–139.

Knoops, Geert-Jan Alexander (2005), *Theory and Practice of International and Internationalized Criminal Proceedings*, Kluwer Law International, pp. 4–5.

Kornhauser, Lewis A. (1989), 'An Economic Perspective on *stare decisis*', *Chicago Kent Law Review*, **65**: 63–92.

Maggi, Giovanni and Robert W. Staiger (2008), 'On the Role and Design of Dispute Settlement Procedures in International Trade Agreements', NBER Working Paper #14067.

Prusa, Thomas J. and Edwin Vermulst (January 2009), 'A One-Two Punch on Zeroing: US–Zeroing (EC) and US–Zeroing (Japan)', *World Trade Review*, **8**: 187–241.

Schott, Peter K. (2008), 'The Relative Sophistication of Chinese Exports', *Economic Policy*, **53** (January): 5–49.

Staiger, Robert W. and Frank A. Wolak (1992), 'The Effects of Domestic Antidumping Law in the Presence of Foreign Monopoly', *Journal of International Economics*, **32** (3–4): 265–287.

Staiger, Robert W. and Frank A. Wolak (1994), 'Measuring Industry Specific Protection: Antidumping in the United States', *Brookings Papers on Economic Activity: Microeconomics*, Volume 1.

Tyner, Davis B. (2006), 'Internationalization of War Crimes Prosecutions: Correcting the International Criminal Tribunal for the Former Yugoslavia's Folly in Tadic', *Florida Journal of International Law*, **18**: 843–885.

Continued suspense: *EC–Hormones* and WTO disciplines on discrimination and domestic regulation
Appellate Body Reports: *Canada/United States – Continued Suspension of Obligations in the EC – Hormones Dispute,* WT/DS320/AB/R,WT/DS321/AB/R, adopted 14 November 2008

BERNARD HOEKMAN

World Bank and CEPR

JOEL TRACHTMAN

Tufts University[1]

Abstract: Based on the reasoning of the Appellate Body in *Canada/United States – Continued Suspension of Obligations in the EC–Hormones Dispute* ('*Continued Suspension*'), this paper analyzes the distinction between the national-treatment obligation under Article III of GATT and the requirement under the Agreement on Sanitary and Phytosanitary (SPS) Measures that such measures be based on a risk assessment that takes into account available scientific evidence. The Appellate Body's reasoning makes clear that the primary purpose of the SPS Agreement is to discipline discriminatory regulation, and not the level of protection. We argue that the case clarifies that *de facto* protection (market segmentation) created by an SPS measure must be motivated by demonstrating that the measure is addressing a market failure, as reflected in the existence of some scientific basis for a health or safety concern. The scientific-basis requirement is a means for determining the intent of an SPS measure. While this is a factor that is ostensibly not relevant in GATT national-treatment cases, the need for scientific justification is not a move away from a concern with preventing illegitimate discrimination against imported products.

1 This paper was prepared for The American Law Institute Principles of World Trade Law project. We are grateful for comments by participants in that project, and especially Henrik Horn and Joost Pauwelyn. The views expressed are personal and should not be attributed to the World Bank.

Introduction

In the case of *Canada/United States – Continued Suspension of Obligations in the EC – Hormones Dispute* (*Continued Suspension*), the European Communities (EC) challenged continued suspension of WTO concessions by the US and Canada. The US and Canada justified the suspension of concessions on the basis of the EC's alleged violation of the Agreement on Sanitary and Phytosanitary Measures (the SPS Agreement), continuing from an earlier case in which a WTO dispute-settlement proceeding concluded that the EC violated its obligations under the SPS Agreement, and in which the US and Canada were authorized to suspend concessions.

While this decision addresses important adjectival issues, the main substantive issue in this case is the question of the scope of disciplines on domestic regulation for sanitary and phytosanitary purposes. The SPS Agreement intensifies the disciplines on domestic regulation compared to the General Agreement on Tariffs and Trade (GATT) alone. The GATT only requires that domestic regulation of products be applied on a non-discriminatory basis, both in the national-treatment and in the most-favored-nation (MFN) sense. The SPS Agreement goes beyond this by specifying additional conditions that must be satisfied by SPS product regulations. *Continued Suspension* clarified what those conditions are and how they should be applied and interpreted in practice.

This paper seeks to better understand the precise parameters and nature of the difference between the pre-1995 GATT tests for discrimination and the post-1995, 'post-discriminatory', additional disciplines that are embodied in the SPS Agreement. We will argue that the approach taken by the Appellate Body is consistent with a view of SPS regulation as a mechanism that is (and should be) focused on addressing consumption externalities in the importing country, and that the specific criteria that are imposed to determine the WTO legitimacy of SPS measures are an effort to ensure that regulation is indeed directed towards addressing a non-pecuniary externality as opposed to an effort to improve the terms of trade. As is the case in other areas of WTO law affecting domestic 'behind the border' policy instruments, the disciplines are relatively weak in the sense that they allow for substantial discretion regarding the specific features of the product regulation that may be imposed by an importing government: what the SPS Agreement does is to impose (weak) conditions on governments aimed at ensuring that the aim of the regulation is to address a true consumption externality — through the requirement that any regulation, whatever the level chosen, has an objective (scientific) basis.

Thus, our interpretation of the Appellate Body's reasoning is that the primary purpose of the SPS Agreement is to discipline discriminatory regulation, and not to address instances of inefficient non-discriminatory product regulation, including inefficient choices of excessive levels of protection. Based on our reasoning, it is not impossible to infer that the SPS Agreement is designed to discipline regulation that is simply ignorant, failing to achieve its purported goal without discrimination. However, we argue that the distinction between discrimination analysis and rationality analysis is not as great as it might at first appear. The SPS Agreement is aimed at overcoming specific difficulties that arise in applying the general GATT non-discrimination rules to this area of regulation as it affects imported products.

This paper is organized as follows. Section 1 briefly reviews basic analytical insights and considerations that arise in connection with product regulation in the area of food, plant, and animal health and safety. In Section 2 we describe the facts and main holdings of *Continued Suspension*. In Section 3, we evaluate the distinction between the national-treatment obligation under Article III of GATT, and the requirement under the SPS Agreement that SPS measures be based on a risk assessment that takes into account available scientific evidence (Art. 5.1), as modified by Article 5.7 in situations where such evidence is insufficient. We evaluate this distinction from a doctrinal and jurisprudential standpoint, seeking to compare the distinct elements of each of these two disciplines on domestic regulation. In Section 4 we discuss the relationship between discrimination and 'post-discrimination' disciplines and a number of 'gaps' in the GATT discrimination rules that help to understand the 'additionality' of the SPS Agreement as it has been interpreted by the Appellate Body. Section 5 concludes.

1.   Conceptual considerations

Key provisions in the SPS Agreement provide that Members must ensure that any SPS measure be applied only to the extent necessary to protect human, animal, or plant life or health, that SPS measures must be based on scientific principles (Art. 2.2), and that a reflection of this requirement is that governments must base any SPS measure on an assessment of the risks to human, animal, or plant life or health, taking into account risk-assessment techniques developed by relevant international organizations (Art. 5.1). The risk assessment must identify the diseases, pests, etc. a Member wants to prevent in its territory, identify the potential biological and economic consequences associated with such diseases, and evaluate the likelihood of entry, establishment, or spread of these diseases (Art. 5.3). In the assessment of risks, available scientific evidence must be considered, as well as relevant processes and production methods; inspection, sampling, and testing methods; and the prevalence of specific diseases or pests and environmental conditions (Art. 5.2). In cases where relevant scientific evidence is insufficient, a Member may provisionally adopt SPS measures on the basis of available pertinent information, including that from the relevant international organizations as well as from SPS measures applied by other Members (Art. 5.7). If such provisional measures are imposed, Members must seek to obtain the additional information necessary for a more objective assessment of risk and review the SPS measure accordingly within a reasonable period of time.

From a social-welfare perspective, technical product regulations – of which SPS measures are a specific subcategory – are measures that can be justified as instruments to deal with specific market failures. Possible rationales for product regulation include imperfect information, uncertainty, market power, and other sources of externalities in production or consumption. Although product regulation can improve welfare if it succeeds in internalizing spillovers at acceptable transaction costs (i.e., improves allocative efficiency), this need not be the purpose or outcome. The intervention may also allow incumbent firms in an industry to exploit market power. Product standards are one of the possible instruments through which a firm or industry can induce government to raise rivals' costs. Given compliance costs, regulation may reduce the contestability of a market, because potential entrants find it less attractive to compete or to enter. The greater are the barriers to entry created by the regulation for foreign firms (the fixed compliance costs), the greater will be the profit-enhancing (shifting) effect of the product-regulation measure for the domestic firms or industry, all other things being equal. Thus, regulation can be employed strategically to shift rents.

In general, if product regulations differ across countries, this will segment markets, even if each country applies identical norms to domestic and foreign goods (i.e. the national-treatment rule is satisfied). Prices for similar goods of uniform quality will then not be equal across countries, as the different standards inhibit arbitrage. Thus, non-discriminatory product regulation can have effects on trade – and afford *de facto* protection to a domestic industry.

There are many types of market failures that can justify government intervention in the form of product regulation. In the case of SPS measures, the primary rationales are either imperfect/asymmetric information problems or negative externalities. Consumption externalities may arise as a result of certain types of production processes giving rise to product characteristics that cannot be readily observed by buyers and that may be harmful to animal, plant, or human health and safety, especially in the medium or longer term. To a significant degree, consumer food products are credence goods, especially when it comes to the extent to which non-noticeable factors associated with the production process – e.g. hormone residues – have potential long-term consequences for health.

The negative externality may arise as a result of the consumption of imported foreign products that embody or carry pests or diseases that may harm consumers or have seriously detrimental effects on local production of crops, livestock, or biodiversity assets. In the case of information problems, consumers may not have the means to determine whether producers use inputs that result in harmful substances being embodied in a product that will generate detrimental consequences over time, not just for the consumer directly, but for society more broadly. For example, milk used to be a product that killed thousands in the late nineteenth and early twentieth centuries – product regulation helped to improve quality greatly over time (Olmstead and Rhode, 2009).[2]

The SPS Agreement applies to a limited set of measures that are identified by their purpose. The market-failure case for SPS regulation distinguishes this area from the more general taxation and regulation that is covered by the GATT national-treatment principle. In the case of general taxation and regulation, the objective of intervention often will *not* be to address the types of externalities that (should!) motivate SPS regulation. As extensively analyzed in the literature on trade agreements, although some subset of non-SPS-related domestic taxation and regulation will be aimed at internalization of specific externalities (i.e. addressing market failures), the reason trade agreements include disciplines on the use of domestic taxes and regulation is that these instruments can be used as substitutes for trade barriers to influence the terms of trade. A rationale for the national-treatment rule for domestic taxes and regulation is that it is a necessary condition for tariff commitments to be meaningful.

In the SPS area, the presumption is that government intervention is needed to protect consumers and producers from product characteristics that can be harmful at either the individual or social/industry level. The problem from a trade perspective is that SPS regulation may inadvertently have negative effects on foreign producers or may be deliberately abused for protectionist purposes. Moreover, the standard may not be set at the level appropriate to internalize the local consumption externality.

The negative trade effect of an *efficient* non-discriminatory product regulation – i.e. one that addresses the information problems or consumption externality that give rise to market failure – on foreign producers is not something that should be dealt with through a change in the regulation that is applied, as (by construction – given that the regulation is efficient) that would result in the local externality no longer being fully offset. If the problem is a local consumption externality or market failure and the product regulation deals with that in an efficient manner, the importing country has achieved the first-best solution.

However, if the regulation is not efficient, either because standards are set in a way that increases domestic profits (by reducing foreign competition) by less than the losses incurred by consumers (either directly in pecuniary terms or indirectly in terms of the relevant externalities continuing to persist), or because of imperfect information, foreign interests may help identify a measure that reduces costs of compliance (differential effects) and/or comes closer to dealing with the market failure. In these cases, objective analysis and information is a key input into informed debate and deliberation on the source and magnitude of the market failure, and on whether a specific SPS regulation serves to address the problem in an

---

2 Alan Olmstead and Paul Rhode (2009), 'The battles against animal diseases: science, policy, and the origins of economic regulation in the United States', http://ele.arizona.edu/papers/ELErhode2-6-09.pdf.

effective and efficient manner. This will often be a public good, affected by the classic collective-action constraints identified by Mancur Olson.[3]

In general, given differences in circumstances, social preferences, and risk attitudes across countries, product regulation will need to differ. It is of course in practice very difficult to identify what constitutes an efficient regulation as there is much uncertainty regarding the health effects of specific substances, both *ex ante* and *ex post*. This suggests that international cooperation can be beneficial by increasing information and scrutiny of the effects, efficacy, and equivalence of specific product regulations.[4] The various provisions in the SPS Agreement that call for adoption of international SPS norms where these exist or are developed and the process of notification and discussion in the SPS Committee are important elements of such cooperation that have already been put in place. However, absent agreement that countries will accept products that meet certain minimum standards, the fact that governments are free to adopt idiosyncratic norms will always bring with it differential trade effects, as firms will confront differences in market-specific costs of contesting different foreign markets. Absent a willingness to agree to abide by international norms or to accept mutual recognition (both of which may result in inefficiency at the local level), the challenge confronting WTO members is to ensure that national norms indeed are directed towards dealing with national consumption externalities, while seeking to minimize as much as possible the scope for protectionist abuse of SPS norms.

As we argue below, the SPS Agreement and the way its provisions have been interpreted by the Appellate Body are an effort to address this challenge in a way that gives governments great leeway regarding the substance and thus the level of the market segmenting effects created by specific SPS norms. As a result, the effective disciplines that are imposed through the requirement that SPS measures be justified on the basis of scientific principles (risk assessment, etc.) are in practice rather weak. The implication is that the SPS Agreement does not take the WTO very far towards imposing 'post-discrimination' disciplines on domestic regulation.

2. Continued Suspension

Facts

In the original 1998 *EC–Hormones* case,[5] the European Communities' (EC) import ban on meat and meat products from cattle treated with six

---

3 Mancur Olson (1965), *The Logic of Collective Action: Public Goods and the Theory of Groups*, Cambridge, MA: Harvard University Press.

4 See Robert Howse (2000), 'Democracy, Science and Free Trade: Risk Regulation on Trial at the World Trade Organization', 98 *Michigan Law Review* 2329.

5 Appellate Body Report, *EC – Measures Concerning Meat and Meat Products (EC–Hormones)*, WT/DS26/AB/R, WT/DS48/AB/R, adopted 13 February 1998, DSR 1998:I, 135.

hormones – oestradiol-17β, testosterone, progesterone, trenbolone acetate, zeranol, and MGA – was found to violate Article 5.1 of the SPS Agreement. The Appellate Body (AB) in the 1998 decision found that the EC's scientific studies were not 'sufficiently specific to the case at hand', because they did 'not address the particular kind of risk … at stake – the carcinogenic or genotoxic potential of the residues of those hormones found in meat derived from cattle to which the hormones had been administered for growth promotion purposes'.[6] Therefore, the AB concluded that 'no risk assessment that reasonably support[ed] or warrant[ed] the import prohibition embodied in the Directives was furnished to the Panel'.[7]

Following the adoption of the AB report in the 1998 *EC–Hormones* case, the European Commission funded 17 scientific studies regarding the effects of hormone residues in meat on human health. The EU Scientific Committee on Veterinary Measures relating to Public Health (SCVPH) issued an opinion regarding the human health effects in 1999, which was revised in 2000 and 2002. The EC argued that the 1999, 2000, and 2002 SCVPH opinions, supported by these 17 scientific studies conducted between 1998 and 2001, constituted the risk assessment upon which the ban under Directive 2003/74/EC on meat treated with these hormones was based. Directive 2003/74/EC maintained the *permanent* prohibition on the importation of meat and meat products from animals treated with oestradiol-17β for growth-promotion purposes originally contained in Directive 96/22/EC. In relation to the five other hormones – testosterone, progesterone, trenbolone acetate, zeranol, and MGA – Directive 2003/74/EC imposed the prohibition on a *provisional* basis.[8]

Despite the EC argument that this work (the SCVPH opinions, based on the 17 scientific studies) constituted an appropriate risk assessment upon which its ban was based, Canada and the US continued to suspend concessions in relation to the earlier finding of violation. The EC argued that the measure found to violate WTO law had been removed, requiring the termination of suspension of concessions under Article 22.8 of the Dispute Settlement Understanding by the US and Canada. The EC argued that the continuation of suspension of concessions violated Article 23.1 of the Dispute Settlement Understanding, which requires Members seeking to redress perceived violations of obligations or other nullification or impairment of benefits under the WTO to have recourse to, and abide by, the rules and procedures of the WTO's dispute-settlement mechanism.

The Panel considered that it was required to address the consistency of Directive 2003/74/EC with Articles 5.1 and 5.7 of the Agreement in order to determine whether the US and Canada's continued suspension of concessions

---

6 *EC–Hormones*, para. 200.
7 *EC–Hormones*, para. 208.
8 Appellate Body Report, *US–Continued Suspension*, para. 267.

was or was not in violation of Article 23.1 of the Dispute Settlement Understanding.

Main salient holdings

SPS 5.1

The Panel determined first that Directive 2003/74/EC constituted an SPS measure
under paragraph 1 of Annex A to the SPS Agreement, and in particular, item (b).[9]
This threshold question determines the applicability of the SPS Agreement, as
opposed to the TBT Agreement, or perhaps only the GATT 1994. This determination was not appealed.

The EC appealed the Panel's finding that the permanent EC ban on meat and
meat products from cattle treated with oestradiol-17β for growth-promotion
purposes provided for in Directive 2003/74/EC violates Article 5.1 of the SPS
Agreement.

The EC argued that the Directive was 'based upon' a risk assessment as required
by Article 5.1, which risk assessment was comprised of the 1999, 2000, and 2002
SCVPH opinions (the 'SCVPH Opinions'), which in turn were based on the 17
studies mentioned above.

The AB began its analysis under Article 5.1 by explaining the disciplines
imposed by the SPS Agreement in this context:

> The *SPS Agreement* recognizes the right of WTO Members to take measures
> necessary to protect human, animal or plant life or health. The right to take a
> protective measure must be exercised consistently with a series of obligations that
> are set forth in that Agreement, and that seek to ensure that such measures are
> properly justified.[10]

As explained in more detail below, the obligations set forth in the SPS Agreement
seem intended to go beyond those of non-discrimination set forth in the GATT.
The AB noted that Member States are free to set their 'appropriate level of
protection' to be effected through their SPS measures. While the Codex
Alimentarius Commission – the relevant international standards-setting body, a
joint office of the Food and Agricultural Organization (FAO) and the World
Health Organization (WHO) – has adopted an international standard for oestra-
diol-17β, based on evaluations carried out by the Joint FAO/WHO Expert
Committee on Food Additives (JECFA), the EC had decided on a higher level of
protection, involving zero avoidable risk.[11] It was in order to achieve this higher
level of protection that the EC adopted Directive 2003/74/EC.

The AB cited the original *EC–Hormones* decision for the proposition that
Article 5.1 is a 'specific application of the basic obligations contained in Article 2.2

---

9 Panel Report, *US–Continued Suspension*, para. 7.434.
10 Appellate Body Report, *US–Continued Suspension*, para. 522.
11 Panel Report, *US–Continued Suspension*, para. 7.607.

of the *SPS Agreement*'. Article 5.1 must constantly be read together with Article 2.2. Article 2.2 provides as follows:

> Members shall ensure that any sanitary or phytosanitary measure is applied only to the extent necessary to protect human, animal or plant life or health, is based on scientific principles and is not maintained without sufficient scientific evidence, except as provided for in paragraph 7 of Article 5.

The risk assessment called for by Article 5.1 is a process by which to establish the scientific basis for the relevant SPS measure. When Article 5.1 requires that SPS measures be 'based on' the relevant risk assessment, it means that there must be a rational relationship between the SPS measure and the risk assessment.[12]

The Panel applied a four-prong test for determining whether the SCVPH Opinions constituted a valid risk assessment under Article 5.1: (i) whether the SCVPH Opinions took into account risk-assessment techniques of the relevant international organizations; (ii) whether they took into account the factors listed in Article 5.2, including available scientific evidence; (iii) whether they satisfied the definition of 'risk assessment' contained in Annex A, paragraph 4, of the SPS Agreement, including evaluation of the likelihood and consequences of entry of a product; and (iv) whether the conclusions of the SCVPH Opinions are supported by the scientific evidence evaluated.

The US had alleged that the SCVPH Opinions had failed to take into account available scientific evidence, and relevant inspection, sampling, and testing methods, as required under Article 5.2. However, the Panel found that the SCVPH Opinions had specifically taken into account the scientific evidence cited by the US, and that the EC had taken into account all relevant inspection, sampling, and testing methods.[13]

The Panel found that the EC had 'not satisfied the requirements of the definition of a risk assessment contained in Annex A(4) because it ha[d] not evaluated specifically the possibility that these adverse effects come into being, originate, or result from the consumption of meat or meat products which contain veterinary residues of oestradiol-17β as a result of the cattle being treated with the hormone for growth promotion purposes'.[14] Although the EC had shown the general association between excess hormones and neurobiological, developmental, reproductive, and immunological effects, as well as immunotoxicity, genotoxicity, and

---

12 Appellate Body Report, *US–Continued Suspension*, para. 528, citing Appellate Body Report, *EC–Hormones*, para. 193.

13 Panel Report, *US–Continued Suspension*, paras. 7.483 and 7.484.

14 Paragraph 4 of Annex A of the SPS Agreement provides as follows: 4. *Risk assessment* – 'The evaluation of the likelihood of entry, establishment or spread of a pest or disease within the territory of an importing Member according to the sanitary or phytosanitary measures which might be applied, and of the associated potential biological and economic consequences; or the evaluation of the potential for adverse effects on human or animal health arising from the presence of additives, contaminants, toxins or disease-causing organisms in food, beverages or feedstuffs.'

carcinogenicity, it failed to show the specific association between these particular residues and these adverse effects.[15] The AB agreed with the Panel:

> The definition of a risk assessment in paragraph 4 of Annex A, as interpreted by the Appellate Body, required the European Communities to conduct a risk assessment that addresses the specific risk at issue. The particular risk being evaluated by the European Communities in this case was the potential for neurobiological, developmental, reproductive, and immunological effects, as well as immunotoxic, genotoxic and carcinogenic effects from the residues of oestradiol-17β found in meat derived from cattle to which this hormone was administered for growth-promoting purposes. Although the European Communities is correct in arguing that it was not required to demonstrate that these adverse health effects would actually arise, it was nevertheless required to demonstrate that these adverse effects could arise from the presence of residues of oestradiol-17β in meat from treated cattle.[16]

Of course, all scientific work involves extrapolation. For example, a scientific risk assessment might extrapolate from the risks of a particular formulation or application of oestradiol-17β to the risks of a slightly varying formulation or application. So, when the AB calls for a more specific risk assessment, even though it does not require that the contribution to risk be isolated, it is making a judgment regarding the permissible extent of extrapolation. It is interpreting the SPS Agreement to require *some* relevant scientific basis, rather than a relatively broad extrapolation.

The Panel also went on to find that the EC had failed to satisfy the fourth requirement of the definition of risk assessment: the requirement that the scientific evidence support the conclusions. Here, importantly for the subsequent analysis in this paper, the Panel found that the scientific evidence referred to in the SCVPH Opinions did not support the conclusion that the genotoxicity of oestradiol-17β had been demonstrated and that residues of oestradiol-17β in meat lead to increased risk of cancer or adverse immunological and developmental effects.[17]

At the core of the EC appeal was the argument that the Panel had substituted its own judgment for that of the relevant WTO member.[18] The AB clarified that 'the review power of a panel is not to determine whether the risk assessment undertaken by a WTO Member is correct, but rather to determine whether that risk assessment is supported by coherent reasoning and respectable scientific evidence and is, in this sense, objectively justifiable'.[19] That is, the disciplines that are imposed are more of a procedural nature. This approach is comparable to the AB's approach to objective indicia of intent in *Japan–Alcoholic Beverages*, discussed below.

---

15 Panel Report, *US–Continued Suspension*, para. 7.537.
16 Appellate Body Report, *US–Continued Suspension*, para. 559 (citation omitted).
17 Panel Report, *US–Continued Suspension*, para. 7.572.
18 European Communities' Appellant's Submission, para. 248.
19 Appellate Body Report, *US–Continued Suspension*, para. 590.

A panel must also determine whether the results of the risk assessment 'sufficiently warrant' the SPS measure.[20] In first looking at expert opinion, and then examining whether the EC risk assessment agreed with this opinion, the Panel gave too little deference to the member's retained autonomy to engage in its own risk assessments.[21] Therefore, the AB determined that 'the Panel failed to conduct an objective assessment of the facts of the case, as required by Article 11 of the DSU, in determining whether the European Communities' risk assessment satisfied the requirements of Article 5.1 and Annex A of the SPS Agreement.'[22]

Accordingly, the AB reversed the Panel's finding that the EC failed to satisfy the requirements of Article 5.1 and Annex A, paragraph 4, of the *SPS Agreement*. The AB declined to complete the analysis, in light of the 'numerous flaws' in the Panel's analysis.[23]

The AB also reversed the Panel's exclusion from consideration of the risks of abuse or misuse of hormones.[24] Although the Panel found that it need not consider risks of abuse or misuse where there was no evidence of a specific link between use of oestradiol-17β in meat and the adverse effects cited, the AB found some evidence in the record that abuse or misuse could be relevant to the determination of this specific link.[25]

SPS Article 5.7
Where there is sufficient scientific evidence, Article 5.1 must be satisfied. Where there is not, Article 5.7 provides that:

> In cases where relevant scientific evidence is insufficient, a Member may provisionally adopt sanitary or phytosanitary measures on the basis of available pertinent information, including that from the relevant international organizations as well as from sanitary or phytosanitary measures applied by other Members. In such circumstances, Members shall seek to obtain the additional information necessary for a more objective assessment of risk and review the sanitary or phytosanitary measure accordingly within a reasonable period of time.

There is thus a continuum of application of Articles 5.1 and 5.7, determining the alternative necessary to be met in connection with SPS measures.[26] The application of Article 5.1 or 5.7 is based on the determination of whether there is sufficient evidence necessary to support a risk assessment under Article 5.1.[27]

The EC argued before the Panel that the SCVPH Opinions and supporting studies provided the 'available pertinent information' within the meaning of

20 Ibid., para. 591.
21 Ibid., paras. 598–602.
22 Ibid., para. 616.
23 Ibid., para. 620.
24 Ibid., para. 545.
25 Ibid., paras. 547–555.
26 Ibid., para. 674.
27 Ibid., para. 702, citing Appellate Body Report, *Japan–Apples*, para. 179.

Article 5.7 on the basis of which the provisional ban on the five hormones had been enacted.[28] The Panel found that the EC's provisional ban under Directive 2003/74/EC failed to comply with Article 5.7 of the SPS Agreement because the relevant scientific evidence was not insufficient within the meaning of that provision.[29]

The AB disagreed with the Panel's finding that 'the determination of whether scientific evidence is sufficient to assess the existence and magnitude of a risk must be disconnected from the intended level of protection'. The fact that there was patently sufficient scientific evidence for the establishment of an international standard is not determinative. Rather, 'the fact that the WTO Member has chosen to set a higher level of protection may require it to perform certain research as part of its risk assessment that is different from the parameters considered and the research carried out in the risk assessment underlying the international standard'.[30]

One question that arose in this case has to do with the dynamic nature of science, by virtue of which a body of evidence deemed sufficient at a particular moment to support an international standard might later become insufficient. Here, the AB rejected the Panel's finding that, where international standards exist, 'there must be a *critical mass* of new evidence and/or information that calls into question the fundamental precepts of previous knowledge and evidence so as to make relevant, previously sufficient, evidence now insufficient' within the meaning of Article 5.7.[31] Rather, 'it suffices that new scientific developments call into question whether the body of scientific evidence still permits of a sufficiently objective assessment of risk'.[32]

In light of the above, the AB reversed the Panel's finding that 'it has not been demonstrated that relevant scientific evidence was insufficient, within the meaning of Article 5.7 of the *SPS Agreement*, in relation to any of the five hormones with respect to which the European Communities applies a provisional ban'.[33] It did not consider it possible to complete the analysis.

3. WTO Discipline of Domestic Regulation: Comparing the GATT III/XX Complex to the SPS 2.2/5.1/5.7 Complex

One of the most contentious issues in WTO law is the discipline applied to domestic prudential regulation.[34] This discipline was substantially changed, and is

28 Panel Report, *US–Continued Suspension*, para. 7.581. The five hormones were progesterone, testosterone, zeranol, trenbolone acetate, and MGA.
29 Appellate Body Report, *US–Continued Suspension*, para. 621.
30 Ibid., paras. 685–688.
31 Ibid., para. 712, quoting Panel Report, *US–Continued Suspension*, para. 7.648.
32 Ibid., para. 725.
33 Ibid., para. 734, quoting Panel Report, *US–Continued Suspension*, para. 7.835.
34 By 'prudential regulation', we mean regulation whose primary purpose is consumer protection, environmental protection, or other broad societal protection, but not regulation designed to engage in economic management, such as subsidies, protection from imports, monetary policy, etc.

commonly understood to have been substantially extended in 1995 with the advent of the SPS Agreement and the revised TBT Agreement. Hudec described the change as a move from the pre-1995 test for discrimination to a 'post-discriminatory'[35] discipline on domestic regulation as follows:

> Traditionally, trade agreements have focused on limiting or eliminating discrimination against foreign trade by disciplining governmental measures that impose competitive disadvantages on foreign goods vis-à-vis domestic goods with which they compete. In the recent Uruguay Round trade agreements, however, it appears that the draftsmen of two key agreements added another goal, one that can be described as the prevention of unjustified regulation per se, whether or not such a regulation creates a competitive disadvantage for foreign goods vis-à-vis domestic goods. Thus, for example, a food safety measure that is not based on scientific principles would be a violation of Article 2 of the Agreement on the Application of [SPS] Measures, whether or not it discriminates against foreign goods. While other rules of the SPS Agreement are directed at traditional trade agreement concerns about discrimination, it is clear that violations of provisions like Article 2 do not require findings of discrimination.[36]

However, we argue below that the distinction between discrimination analysis and 'rationality' analysis is not as great as it might at first appear. Hudec suggested this as well:

> The place to start is to recognize that the word 'discrimination' that we use in all these cases is a normative term expressing a judgment of disapproval. When we see a regulation that has the effect of putting foreign goods at a competitive disadvantage, the neutral descriptive term for that situation is that the regulation has a 'differential impact.' If we think there is nothing wrong with that differential impact, we continue to call it a differential impact. If we think there is something wrong about the differential impact, then we call it discrimination.

Thus, differential impact that has adequate rational justification in terms of achieving a regulatory objective is not understood as discrimination. But this leaves open the question of whether treatment that does not result in differential impact, but that lacks adequate rational justification, is acceptable or not. Does WTO law impose a 'free-standing' requirement of rationality in regulation, regardless of whether there are differential impacts? The *Continued Suspension* case does not present this specific question, because it is widely assumed that the European limits on hormones have a differential impact on Canadian and US producers. But this differential impact was not a formally salient feature of the argument.

A close analysis of the way in which the AB has applied SPS Articles 2.2., 5.1, and 5.7 (the 'SPS 2.2/5.1/5.7 Complex'), and a comparison with the way the AB

---

35 See Robert E. Hudec (2003), 'Science and post-discriminatory WTO law', 26:2 *Boston College International and Comparative Law Review* 185.

36 Ibid. at 187.

has applied GATT Articles III, XI, and XX (the 'GATT Article III/XX Complex'), helps illuminate the types of cases that might be covered by the SPS Agreement that are not covered by the GATT. Interestingly, from the standpoint of this relationship, a measure that complies with the SPS Agreement, including the SPS 2.2/5.1/ 5.7 Complex, is presumed under SPS Article 2.4 'to be in accordance with the obligations of the Members under the provisions of GATT 1994 which relate to the use of sanitary or phytosanitary measures, in particular the provisions of Article XX(b)'.

Therefore, a measure that complies with the SPS Agreement is presumed not to illegally discriminate under Article III of GATT. Of course, SPS Articles 2.3 and 5.5 contain their own antidiscrimination prohibitions, making it seem ordinarily unnecessary as a matter of judicial economy to test a measure for discrimination under Article III where it complies with the SPS Agreement. While these antidiscrimination prohibitions have different formulations, the differences are unlikely to produce different outcomes. Furthermore, SPS Article 2.4 only sets up a presumption, which we may assume is rebuttable. But we still have the question, what is prohibited by the SPS 2.2/5.1/5.7 Complex that is not already prohibited by the national-treatment provisions of either the SPS Agreement or GATT?

The remainder of this section analyzes the substantive components and effects of the additional disciplines on domestic regulation in the SPS 2.2/5.1/5.7 Complex, beyond the disciplines that result from the GATT III/XX Complex. In Section 4, we discuss public policy and economic dimensions of the additional disciplines.

National Treatment Jurisprudence: The GATT III/XX Complex

Before the inception of the WTO in 1995, the only multilateral trade discipline on domestic product regulation was provided by Articles III and XI of GATT. Article III requires national treatment, and Article XI applies, where Article III does not apply, to prohibit quantitative restrictions on imports (and exports). We will not discuss Article XI in further detail. Article XX provides a range of exceptions for measures that may otherwise violate Article III. Let us begin with the text of Articles III:1 and 4 of the GATT, which provide:

> 1. The contracting parties recognize that internal taxes and other internal charges, and laws, regulations and requirements affecting the *internal* sale, offering for sale, purchase, transportation, distribution or use of products, and internal quantitative regulations requiring the mixture, processing or use of products in specified amounts or proportions, should not be applied to imported or domestic products so as to afford protection to domestic production. [emphasis added]
> 4. The products of the territory of any contracting party imported into the territory of any other contracting party shall be accorded treatment no less favourable than that accorded to like products of national origin in respect of all laws, regulations and requirements affecting their internal sale, offering for sale, purchase, transportation, distribution or use.

This language has been interpreted in several GATT and WTO cases. In its first report, *Japan–Alcoholic Beverages*, the AB declared that the broad purpose of Article III is to prohibit 'protectionism',[37] a concept that it did not define. It also rejected Hudec's 'aims-and-effects' approach to the obligation of national treatment, at least as a search for subjective intent.[38] It refused to see any issue of the subjective intent of the member state in Article III determination:

> [I]t does not matter that there may not have been any desire to engage in protectionism in the minds of the legislators or the regulators who imposed the measure. It is irrelevant that protectionism was not an intended objective if the particular tax measure in question is nevertheless, to echo Article III:1, applied to imported or domestic products so as to afford protection to domestic production.[39]

The AB stated that 'it is possible to examine objectively the underlying criteria used in a particular tax measure, its structure, and its overall application, to ascertain whether it is applied in a way that affords protection to domestic products'[40] (emphasis added). As noted above, this search for the underlying structure is comparable to the search for a scientific basis under the SPS Agreement. The *EC–Asbestos* AB Report reiterated that the text of Article III:4 reflected the general principle of paragraph 1 of Article III in seeking 'to prevent Members from applying internal taxes and regulations in a manner which affects the competitive relationship, in the marketplace, *between the domestic and imported products involved*, "so as to afford protection to domestic production"'.[41]

---

37 'The broad and fundamental purpose of Article III is to avoid protectionism in the application of internal tax and regulatory measures. More specifically, the purpose of Article III "is to ensure that internal measures not be applied to imported and domestic products so as to afford protection to domestic production". Toward this end, Article III obliges Members of the WTO to provide equality of competitive conditions for imported products in relation to domestic products ... Article III protects expectations not of any particular trade volume but rather of the equal competitive relationship between imported and domestic products ....' *Japan – Taxes on Alcoholic Beverages (Japan–Alcoholic Beverages II)*, WT/DS8/AB/R, WT/DS10/AB/R, WT/DS11/AB/R, adopted 1 November 1996, at p. 16.

38 See Appellate Body Report, *Japan–Alcoholic Beverages II*, at p. 27: 'This third inquiry under Article III:2, second sentence, must determine whether "directly competitive or substitutable products" are "not similarly taxed" in a way that affords protection. This is not an issue of intent. It is not necessary for a Panel to sort through the many reasons legislators and regulators often have for what they do and weigh the relative significance of those reasons to establish legislative or regulatory intent'; and at p. 29: 'Although it is true that the aim of a measure may not be easily ascertained, nevertheless its protective application can most often be discerned from the design, the architecture, and the revealing structure of a measure.' See Robert E. Hudec (1998), 'GATT/WTO Constraints on National Regulation: Requiem for an Aims and Effects Test', 32 *International Lawyer* 619. See also Amelia Porges and Joel P. Trachtman (2003), 'Robert Hudec and Domestic Regulation: The Resurrection of "Aim and Effects"', 37 *Journal of World Trade* (commissioned paper).

39 Appellate Body Report, *Japan–Alcoholic Beverages II*, at p. 28.

40 Ibid., at p. 29.

41 Appellate Body Report, *European Communities – Measures Affecting Asbestos and Asbestos-Containing Products (EC–Asbestos)*, WT/DS135/AB/R, adopted 5 April 2001, at para. 98.

For a violation of Article III:4 to be established, the complaining Member must prove that the measure at issue is a 'law, regulation, or requirement affecting their internal sale, offering for sale, purchase, transportation, distribution, or use'; that the imported and domestic products at issue are 'like products'; and that the imported products are accorded 'less favorable' treatment than that accorded to like domestic products.[42]

Imported and domestic like products

The prohibition against discrimination in the national-treatment obligation can apply only when imported and domestic products are 'like'. The majority of the AB in *EC–Asbestos* found that 'likeness' under Article III:4 is, 'fundamentally, a determination about the nature and extent of a competitive relationship between and among products'.[43] To perform such an assessment, the AB recalled that four basic criteria, derived from the *Border Tax Adjustment* report – (i) the physical properties of the products in question; (ii) their end-uses; (iii) consumer tastes and habits *vis-à-vis* those products; and (iv) tariff classification[44] – are to be used as tools in the determination of this competitive relationship between products. These criteria do not exhaust inquiry.[45]

The competitive relationship between imports and domestic goods is the determinant of likeness. 'If there is – or could be – no competitive relationship between products, a Member cannot intervene, through internal taxation or regulation, to protect domestic production.'[46] This competitive relationship is to be determined using the basic criteria of the *Border Tax Adjustments* report. The balancing of the criteria identified in the *Border Tax Adjustments* report is intended to approximate the competitive relationship between the relevant goods. A more precise and refined, and quantitative, measure of whether a competitive relationship exists is the economic concept of cross-elasticity of demand.[47] Roughly speaking, this measures the extent to which a rise in the price of one good induces a shift in demand by

---

42 Appellate Body Report, *Korea – Measures Affecting Imports of Fresh, Chilled and Frozen Beef* (*Korea–Various Measures on Beef*), WT/DS161/AB/R and WT/DS169/AB/R, adopted 10 January 2001, at para. 133.

43 Appellate Body Report, *EC–Asbestos*, at para. 99. Note the different opinion with regard to the very specific aspects mentioned in para. 154. See the analysis of the *Asbestos* report in Henrik Horn and J.H.H. Weiler (2003), '*European Communities – Measures Affecting Asbestos and Asbestos-Containing Products*', in Henrik Horn and Petros C. Mavroidis (eds.), *The WTO Case Law of 2001: The American Law Institute Reporters' Studies*, Cambridge: Cambridge University Press.

44 Working Party Report, Border Tax Adjustments, adopted 2 December 1970, BISD 18S/97.

45 Appellate Body Report, *EC–Asbestos*, at para. 101.

46 Ibid., at para. 117.

47 See, for instance, the criteria of cross-elasticity of demand to determine whether imported and domestic products are directly competitive or substitutable in the Appellate Body Report in *Japan–Alcoholic Beverages II*, at p. 26, or in Appellate Body Report, *Korea – Taxes on Alcoholic Beverages* (*Korea–Alcoholic Beverages*), WT/DS75/AB/R, WT/DS84/AB/R, adopted 17 February 1999, at paras. 108–124, or in the Appellate Body Report, *United States – Transitional Safeguard Measure on Combed Cotton Yarn from Pakistan* (*US–Cotton Yarn*), WT/DS192/AB/R, adopted 5 November 2001, paras. 89–102.

consumers to the other good being tested. Although not as accurate or refined as using the cross elasticity of demand to determine a competitive relationship, the qualitative *Border Tax Adjustment* factors may be used to assess a competitive relationship between products.

The *Border Tax Adjustment* test, emphasizing competitive relationships as specified by the AB in *Asbestos*, is relatively ignorant of factors that motivate regulation. An alternative approach to like products would examine the rationality of the domestic regulatory distinction that results in differential regulatory treatment – determining whether to respect the rationality of the national regulatory categories and thus to accept that the products are not 'like'. This search for the rationality of the domestic regulation, if effected, would be comparable to the search for a scientific basis in the SPS Agreement.

The economic theory of regulation suggests that regulation is necessary precisely where consumers cannot adequately distinguish relevant goods – where, but for the regulation, they would be in close competitive relation. Thus, a competitive relationship test for likeness could often result in a finding that goods that differ by the parameter addressed by regulation are indeed like, and should be treated the same.[48] Hence, many domestic regulations would prima facie violate Article III – as like products would be treated differently, they would need the justification of Article XX to be WTO-compatible. This is why the AB's two-step analysis, used first in *Korea–Various Measures on Beef*[49] and described more precisely in paragraph 100 of the *EC–Asbestos* decision, discussed hereafter, is important. Note that it is important in order to ensure that rational regulation with differential impact does not violate Article III.

Less favorable treatment
The less-favorable-treatment criterion involves an 'effects test'. In *Korea–Various Measures on Beef*, the AB reversed the Panel, which had concluded that a regulatory distinction based exclusively on the origin of the product necessarily violated Article III. The AB emphasized the fact that 'differential treatment' may be acceptable, so long as it is 'no less favorable'. Article III only prohibits discriminatory treatment, which 'modifies the conditions of competition in the relevant market to the detriment of imported products'.[50]

Is this 'modification of the conditions of competition to the detriment of imported products' the benchmark to assess the existence of 'protectionism' condemned by Article III? In *EC–Asbestos*, the AB reiterated that the 'broad and fundamental purpose' of the obligation of national treatment (Article III GATT) is 'to avoid' the application of 'protectionist' internal measures; this determination is based on whether such internal measures are applied in a manner that affects the

---

48 Moreover, if it is true that consumers would not consider them interchangeable, then some may say that the regulation was not necessary.
49 Appellate Body Report, *Korea–Various Measures on Beef*, at paras. 133–149.
50 Ibid., at para. 137.

competitive relationship, in the marketplace, between the domestic and imported products involved, 'so as to afford protection to like domestic production'.[51] This decision established a two-step analysis, wherein the first step requires a determination whether like products are treated differently, and the second step determines whether this differential treatment amounts to 'less favorable treatment'.

In paragraph 100 of its opinion in *EC–Asbestos*, the AB made the following statement:

> A complaining Member must still establish that the measure accords to the group of 'like' imported products 'less favourable treatment' than it accords to the group of 'like' domestic products. The term 'less favourable treatment' expresses the general principle, in Article III:1, that internal regulations 'should not be applied ... so as to afford protection to domestic production.'[52]

And as the AB had stated in *Korea–Various Measures on Beef*, 'a formal difference in treatment between imported and like domestic products is thus neither necessary, nor sufficient, to show a violation of Article III:4'. Whether or not imported products are treated less favorably than like domestic products should be assessed instead by examining whether a measure modifies the conditions of competition in the relevant market to the detriment of imported products as a class. Thus, it is not enough to find a single foreign like product that is treated differently from a single domestic like product. Rather, the class of foreign like products must be treated less favorably than the class of domestic like products. In order for this to occur, it would seem necessary that the differential regulatory treatment be predicated, either intentionally or unintentionally, on the foreign character of the product. However, in *Korea–Various Measures on Beef*, the AB made clear that differential treatment based on nationality, alone, would not necessarily amount to 'less favorable' treatment.[53] Thus, a violation would only occur if after respecting the legitimate (non-national origin) categories, the measure is still found to treat the import less favorably.

As the AB applies this principle in future cases, we may be able to determine whether a regulation allowing for distinctions (different treatment) based on non-protectionist prudential goals and considerations is captured by the less-favorable-treatment provision and therefore condemned by the application of Article III just because it affects negatively market opportunities for imports. It may be that the less-favorable-treatment criterion only condemns protectionist or other

---

51 Appellate Body Report, *EC–Asbestos*, at paras. 96 and 98: 'in endeavoring to ensure "equality of competitive conditions", the "general principle" in Article III seeks to prevent Members from applying internal taxes and regulations in a manner which affects the competitive relationship, in the marketplace, between the domestic and imported products involved, "so as to afford protection to domestic production"'.

52 Ibid., at para. 100.

53 Appellate Body Report, *Korea–Various Measures on Beef*, at para. 134.

illegitimate regulatory distinctions. If so, then Article III would include a search for legitimate regulatory rationales comparable to the search for a scientific basis under the SPS Agreement; the gap between discrimination and post-discrimination would be narrow. It is worth noting that a similar consideration motivated the aims-and-effects test.[54] It is also possible that 'less favorable treatment' could be interpreted broadly so as to include any market distortion favoring domestic products, even if the goal, object, and purpose of the measure are not protectionist. In such case, reliance on Article XX to justify such measure would remain possible.

Since *Japan–Alcohol*, the AB has purported to reject inquiry into the subjective intent of governments. However, it allowed in that case that intent might be discerned from the objective structure of a regulatory measure. Discussing the *Reformulated Gasoline* decision, Hudec noted that where tribunals are concerned with the intent of regulators, they do not examine subjective intent:

> The standard way of deciding such purpose questions in GATT law, US Constitutional law, and European Community law is by reference to what I usually refer to as 'objective indicators.' The objective indicators, when applied, look a great deal like second-guessing the judgments of governments. In general, one looks to whether the measure was really necessary to obtain the declared goal. For example, one examines whether less restrictive alternatives were available and not used, or whether the decision in areas affecting foreign goods is in fact consistent with the kinds of decisions that are taken in analogous areas which affect sellers of domestic goods.[55]

We suggest below that the scientific-evidence test of the SPS Agreement may be understood in just these terms: as an objective indicator of protectionist intent. This is just a possible characterization, but it is especially appealing assuming that the scientific-evidence test is not a free-standing rationality requirement, independent of trade effects – that is, assuming that the inquiry is not just into aim, but also into effects. Even if the scientific-evidence test is doctrinally a free-standing rationality requirement, once we consider the remedies available for violation, we might see that trade effects are considered.

To conclude this discussion, we may say that an Article III:4 case is comprised of the following elements: (i) a product comparison to determine whether the imported goods are 'like' a domestically produced good, (ii) a treatment comparison to determine whether the imported goods are treated 'less favorably', and (iii) a potential exercise of discretion to determine whether the less favorable treatment is of the requisite type. What could be involved in the last determination? Assuming that the first examination of 'less favorable treatment' considers the effects of the domestic measure under consideration, there is only one

---

54 See Hudec, supra note 35; and Frieder Roessler (1996), 'Diverging Domestic Policies and Multilateral Trade Integration', in Robert E. Hudec and Jagdish Bhagwati (eds.), *Fair Trade and Harmonization, Pre-requisite for Free-Trade*, Vol. II, Cambridge, MA: MIT Press.
55 Hudec, supra note 35, at 193.

other area for consideration: the legitimacy of the aim of the domestic measure. Again, this is the same consideration as that included in the 'post-discriminatory' SPS Agreement.

Article XX Necessity
Assuming that a violation of Article III:4 is found, this does not necessarily mean that the subject measure will constitute a violation of GATT. Rather, measures may be eligible for an exception under Article XX. We will examine Article XX(b), as it relates closely to the SPS context. In particular, we may see in Article XX(b) a type of rationality analysis that presages and parallels the scientific-basis requirements of the SPS 2.2/5.1/5/7 Complex.

Since its inception, GATT has always recognized that prudential government policies may justify measures contrary to basic GATT market-access rules. Traditionally in GATT, the exceptional provisions of Article XX(b) and (d) are available to justify measures – otherwise incompatible with other GATT provisions – if they are 'necessary.' This has been interpreted to require that the country invoking these exceptions demonstrate that no other WTO-compatible or less-restrictive alternative was reasonably available to pursue the desired policy goal.[56]

The Article XX necessity test was addressed in *Korea–Various Measures on Beef*, where Korea attempted to justify its dual retail system for beef by arguing the need for compliance with a domestic regulation against fraud. The AB interpreted the necessity test of Article XX(d) to imply a requirement for balancing among at least three variables:

> In sum, determination of whether a measure, which is not 'indispensable', may nevertheless be 'necessary' within the contemplation of Article XX(d), involves in every case a process of weighing and balancing a series of factors which prominently include the contribution made by the compliance measure to the enforcement of the law or regulation at issue, the importance of the common interests or values protected by that law or regulation, and the accompanying impact of the law or regulation on imports or exports.[57]

After reiterating that WTO Members have the right to determine for themselves the level of enforcement of their domestic laws[58] (a concept close to the 'appropriate level of protection' referred to in the SPS Agreement), the AB called for an authentic balancing and weighing of (at least) these variables: 'The more vital or important those common interests or values are, the easier it would be to accept as

---

56 See GATT Panel Report, *United States – Section 337 of the Tariff Act of 1930 (US–Section 337)*, adopted 7 November 1989, BISD 36S/345, at para. 5.26; GATT Panel Report, *United States – Measures Affecting Alcoholic and Malt Beverages (US–Malt Beverages)*, adopted 19 June 1992, BISD 39S/206), at para. 5.52; and GATT Panel Report, *Thailand – Restrictions on Importation of and Internal Taxes on Cigarettes (Thailand–Cigarettes)*, adopted 7 November 1990, BISD 37S/200, at para. 223.
57 Appellate Body Report, *Korea–Various Measures on Beef*, at para. 164.
58 Ibid., at para. 177.

"necessary" a measure designed as an enforcement instrument';[59] 'The greater the contribution [to the realization of the end pursued], the more easily a measure might be considered to be "necessary"';[60] or: 'A measure with a relatively slight impact upon imported products might more easily be considered as "necessary" than a measure with intense or broader restrictive effects.'[61] Note the relationship between these variables and the requirement for a scientific basis under the SPS 2.2/5.1/5.7 Complex.

It is not clear how these variables affect each other, nor is it clear how their balancing would affect the final determination that a measure qualifies under Article XX and how this new test relates to the traditional 'least trade restrictive alternative reasonably available' test. Yet in *EC–Asbestos*, the AB tried to reconcile its new balancing test with the traditional least-trade-restrictive-alternative test. For the AB, the balancing referred to in *Korea–Various Measures on Beef* is part of the determination of whether a WTO-compatible or less-trade-restrictive alternative exists to obtain the end pursued (as called for by the traditional necessity test of Article XX(b)).[62] In light of France's chosen level of protection, and noting that the protection of human life is vital and important to the highest degree,[63] the *EC–Asbestos* AB report concluded that '[t]he remaining question, then, is whether there is an alternative measure that would achieve the same end and that is less restrictive of trade than a prohibition'.[64]

In *Korea–Various Measures on Beef* the possibility of an unreasonable or inauthentic policy goal was raised:

> The application of such [different] measures for the control of the same illegal behaviour for like, or at least similar, products raises doubts with respect to the *objective necessity* of a different, much stricter, and WTO-inconsistent enforcement measure.[65]

This search for reasonableness or authenticity has a direct parallel in the SPS 2.2/5.1/5.7 Complex, as well as in Article 5.5 of the SPS Agreement.

59 Ibid., at para. 162.
60 Ibid., at para. 163.
61 Ibid.
62 Appellate Body Report, *EC–Asbestos*, at para. 172: 'We indicated in *Korea–Beef* that one aspect of the "weighing and balancing process ... comprehended in the determination of whether a WTO-consistent alternative measure" is reasonably available is the extent to which the alternative measure "contributes to the realization of the end pursued". In addition, we observed, in that case, that "[t]he more vital or important [the] common interests or values" pursued, the easier it would be to accept as "necessary" measures designed to achieve those ends. In this case, the objective pursued by the measure is the preservation of human life and health through the elimination, or reduction, of the well-known, and life-threatening, health risks posed by asbestos fibres. The value pursued is both vital and important in the highest degree. The remaining question, then, is whether there is an alternative measure that would achieve the same end and that is less restrictive of trade than a prohibition.'
63 Ibid.
64 Ibid.
65 Appellate Body Report, *Korea–Various Measures on Beef*, at para. 172.

In *Brazil–Tyres*, it was seen that this type of balancing test may be very demanding to apply in technical terms, and that panels may avoid carrying out these tests as described.[66] In fact, these tests may require the panel to second-guess some of the public-policy evaluations that governments often carry out in order to determine their measures. This type of second-guessing is precisely the type of judicial exercise that has been rejected under the scientific-basis provisions of the SPS Agreement. Indeed, the AB decision in the *Continued Suspension* case may be understood along parallel lines as an interpretation of the SPS Agreement that limits the scope of judicial scrutiny of national use of science as a basis for public policy.

Post-discrimination rules and jurisprudence

We have already discussed the main relevant features of the SPS Agreement, as applied in the *Continued Suspension* case. The SPS Agreement should be understood, to some extent, as a conversion of Article XX of GATT from a defense applicable only after a primary violation is established to a positive obligation, and an expansion of its disciplines. Its drafters were concerned with the need to (1) expand the scientific and procedural requirements for a Member to impose an SPS measure and (2) encourage reliance on and participation in international standard-setting bodies. Yet the obligations of the SPS Agreement stand alone, and the Panel in *EC–Hormones* stated that since the SPS Agreement adds to Articles III, XI, and XX of GATT, there is no obligation to prove a violation of Articles III or XI before the SPS Agreement can be invoked.[67] The SPS obligations are *additional* to the GATT obligations, except to the extent that they may be doctrinally coterminous with or included in the GATT obligations.

In all cases where a standard other than an international standard is used, the Member imposing an SPS measure must be able to rely on a relevant risk assessment pursuant to Article 5.1 to 5.4 of the SPS Agreement, unless there is insufficient

---

66 Chad Bown and Joel P. Trachtman (2009), '*Brazil – Measures Affecting Imports of Retreaded Tyres*: A Balancing Act', 8 (Special Issue 1) *World Trade Review* 85.

67 In *EC–Hormones* (US), the European Communities submitted that 'the "substantive" provisions of the SPS Agreement can only be addressed if recourse is made to GATT Article XX(b), i.e., if, and only if, a violation of another provision of GATT is first established'. The Panels rejected this argument, indicating as follows: 'The SPS Agreement contains, in particular, no explicit requirement of a prior violation of a provision of GATT which would govern the applicability of the SPS Agreement, as asserted by the European Communities' (para. 8.36). The Panels added: 'on this basis alone we cannot conclude that the SPS Agreement only applies, as Article XX(b) of GATT does, if, and only if, a prior violation of a GATT provision has been established. Many provisions of the SPS Agreement impose "substantive" obligations which go significantly beyond and are additional to the requirements for invocation of Article XX(b). These obligations are, *inter alia*, imposed to "further the use of harmonized sanitary and phytosanitary measures between Members" and to "improve the human health, animal health and phytosanitary situation in all Members". They are not imposed, as is the case of the obligations imposed by Article XX(b) of GATT, to justify a violation of another GATT obligation (such as a violation of the non-discrimination obligations of Articles I or III)' (para. 8.38). Panel Report, *EC Measures Concerning Meat and Meat Products (Hormones)* – Complaint by the United States (*EC–Hormones* (US)) WT/DS26/R/USA, adopted 13 February 1998 as modified by the Appellate Body Report, WT/DS26/AB/R, DSR 1998:III, p. 699.

evidence in accordance with Article 5.7. These requirements[68] were interpreted in each of the four prior cases under the SPS Agreement: *EC–Hormones*,[69] *Australia–Salmon*,[70] *Japan–Agricultural Products*,[71] and *EC–Biotech*.[72]

4. The relationship between discrimination and post-discrimination disciplines

A comparison between the disciplines of the GATT III/XX Complex and the SPS 2.2/5.1/5.7 Complex can only operate at a rather high level of generality. However, the preceding discussion provides a basis for showing, in realistic terms, the actual operation of these tests and how they relate to one another. Their general purpose appears to be the same: to discipline protectionist national regulation.

Imagine a conversation between two trade negotiators. After agreeing on tariff reduction-based liberalization, they are concerned about defection from the agreed commitments. They agree not to discriminate in the application of domestic tax and regulatory measures (i.e. abide by national treatment) but recognize that there is both *de jure* and *de facto* discrimination. *De facto* discrimination is more difficult to identify reliably, because it is possible to write facially general rules that have differential, and protectionist, effects.

The negotiators decide that the history of application of national-treatment rules provides too much flexibility to judges to determine whether a national measure is impermissibly *de facto* discriminatory, and inevitably requires the judges to evaluate the good faith, or the prudential regulatory basis, of the domestic regulation. It is possible, though, to give the judges more guidance, and to discipline a broader range of national measures where it may otherwise be difficult to identify discrimination. In addition to prohibiting discrimination, the negotiators agree, they will also make sure that a certain category of regulatory measures where they expect a high level of protectionism – domestic political pressure for protection – is supported by a prudential regulatory basis: that it has an objective and sufficient non-protectionist 'aim' or purpose. They agree that all regulation in

---

68 In *Australia–Salmon*, the Appellate Body stated: 'On the basis of [the] definition [prescribed in the first part of paragraph 4 of Annex A], we consider that, in this case, a risk assessment within the meaning of Article 5.1 must: (1) identify the diseases whose entry, establishment or spread a Member wants to prevent within its territory, as well as the potential biological and economic consequences associated with the entry, establishment or spread of these diseases; (2) evaluate the likelihood of entry, establishment or spread of these diseases, as well as the associated potential biological and economic consequences; and (3) evaluate the likelihood of entry, establishment or spread of these diseases according to the SPS measures which might be applied.' Appellate Body Report, *Australia–Salmon*, WT/DS18/AB/R, adopted 16 November 1998, at para. 121.

69 Appellate Body Report, *EC–Hormones*.

70 Appellate Body Report, *Australia–Salmon*.

71 Appellate Body Report, *Japan – Measures Affecting Agricultural Products (Japan–Agricultural Products II)*, WT/DS76/AB/R, adopted 19 March 1999.

72 *European Communities – Measures Affecting the Approval and Marketing of Biotech Products (EC–Biotech)*, WT/DS291,292,293/R, adopted 21 November 2006.

this category will be required to have a scientific basis. As discussed in Section 1, this can be justified from an economic perspective insofar as the presumption is that there are market failures because of imperfect information or negative consumption or production externalities (from pests, diseases, etc.).

Although it might be argued à la Hudec that the SPS 2.2/5.1/5.7 Complex goes beyond protectionism, a reasonable argument can be made that it was not intended to do so, and that it has been interpreted in a way that does not do so. If this is correct, it might well be asked why the SPS 2.2/5.1/5.7 Complex was considered necessary to supplement the GATT III/XX Complex. There are two potential responses. The first can be expressed in a single word: agriculture.[73] Given the intent to begin a process of liberalization of agricultural imports under the Agreement on Agriculture, it made sense in 1994 to develop also a specialized set of disciplines on domestic regulation in the field of agriculture. Perhaps it was hoped that this specialized set of disciplines would also respond to the second possible purpose: to fill gaps in the disciplines of the GATT III/XX Complex.

There are three distinct types of gaps in the GATT III/XX Complex.

First, it may be difficult from an evidentiary or burden-of-proof standpoint to prove the requisite discrimination. One response to this first gap would be to establish a 'presumption' of discrimination, or a proxy for an actual finding of discrimination. The scientific-basis requirement of the SPS 2.2/5.1/5.7 Complex may be understood to fill this gap (the 'evidentiary gap'). In economic terms, a (minimum) test is imposed that increases the likelihood that the objective of the national measure is to address a consumption externality, as opposed to improving the terms of trade, shifting rents, etc.

Second, assuming for a moment that the differentiating factor in the GATT III/XX complex between legal and illegal domestic measures is the legitimacy or prudential basis of the regulatory measure, a gap in the GATT III/XX Complex from a trade-liberalization standpoint is the possibility that measures that do not 'discriminate' in terms of aim and thus are not thereby prohibited nevertheless have a substantial and unjustified differential effect (see discussion above). Because it might be assumed that this type of differential effect is only sustainable against those who are not adequately represented in the domestic political process, we might term this effect the 'representation gap'. While it might be appropriate to exclude foreign interests from the domestic political process addressing a *local* consumption externality, it may also be appropriate to address any negative external consequences through international negotiations and perhaps an international legal rule.

Third, there may be circumstances in which the domestic regulation is inefficient. This may occur because domestically enfranchised persons who are harmed are not sufficiently harmed to induce them to take sufficient political action to

---

73 It should be noted, of course, that the TBT Agreement, dealing with non-SPS technical regulations and standards, also addresses 'post-discriminatory' measures.

terminate the domestic regulation. As Mancur Olson showed, political action can be a public good that is under-supplied. We might term this effect the 'efficiency gap'. The solution may involve external pressure and engagement in negotiations that center on the substantive content/level of domestic product regulation and that result in either harmonization or mutual recognition of standards. It might alternatively involve a process-of-information provision and 'learning' that is aimed at changing the incentives of groups to engage in the standards setting (political) process and/or the views of consumers regarding the appropriate level of regulation.

As recounted above, the AB has said that it does not consider the legislative 'aim' in connection with measures evaluated under Article III. However, as a practical matter, panels and the AB have done so, even after *Japan–Alcoholic Beverages*.[74] But we might say that the SPS 2.2/5.1/5.5 Complex does what the AB suggested: it calls for an examination of the objective structure of the regulation – in this case, whether it is objectively justified by scientific evidence – in order to deduce whether it is motivated by illegitimate protectionism.

It must be conceded that discrimination is not easily defined, and that its determination often cannot avoid judicial evaluation of national regulatory categories. In fact, determination of difficult cases of *de facto* discrimination requires judicial evaluation of national regulatory categories. Thus, it is simply incorrect to say that pre-1995 GATT law did not involve critique of national regulatory categories. The distinction between discrimination regulation and post-discrimination regulation is therefore nuanced. Hudec cataloged the distinctions as follows:

> The second-guessing of government regulatory decisions that goes on in a trade discrimination case occurs in a much different setting from, and for a much different purpose than, the second-guessing that seems so unwarranted in the post-discriminatory part of the SPS Agreement ... First, the typical discrimination case concerns a situation in which foreign goods are in fact being placed at a disadvantage *vis-à-vis* domestic goods. There is a differential impact, the central problem at which the international trading system is directed. Second, a discrimination case concerns a question of wrongful purpose, not just a mistake in judgment. Third, discrimination cases involve a situation in which government wrongdoing is a highly possible element – not probable, but possible.[75]

The first distinction noted by Hudec – that discrimination cases necessarily involve differential effects, while post-discrimination cases do not – may be more important as form than as substance. Although in principle an SPS measure may lack a scientific basis yet not produce differential effects, none of the post-discrimination cases decided so far has been argued to involve equivalent effects on

---

74 Amelia Porges and Joel P. Trachtman (2003), 'Robert Hudec and Domestic Regulation: The Resurrection of "Aim and Effects"', 37 *Journal of World Trade*.

75 Hudec, supra note 35, at 194.

domestic and imported goods. Perhaps there is an implicit understanding among the member states that would require differential effects as a basis for legitimate litigation under these provisions, even where the formal language of the SPS Agreement does not require differential effects. To the extent that SPS measures are intended to address consumption externalities, then differential effects (in the national-treatment sense) would arise to the extent that imported products are treated differently and adversely because they generate consumption externalities greater than those generated by domestic products. Under these circumstances, differential effects in the market should not be a sufficient basis for a finding of violation of Article III, nor should they be a basis for a finding of violation of the SPS Agreement. Rather, in both cases, the requisite finding appears to be one of illegitimacy of purpose, rather than disproportionality of effects.

Hudec's second distinction, that discrimination cases necessarily involve a prohibited aim – protectionism – is also not necessarily persuasive: as the risk-assessment requirement has evolved under the WTO, it increasingly can be seen as a proxy test for protectionist aim. According to this perspective, scientific-basis requirements address the evidentiary gap: they address the question of whether there is indeed a consumption externality of the type that is amenable to govern-ment reaction. Necessity tests may be understood in the same way. After all, where governments act irrationally in a way that has protective effects, one possible inference is that there is a protective aim. It is not the only possible inference, but it may be an attractive one.

Hudec's third distinction seems to track the second one: government wrong-doing in the form of protectionist intent may be identified using direct evidence, or using proxy evidence. As noted above, protectionist intent is rarely identified using direct evidence. Rather, as the AB stipulated in *Japan–Alcoholic Beverages*, it may be inferred from the objective structure of the measure. In this light, we might understand the SPS 2.2/5.1/5.7 Complex as a refined legislatively designed mech-anism for inference of protectionism based on the structure of the measure. This is not the only way to understand it, but it is an increasingly plausible way to understand it.

So, can the SPS 2.2/5.1/5.7 Complex be understood as a subtle, rule-based (as opposed to standard-based) prescription for evaluation of the aim of a national measure? It seems to evaluate directly the extent and quality of the non-protectionist aim: by asking whether the measure is based on a risk assessment, it asks whether an agreed predicate for non-protectionist SPS measures has been satisfied. It might alternatively be understood as establishing a presumption of a protectionist aim where the risk-assessment criterion has not been met.

While a measure may be found illegal under the SPS 2.2/5.1/5.7 Complex even where it has no trade effects, the Dispute Settlement Understanding, by limiting retaliation to the level of nullification or impairment – to the level of trade ef-fects – may be understood as establishing an effective requirement of trade effects, in a legal-realist sense.

Table 1. Key features of the SPS and GATT Art. III/XX disciplines

	SPS 2.2/5.1/5.7	GATT III/XX
Domain of application	SPS measures (agricultural products)	Domestic taxation and regulation
Appropriate level of protection	Member-state discretion	Member-state discretion
Required prudential basis	Scientific; (implicit) presumption of a market failure justifying product regulation	Tax/regulatory justification
Standard of review/deference	Coherent reasoning; respectable science; objectively justifiable; sufficient warrant for measure; need not reflect a 'majority view' or existing international norms	Unspecified in Art. III; plausible nonprotectionist aim; in Art. XX, balancing test includes contribution
Aim	Scientific evidence as proxy for aim; presumption that SPS measures address negative externalities	Direct evidence rejected in *Japan–Alcohol*; indirectly derived from objective structure of measure; possibly embedded in like-products determination; or less-favorable-treatment determination; or in necessity under *Korea–Beef*.
Effect	Not explicitly addressed	Possibly embedded in like-products determination; or less-favorable-treatment determination; or in necessity under *Korea–Beef*
Remedy	Determined by trade effects	Determined by trade effects

Table 1 summarizes the salient features of the comparison between the SPS 2.2/5.1/5.7 Complex and the GATT III/XX Complex. For convenience, the table also summarizes some of the key differences between the possible welfare-enhancing justifications for intervention in the SPS area as distinct from more general motivations for taxation/regulation of products circulating in the economy.

5. Concluding remarks

The trade dispute between the US and Canada, and the EU, on hormones and beef has been one of the longest-running conflicts in the trading system – the first formal dispute dates back to 1988 when the US brought a case to GATT (invoking the then TBT agreement). Indeed, one of the drivers for the negotiation of the SPS Agreement was this dispute. If evaluated on the basis of resolving the dispute, it would appear that the addition of specific disciplines on the use of SPS measures has not (yet) been successful. However, the latest AB report has clarified how the disciplines of the SPS Agreement should be applied and in the process made clearer how the Agreement goes beyond the GATT Article III/XX Complex.

What the SPS Agreement does is to somewhat reduce the incompleteness of the WTO contract by requiring that SPS measures be motivated by ('aim at') reducing national product-specific consumption externalities. It is often stressed by economists that the WTO is an 'incomplete contract'. This implies that it does not (and cannot) specify what is permitted of governments in every state of the world. Instead, the WTO contains only a few specific, unambiguous disciplines (the most obvious being the tariff bindings). From an economic perspective, both the GATT III/XX Complex and the SPS 2.2/5.1/5.7 Complex can be regarded as responses to contractual incompleteness in the WTO treaty.[76]

Horn (2006) notes that a complete contract that specifies permissible policies in all possible states of the world is simply infeasible: the costs of writing and enforcing any such agreement are prohibitive, even assuming heroically that governments are able to specify *ex ante* all the regulatory needs that may arise in the future.[77] Both the GATT III/XX Complex and the SPS 2.2/5.1/5.7 Complex can be regarded as components of a state-contingent contract, delegating to the dispute-settlement process the task of determining the state. But these provisions refer to a state that is described by virtue of conditions such as like products, less favorable treatment, lack of scientific basis, etc. The implication is that the degree to which state contingencies result in beneficial internalization of externalities (i.e. in contract completeness) needs to be examined.

Horn develops a model in which for given tariff commitments, a marginally binding national-treatment provision will increase government welfare, but moving beyond this and further tightening national treatment may reduce welfare. The problem caused by tariff bindings combined with a hypothesized strict national-treatment rule (one that is unable to use regulatory categories to distinguish between products) is that insofar as imported products cause externalities, governments no longer can use the tariff to offset these. Instead they must use domestic instruments, which, because of national treatment, must apply equally to local and imported goods. As a result, an importing country that is being forced to abide by an equal-taxation dictum will set a uniform tax that is, from an international efficiency point of view, too high with regard to the domestic product, and too low with regard to the imported product. As a consequence, provided the externality problem is sufficiently severe, the imposition of national treatment may be internationally inefficient.[78] Horn explains that information about government

---

76 See, e.g., Henrik Horn, Giovanni Maggi, and Robert Staiger (2008), 'Trade Agreements as Endogenously Incomplete Contracts', mimeo, forthcoming in the *American Economic Review*, 2009.

77 Henrik Horn (2006), 'National Treatment in the GATT', 96:1 *American Economic Review* 394.

78 Costinot develops a model showing that national treatment results in standards that are excessively restrictive, due to failure to take account of the interests of foreign producers exporting to the regulating market. On the other hand, under a regime of mutual recognition in which each state undertakes to accept as satisfactory the regulation of the home state of the exported good, standards will be too low due to a race-to-the-bottom effect in which the regulating government fails to account for foreign externalities. See Arnaud Costinot (2008), 'A Comparative Institutional Analysis of Agreements on Product Standards', 75 *Journal of International Economic Law* 197.

preferences is at the core of the problem that national treatment is intended to solve:

> If we were to assume that such information [regarding government preferences in order to determine the first-best solution] is verifiable, in the context of the present model there would exist an even simpler solution than the market access rule: a provision simply requesting the parties to 'set internal taxes to their first-best levels.' This would implement the first-best outcome even if tariff negotiators were myopic, as long as the tariffs were set sufficiently low, since this would leave room to set total taxes at the first-best level, once the state of nature is realized. Presumably, the reason why we do not see such a provision lies in the difficulty to prove whether a set of taxes that benefits domestic interests, and harms foreign interests, is chosen to exploit neighbors, or because the importing government's preferences are such as to make the chosen taxes efficient from a global point of view. That is, it requires the adjudicator to effectively determine the intent behind the de facto discriminatory taxes, something the Appellate Body in the WTO has repeatedly (but not always very convincingly) claimed to be irrelevant to its decisions.[79]

The question raised by Horn is precisely the one discussed above regarding the ability to determine whether domestic regulators are engaging in first-best regulation, or protectionism. The scientific-basis requirement imposed by the SPS 2.2/5.1/5.7 Complex may be said to respond to precisely this question: how do we determine the intent behind *de facto* discrimination – how do we get closer to a requirement to set internal regulation at its first-best level? While there is no WTO law requirement that domestic regulators set internal regulations to their first-best levels, the scientific-basis requirement achieves a closer approximation of this test than mere national treatment. In order to get closer to a first-best level, it might be necessary to discipline 'appropriate level of protection'.

The nature of the externality arising from imports is left unclear in the Horn analysis, which is very general. In the case of SPS, tariffs would often be very poor substitutes for regulation – tariffs cannot address the local consumption externality or information problem that is created by or associated with the characteristics of the product or its by-products. If the imported products cause negative externality problems because they are different from domestic products, the imported products may well not be 'like' the domestic products, and so Article III would not require 'no less favorable' treatment. To revert to the case of hormones, if products with and without hormone residues are sufficiently different, the GATT Article III/XX Complex may not provide disciplines to preclude the protectionist use of product regulation.

Substantively, the SPS disciplines requiring there to be a scientific basis for SPS measures are closely related to the GATT non-discrimination doctrine, in that they define the necessary (but not sufficient) conditions for concluding that specific SPS

---

79 Horn, supra note 78, at 402.

measures cannot be justified. The SPS Agreement goes beyond the GATT Article III/XX Complex by imposing requirements on governments regarding the criteria that must be satisfied as a precondition for imposing a specific SPS measure, while leaving the level of the measure to the discretion of the government. The constraint is a weak one, in that a minimum threshold criterion applies: there must be a scientific basis for the measure, even if the scientific evidence represents divergent or minority views in the profession. The *de facto* protection (market segmentation) created by an SPS measure must be motivated by demonstrating that the measure is addressing a market failure (consumption externality), as reflected in the existence of some scientific basis for a health or safety concern.

The scientific-basis requirement is a means for determining the intent of an SPS measure, a factor that is ostensibly not relevant in GATT national-treatment cases. But scientific justification is not a move away from a concern with preventing illegitimate discrimination against imported products. Instead this element of post-discrimination regulation in the WTO is the test that is used to determine whether there is *de facto* discrimination and a protectionist effect created by an SPS measure. Although the 'scientific basis' test can therefore be regarded as a proxy measure of intent needed to justify an SPS measure, the AB report in *Continued Suspension* makes clear it is a weak test: governments are free to apply whatever level of protection they deem appropriate, a minority scientific view is enough to justify a measure, and panels have no business assessing what is 'good science', evaluating whether the risk assessment undertaken by a government is 'correct', or giving more weight to the majority view in the scientific community.

Insofar as the specific SPS measures that are adopted by governments are targeted at market failures that have effects on national objectives/territory, any international negative spillovers associated with the SPS norms that are adopted will reflect the national preferences and attitudes towards risk and the fact that such preferences and attitudes will differ across countries. Given the unwillingness of WTO Members to accept strong disciplines regarding harmonization or acceptance of minimum standards in this area, the outcome of the *Continued Suspension* case seems to represent an appropriate application of the SPS Agreement. The SPS Agreement makes a marginal additional contribution in further completing the WTO 'contract' compared to the potential outcome of litigation of such cases under GATT alone. That said, there is extensive economic literature concluding that from a cost–benefit perspective the levels at which SPS measures are set is often excessive, imposing high costs with very little to show in terms of greater safety or health.[80] Ultimately, improving the cost–benefit ratio of product regulation requires economic analysis and public-policy debate informed by assessments of actual risks and the impacts of specific measures.

---

80 See Bernard Hoekman and Michel Kostecki (2009), *The Political Economy of the World Trading System*, Oxford University Press, for a brief review of some of this literature.

United States – Subsidies on Upland Cotton Recourse to Article 21.5 by Brazil, WT/DS267/AB/RW (2 June 2008)

WILLIAM J. DAVEY

Guy Raymond Jones Chair in Law Emeritus, University of Illinois

ANDRÉ SAPIR

Professor of Economics, ECARES, Université Libre de Bruxelles, Brussels, Senior Fellow, Bruegel, Brussels Research Fellow, CEPR, London

Abstract: Two of the four issues in this Appellate Body Report concerned the proper scope of Article 21.5 DSU compliance panel proceedings; the other two issues concerned the Appellate Body's review of the Panel's use of evidence. On the Article 21.5 issues, the Appellate Body essentially ruled that an Article 21.5 compliance proceeding could evaluate the WTO consistency of: (i) the entirety of an implementation measure (including parts of the measure that did not specifically implement DSB recommendations and rulings) and (ii) new subsidy grants made under a program in respect of which prior subsidy grants had been found to cause serious prejudice so as to determine whether the new grants also resulted in serious prejudice. On the evidentiary issues, the Appellate Body upheld the Panel's conclusions, although it modified certain of the Panel's reasoning. Probably the most interesting aspect of the case was the substantial deference showed by the Appellate Body to the Panel's consideration of causation and non-attribution issues. This deference was striking compared to the lack of deference that the Appellate Body has given to national authorities on those issues. We detect, however, a welcome interest on the part of the Appellate Body to require the use of analytical tools on the part of panels evaluating serious-prejudice cases.

1. Background

This paper examines certain issues presented by the Appellate Body Report in a compliance proceeding brought by Brazil in respect of US subsidies benefitting upland cotton.[1] The case initially arose in 2002, when Brazil challenged certain US

---

1 *United States – Subsidies on Upland Cotton – Recourse to Article 21.5 of the DSU by Brazil*, WT/DS267/AB/RW (2 June 2008) (hereinafter 'Appellate Body 21.5 Report'). The Panel and Appellate Body reports in the original proceedings were analyzed in André Sapir and Joel Trachtman, 'Subsidization, Price Suppression, and Expertise: Causation and Precision in Upland Cotton', The WTO Case Law of 2004–2005 (ALI, 23 February 2007), also published in 7 *World Trade Review* 183–209 (2008).

181

measures as subsidies prohibited by or actionable under WTO rules.[2] The original
Panel Report, issued in 2004, concluded *inter alia*:[3]

– US government export credit guarantees provided to unscheduled products
(including upland cotton) and one scheduled product (rice) under three US
programs – known as GSM 102, GSM 103, and SCGP – were export subsidies
applied so as to result in circumvention of US export subsidy commitments in the
WTO Agreement on Agriculture;

– such subsidies to the extent subject to the SCM Agreement were prohibited
export subsidies because the premiums charged for the guarantees did not cover
their long-term costs;

– export credit guarantees provided in respect of other scheduled products
(including in particular pig meat and poultry meat) did not violate any WTO
rules;

– certain US domestic subsidy measures – namely marketing loan program
payments, Step 2 payments,[4] market loss assistance payments and countercyclical
payments – were actionable subsidies in that they caused significant price suppression resulting in serious prejudice to Brazil in terms of Article 5(c) SCM; and

– the United States should withdraw the export subsidies within six months of
the adoption of the report (or, if earlier, by 1 July 2005) and take appropriate
steps to remove the adverse affects of or withdraw the subsidies found to cause
serious prejudice to Brazil. Article 7.9 DSU effectively requires the latter to be
accomplished within six months of the adoption of the report in question (i.e., by
21 September 2005 in this case).

On appeal, the Appellate Body upheld the results reached in the Panel Report to
the extent appealed, except for the findings on pig meat and poultry meat.[5] As to
them, the Appellate Body found itself unable to complete the analysis of the issues.
Thus, there was no finding of WTO inconsistency with regard to those two products, but also no finding of WTO consistency (which was the case of the other
scheduled products besides rice). The reports were adopted on 21 March 2005.[6]

The United States stated that it would implement the DSB recommendations.[7]
As to the export credit programs, the US eliminated the GSM 103 program and

2 *United States – Subsidies on Upland Cotton*, WT/DS267/1 (3 October 2002).
3 *United States – Subsidies on Upland Cotton*, WT/DS267/R (8 September 2004) (hereinafter 'Panel Report').
4 The Step 2 payments were also found to constitute export and import substitution subsidies under Article 3 SCM.
5 *United States – Subsidies on Upland Cotton*, WT/DS267/AB/R (3 March 2005) (hereinafter Appellate Body Report').
6 WT/DS267/20 (24 March 2005).
7 WT/DSB/M/188, at 7 (18 May 2005) (minutes of meeting held on 20 April 2005).

announced a new fee structure for the GSM 102 and SCGP programs in June 2005. In October 2005, it stopped issuing guarantees under the SCGP program. Then, in February 2006, it eliminated the Step 2 program.[8]

Brazil claimed that these actions failed to bring the United States into compliance with its WTO obligations, and the Article 21.5 DSU compliance proceeding that is the subject of this paper ensued.[9] In its report,[10] the compliance Panel concluded that the revised GSM 102 program continued to provide guarantees for fees that did not cover its total costs and thus was still an export subsidy in violation of the Agriculture Agreement and a prohibited export subsidy under the SCM Agreement. These findings applied to unscheduled products (such as upland cotton) and to three scheduled products (rice, pig meat, and poultry meat). The Panel also concluded that the marketing loan and countercyclical payments that were unchanged continued to cause serious prejudice to Brazil. The Panel also made two procedural rulings regarding the scope of the Article 21.5 proceeding. First, the Panel concluded that Brazil could renew its claim that the US was providing export subsidies in excess of the applicable scheduled amounts with regard to pig meat and poultry meat. Second, the Panel determined that, in examining the serious-prejudice issue, it could consider marketing loan and countercyclical payments made subsequent to the date by which the United States should have implemented the original Panel Report.

On appeal, the Appellate Body upheld the results of the Panel Report,[11] although it modified the Panel's analysis. The reports were adopted on 20 June 2008.[12] As noted, Brazil had previously requested authority to take retaliatory measures against the United States for its failure to comply, and following adoption of the Article 21.5 reports, the arbitrations to determine the level of permitted retaliation measures were reactivated[13] and were pending as of 1 August 2009.

For the most part, the Appellate Body's rulings in this case focused on rather narrow issues: two of the four contested issues concerned the permissible scope of Article 21.5 proceedings; the other two issues essentially involved a review of the conclusions that the Panel had drawn from the evidence it examined. Regarding

---

8 Appellate Body 21.5 Report, para. 8.

9 Brazil initially requested authorization to take countermeasures for non-implementation on 4 July 2005. WT/DS267/21 (5 July 2005). That action led to an agreement on sequencing between the United States and Brazil, pursuant to which the United States requested arbitration of the level of countermeasures; the arbitrations (technically there are two arbitrations – one under Article 4 SCM and one under Article 7 SCM) were suspended until completion of the Article 21.5 DSU proceedings, and Brazil was allowed to have a 21.5 panel established without further consultations or a second DSB meeting. The agreement is found at WT/DS267/22 (8 July 2005). Brazil requested the establishment of a 21.5 panel on 18 August 2006, WT/DS267/30 (21 August 2006), and it was established on 28 September 2006. WT/DSB/M/220, item 4 (2 November 2006).

10 *United States – Subsidies on Upland Cotton – Recourse to Article 21.5 of the DSU by Brazil*, WT/DS267/RW (18 December 2007) (hereinafter 'Panel 21.5 Report').

11 Appellate Body 21.5 Report, para. 448.

12 WT/DS267/37 (26 June 2008).

13 WT/DS267/38 & 39 (15 October 2008).

the issues arising under the Agriculture and SCM Agreements, the Panel largely followed the same basic approach that it had in the original proceeding. Thus, the case does not present new issues under those agreements. As noted below, however, it is interesting to contrast the rather 'light touch' review the Appellate Body applied to the Panel's findings on serious prejudice with the intensive review that it has instructed panels to undertake when they are reviewing decisions of national authorities on injury in dumping, subsidy, and safeguard cases.

We turn first to the Article 21.5 scope issues and then to the evidentiary issues.

2. Article 21.5: Scope of 'Measures Taken to Comply'

Article 21.5 DSU provides an expedited panel procedure in the event that 'there is disagreement as to the ... consistency with a [WTO] agreement of measures taken to comply with the [DSB's] recommendations and rulings'. Under Article 21.5, the matter is to be referred to the original panel (wherever possible) and the report is to be circulated within 90 days. In practice, so-called compliance panels have usually taken much longer than 90 days to circulate their reports and the reports have often been appealed. Nonetheless, compliance panel proceedings are typically a bit quicker than regular panel proceedings.[14]

A responding party may well prefer to limit the scope of issues referred to compliance panels under Article 21.5. After all, the matter will be heard by the original panel, which has already found the respondent to be in violation of WTO rules in the initial proceeding.[15] Moreover, if the respondent loses in an Article 21.5 proceeding, it will not benefit from any reasonable period of time in which to implement, but rather will be immediately subject to retaliatory measures (subject to a relatively short delay while the level of retaliation is arbitrated). Thus, there are clear strategic reasons why respondents urge a narrow view of the scope of the phrase 'measures taken to implement'.

Complaining parties, of course, have precisely the opposite interests. For the WTO dispute-settlement system itself, it would seem that allowing more scope to Article 21.5 DSU proceedings is probably desirable. As discussed in more detail below, such a result promotes efficiency and avoids splitting closely related issues between two separate proceedings.

2.1 Raising previously litigated but unresolved issues in Article 21.5 DSU proceedings

The first scope issue in this case concerned certain US export credit guarantee programs. As noted above, the United States was found to have violated WTO rules because the fees charged for these programs did not cover their costs. As a

---

14 William J. Davey (2008), 'Expediting the Panel Process in WTO Dispute Settlement', in Merit E. Janow, Victoria Donaldson, and Alan Yanovich (eds.), *The WTO: Governance, Dispute Settlement and Developing Countries*, New York: Juris Publishing, pp. 409, 415–421.

15 More often than not, the original panelists are available and do serve. See ibid., at 464–470.

consequence, it was found to have provided WTO-illegal export subsidies with regard to products not subject to WTO export subsidy commitments (i.e., so-called unscheduled products, including upland cotton) and with regard to one product – rice – where it had scheduled export subsidy commitments. In respect of two other scheduled products – pig meat and poultry meat – the Appellate Body reversed the Panel's conclusion that it had not exceeded its export subsidy commitments, but the Appellate Body did not complete the analysis of the issue, which meant that there were no findings regarding these two products. The Panel's conclusion that there was no violation of export subsidy commitments in other scheduled products was not challenged.

The United States claimed that it had corrected the export credit violations by eliminating two of the three export credit guarantee programs at issue and generally restructuring the remaining program. In challenging the restructured program – GSM 102 – Brazil argued that GSM 102 continued to constitute an export subsidy and requested findings in respect of unscheduled products and three scheduled products – rice, as to which a violation had been found in the original proceeding, and pig meat and poultry meat, as to which no findings were made, as described above. The United States asked the Panel to exclude pig meat and poultry meat from the scope of the proceedings. The Panel declined to do so. In its view, the fact that no violation had been found and that therefore no implementing measure needed to be taken did not mean that Brazil's claims were not related to 'measures taken to comply', as used in Article 21.5 DSU.[16] In reaching this conclusion, the Panel viewed the export guarantee arrangements for pig and poultry meat as measures separate from the implementing measure – the revised GSM 102 program – but it relied on *US–Softwood Lumber IV*[17] as supporting the notion that measures 'with a particularly close relationship' to an implementation measure could be considered to be within the scope of an Article 21.5 proceeding.[18] The Panel also noted that this situation was analogous to a case where the Appellate Body had ruled that a claim in respect of which a panel had exercised judicial economy in the original proceeding could be properly heard in an Article 21.5 proceeding.[19]

On appeal, the Appellate Body rejected the Panel's analysis – in particular, its view that multiple measures were at issue – as inapplicable. In its view, the first step was to identify the 'measure taken to comply'.[20] In that regard, it took the

16 Panel 21.5 Report, para. 9.23.

17 *United States – Final Countervailing Duty Determination with respect to Certain Softwood Lumber from Canada – Recourse to Article 21.5 of the DSU by Canada*, WT/DS257/AB/RW (adopted 20 December 2005).

18 Panel 21.5 Report, paras. 9.24–9.25.

19 Panel 21.5 Report, para. 9.26, citing *European Communities – Anti-Dumping Duties on Imports of Cotton-Type Bed Linen from India – Recourse to Article 21.5 of the DSU by India*, WT/DS141/AB/RW (adopted 24 April 2003).

20 Appellate Body 21.5 Report, para. 201.

view that the measure taken to comply was the revised GSM 102 program as a whole, and it noted various examples of where the United States had so described it.[21] The Appellate Body stressed that WTO Members have discretion to adopt either narrowly focused measures or broader measures when they implement DSB recommendations and rulings. It saw no reason why the definition of 'measures taken to comply' should be limited to what a Member was required to implement. Thus, since it viewed the new GSM 102 program as a single measure, it naturally encompassed the contested provisions on pig and poultry meat.[22]

In reaching its conclusion, the Appellate Body rejected the US arguments that its interpretation would lead to Members making the least possible changes to measures and would result in tangles of separate regimes, all done to avoid possible expansive challenges in Article 21.5 proceedings. The Appellate Body's position was simple: the choice of how to implement is up to the WTO Member concerned, and the DSU is neutral as to that choice.[23] It also rejected the US argument that it was unfair to include pig and poultry meat because they would be subject to an expedited challenge and benefit from no reasonable period of time for implementation, even though they had never been subject to a finding of WTO inconsistency. Again, the Appellate Body saw these consequences as flowing from the US choice as to the scope of its implementation measure.[24] Moreover, as the Appellate Body later noted, there are strong efficiency reasons for treating such related claims in one proceeding.

The Appellate Body did, however, place certain limits on the claims that could be raised. For example, it indicated that a complainant could not raise (i) claims that were raised in the original proceeding but were rejected or not pursued[25] and (ii) claims that could have been, but were not, raised in the original proceeding.[26] It would be possible, however, to raise claims that had been pursued in the original proceeding but not decided for reasons of judicial economy or, as in this case, the Appellate Body's inability to complete the analysis of an issue. And, of course, to the extent that the new measure taken to comply implicates new WTO issues, those could be raised.

---

21 Appellate Body 21.5 Report, paras. 203–204.

22 As to the Panel's reliance on the *US–Softwood Lumber IV* case, the Appellate Body noted that the case applied where there was a measure taken to comply and another closely related measure that could not be so characterized. That issue was explored in much more detail in *United States – Laws, Regulations and Methodology for Calculating Dumping Margins (Zeroing)*, WT/DS294/AB/RW (adopted 11 June 2009).

23 Appellate Body 21.5 Report, para. 206.

24 Appellate Body 21.5 Report, para. 207. The Appellate Body could have noted, but did not, that Article 21.5 proceedings are typically not all that expedited. See note 14 supra.

25 Appellate Body 21.5 Report, para. 210. An example would be a claim in respect of which a prima facie case had not been established. See *European Communities – Anti-Dumping Duties on Imports of Cotton-Type Bed Linen from India – Recourse to Article 21.5 of the DSU by India*, WT/DS141/AB/RW (adopted 24 April 2003).

26 Appellate Body 21.5 Report, para. 211. An example would be a new claim against an unchanged part of the contested measure.

To us, the Appellate Body's position seems textually based and eminently reasonable, particularly for reasons of efficiency. An attempt to limit the scope of 'measures taken to comply' in the way suggested by the United States would likely lead to many instances of cases that belonged together being split between regular and compliance proceedings. That would obviously be inefficient, especially if different panelists were involved.[27] While determination of whether a measure qualifies as a 'measure taken to comply' for purposes of Article 21.5 DSU may at times be difficult, that was not true in this case. The revision of the GSM 102 program was clearly a 'measure taken to comply'.

2.2 Subsequent subsidy payments and Article 21.5 proceedings

The second Article 21.5 scope issue concerned the challengeability of subsidy payments made subsequent to 21 September 2005 (the date by which the United States was required to remove the adverse affects of or withdraw the subsidies found to be causing serious prejudice in the initial panel proceeding). As described above, in the original proceeding, payments under several US programs – the so-called Step 2 program, as well as the programs providing marketing loan, market loss assistance, and counter-cyclical payments – were found to have caused serious prejudice to Brazil. The United States terminated the Step 2 program, but continued payments under the marketing loan and counter-cyclical programs on the same terms as before. In the Article 21.5 proceeding, the United States argued that the findings in the original proceeding had been made in respect of payments made in the 1999–2002 marketing years and that it was required only to remove the adverse effects of those payments. According to the United States, later payments had to be challenged in a new proceeding.[28] In this regard, it noted that Brazil had chosen to challenge the payments and not the programs 'as such'. The Panel rejected this reasoning and took the position that the obligation in Article 5 SCM not to cause adverse effects through subsidies would not be met if a Member continued to provide payments under the same conditions as the original subsidy found to have caused adverse effects.[29] The Panel also cited the 'particularly close relationship' language discussed in the prior section.[30]

On appeal, the Appellate Body reached the same result, but based it on somewhat different reasoning. It focused on the requirement in Article 7.8 SCM that 'the Member granting *or maintaining* such subsidy [i.e., one found to cause adverse effects] shall take appropriate steps to remove the adverse effects or shall

---

27 It is likely that there would be different panelists, since the respondent could object to the same panelists and the Director-General might hesitate to appoint the same panelists, as different issues would be at stake.

28 The Panel determined that the DSB recommendations and rulings addressed only payments made under the subsidy programs and not the programs themselves. Brazil conditionally appealed this finding, but the Appellate Body found it unnecessary to decide the issue. Appellate Body 21.5 Report, paras. 250–254.

29 Panel 21.5 Report, paras. 9.79.

30 Panel 21.5 Report, para. 9.80.

withdraw the subsidy'. The Appellate Body was of the view that the implementation obligation was not limited to the subsidies granted in the past that had given rise to the Panel's rulings. In its view, the word 'maintain' suggests that the Article 7.8 obligation is of a 'continuous nature', which means that it would apply to recurring annual payments subsequent to those that had been evaluated by the Panel.[31] Otherwise, it thought that the commitment to take appropriate steps to remove the effects would be virtually meaningless. The respondent could do nothing, and the effects of the previously granted subsidies would dissipate. while the same effects would continue as a result of the newly granted subsidies.[32]

The United States disputed this. In its view, Brazil could have obtained broader relief of the sort that it was seeking in the Article 21.5 proceeding if it had challenged the US subsidy program 'as such' or claimed that the program created a threat of serious prejudice in the future. The Appellate Body responded that there was little difference between an 'as such' challenge and that made by Brazil, because in both cases the past actual payments would have to be examined to determine if the program was causing serious prejudice.[33] As to the possibility of alleging the threat of serious prejudice, the Appellate Body noted that that claim differed in substance from a claim of current serious prejudice. It also noted that in countervailing duty cases, a finding of serious injury entitled one to a remedy against future imports.[34] Overall, the Appellate Body was concerned that accepting the US argument would make it difficult to obtain relief even after serious prejudice had been established and that the US position would undermine the DSU goal of prompt compliance.

On reflection, the Appellate Body seems to have come to the best result, although one can criticize its reasoning in some respects. For example, the use of the term 'maintain' in Article 7.8 SCM would seem to cover the situation where a subsidy has been granted in the past, but is still being paid out (e.g., a ten-year grant of $1 million per year), rather than the Appellate Body's interpretation, which seems to suggest that it covers future independent grants. Moreover, the relevance of its citation to CVD practice as context supporting its position is difficult to understand, as such different anti-subsidy provisions are concerned.[35]

---

31 Appellate Body Report, para. 237.

32 Ibid. The Appellate Body found support for its view of Article 7 in the operation of Article 4 SCM (prohibited subsidies). It noted that where a Member replaced condemned prohibited subsidies with new subsidies, those new subsidies could be challenged in an Article 21.5 proceeding. *United States – Tax Treatment of 'Foreign Sales Corporations' – Second Recourse to Article 21.5 of the DSU by the European Communities*, WT/DS108/AB/RW2 (adopted 14 March 2006).

33 Appellate Body 21.5 Report, para. 237.

34 Appellate Body 21.5 Report, para. 238.

35 The rules at issue in *US–Cotton* effectively limit the right of a WTO Member to provide subsidies, while the rules on CVDs concern a Member's right to impose compensatory duties to offset subsidized exports from other members. It is true, of course, that an investigation of past conduct in a CVD case serves as the basis for a prospective remedy.

Nonetheless, the US argument would unduly narrow the scope of Article 21.5 proceedings. In essence, it resembles the argument that if a measure is found to violate WTO rules, compliance is achieved by the simple act of withdrawing the contested measure and that Article 21.5 cannot be used to challenge a replacement measure. That position was long ago rejected.[36] To us, it seems that if a WTO Member is found to have violated WTO rules, then it is appropriate to allow an Article 21.5 challenge to the 'new' regime that the Member puts in its place – whether that regime is a truly new regime, a somewhat revised regime, or essentially a continuation of the old regime.

Interestingly, the issue in this case is not so dissimilar from the issues that arise under antidumping cases involving the United States since the US system of retrospective assessment of antidumping duties on an annual basis means that by the time that a WTO proceeding – original or compliance – has been completed there will technically be a new US measure in place. The United States has to date also been unsuccessful in arguing that such 'new' measures are not challengeable in Article 21.5 proceedings.[37]

The US defense that Brazil should have challenged the US programs on an 'as such' basis is somewhat disingenuous. Such a challenge is a particularly difficult one to make when subsidies are involved. For example, the subsidies Brazil challenged under Article 5 SCM are not prohibited. They are a WTO problem only if they result in certain adverse effects, such as the serious prejudice to its interests that Brazil claimed in this case. Thus, an 'as such' challenge under Article 5 would have to show that the program at issue inherently led to serious prejudice, which would involve, as noted by the Appellate Body, looking at exactly the same material as was considered in this case. The difference would be that a stronger finding would have to be made – the program inherently causes serious prejudice, as opposed to a finding that the program has caused serious prejudice in the specific years examined. Since the existence of serious prejudice will depend on so many other market factors that will change over time, it will not be easy to conclude that a subsidy program inherently results in serious prejudice.

Basically the issue comes down to two questions: What is the nature of the obligation found in Article 5 SCM? If violated, what sort of remedial action is required? The obligation is not to cause 'adverse effects' such as 'serious prejudice'. That obligation is a continuing one. Once such adverse effects are found, the respondent is required by Article 7.8 SCM to remove the adverse effects or withdraw the subsidy. Since WTO remedial obligations are commonly viewed as prospective in nature, this obligation would seem to require the subsidy program to be withdrawn or the adverse effects of the program to be removed. If the subsidy

---

36 *European Communities – Regime for the Importation, Sale and Distribution of Bananas – Recourse to Article 21.5 by Ecuador*, WT/DS27/RW/ECU, paras. 6.3–6.12, especially para. 6.09 (adopted 6 May 1999).

37 See, e.g., *United States – Measures Relating to Zeroing and Sunset Reviews – Recourse to Article 21.5 of the DSU by Japan*, WT/DS322/RW (24 April 2009) (on appeal, report expected 18 August 2009).

program is only modified, as here, the implementation issue will be whether the revised program will still cause serious prejudice. As such, that issue is an appropriate one for Article 21.5 DSU proceedings. And that is the result achieved here. Indeed, it would make little sense to say that the nature of the finding and the obligation to remove the adverse effects had no future implications for the programs found to have caused the problems.

2.3 Summary

In our view, the Appellate Body's resolution of the DSU Article 21.5 scope issues seems eminently reasonable.

3. Evidentiary issues

There were two evidentiary issues on the appeal – one relating to whether the US export credit guarantee program covered its costs and the other related to the Panel's finding of significant price suppression.

3.1 GSM 102 export credit guarantees

The third issue on appeal was the US claim that the evidence did not support a conclusion that its continuing export credit guarantee program – GSM 102 – still operated at a loss. The Panel examined four items of what the Appellate Body characterized as quantitative evidence in its assessment of whether or not the GSM 102 program was operated at a loss.

   (i) US estimates showing losses for the 2006–2008 GSM 102 guarantees in the 2007 and 2008 US budgets;
  (ii) US re-estimates for the 1992–2006 period that showed no losses overall;
 (iii) consolidated financial statements of the granting agency (CCC), which showed an overall liability for the guarantee programs; and
 (iv) cash accounting data compiled by Brazil for the 1992–2005 period, which showed a loss for the programs.[38]

In its evaluation of this evidence, the Panel relied in particular on item (i), which it found was confirmed by items (iii) and (iv).[39] It discounted item (ii), offered by the United States, because even though that data had shown some older cohorts (the guarantees granted in a given year) did not incur losses, the data did not demonstrate that more recent years would not result in losses. Moreover, the Panel noted that the re-estimates were only estimates.[40] Although the Panel did not comment on it, the re-estimates seemed to continue to show recent cohorts operating at a

---

38 Appellate Body 21.5 Report, para. 279.
39 Panel 21.5 Report, para. 14.89.
40 Ibid., para. 14.81.

loss (i.e., the overall profitability of the program as re-estimated by the United States fell significantly by including the 2003–2006 cohorts).[41]

For the Appellate Body, the Panel's evaluation was seriously flawed. With the exception of two cohorts that had closed out profitably (1994 and 1995), all the evidence consisted of estimates and projections. Yet the Panel seemed to dismiss the US re-estimates because they were merely estimates and yet gave credence to the other estimates. Moreover, it did not attempt to reconcile the various estimates or explain why such a reconciliation was not possible. In the Appellate Body's words: 'The Panel's internally incoherent treatment of the same class of quantitative evidence thus vitiates the conclusion it drew based on the financial data submitted by the parties.'[42] Thus, the Appellate Body concluded that the Panel had not made an 'objective assessment' of the matter and facts as required by Article 11 DSU.[43]

Having reversed the Panel's conclusion based on the quantitative evidence, the Appellate Body turned to whether it could complete the analysis of the issue. In this regard, it essentially concluded that the evidence offered by the United States and Brazil was of similar reliability, but supported irreconcilable results.[44] It noted that its attempt to reconcile some of the conflicting estimates at the appellate hearing was unsuccessful.[45] Thus, the Appellate Body concluded that the quantitative evidence did not resolve the issue of whether the GSM 102 program operated at a loss.

This conclusion did not end the matter, because the Panel had also based its finding that the US program did not cover its overall costs on the structure, design, and operation of the GSM 102 program.[46] In that regard, the Panel had noted (i) that there was a statutory cap of 1% on GSM 102 fees; (ii) that the fees did not increase in respect of risk as fast as they did under certain other US export credit programs (probably because of the cap); and (iii) that foreign obligor risk was not reflected in the fees. The Appellate Body rejected the US criticisms of the Panel's analysis of these factors[47] and concluded that it was 'not persuaded that the Panel

---

41 See figures in Appellate Body 21.5 Report, para. 262.
42 Appellate Body 21.5 Report, para. 294.
43 Ibid., para. 295.
44 Ibid., para. 301.
45 Ibid., para. 300.
46 The Panel also compared the GSM 102 program fees with the OECD's minimum premium rates (MPRs), established under the OECD's 'Arrangement on Officially Supported Export Credits – 2008 Revision', OECD Doc. TAD/PG(2007)28/Final (see paras. 23–25 thereof) and noted that there was a significant difference. While the OECD MPRs are set to ensure that certain, non-agricultural credit guarantee programs charge appropriate premia to reflect non-payment risks, their scope of application is sufficiently different that the Panel did not place much reliance on the OECD MPRs, except to note that the difference in fees was of considerable magnitude. The Appellate Body also did not place much emphasis on the differences. Appellate Body 21.5 Report, paras. 302–307.
47 The US criticisms were largely an attempt to suggest that these other comparators were different than the GSM 102 program, which the Panel and Appellate Body accepted. The US arguments that they were therefore irrelevant was not so persuasive and was rejected.

erred in finding that "the GSM 102 program is not designed to cover its long term operating costs and losses'''.[48]

Given its foregoing analysis, the Appellate Body concluded that 'The Panel's finding on the structure, design and operation, in light of the two plausible outcomes with similar probabilities that emerge from the quantitative evidence, provides a sufficient evidentiary basis for the conclusion that it is more likely than not that the revised GSM 102 program operates at a loss.'[49]

This conclusion is defensible – but only barely. The key evidence was the so-called quantitative evidence. The Appellate Body characterized that evidence as supporting two plausible outcomes, but since the outcomes were polar opposites, it would have been more appropriate to characterize the quantitative evidence as inconclusive. In that situation, one can legitimately ask whether indirect evidence regarding the design of the program should be sufficient to conclude that a violation had occurred. After all, evidence on design, structure, and operation is only indicative of a potential problem with meeting costs; the key evidence is the quantitative evidence, which was inconclusive. One can argue that Brazil or the Panel needed to do much more to explain the inconsistencies in that key evidence. The changes made by the United States should have reduced its losses (if any). The fact that the only cohorts that had closed in the past were profitable certainly could be taken to suggest that those changes would make it likely that the more recent cohorts would also be profitable. At a minimum, some more detailed analysis of the differences between the terms under which the profitable cohorts and the current cohorts operated should have been undertaken. These unexplored areas certainly raise some serious questions about the Panel and the Appellate Body's conclusions. Ultimately, of course, it is not the role of the Appellate Body to revisit a Panel's factual findings, but where it has reversed part of the findings supporting a specific factual conclusion, this raises questions about the conclusion itself. Thus, while the conclusion may have been correct,[50] the issue presented a very close call and a more thorough analysis of the evidence should have been undertaken. This case is one where a remand would have been useful.

48 Appellate Body 21.5 Report, para. 320.

49 Ibid., para. 321.

50 As panelists, we would have analyzed the evidence in its totality and concluded that it all supported Brazil – including the re-estimates of recent cohorts – except for the re-estimates of cohorts from the past. Absent more evidence on why the experience of those cohorts should outweigh the current US government view of whether the program would lose money, that counter-evidence would not outweigh what Brazil had presented. By dividing the evidence into two groups – quantitative and other – and essentially determining that the more important group was inconclusive, the Appellate Body arguably made the issue a closer one than it really was. After all, the US government issued the guarantees on the assumption that they would lose money and, to the extent that the cost of the guarantees at issue here was re-estimated, they still showed losses.

3.2 Serious prejudice

The United States also appealed the Panel's finding that its domestic subsidies to cotton producers caused serious prejudice to Brazil through the suppression of cotton prices internationally. In that respect, the United States raised two particular points.[51]

First, the United States objected that the Panel did not indicate the degree of price suppression that it found to be significant. In the original proceeding, the Panel had used a 'binary' approach in that it first determined whether price suppression had occurred and then considered whether it was significant. In this Article 21.5 proceeding, the Panel followed a unitary approach in which it considered three issues together: the existence of price suppression, its significance, and its causation.[52]

The Appellate Body considered that a unitary approach was acceptable given the conceptual nature of the inquiry – which essentially involved an evaluation of a comparison of what did happen and what would have happened if there had been no US subsidization.[53] In that regard, the Appellate Body noted that the Panel had used an economic model proposed by Brazil in order to undertake the counterfactual assessment. Using that model, but substituting US parameters for the Brazilian ones, the Panel found that US production was 12–18% higher with the subsidies and that elimination of the subsidies would have increased prices by 1.4–2.3% (compared to an increase of 8.2–8.9% using Brazil's parameters).[54] The Panel did not choose between the US and Brazilian parameters, but suggested that even with the US numbers, there was significant price suppression because of the commodity status of the product involved:

> [F]or a basic and widely traded commodity, such as upland cotton, a relatively small decrease or suppression of prices *could be significant* because, for example, profit margins *may* ordinarily be narrow, product homogeneity means that sales are price sensitive or because of the sheer size of the market in terms of the amount of revenue involved in large volumes trade on markets experiencing price suppression.[55]

Noting that the United States had not challenged the accuracy of this statement, the Appellate Body concluded: 'Thus, the range of price effects resulting from the simulations would fall within the Panel's view of what constitutes "significant" price suppression in the specific context of the world price of upland cotton.'[56]

---

51 The United States raised several other evidentiary issues that the Appellate Body grouped together in one section and rejected – in part because they involved questions of fact and in part because the Appellate Body thought the Panel's decision to follow the approach of the original panel on a number of issues was appropriate. Appellate Body 21.5 Report, paras. 382–446.

52 Appellate Body 21.5 Report, paras. 352–353.

53 Ibid., paras. 354 *et seq.*

54 Ibid., paras. 363–365.

55 Panel 21.5 Report, para. 10.50, quoting Panel Report (emphasis added).

56 Appellate Body 21.5 Report, para. 365.

One would have wished for more analysis by the Panel than speculation that a small suppression of prices *could* be significant. Indeed, one could argue that the Panel never found that price suppression was significant in fact, but only speculated that it could be. Nonetheless, given the role of the Appellate Body, which is not to review factual questions, its decision not to disturb the Panel finding may be defensible.

Second, the United States objected to the Panel's conclusion because it had failed to consider the influence of China on cotton prices. China has become the major cotton importer. For us, as well as the Appellate Body, the US evidence that the lack of transparency about Chinese demand had a price-suppressing effect was not all that persuasive.[57] However, the US argument was theoretically sound; it was a matter of whether there was evidence to support it. Nonetheless, the Panel's analysis of this issue was rather terse. In its entirety, it read:

> [B]ased on the evidence before it, that while China may play a significant role in the market for upland cotton, this does not diminish the significance of the impact of [US] subsidies on the world price for upland cotton as a result of their effect on [US] supply to the world market.[58]

Given the weakness of the US evidence, the Appellate Body essentially concluded that the Panel had done enough.[59]

In respect of both of these evidentiary issues, the difference in the level of deference accorded by the Appellate Body to panel factfinding and analysis as opposed to national authority factfinding and analysis is striking. In particular, one is struck by the stark difference between the Appellate Body's approach to non-attribution analysis here and its approach to non-attribution analysis by national authorities in trade-remedy cases. In apparent recognition of this gulf, the Appellate Body stressed that the 'serious-prejudice' provisions of the SCM Agreement do not contain the detailed language on causation and non-attribution applicable to CVD investigations under the same agreement.[60] Nonetheless, there is an explicit causation requirement in Article 5(c) SCM (not mentioned by the Appellate Body) and, according to the Appellate Body, there is a causation requirement inherent in Article 6.3 SCM. Also inherent in these causation requirements is a requirement not to attribute price-suppression effects attributable to other causes than the subsidy to the subsidy. While the lack in Articles 5 and 6 SCM of the more specific language found in the trade-remedy provisions may argue for a bit more flexibility for a panel's consideration of the issue, no reasonable degree of flexibility can justify the difference. The Panel's analysis here

---

57 Appellate Body 21.5 Report, para. 378.
58 Panel 21.5 Report, para. 10.243.
59 Appellate Body 21.5 Report, para. 381.
60 Ibid., para. 368.

does not at all measure up to the Appellate Body's language, for example, in *Japan–Hot-Rolled Steel*:[61]

> In order that investigating authorities … are able to ensure that the injurious effects of the other known factors are not 'attributed' to dumped imports, they must appropriately assess the injurious effects of those other factors. Logically, such an assessment must involve separating and distinguishing the injurious effects of the other factors from the injurious effects of the dumped imports. If the injurious effects of the dumped imports are not appropriately separated and distinguished from the injurious effects of the other factors, the authorities will be unable to conclude that the injury they ascribe to dumped imports is actually caused by those imports, rather than by the other factors. Thus, in the absence of such separation and distinction of the different injurious effects, the investigating authorities would have no rational basis to conclude that the dumped imports are indeed causing the injury.

While one could argue that the apparent difference in approach can be justified on the ground that national investigating authorities may tend to be biased, whereas WTO panels are more objective, the Appellate Body expressly rejected the idea of a different standard, as noted below. Nonetheless, in this case the difference in approach is real (and significant under any evaluative standard).

It is noteworthy, however, that the Appellate Body's position with respect to the role of economic analysis, and in particular of economic models, has evolved significantly since the original proceeding.

In the original proceeding, Brazil submitted a quantitative simulation of an economic model in support of its 'serious-prejudice' arguments, which showed that, but for the US subsidies to the US upland cotton industry, world cotton prices would have been higher by an average of 12.6% during the period 1999–2002. The United States objected to the accuracy and adequacy of the simulation and to the fact that Brazil provided the model itself.

The Panel decided to 'take note' of the outcomes of the simulation, but refused to rely 'upon the quantitative results of the modeling exercise – in terms of estimating any numerical value of the effects of the United States subsidies'.[62] It further indicated that 'Without prejudice to the relevance or utility of such simulations generally to a serious-prejudice analysis under Part III of the SCM Agreement, we would point out our particular concern here, in ensuring procedural fairness between the parties and the reliability of the evidence, that the model was not equally accessible to the parties and, as relevant, to the Panel in these proceedings.'[63]

On appeal, neither party contested the Panel's decision to take the modeling results 'into account where relevant to our analysis … and [to attribute] to them

---

61 *United States – Anti-Dumping Measures on Certain Hot-Rolled Steel Products from Japan*, WT/DS184/AB/R, para. 223 (adopted 23 August 2001).
62 Panel Report, para. 7.1205.
63 Ibid., para. 7.1206.

the evidentiary weight we deemed appropriate'.[64] The United States, however, contended that the Panel failed to include in its analysis the supply response of third countries that would have resulted in the absence of US subsidies. For its part, Brazil argued that the Panel did take this factor into account, since the models it used incorporate such supply response. Both parties agreed on the features of the models, but disagreed on 'whether the Panel *took into account* supply responses of third countries, as reflected in these models or otherwise.'[65]

The Appellate Body was unable to decide on what is ultimately an empirical issue. It simply indicated:

> We note that the Panel indicated expressly that it had taken the models in question into account. It would have been helpful had the Panel revealed how it used the models in examining the question of third country responses. Nevertheless, we are not prepared to second-guess the Panel's appreciation and weighting of the evidence before it, and we do not see any error on the part of the Panel in the application of the law to the facts in addressing this question.[66]

This amounted to accepting the Panel's decision, while at the same time faulting it for insufficient economic analysis. In the ALI project's examination of those reports, the authors (including one of the present coauthors) concluded:

> The *Upland Cotton* case illustrates the challenges that panels face when they are required to evaluate complex economic matters. The serious-prejudice provisions of the SCM Agreement call for an initial determination by the Panel ... In these cases, requirements to determine issues such as 'causation', 'price suppression', and 'significant' must be understood as requirements that panels use the best analytical tools reasonably available to make such determinations.[67]

In this Article 21.5 proceeding, the Panel seems to have heeded the criticism by the Appellate Body and the advice of the ALI project. Here Brazil again submitted an economic model to simulate the effects of US subsidies on the world market for upland cotton, a fact welcomed by the Panel. In its entirety, the relevant paragraph read:

> In this case, we have taken the analysis of the model one step further by considering is some details the arguments made by the parties about the model, its assumptions and results. To the extent possible, we have provided our assessment of these arguments, and based on that arrived at an overall conclusion about the simulation results.[68]

---

64 Ibid., para. 7.1209.
65 Appellate Report, para. 447.
66 Ibid., para. 448 (footnote omitted).
67 André Sapir and Joel Trachtman, *World Trade Review*, see note 1 supra, p. 208.
68 Panel 21.5 Report, para. 10.198. The omitted footnote 491 at the end of the first sentence noted the transparency of the model, with Brazil providing to the United States and to the Panel 'full access to the model, its assumptions and the results'. We recall that in the original proceeding the Panel had deplored that the model used by Brazil was not equally available to the parties and to the Panel itself.

In its evaluation, the Panel noted the advantage of the modeling approach used by Brazil, but was 'also mindful of the criticism by the United States that Brazil's model "has no foundation within economic circles"'.[69] Furthermore, it noted that the magnitude of the impact of US subsidies on the world cotton price depends on the parameter values assigned to the model, and that the two parties presented arguments in favor of different parameter values. The Panel decided not to take a position on which parameter values were better, but nonetheless took 'note of the fact that price suppression has been the outcome of all the simulation results whether one uses the parameter values proposed by Brazil or [those] proposed by the United States'.[70]

Hence, contrary to the original proceeding, where the Panel simply took the model into account, here the model simulation results were central to the Panel's finding of price suppression due to the US subsidies. However, by refusing to take a position on the parameter values, the Panel was still unable to reach a judgment, simply based on the model, about the magnitude of the impact of US subsidies and, therefore, about whether price suppression was 'significant'. For this, as noted above, it needed to invoke the fact referred to previously that upland cotton is a 'basic and widely traded commodity'.

On appeal, the United States claimed that the Panel had failed to determine the degree of price suppression that it found to be 'significant'. In its evaluation of the US claim, the Appellate Body started by focusing on price suppression. It credited the Panel for its extensive discussion of the model simulations presented by both parties, insisting that such simulations are essential in serious-prejudice cases: 'Because the examination of price suppression necessarily involves an analysis of what would have been the case in the absence of an intervening event, modeling exercises are likely to be an important analytical tool that a panel should scrutinize.'[71]

However, the Appellate Body faulted the Panel for refusing to take a stand on which parameters were more appropriate to measure the effect of the subsidies at issue on prices, or on the appropriateness of the model itself. In support of its view that 'the Panel could have gone further in its evaluation and comparative analysis of the economic simulations and the particular parameters used',[72] the Appellate Body noted:

> The relative complexity of a model and its parameters is not a reason for a panel to remain agnostic about them. Like other categories of evidence, a panel should reach conclusions with respect to the probative value it accords to economic

---

69 Ibid., para. 10.220.
70 Ibid. Para. 10.222.
71 Appellate Body 21.5 Report, para. 357.
72 Ibid., para. 358.

simulations or models presented to it. This kind of assessment falls within the panel's authority as the initial trier of facts in a serious-prejudice case.[73]

The Appellate Body had already noted in an earlier footnote that 'where a panel operates as an initial trier of facts, such as this one, it would ... be expected to provide reasoned and adequate explanations and coherent reasoning'.[74] The Appellate Body explicitly stated that this requirement was similar to what a panel is expected to do when examining determinations of domestic investigating author-ities in trade-remedy cases. Perhaps this statement indicates that the Appellate Body in the future will hold panel determinations in these circumstances to the higher standard it expects of national authorities. It did not do so in this case.

Nor did the Appellate Body suggest how panel determinations in future 'serious-prejudice' cases could achieve a higher standard of economic expertise than in the past. Perhaps the earlier advice by the ALI project could usefully be repeated here, namely that:

> The determination of significant price suppression and its causation would seem amenable to a report from an expert review group comprised of economic experts in relevant disciplines...Engaging expert review groups to work through issues of appropriate assumptions and modeling techniques would relieve panels of a burden that they generally cannot bear. Article 13 of the DSU has been found to provide panels with broad flexibility to utilize experts. So it is curious that economic experts have not been used.[75]

4. Conclusion

US–Upland Cotton is one of only three serious-prejudice WTO disputes, one of only two with a positive decision, and the only one with a decision that has been appealed to the Appellate Body. It is also the only serious-prejudice case to have been adjudicated under Article 21.5 DSU.

Regarding the scope of compliance proceedings under Article 21.5 DSU, the Appellate Body upheld the Panel's findings that the two Brazilian claims contested by the United States were properly within the scope of the Article 21.5 proceed-ings. We concur with the Appellate Body's reasoning on these matters.

As far as substantive, evidentiary issues are concerned, the Appellate Body first upheld the Panel's finding that the United States had failed to comply with the DSB's recommendations and rulings concerning export subsidies. It did so despite having faulted the Panel for failing to make an 'objective assessment' of the matter and facts as required by Article 11 DSU, which necessitated that the Appellate Body complete the analysis. Our view, however, is that the Appellate Body's

---

73 Ibid., para. 357.
74 Ibid., para. 293, n.618.
75 André Sapir and Joel Trachtman, see note 1 supra, p. 206.

analysis was too rudimentary to uphold the Panel's finding with sufficient confidence. A remand would therefore have been useful.

Finally, the Appellate Body upheld the Panel's finding that the United States failed to comply with the DSB's recommendations and rulings, in that certain payments to US cotton producers resulted in serious prejudice for Brazil. In doing so, the Appellate Body did not subject the Panel's analysis to the type of searching examination that it has required panels to undertake in respect of injury analyses of national authorities. Of particular interest, the Appellate Body credited the Panel for its discussion of the modeling exercises presented by the parties, although it faulted the Panel for not going far enough in its own evaluation of these exercises. Here we clearly detect a will on the part of the Appellate Body to insist on the necessity for future panels to make full use of analytical tools, such as simulation models, in serious-prejudice cases. We suggest that in order to fulfill this requirement, panels may well have to engage experts under Article 13 DSU.

China – Measures Affecting Imports of Automobile Parts

JASPER WAUTERS

White and Case, LLP

HYLKE VANDENBUSSCHE

Université Catholique de Louvain

Abstract: This paper reviews the WTO Appellate Body Report on
China – Measures Affecting Imports of Automobile Parts (WT/DS342/AB/R,
15 December 2008). This dispute concerns a set of regulatory measures imposing
a 25% 'charge' on imported automobile parts used in the manufacture of motor
vehicles in China. The main legal question in this case consisted of the nature of
this charge as either a border charge subject to China's tariff concessions or an
internal charge, subject to the basic nondiscrimination requirement of GATT
Article III. In our report, we examine the reasoning of the Appellate Body relating
to the difference between these two types of charges. We discuss the role and
relevance of this distinction in the GATT/WTO legal system in general, and for
the purposes of resolving this dispute in particular. We also address the important
systemic question relating to the review of a Member's domestic laws for
purposes of determining their GATT/WTO consistency. This was an important
issue in this case, as China claimed that the Panel misunderstood the meaning of
the relevant Decree and requested the Appellate Body to review the Panel's
erroneous reading of this Decree. We discuss the Appellate Body's reasoning
relating to the review of domestic laws by Panels and the Appellate Body and
express concern over the distinction drawn by the Appellate Body between legal
and factual elements of relevance in the interpretation of such laws.

The 'economic bone' in this case is less straightforward to split than the legal
one. In legal terms, the Appellate Body's decision is a time-consistent one, but, in
economic terms, it is not clear if it is also a welfare-optimal one. The main reason
is that many questions relevant to the case were left unaddressed by the Appellate
Body. Due to the lack of factual evidence to substantiate its allegations, the
Panel's ruling remains rather speculative on certain accounts. For this purpose,
we engage in our own examination of the facts, using mainly a unique dataset of
Chinese firm-level data. We analyze issues of ownership in China's car industry,
the growth of the import-competing Chinese industry over time, the elasticity of

This paper reviews the WTO Appellate Body Report on *China – Measures Affecting Imports of
Automobile Parts* (WT/DS342/AB/R, 15 December 2008) (hereinafter Appellate Body Report). It is
prepared for the American Law Institute project on 'Principles of Trade Law: The World Trade
Organization.'

The views expressed in this paper are those of the author only and do not represent the views of the firm
that he works for. We thank Marco Bronckers for a useful discussion and Rob Howse for comments on an
earlier version.

201

the demand for cars, and duty pass-through, etc. The purpose is to verify more closely who 'benefits' and who 'loses' from the Chinese import duty so as to understand the economic incentives involved. In this respect, we attempt to determine whether the economics support the conclusion that China pursued a beggar-thy-neighbor policy in the car-part industry.

1. The dispute

1.1   The measure at issue

This dispute concerns a set of regulatory measures imposing a 25% 'charge' on imported automobile parts used in the manufacture of motor vehicles in China. The charge is due if the imported auto parts have the character of a 'complete vehicle', something that is determined by the Chinese authorities based on criteria prescribed under three instruments enacted by the Chinese government.[1]

The criteria for such a determination are expressed in terms of particular combinations or configurations of imported auto parts or the value of imported parts used in the production of a particular vehicle model. The use in the production of a vehicle model of specified combinations of 'major parts' or 'assemblies'[2] that are imported requires characterization of *all* parts imported for use in that vehicle model as 'complete vehicles'.

Various combinations of assemblies will meet the criteria, for example: a vehicle body (including cabin) assembly and an engine assembly, or five or more assemblies other than the vehicle body (including cabin) and engine assemblies. The use, in a specific vehicle model, of imported parts with a total price that accounts for at least 60% of the total price of the complete vehicle also requires characterization of *all* imported parts for use in that vehicle model as complete vehicles. Imports of Completely Knocked Down (CKD) and Semi-Knocked Down (SKD) kits[3] are also characterized as imports of complete vehicles.

---

1 These instruments are:

- Policy on Development of the Automotive Industry (Order of the National Development and Reform Commission (No. 8)) ('Policy Order 8'), which entered into force on 21 May 2004;
- Administrative Rules on Importation of Automobile Parts Characterized as Complete Vehicles (Decree of the People's Republic of China, No. 125) ('Decree 125'), which entered into force on 1 April 2005;
- Rules on Verification of Imported Automobile Parts Characterized as Complete Vehicles (Public Announcement of the Customs General Administration of the People's Republic of China, No. 4 of 2005) ('Announcement 4'), which entered into force on 1 April 2005.

2 An 'assembly' is defined in Article 4 of Decree 125 to include the vehicle body (including cabin) assembly, the engine assembly, the transmission assembly, the driving axle assembly, the driven axle assembly, the frame assembly, the steering system, and the braking system. The Panel found that an 'assembly' corresponds roughly to the major parts of a vehicle (Panel Reports, *China – Measures Affecting Imports of Automobile Parts* (WT/DS342/R) (hereinafter Panel Reports), paras. 7.88 and 7.89).

3 Although CKD and SKD kits are specifically mentioned in Article 21(1) of Decree 125, they are not defined under the challenged measures. The Panel found that, for purposes of this dispute, CKD and SKD

In other words, the measures at issue set up a regulatory regime and impose a charge with respect to imported auto parts used in the production or assembly of certain models of motor vehicles that are sold in the Chinese domestic market. They prescribe thresholds regarding the type or value of imported auto parts used to assemble specific vehicle models. If the imported parts used in a given vehicle model meet or exceed these thresholds, then *all* of the imported parts used to assemble that model are characterized as complete vehicles and are subject to the charge under the measures at issue.

The charge is imposed following assembly of the vehicles. The measures set out a number of procedural and administrative steps designed to determine whether the charge applies and ensure tracking and reporting of the imported auto parts, along with payment of the charge, in respect of the relevant auto parts. The amount of the charge imposed corresponds to the tariff rate applicable to complete vehicles, that is 25 %. Imported auto parts that are not 'characterized as complete vehicles' under the measures at issue are subject to duties at the tariff rates for auto parts in China's Schedule of Concessions, that is 10 % on average.

The system is based on the principle of 'self-evaluation' to be performed by the automobile manufacturer prior to beginning production of a new vehicle model that will incorporate imported parts and that will be sold in China. In case of a positive self-evaluation, the manufacture will apply to the Ministry of Commerce for an import license for the parts to be used in the vehicle model. The automobile manufacturer must provide a duty bond,[4] the amount of which is calculated on the basis of the projected quantity and value of the auto parts that will be imported each month. In practice, the amount corresponds to the applicable tariff rate for auto parts (10 % on average) applied to the projected monthly importations of auto parts. The automobile manufacturer may then begin to import parts to be used in the production of its new vehicle model. When the auto parts characterized as complete vehicles for use in a registered vehicle model are then actually imported into China, they are subject to the duty bond as well as to ongoing tracking and reporting requirements imposed on the manufacturer importing those parts. The parts are not, however, subject to any ongoing physical confinement or any other restriction by customs authorities on their use in the internal market.

Article 13 of China's Decree 125 states that auto manufacturers importing auto parts characterized as complete vehicles must declare their importation of such auto parts and *pay duties* to the district customs office. Article 13 thus refers to the obligation not only to declare the importation of auto parts, but also to pay duties.

---

kits refer to all or nearly all of the auto parts and components necessary to assemble a complete vehicle, which must be packaged and shipped in a single shipment, and which must go through the assembly process to become a complete vehicle once they have been imported into the importing country (see, Panel Reports, paras. 7.644–7.647).

4 Panel Reports, paras. 7.51–7.52. Third-party auto suppliers and auto-part manufacturers are not covered by this requirement, as they are subject to normal customs procedures and thus pay the import duty at the tariff rate applicable to auto parts at the time of importation (Panel Reports, para. 7.51).

However, actual payment of the duty/charge under the measures does not occur until the Verification Centre has completed the verification that the imported parts actually possessed the essential character of 'complete vehicles'. This occurs after the manufacturers have finished the assembly of auto parts into complete vehicles.[5] It is this 'duty' that is to be paid by the manufacturers following verification that constitutes the 'charge' under the measure which is being challenged by the complainants.

1.2   The complainants' claims and China's defense

The United States, Canada, and the European Communities (the 'complainants') claimed that the charge imposed under the measures was an 'internal charge' that was inconsistent with Article III:2 of the GATT 1994 because it applied to imported auto parts, while no similar charge applied to like domestic parts. In addition, they argued that the additional administrative requirements on automobile manufacturers that use imported auto parts in excess of specified thresholds violated China's obligations under Article III:4 of the GATT 1994. According to the complainants, these requirements provided an incentive to prefer domestic auto parts. By using domestic parts, the manufacturers would be able to avoid all of the reporting and verification requirements.

In the alternative, if the measures were considered to impose customs duties, as argued by China, the complainants claimed that such a 'duty' (25%) was in excess of the relevant tariff bindings in China's Schedule of Concessions for automobile parts (10%) and was therefore inconsistent with Article II:1(a) and (b) of the GATT 1994.

The complainants also argued that the charge imposed by the measures equally applied to imports of certain unassembled or partially assembled motor vehicles, that is completely CKD and SKD kits.[6] The complainants claimed that China's tariff treatment of such kits under the measures was inconsistent with Article II:1(a) and (b) of the GATT 1994, as it exceeded the 10% import duty rate set for imported parts. Two of the complainants, the United States and Canada, claimed that the measures were also inconsistent with paragraph 93 of China's Accession Working Party Report, in which China promised to set at 10% the level of the

---

5 Once production of the relevant vehicle model begins, the automobile manufacturer must submit a verification application to the relevant authorities. Following verification by the authorities, the automobile manufacturer must make a declaration of duty payable, and submit additional documentation in respect of all relevant complete vehicles assembled from when production of the vehicle model began. The authorities then proceed to classify the auto parts as complete vehicles and to collect the 'duty' and VAT for all imported auto parts used in assembling those complete vehicles.

6 The Panel explained that, although the measures at issue do not define CKD and SKD kits, it considered CKD and SKD kits under the measures to refer to all or nearly all of the auto parts and components necessary to assemble a complete vehicle, which must be packaged and shipped in a single shipment, and which must go through the assembly process to become a complete vehicle once they have been imported into the importing country (Panel Reports, paras. 7.644–7.647).

duties due in respect of the importation of such kits, in case it would create a separate tariff line for kits.[7]

China responded that the charge under the measures was an ordinary customs duty, within the meaning of Article II:1(b), and not an internal measure subject to Article III. China argued that the measures were not inconsistent with Article II of the GATT 1994 because they give effect to a proper interpretation of 'motor vehicles' in China's Schedule of Concessions. China explained that the measures ensured 'substance over form' in the administration of China's national customs law in that they allow customs authorities to classify, as complete motor vehicles, groups of auto parts and components that have the essential character of a complete vehicle, irrespective of how an importer chooses to structure the importation of these parts. China contended that the measures thereby prevent the 'circumvention' of China's tariff headings for motor vehicles. China argued that the treatment of the CKD or SKD kits was in line with its tariff binding for complete vehicles and thus consistent with GATT Article II. In China's view, it was consistent with China's obligation under its Schedule and Article II:1(b) of the GATT 1994 to treat CKD and SKD kit imports as complete vehicles in light of the principle that a complete set of parts 'presented unassembled or disassembled' (e.g., in a kit) is classified as the complete article, not as parts of that article.

China argued that, insofar as the measures were found to be inconsistent with either Article II or Article III, they were justified under Article XX(d) of the GATT 1994. China expressed the view that the measures were necessary to address circumvention of the obligation to pay 25% duties on complete vehicles through the shipment of auto parts at 10% when those parts were later assembled into a complete vehicle.

2. The Panel's findings

The Panel found that the charge imposed by China was an internal charge that was inconsistent with GATT Article III and that could not be justified under GATT Article XX. In the alternative, and assuming the charge was considered to be a customs duty, the Panel found that the charge violated China's tariff commitments under GATT Article II.

With regard to the CKD and SKD kits, however, the Panel was of the view that the 'duties' imposed by the measure were not internal charges, but customs duties covered by GATT Article II. The Panel found that the duties imposed on kits were consistent with China's tariff commitments for complete vehicles under GATT

---

7 Paragraph 93 of China's WPR states as follows: 'Certain members of the Working Party expressed particular concerns about tariff treatment in the auto sector. In response to questions about the tariff treatment for kits for motor vehicles, the representative of China confirmed that China had no tariff lines for completely knocked-down kits for motor vehicles or semi-knocked down kits for motor vehicles. If China created such tariff lines, the tariff rates would be no more than 10%. The Working Party took note of this commitment.'

Article II. However, the Panel considered that China had violated the commitment made at the time of its accession to the WTO that it would not impose duties of more than 10 % on such kits in the event it created a new tariff line for kits. We briefly expand on the Panel's reasoning below.

China's charge on imported auto parts is an internal charge covered by GATT Article III

The Panel first considered as a threshold matter whether, as contended by the complainants, the charge imposed on automobile manufacturers under the measures at issue constituted an 'internal charge' under Article III:2, or, as contended by China, an 'ordinary customs duty' under Article II:1(b).[8] The Panel observed that 'a charge cannot be at the same time an "ordinary customs duty" under Article II:1(b) of the GATT 1994 and an 'internal tax or other internal charge' under Article III:2 of the GATT'.[9]

The Panel found that 'the obligation to pay internal charges does not accrue because of the importation of the product at the very moment it enters the territory of another Member but because of the internal factors (e.g., because the product was resold internally or because the product was used internally), which occur once the product has been *imported* into the territory of another member. The status of the *imported* good, which does not necessarily correspond to its status at the moment of *importation*, seems to be the relevant basis to assess this internal charge.'[10] In sum, according to the Panel:

> [I]f the obligation to pay a charge does not accrue based on the product at the moment of its importation, it cannot be an 'ordinary customs duty' within the meaning of Article II:1(b), first sentence of the GATT 1994: it is, instead, an 'internal charge' under Article III:2 of the GATT 1994, which obligation to pay accrues based on internal factors.[11]

The Panel applied its interpretation to the measures at issue to conclude that they imposed an internal charge rather than an ordinary customs duty. The Panel considered the following facts relevant:

- that the obligation to pay the charge accrues internally after the auto parts have been assembled into motor vehicles within China;[12]
- that the charge is imposed on automobile manufacturers rather than on importers in general;
- that the imposition of the charge on specific imported parts is based on which *other* imported or domestic parts are used together with those imported parts in

8 Panel Reports, para. 7.105.
9 Ibid.
10 Ibid., para. 7.185.
11 Ibid., para. 7.204.
12 Ibid., para. 7.205.

assembling a vehicle model, rather than upon the specific parts at the moment of importation;[13]
- that identical imported parts imported at the same time in the same container or vessel can be subject to different charge rates depending on whether or not the vehicle model into which they are later assembled meets the criteria set out in the measures.[14]

On this basis, the Panel concluded that the 25% charge imposed on automobile manufacturers was an internal charge within the meaning of Article III:2 of the GATT 1994.[15] It held that the Chinese regulatory measures were inconsistent with GATT Article III:2, first sentence, because they subjected imported auto parts to an internal charge in excess of that applied to like domestic auto parts.[16] In addition, The Panel was of the view that the measures were inconsistent with GATT Article III:4 because imported auto parts were accorded less favorable treatment than like domestic auto parts, mainly due to the disincentive created in respect of imported auto parts by the administrative requirements relating to the use of imported parts.[17]

Despite the fact that the Panel thus resolved the issue before it, the Panel went on to make alternative findings under GATT Article II, assuming *arguendo* that the measures would be considered as 'ordinary customs duties' within the scope of the first sentence of Article II:1(b). The Panel concluded that, insofar as this was a correct assumption, the measures were inconsistent with China's tariff binding commitments in respect of auto parts and were thus inconsistent with Article II:1(a) and (b) of the GATT 1994.[18]

The Panel also concluded that the measures at issue were not justified under Article XX(d) of the GATT 1994.[19] In the course of its analysis under Article XX(d) of the GATT 1994, the Panel rejected China's arguments relating to tariff 'circumvention'[20] and made certain observations regarding the operation of the automotive industry in general. The Panel considered that 'the language of Policy Order 8, which is a legal authority giving rise to the implementing measures at issue (Decree 125 and Announcement 4), as well as the circumstances leading up to the introduction of the measures as explained by China cast doubt on China's claim that the measures are "designed" to address the evasion or circumvention of higher tariff rates that apply to motor vehicles under China's tariff schedule'.[21]

---

13 Ibid., para. 7.207.
14 Ibid.
15 Ibid., para. 7.212. The Panel excluded from the scope of this finding the 'charge' imposed on CKD and SKD kits imported under Article 2(2) of Decree 125, which it considered to be an ordinary customs duty.
16 Ibid., para. 7.223.
17 Ibid., para. 7.272.
18 Ibid., para. 7.523.
19 Ibid., para. 7.365.
20 Ibid., para. 7.346. China did not appeal the Panel's finding under Article XX(d).
21 Ibid., para. 7.312. The Panel noted that the title of Policy Order 8 – 'the Policy on Development of the Automotive Industry' – refers to the development of China's automotive industry, not enforcement of

In response to the question of circumvention, the Panel explained that 'to circumvent one tariff duty for another as claimed by China, an importer at least needs to have the intent to do so'.[22] It considered that, to the extent the action China submits as inconsistent under its tariff schedule includes the importation and assembly of auto parts without any intention to avoid the higher tariff duties imposed on motor vehicles, China has not explained why and how such an action is inconsistent with its tariff schedule.

The Panel concluded that Chinese law provided an incentive to export parts rather than complete cars and that there was therefore nothing 'wrong' with exporters acting on that incentive. According to the Panel, 'China has neither provided evidence showing such practices by importers, nor proved to our satisfaction why such actions are inconsistent with importers' obligations under China's tariff schedule.'[23] Insofar as 'circumvention' refers to fraudulent declarations, the Panel considered that this issue was adequately dealt with under Chinese law as it is in most domestic legal systems. The Panel thus found that China had not discharged its burden to prove that the measures 'secure compliance' with its tariff schedule.[24] Neither could the measure be considered as 'necessary' to secure compliance, according to the Panel. The Panel was of the view that the scope of the measures was too broad to be viewed as necessary for the prevention of such an action, since it encompassed even a situation where automobile manufacturers/importers use imported auto parts for their assembly into motor vehicles in the normal course of their business operations without any intention to avoid the higher tariff duties imposed on motor vehicles, let alone any intention to falsely declare or document the specific content of importation. In the Panel's view, this type of measure went well beyond what was necessary to enforce China's tariff provisions for motor vehicles.[25]

With regard to CKD and SKD kits, the Panel found that the measures were not inconsistent with Article II:1(b) of the GATT 1994,[26] since China's tariff commitment of 25% for complete cars can be read to include these types of kits. However, the Panel upheld the argument that the measures were inconsistent with China's commitment under paragraph 93 of China's Accession Working Party Report, since China had *de facto* created a new tariff line for such kits and imposed duties at a level above the level indicated in the WPR.[27]

China's tariff provisions for motor vehicles or vehicle parts. Further, as submitted by the complainants, the text of the preamble of Policy Order 8 also shows that the main reason for introducing the Policy is to further develop China's automotive industry (Ibid., para. 7.306).

22 Ibid., para. 7.326
23 Ibid., para. 7.337.
24 Ibid., para. 7.346.
25 Ibid., para. 7.361.
26 Ibid., para. 7.736.
27 Ibid., para. 7.758. The Panel exercised judicial economy with respect to the claims under the *TRIMs Agreement*, Article III:5 of the GATT 1994, and Articles 3.1(b) and 3.2 of the *SCM Agreement*.

3.   China's appeal and the Appellate Body's findings

China appealed the Panel's characterization of the nature of the 'charge' imposed under the measures at issue. In China's view, the Panel reached its finding on the basis of an erroneous interpretation of the first sentence of Article II:1(b) of the GATT 1994, which failed to take into account the context provided by the rules of the Harmonized Commodity Description and Coding System (the 'Harmonized System'). China asserted that Rule 2(a) of the General Rules for the Interpretation of the Harmonized System (GIR 2(a))[28] enables national customs authorities to classify unassembled auto parts as a complete motor vehicle, including in the situation where auto parts that are related through their subsequent common assembly arrive in multiple shipments. China was of the view that a correct approach would have led the Panel to the conclusion that the charge in question was an ordinary customs duty subject to the tariff bindings in respect of complete vehicles of GATT Article II and China's tariff schedule.

The Appellate Body basically rejects all of China's arguments on appeal, with the exception of the arguments relating to the Panel's treatment of CKD and SKD kits.

Distinguishing between customs duties and internal charges
The Appellate Body agrees with the analytical approach of the Panel to determine as a threshold matter whether the charge imposed by the measure was an internal measure or rather a border measure/customs duty, noting the Panel's view that 'a charge cannot be at the same time an "ordinary customs duty" under Article II:1(b) of the GATT 1994 and an "internal tax or other internal charge" under Article III:2 of the GATT'.[29]

In response to China's argument about the relevance of the correct classification of the product under the rules of the harmonized system, the Appellate Body clarifies that it is of the view that the question was not whether China could treat car parts as complete vehicles. Rather, in its view the relevant question concerns the nature of the measure as either an internal charge or a customs duty. Therefore, the Appellate Body finds, the Harmonized System rules and commentaries do not constitute relevant context that should have been considered by the Panel.[30] The Appellate Body considers that classification issues have some bearing on the question of whether a Member applying a customs duty is in conformity with its

---

28 The text of GIR 2(a) provides:

Any reference in a heading to an article shall be taken to include a reference to that article incomplete or unfinished, provided that, as presented, the incomplete or unfinished article has the essential character of the complete or finished article. It shall also be taken to include a reference to that article complete or finished (or falling to be classified as complete or finished by virtue of this Rule), presented unassembled or disassembled.

29 Appellate Body Report, para. 139.
30 Ibid., para. 152.

obligation, under Article II:1(b), not to impose duties in excess of the bound rate set out in the Member's Schedule for the product concerned. Yet this issue (whether a duty applied to a *product* by virtue of its classification is consistent with Article II:1(b)) is separate from the issue of whether a *charge* falls under the first sentence of Article II:1(b) at all (as opposed to under Article III:2).[31]

The Appellate Body then states its view in respect of the difference between ordinary customs duties and internal charges. According to the Appellate Body, for a charge to constitute an ordinary customs duty in the sense of GATT Article II, 'the *obligation* to pay it must accrue at the moment and by virtue of or, in the words of Article II:1(b), "on", importation'.[32]

In contrast, the Appellate Body[33] is of the view that the charges falling within the scope of GATT Article III are charges that are imposed on goods that have already been 'imported', and that the obligation to pay them is triggered by an 'internal' factor, 'something that takes place *within* the customs territory'.[34] The time at which a charge is collected or paid is not decisive. What is important, however, is that the *obligation* to pay a charge must accrue due to an internal event, such as the distribution, sale, use, or transportation of the imported product.

The Appellate Body thus reaches the following conclusion in paragraphs 163 and 165 of its report:

> This leads us, like the Panel, to the view that a key indicator of whether a charge constitutes an 'internal charge' within the meaning of Article III:2 of the GATT 1994 is 'whether the obligation to pay such charge accrues because of an *internal* factor (e.g., because the product was *re-sold* internally or because the product was *used* internally), in the sense that such 'internal factor' occurs *after the importation* of the product of one Member into the territory of another Member.'[35] We also observe that the Harmonized System does not serve as relevant context for the interpretation of the term 'internal charges' in Article III:2.
>
> ...
>
> In our view accepting that a charge imposed on auto parts following, and as a consequence of, their assembly into a complete motor vehicle can constitute an ordinary customs duty would significantly limit the scope of 'internal charges' that fall within the scope of Article III:2 of the GATT 1994. We also share the concerns expressed by the Panel to the effect that the security and predictability of tariff concessions would be undermined if ordinary customs duties could be applied based on factors and events that occur internally, rather than at the moment and by virtue of importation, and that this, in turn, would upset the carefully negotiated and balanced structure of key GATT rights and obligations,

31 Ibid., para. 155.
32 Ibid., para. 158.
33 Ibid., para. 161.
34 Panel Reports, paras. 7.128 and 7.129.
35 Ibid., para. 7.132 (original emphasis).

including the different disciplines imposed on ordinary customs duties and internal charges.

Characterization of China's 25% charge on imported parts as an
'internal charge'
The Appellate Body considers that 'the same measure may exhibit some characteristics that suggest it is a measure falling within the scope of Article II:1(b), and others suggesting it is a measure falling within the scope of Article III:2', but that one must identify the features that 'are the most central to that measure itself, and which are to be accorded the most significance for purposes of characterizing the relevant charge'[36]

The Appellate Body agrees with the Panel that the characteristics of the charge it had identified – and to which we referred above in the context of the Panel's decision – were of 'particular significance for legal characterization purposes'.[37] It adds to the factors identified by the Panel the fact that it is not the declaration made at the time of importation, but rather the declaration of duty payment made subsequent to the assembly/production of complete motor vehicles, that determines whether the charge will be applied.[38] This, according to the Appellate Body, may lead to the charge being applied to imported parts not originally declared as complete vehicles as well as the nonapplication, following reverification, of the charge in respect of parts originally declared as complete vehicles.

The Appellate Body rejects China's arguments based on the terms used in Chinese law ('duties') to describe the charges as being determinative. The Appellate Body confirmed its earlier expressed view that the way in which a Member's domestic law characterizes its own measures, although useful, cannot be dispositive of the characterization of such measures under WTO law.

In sum, the Appellate Body agrees with the Panel that the 25% charge imposed on imported auto parts under the conditions set forth in the challenged measures is an internal charge subject to the obligations of GATT Article III.[39]

Since China accepted that, if the Appellate Body were to uphold the Panel's finding that the charge imposed under the measures is an internal charge falling within the scope of Article III:2, it must also uphold the Panel's finding that the charge is inconsistent with China's obligations under the first sentence of Article III:2 of the GATT 1994, the Appellate Body agrees with the Panel that the charge violates GATT Article III.2.[40]

---

36 Appellate Body Report, para. 171.
37 Ibid., para. 172.
38 Ibid., para. 173. The Appellate Body refers to the scenario where an automobile manufacturer does not import parts directly, but instead purchases them from an independent third-party supplier within China who paid 10% import duty on the imported parts, while the manufacturer may be liable to pay 25% duties depending on the amount of imported parts used in the assembly of the vehicle (Ibid., para. 174).
39 Ibid., para. 182.
40 Ibid., para. 184.

The Appellate Body also agrees with the Panel that the measures create an incentive to prefer domestic auto parts and thus distort competitive opportunities for imported products in a manner inconsistent with GATT Article III.4. According to the Appellate Body, the administrative procedures and associated delays imposed on automobile manufacturers using imported parts, which could be avoided entirely if a manufacturer were to use exclusively domestic auto parts, provide incentives that negatively 'affect' the conditions of competition for imported auto parts on the Chinese internal market.[41]

Given the fact that it had upheld the Panel's finding under GATT Article III, the Appellate Body saw no reason to examine the Panel's alternative findings under Article II, even though some of the complainants (EC and Canada) considered that it would be useful and systemically important for the Appellate Body to do so. Nor did the Appellate Body see any reason to accede to China's request to declare such alternative findings 'moot and of no legal effect'.[42]

Treatment of CKD kits under the challenged measure

The Appellate Body then turns to the Panel's finding that China's imposition of the 25% charge on CKD and SKD kits is a violation of China's accession commitments under paragraph 93 of its WPR. We recall that the Panel had found that the 'exemption' created by the Decree 125 for kits that were declared as complete vehicles and subject to ordinary customs procedures implied that they were subject to the 25% charge of the measure but not subject to the administrative aspects of the measure. According to the Panel, the 25% charge imposed on such kits was therefore not an internal charge, but rather a customs duty.

China argues that the Panel misread the 'exemption' for kits as set forth in the measure. China explains that the provision of the challenged Chinese Decree 125 relating to CKD and SKD kits exempts such kits from the measures altogether, and thus also from the charge.

The Appellate Body first rejects the suggestion that the Panel's understanding of the Chinese Decree and of the scope of the exemption is a factual determination that it cannot review. The Appellate Body considers that it can review the interpretation of the Panel as to the meaning of China's municipal law. According to the Appellate Body, 'When a panel examines the municipal law of a WTO Member for purposes of determining whether the Member has complied with its WTO obligations, that determination is a legal characterization by a panel, and is therefore subject to appellate review under Article 17.6 of the DSU'.[43]

The Appellate Body examines Article 2 of the Decree and expresses some 'difficulty understanding how the Panel could read Article 2(2) to mean that CKD and SKD kits that are declared and paid for at the border, prior to assembly, and that are not subject to verification or other procedural steps under the measures at

---

41 Ibid., paras. 195–196.
42 Ibid., para. 209.
43 Ibid., para. 225.

issue, can nonetheless be subject to the charge under the measures at issue'.[44] In the view of the Appellate Body, the 'duties' referred to in Article 2(2), which are to be declared and paid upon importation, are not 'duties' or charges imposed under Decree 125. Consequently, it finds that the Panel's construction of Article 2(2), read together with Article 21(1), 'amounts in our view to legal error'.[45]

The Appellate Body faults the Panel for not explaining how the same charge of 25% could be, in one context, an internal charge, while in the context of the CKD and SKD kits it allegedly constitutes a border duty, if indeed this distinction is to be treated as a threshold issue.[46]

The Appellate Body also reverses the Panel's subsequent finding that the measures at issue are inconsistent with China's conditional commitment in paragraph 93 of its Accession Working Party Report, as this finding was premised upon the erroneous view that the measures impose a charge that is an ordinary customs duty on CKD and SKD kits imported under Article 2(2) of Decree 125. The Appellate Body does not see how the charge imposed under the measures at issue could, as an internal charge within the meaning of Article III:2, somehow have violated China's commitment regarding its tariff treatment of CKD and SKD kits in paragraph 93 of its Accession Working Party Report.[47]

4.   Legal analysis

4.1   Border measure or internal charge – a fine line

The main legal issue to be resolved in this case was the question whether the charge imposed by China on imported auto parts was to be characterized as a customs duty (i.e., a border charge) *on the importation of* auto parts, or rather as an internal charge *on imported* auto parts (i.e., an internal measure). Under GATT, different rules apply to these different types of charges.

Ordinary customs duties, as well as all other duties and charges imposed on the importation of goods, are covered by the tariff commitments set forth in a Member's schedule of concessions. GATT Article II provides that no ordinary customs duties are to be levied 'on the importation' of products above the bound tariff rate. In addition, it provides that products shall be exempt from all other duties or charges of any kind 'imposed on or in connection with importation'. GATT Article II is the basic market-access provision that determines the maximum price of the entry ticket to be paid in order to obtain market access in a given Member country. GATT Article XI is the corollary of Article II, as it prohibits any 'restrictions or prohibitions other than duties, taxes or charges ... on importation'.

44 Ibid., para. 235.
45 Ibid., para. 238.
46 Ibid., para. 243.
47 Ibid., para. 245.

GATT Article XI thus confirms that duties and charges as circumscribed by GATT Article II are the only type of border measure allowed for under GATT.

In contrast, the only obligation that Members have in respect of 'internal taxes or other internal charges of any kind' is to ensure that imported products that have paid their entry ticket into the market are treated no differently from like domestic products. That is basically what GATT Article III stands for. It imposes a requirement that internal taxes, and more generally any measures affecting the internal sale, purchase, transportation, distribution or use of products, 'should not be applied to imported or domestic products so as to afford protection to domestic production'. This is translated into two practical obligations: (1) in respect of internal taxes or charges, not to impose internal taxes or other internal charges of any kind in excess of those applied on like domestic products; and (2) in respect of any other internal measures, to ensure that imported products are treated no less favourably than like domestic products. GATT Article III thus acts as an 'anti-circumvention' provision, as it intends to prevent a Member from retreating from its market-access commitments by imposing internal charges or introducing internal measures more generally in a manner that distorts competitive opportunities to the detriment of imported products. The Panel in the case discussed in our report correctly summarized the role played by both provisions in the system in the following manner:

> As the Appellate Body clarified, a basic object and purpose of the GATT 1994, as reflected in Article II of the GATT, is 'to preserve the value of tariff concessions negotiated by a Member with its trading partners and bound in that Member's Schedule'.[48] At the same time, the broad purpose of Article III is 'to avoid protectionism in the application of internal tax and regulatory measures'.[49] While serving their own objects and purposes, these two provisions are also interrelated such that the disciplines contained in these two provisions aim to ensure 'the security and predictability of the reciprocal and mutually advantageous arrangements directed to the substantial reduction of tariffs and other barriers to trade.'[50] To achieve this overall object and purpose of the WTO Agreement,

---

48 Appellate Body Report, *Argentina – Measures Affecting Imports of Footwear, Textiles, Apparel and Other Items* (WT/DS56/AB/R, adopted 22 April 1998), para. 47.

49 Appellate Body Report, *Japan – Taxes on Alcoholic Beverages* (WT/DS8/AB/R, WT/DS10/AB/R, WT/DS11/AB/R, adopted 1 November 1996), DSR 1996:I, pages 16–17; 109–110 (original footnotes omitted). See also Appellate Body Report, *United States – Tax Treatment for 'Foreign Sales Corporations' – Recourse to Article 21.5 of the DSU by the European Communities* (WT/DS108/AB/RW, adopted 29 January 2002), para. 204. The GATT Panel in *Italy–Agricultural Machinery* also provides insight on the object and purpose of Article III, stating that 'the intention of the drafters of the Agreement was clearly to treat the imported products in the same way as the like domestic products once they had been cleared through customs. Otherwise indirect protection could be given' (GATT Panel Report, *Italian Discrimination Against Imported Agricultural Machinery* (adopted 23 October 1958), para. 11).

50 Appellate Body Report, *European Communities – Customs Classification of Frozen Boneless Chicken Cuts* (WT/DS269/AB/R, WT/DS286/AB/R, adopted 27 September 2005), para. 243.

Members are obliged to respect the boundaries between Article III and Article II of the GATT 1994.[51]

However, the distinction between import duties/border charges, on the one hand, and internal charges, on the other hand, is not always an easy one to make. Both GATT Article II on import duties/charges and GATT Article III on internal taxes and charges contain references to the possibility that additional charges may lawfully be imposed or collected at the border, even though their imposition would exceed the bound rate.

GATT Article II.2 provides that nothing in Article II on border charges shall prevent a Member from imposing at any time 'on the importation' of any product 'a charge equivalent to an internal tax imposed consistently with' the non-discrimination obligation of GATT Article III.2 on like domestic products. Similarly, the *Ad* Note to GATT Article III states that any internal charge that applies to an imported product and to the like domestic product and is 'collected or enforced in the case of the imported product at the time of importation, is nevertheless to be regarded as an internal tax or other internal charge' and is thus subject to the provisions of GATT Article III. Both provisions thus warn against simplistic conclusions about the nature of a measure from the mere fact that certain payments are imposed at the border or at the time of importation.

In the case discussed in this report, the Appellate Body had to determine whether the charge imposed by China on imported auto parts was an internal charge covered by GATT Article III or an ordinary customs duty/border charge covered by GATT Article II. The approach followed by the Panel and the Appellate Body in answering this question is in line with the approach adopted in prior GATT/WTO case law relating to the different nature of border measures and internal measures.

In older GATT cases like *Belgian Family Allowances*[52] or *EEC–Parts and Components*,[53] Panels have concluded that if the event that gives rise to the liability to make the payment is an internal event that takes places following importation, such as their assembly, and if the charge is thus imposed on 'imported products' – i.e., products that have been imported already – the charge is of an internal nature, even when this charge is collected at the border. Similarly, the WTO

---

51 Panel Reports, para. 7.201.

52 In this case the 1952 GATT Panel reached the following conclusion:

> After examining the legal provisions regarding the methods of collection of that charge, the Panel came to the conclusion that the 7.5% levy was collected only on products purchased by public bodies for their own use and not on imports as such, and that the levy was charged, not at the time of importation, but when the purchase price was paid by the public body. In those circumstances, it would appear that the levy was to be treated as an 'internal charge' within the meaning of paragraph 2 of Article III of the General Agreement, and not as an import charge within the meaning of paragraph 2 of Article II. GATT Panel Report, *Belgian Family Allowances (allocations familiales)* ('*Belgium–Family Allowances*'), G/32, adopted 7 November 1952, BISD 1S/59.

53 GATT Panel Report, *European Economic Community – Regulation on Imports of Parts and Components* ('*EEC–Parts and Components*'), adopted 16 May 1990, BISD 37S/132.

Panel on *Argentina–Hides and Leather*, found that the prepayment at the border of a Value-Added Tax (VAT) was an internal measure because the measure applied to 'definitive import transactions, but only if the products imported were subsequently re-sold in the internal Argentinean market'.[54] The Panel referred to *Ad* Note to GATT Article III to conclude that 'the fact that [the payment] is collected at the time and point of importation does not preclude it from qualifying as an internal tax measure'.[55]

In contrast, if the charge is 'on' or 'connected with' importation – i.e., in respect of a product that is being imported – and the liability to pay the charge arises as a consequence of importation, it will be considered as a border charge covered by GATT Article II.[56] As noted by the GATT Panel in *EEC – Measures on Animal Feed Proteins*, recalling the GATT negotiating history, 'The Sub-Committee at the Havana Conference considered (Havana Reports pp. 62–63, paragraphs 42–43, E/CONF.2/C.3/A/W.30 page 2) that "certain charges ... were import duties and not internal taxes because ... (a) they are collected at the time of, and as a condition to, the entry of the goods into the importing country, and (b) they apply exclusively to imported products without being related in any way to similar charges collected internally on like domestic products"'.[57]

The same approach to border measures as measures that condition access to the market and impose a condition on entry into the market is found in the WTO case law in respect of GATT Article XI prohibiting restrictions 'on importation'. The Panel on *India–Autos* considered the ordinary meaning of the phrase 're-striction ... on importation' as being a restriction 'with regard to' or 'in connection with' the importation of the product.[58]

The Chinese case discussed in this report shows some resemblance to the GATT case on *EEC–Parts and Components*, relating to so-called 'screwdriver' operations used to circumvent antidumping duties on finished products. In that GATT case, the (then) EEC expressed the view that the antidumping duties it had imposed on finished products were being circumvented by the sale of parts and components

54 Panel Report, *Argentina – Measures Affecting the Export of Bovine Hides and Import of Finished Leather* (WT/DS155/R, adopted 16 February 2001), para. 11.145 (emphasis added, original footnote omitted).

55 Panel Report, *Argentina–Hides and Leather*, para. 11.145.

56 For example, the GATT Panel on *EEC–Parts and Components* came to the following conclusion: 'The text of Articles I, II, III and the Note to Article III refers to charges 'imposed on importation', 'collected ... at the time or point of importation' and applied 'to an imported product and to the like domestic product'. The relevant fact, according to the text of these provisions, is not the policy purpose attributed to the charge but rather whether the charge is due on importation or at the time or point of importation or whether it is collected internally. This reading of Articles II and III is supported by their drafting history and by previous panel reports (e.g. BISD 1S/60; 25S/49, 67)'. GATT Panel report, *EEC–Parts and Components*, para. 5.6.

57 GATT Panel Report, *EEC – Measures on Animal Feed Proteins*, L/4599, adopted on 14 March 1978, 25S/49, para. 4.16.

58 Panel Report, *India – Measures Affecting the Automotive Sector* (WT/DS146/R, WT/DS175/R, adopted 5 April 2002), para. 7.257.

of such products to importers related to or associated with the exporters found to have been dumping their products into the EC market. The EEC considered that 'in order to prevent circumvention, it is necessary to provide for the collection of an antidumping duty on products thus assembled or produced' in the event one could link the assembled products to the products covered by the antidumping duties.[59] The measure imposed by the EEC to fight what it considered to be circumvention of the antidumping duties consisted of imposing the same anti-dumping duties on the finished products assembled in the EEC on the basis of the parts and components exported by exporters that were subject to antidumping duties on the finished products.

The GATT Panel noted that the anti-circumvention duties are levied, according to the EEC regulation, 'on products that are introduced into the commerce of the Community after having been assembled or produced in the Community'. The duties are thus imposed, as the EEC explained before the Panel, not on imported parts or materials, but on the finished products assembled or produced in the EEC. Their imposition is not conditional upon the importation of a product or at the time or point of importation.[60] The GATT Panel found that the internal assembly of the parts into the finished product subject to the antidumping duty triggered the duty liability and thus that the measures imposed by the EEC were internal measures subject to GATT Article III.[61]

In so doing, the GATT Panel rejected arguments by the EEC relating to the policy objective of the charges (to combat circumvention of antidumping duties) or their qualification under domestic law of the EEC as antidumping duties – i.e., border measures. Such arguments were not considered to be relevant to the determination of the nature of the charge, which was either a duty imposed on or in connection with importation within the meaning of Article II or an internal tax within the meaning of Article III.2.[62]

On the nature of the charge imposed by China, the Panel and Appellate Body reach a conclusion similar to that of the GATT Panel on *EEC–Parts and Components*. According to the Appellate Body, for a charge to constitute an ordinary customs duty in the sense of GATT Article II, 'the *obligation* to pay it must

---

59 Article 13 of Council Regulation (EEC) No. 2423/88 as discussed in GATT Panel report, *EEC–Parts and Components*, paras. 2.2–2.7.

60 GATT Panel Report, *EEC–Parts and Components*, para. 5.5

61 The Panel equally rejected the defense that such an anti-circumvention provision was necessary to secure compliance with its GATT-consistent antidumping laws, since the challenged general antidumping Regulation of the EEC did not establish obligations that require enforcement; it merely established a legal framework for the authorities of the EEC. Therefore, in the view of the GATT Panel, the anti-circumvention duties do not serve to enforce the payment of antidumping duties and cannot be justified under GATT Article XX (d). GATT Panel Report, *EEC–Parts and Components*, para. 5.18.

62 According to the GATT Panel, 'the fact that the EEC treats imported parts and materials subject to anti-circumvention duties as not being "in free circulation" therefore cannot, in the view of the Panel, support the conclusion that the anti-circumvention duties are being levied "in connection with importation" within the meaning of Article II:1(b)', GATT Panel Report, *EEC–Parts and Components*, para. 5.7.

accrue at the moment and by virtue of or, in the words of Article II:1(b), "on", importation'.[63] In contrast, the Appellate Body is of the view, like the Panel, that the adjectives 'internal' and 'imported' suggest that the charges falling within the scope of GATT Article III are charges that are imposed on goods that have already been 'imported', and that the obligation to pay them is triggered by an 'internal' factor, 'something that takes place *within* the customs territory'[64]:

> This leads us, like the Panel, to the view that a key indicator of whether a charge constitutes an 'internal charge' within the meaning of Article III:2 of the GATT 1994 is 'whether the obligation to pay such charge accrues because of an *internal* factor (e.g., because the product was *re-sold* internally or because the product was *used* internally), in the sense that such 'internal factor' occurs *after the importation* of the product of one Member into the territory of another Member.[65]

In general, this approach relating to the distinction between border measures and internal charges makes sense – border measures determine the amount that needs to be paid in order to be allowed into a market, while internal charges are triggered by the internal sale, offering for sale, purchase, use, or any other internal event that occurs subsequent to importation. In this case, it was the use of the imported auto parts in a certain combination with other auto parts of foreign origin that led to the imposition of an additional levy to be paid *by the manufacturer of motor vehicles*. Duty liability under the Chinese measure rests with the manufacturer of the vehicle, not the importer of the parts. If the car parts were ultimately not used to manufacture a car that China considered to be an imported vehicle based on the percentage of imported auto parts, the charge was not due, even if the manufacturer had originally informed the authorities to the contrary. It thus seems very clear that it is the use of the parts in a particular combination, once imported, that determines whether the charge is due. In our view, it is correct to conclude, as did the Panel and the Appellate Body, that this charge is not imposed 'on the importation' of the parts but is an internal charge. Arguably, China's measure could be qualified as a 'reverse border adjustment' – China does not impose an additional charge in order to impose the same internal charge levied on domestic products equally on imported products (the normal type of border adjustment measure provided for in *Ad* Note GATT Article III and GATT Article II.2); rather, China imposes the additional charge in order to adjust for a customs duty on cars that was not paid by the importer of the car parts considered as a complete vehicle. In other words, it seems that the internal charge is seen as a means of adjusting for the failure to comply with a border charge (i.e., the customs duty on cars). No GATT provision expressly provides for this type of adjustment

---

63 Appellate Body Report, para. 158.
64 Ibid., para. 161.
65 Ibid., para. 163.

and thus, arguably, such an adjustment is simply a GATT-inconsistent internal charge.

Nevertheless, it seems justified in a case like this one to wonder whether all this discussion about the right 'qualification' of the charge mattered much. Both the Panel and the Appellate Body base their analysis on the fact that Article II refers to charges 'on importation' of a product, while Article III relates to charges imposed on 'imported' products. In line with past GATT/WTO jurisprudence, the Panel considered that 'a charge cannot be at the same time an "ordinary customs duty" under Article II:1(b) of the GATT 1994 and an "internal tax or other internal charge" under Article III:2 of the GATT',[66] and the Appellate Body silently seems to agree with this commonly held view.

However, as became clear in the case of *India–Additional Duties*, the language of GATT Article II.2 casts doubt on this commonly held view that there is such a strict separation. This case suggests that a charge that is imposed at the border and is equivalent to an internal tax may nevertheless be seen as an unjustified border charge that violates GATT Article II, as an internal tax that fails to meet the conditions of GATT Article III, or both.[67] GATT Article II.2 provides that nothing in that Article relating to border measures shall prevent a Member from imposing 'on the importation' of any product a charge equivalent to an internal tax when this charge is imposed consistently with GATT Article III.2. This seems to provide a safe haven for a charge 'on importation' – i.e., a border charge – if it is equivalent to an internal charge. The nature of the charge would be that of a border charge covered by GATT Article II – why else would there be a need for this type of justification under Article II.2? If it were an internal charge, simply collected at the border, GATT Article II would not apply and there would be no need for this type of safe haven. And what is GATT Article II.2 actually saying – that a border charge ('on importation') can be justified as an internal charge so long as there exists a domestic equivalent for this charge and the charge complies with the nondiscrimination requirement of GATT Article III? This type of approach seems to argue against a strict and clean separation between border measures and internal charges based on certain essential characteristics of the measure.

Maybe a more pragmatic approach would be to say that measures that are imposed at the border should prima facie be considered to be border measures

---

66 Panel Report, para. 7.105.

67 The Appellate Body Report, *India – Additional and Extra-Additional Duties on Imports from the United States* (WT/DS360/AB/R, adopted 17 November 2008), found that Indian 'Additional Duty would not be justified under Article II:2(a) of the GATT 1994 insofar as it results in the imposition of charges on imports of alcoholic beverages in excess of the excise duties applied on like domestic products. Consequently, this would render the Additional Duty inconsistent with Article II:1(b) to the extent that it results in the imposition of duties on alcoholic beverages in excess of those set forth in India's Schedule of Concession'. Appellate Body Report, *India–Additional Duties*, para. 214. In other words, it seems that the Appellate Body was saying that a charge imposed at the border which is not consistent with the non-discrimination requirement of Article III.2, even if it perhaps has the character of an internal charge, would be inconsistent with Article II.1(b) on border measures.

subject to GATT Article II. One should not assume that they are actually internal measures simply collected or enforced at the border, unless such charges are clearly linked to a domestic tax equivalent. Such was not the case here, and no argument to this effect was made by China. There obviously was no domestic counterpart to the 25% charge imposed on imported products. China clearly considered the charge to be an import duty, and the Chinese customs authorities were the ones collecting the charge.

It seems that the Panel could have reached the same conclusion of violation simply by accepting that China imposed a duty on imported parts that exceeded the tariff binding on auto parts as set forth in China's Schedule. The only relevant question before the Panel at that stage would be whether China was justified in imposing duties at the level reserved for complete vehicles on parts simply because they were later assembled into a 'complete vehicle' as defined by the Chinese authorities.

The answer to this question has to be 'no': all imported parts will one day be assembled into a complete vehicle and may thus become cars, but what is being imported are parts, not cars.[68] Whether considered as an internal charge or as a customs duty, it is clear that China would be found to have violated its GATT obligations. Maybe the Panel could have done as the 1992 GATT Panel on the *Canadian Liquor Board* case did: it concluded that 'the question whether the restrictions violated Article III.4 [on internal measures] or Article XI:1 [on border restrictions other than duties] of the General Agreement was ... of no practical consequence in the present case'.[69]

4.2 Reviewing the meaning of domestic legislation – a matter of fact or law?

Article 17.6 DSU provides that an appeal 'shall be limited to issues of law covered in the panel report and legal interpretations developed by the panel'. In other words, a challenge to a Panel's finding before the Appellate Body is limited to matters of law, and in principle it is not for the Appellate Body to review factual determinations made by the Panel.

The only indirect way of making the Appellate Body review factual determinations is through Article 11 DSU, which requires a Panel to make an 'objective assessment of the matter' before it. Article 11 DSU thus provides a way of

---

68 The exception could consist of parts 'presented as complete vehicles' under the General Rules for the Interpretation of the Harmonized System, namely, GIR 2(a), which provides:

> Any reference in a heading to an article shall be taken to include a reference to that article incomplete or unfinished, provided that, as presented, the incomplete or unfinished article has the essential character of the complete or finished article. It shall also be taken to include a reference to that article complete or finished (or falling to be classified as complete or finished by virtue of this Rule), presented unassembled or disassembled.

However, as explained through lengthy argumentation by the Panel, this does not justify China's imposition of duties for complete vehicles on parts which it has determined as having the essential character of a complete vehicle based on their subsequent assembly. Panel Report, Section D.

69 GATT Panel Report, *Canada – Import, Distribution and Sale of Certain Alcoholic Drinks by Provincial Marketing Agencies*, DS 17/R, adopted 18 February 1992, 39 S/75–76, para. 5.6.

challenging the Panel's analysis of the evidence or its general approach to establishing the facts. This appeal raised the question whether a Panel's interpretation of
the meaning of municipal law is a legal interpretation by the Panel or a factual
determination that, in the absence of an Article 11 DSU claim, cannot be reviewed
by the Appellate Body.

In particular, the Panel had interpreted a provision in the challenged Chinese
Decree 125 relating to the exemption for CKD and SKD kits to mean that such kits
were subject to the charge under the Decree but not subject to the administrative
requirements of this Decree. China appealed the findings of the Panel regarding
CKD and SKD kits. It did not deny that CKD and SKD kits were subject to a 25%
duty, but argued that this duty was not a duty imposed by the challenged Decree.
China claimed that the Panel misread the Decree's exemption for CKD and SKD
kits as being only a partial exemption. It thus requested the Appellate Body to
examine the Decree and to review the Panel's erroneous reading of this Decree.
The United States on the other hand argued that a Panel's 'constructions of municipal law are factual determinations in WTO dispute settlement' and that the
Appellate Body may not review such findings *de novo*, but must accord them 'the
same deference as other types of factual findings made by Panels in WTO dispute
settlement proceedings'.[70]

The Appellate Body, referring to its report on *US–Section 211 Appropriations
Act*, rejected the US argument and considered that 'When a panel examines the
municipal law of a WTO Member for purposes of determining whether the
Member has complied with its WTO obligations, that determination is a legal
characterization by a panel, and is therefore subject to appellate review under
Article 17.6 of the DSU.'[71] It then added the following qualification of this right to
review a Panel's interpretation of a Member's municipal law, which we find particularly intriguing:

> The Appellate Body has reviewed the meaning of a Member's municipal law, on
> its face, to determine whether the legal characterization by the panel was in error,
> in particular when the claim before the panel concerned whether a specific in-
> strument of municipal law was, as such, inconsistent with a Member's obliga-
> tions.[72] We recognize that there may be instances in which a panel's assessment of
> municipal law will go beyond the text of an instrument on its face, in which case
> further examination may be required, and may involve factual elements.[73] With

---

70 Appellate Body Report, para. 224.

71 Ibid., para. 225.

72 [footnote original] See, for instance, Appellate Body Report, *United States – Section 211 Omnibus
Appropriations Act of 1998* (WT/DS176/AB/R, adopted 1 February 2002), para. 106.

73 [footnote original] The Appellate Body Report, *United States – Sunset Review of Anti-Dumping
Duties on Corrosion-Resistant Carbon Steel Flat Products from Japan* (WT/DS244/AB/R, adopted
9 January 2004), stated that '[i]f the meaning and content of the measure are clear on its face then the
consistency of the measure can be assessed on that basis alone. If, however, the meaning … is not evident
on its face, further examination is required' (Appellate Body Report, *US–Corrosion-Resistant Steel Sunset
Review*, para. 168). See also Appellate Body Report, *United States – Countervailing Duties on Certain*

respect to such elements, the Appellate Body will not lightly interfere with a panel's finding on appeal.[74]

On the point of principle – whether a Panel's interpretation of the meaning of municipal law is a factual determination or rather a legal interpretation subject to Appellate Body review – the Appellate Body's ruling in this case is in line with earlier findings to this effect in *India–Patents (US)* and *US–Section 211 Appropriations Act.* Although we are of the view that this proposition is debatable,[75] we wish to focus our commentary on the new twist given by the Appellate Body to its authority to review a Panel's interpretation of the meaning of municipal law.[76]

In the case discussed in this report, the Appellate Body qualified its 'right to review' a Panel's determination of the meaning of municipal law and stated that it would 'not lightly interfere with a panel's finding' when the Panel's assessment of municipal law goes 'beyond the text of an instrument on its face' and thus involves 'factual elements'.

It is not clear to us what exactly the Appellate Body was trying to say in the bolded part of the above-quoted paragraph. It seems that the Appellate Body was suggesting that, if the determination of the Panel is based on the text of the municipal law without consideration of the application of the law or its interpretation

Corrosion-Resistant Carbon Steel Flat Products from Germany (WT/DS213/AB/R, adopted 19 December 2002), paras. 156 and 157.

74 Appellate Body Report, para. 225. Following its review of the Decree, the Appellate Body concluded that the Panel's construction of Article 2(2) of the Chinese Decree that the kits were exempted from the administrative aspects of the measure but still subject to the charge imposed by the Decree 'amounts in our view to legal error' (Appellate Body Report, para. 238).

75 In our view, there are two different questions at play: First, what does the measure – i.e., the municipal law in question – mean, and what does it require authorities to do? This seems to be a determination of what in fact is required under the law, as interpreted by the domestic courts, etc. A second question is whether what is required by municipal law may correctly be qualified as a violation of the obligations set forth in the international agreement. That second question is clearly a legal assessment, as it involves the application of the international law, as interpreted on the basis of the principles of the Vienna Convention on the Law of Treaties, to the facts as determined by the Panel when determining the meaning of the municipal law. Of course, as with any 'measure', a review that concerns only the second question is limited, as the review of the Panel's application of the law to the facts is based on the assumption that the Panel correctly determined what the facts are. But maybe that limitation was precisely what Article 17.6 DSU intended to impose on the Appellate Body. The arguments offered by the Appellate Body for a more expansive review authority are not very convincing, as the determination of the implications of a Member's municipal law are not more 'legal interpretations' than is the determination of the implications of any other measure. It seems that the Appellate Body is simply keen to review a Panel's interpretation of the meaning of municipal law, while with regard to other types of 'measures', it feels comfortable hiding behind the argument that it is not reviewing the factual determinations of the Panel unless an Article 11 DSU claim has been made. In any case, the Appellate Body construed a way out of the limitation imposed by Article 17.6 DSU through the use of Article 11 DSU ('objective assessment of the matter') as the avenue to bring factual determinations before the Appellate Body. The Appellate Body could have used the same avenue to address a Panel's interpretation of the meaning of municipal law.

76 For an interesting discussion of the question of the treatment of national law in WTO law, see S. Bhuiyan (2007), *National Law in WTO Law, Effectiveness and Good Governance in the World Trading System,* Cambridge University Press, pp. 207–243.

by the domestic courts, then the Panel's reading of the meaning of the municipal law is subject to review by the Appellate Body. However, if the Panel relies on the application of the law or on domestic court rulings to determine the meaning of the law as such, then the Panel's determination rests on 'factual elements' that the Appellate Body would not 'lightly interfere with'. Hence, the Appellate Body would view this interpretation as a factual matter, not subject to review, unless through Article 11 DSU.

The Appellate Body's reasoning appears to deny that, from the standpoint of international law, 'municipal laws are merely facts'.[77] That is why in the past the WTO Appellate Body has stated that the consistency of a Member's domestic laws must be assessed on the basis of the text of the law, its consistent application in practice, if applicable, and possibly the pronouncements of domestic courts on the meaning of such laws, as well as the opinions of legal experts and the writings of recognized scholars:

> A responding Member's law will be treated as WTO-consistent until proven otherwise. The party asserting that another party's municipal law, as such, is inconsistent with relevant treaty obligations bears the burden of introducing evidence as to the scope and meaning of such law to substantiate that assertion. Such evidence will typically be produced in the form of the text of the relevant legislation or legal instruments, which may be supported, as appropriate, by evidence of the consistent application of such laws, the pronouncements of domestic courts on the meaning of such laws, the opinions of legal experts and the writings of recognized scholars. The nature and extent of the evidence required to satisfy the burden of proof will vary from case to case.[78]

In *Dominican Republic–Import and Sale of Cigarettes*, the Appellate Body clearly rejected an attempt by the complainant to impose an analysis of its 'as such' claim based on the text of the legislation in isolation.[79]

---

77 Permanent Court of International Justice, *Certain German Interests in Polish Upper Silesia*, [1926], PCIJ Rep., Series A, No. 7, p. 19, as referred to with approval in Appellate Body Report, *India – Patent Protection for Pharmaceutical and Agricultural Chemical Products* (WT/DS50/AB/R, adopted 16 January 1998), para. 65. Also see GATT Panel Report, *US–Tobacco*, para. 75. This statement by the PCIJ is often quoted without much consideration of what seems to have been meant by it. Basically, it seems that the PCIJ meant to say that an international tribunal does not have to take 'judicial notice' of a country's municipal law but may require proof of the meaning of municipal law and review evidence relating to the meaning of the law. It also implies that an international tribunal is to examine the meaning of municipal law in the domestic factual context – i.e., in the light of its application by the administrative authorities, the interpretation offered by domestic courts, etc. See I. Brownlie (2008), *Principles of Public International Law*, 7th Edition, Oxford University Press, pp. 38–39.

78 Appellate Body Report, *US–Carbon Steel*, para. 157 (footnote omitted); Appellate Body Report, *Dominican Republic – Measures Affecting the Importation and Internal Sale of Cigarettes* (WT/DS302/AB/R, adopted 19 May 2005), para. 111 and Appellate Body Report, *United States – Measures Affecting the Cross-Border Supply of Gambling and Betting Services* (WT/DS285/AB/R, adopted 20 April 2005), para. 138.

79 Appellate Body Report, *Dominican Republic–Import and Sale of Cigarettes*, paras. 112–115.

This was also the approach followed by the WTO Panel on *US–Section 301*, which examined a section of US law, first to determine its meaning in order to subsequently assess whether the challenged section of US law was consistent with the obligations of the US under the WTO Agreements. This Panel correctly considered that it was not to:

> interpret US law 'as such', the way we would, say, interpret provisions of the covered agreements. We are, instead, called upon to establish the meaning of Sections 301–310 as factual elements and to check whether these factual elements constitute conduct by the US contrary to its WTO obligations.[80]

The GATT Panel on *US–Tobacco* similarly considered that an examination of a Member's law required it to refrain from engaging in an independent interpretation of domestic laws and to treat the interpretation of such laws as questions of fact.[81]

In other words, the Appellate Body's distinction between certain textual 'legal' elements and other nontextual 'factual' elements in the case discussed in this report is at odds with the way public international law, as well as established GATT/WTO case law, views the interpretation of municipal law. In addition, it seems that the Appellate Body forgot that in the case of *India–Patents (US)* – to which it expressly refers in support of its position that it can review a Panel's interpretation of domestic law – the Panel and Appellate Body did not simply examine the text of the Indian law in isolation. Rather, there was a considerable amount of evidence available in that case regarding the proper interpretation of the express terms of the Indian Patents Act, all of which was taken into consideration by the Panel and the Appellate Body in its review of the Panel's determination.

Therefore, it would seem proper for the Appellate Body to consider either that any determination by the Panel regarding the meaning of municipal law is a factual determination that is not subject to appeal (other than through Article 11 DSU), and thus to reverse its prior rulings in this respect; or to accept, as it seems to have done in the past, that the interpretation of municipal law in order to determine the law's consistency with the WTO Agreements is a legal interpretation that is subject to review by the Appellate Body, irrespective of the kind of evidence used by the Panel to determine the meaning of the law. A bit of both is not possible, and statements like the one made in this case do not clarify matters; quite to the contrary. The distinction that the Appellate Body seems to make between cases in which the Panel simply bases its understanding of the municipal law on the text of the law as such, without resort to the application of the law, and other cases in which 'factual elements' are incorporated in the analysis is, in our view, misguided.

---

80 Panel Report, *United States – Sections 301–310 of the Trade Act of 1974* (WT/DS152/R, adopted 27 January 2000), para. 7.18.
81 GATT Panel Report, *US–Tobacco*, para. 75.

Such statements, which seem intended only for the Appellate Body in a later case to refer to when it does not feel like reviewing a Panel's interpretation of a Member's municipal law, do not provide the system with 'security' or 'predictability'. To the contrary, they create doubt and uncertainty as to the scope of the Appellate Body's review authority in important cases involving the interpretation of municipal law.

5. Economic analysis

5.1   Incentives for abuse on both sides

It is clear from the above that the 'legal bone' in the case is relatively straightforward in the sense that the Panel's rulings and the Appellate body's decisions are very much in line with earlier rulings and decisionmaking and can therefore be considered as time-consistent. From a legal point of view this case can even be described as highly 'predictable' in the light of similarity with earlier dispute cases. The time consistency by the Panel and the Appellate body reduces uncertainty and enhances transparency in decisionmaking, which is important for trade.

From an economic point of view, time-consistency tends to rank second to the objective of welfare. The ultimate question to an economist is how policy affects the welfare of the parties involved and whether or not a policy is welfare-improving from a unilateral or from a multi-lateral perspective. However, in practice this is a much more difficult objective to verify than time-consistency of policy, but this should not prevent us from striving for better outcomes than a mere pragmatic approach.

Ideally, WTO rules should be in place to make certain that world welfare is maximized; this can be attained by drafting and applying rules to ensure that countries do not pursue their unilateral welfare-maximizing policies at the expense of other countries, which would be a 'beggar-thy-neighbor' policy where one country's gain would be another country's loss. From an economic point of view, what determines who is 'wrong' or who is 'right' in a trade-policy conflict is often the beggar-thy-neighbor policy content of the action undertaken. Policies where one country gains at the expense of another are unlikely to yield stability, which may hurt trade, and they are therefore undesirable. Extrapolated to this dispute case under scrutiny, some insight into who 'gains' and who 'loses' from the higher duty imposed on imported car parts could have helped the Panel to make an even more informed decision. From this perspective several important questions were not raised in the course of the dispute and consequently no factual evidence was gathered on them.

Economists feel particularly uncomfortable if no factual evidence is gathered to substantiate the allegations made on both sides of the fence, with China accusing foreign suppliers of 'circumventing' import duties (GATT Article XX), and importers accusing China of pursuing an '*industrial policy*' aimed at favoring the domestic car industry (Article III:2 of the GATT).

Without sufficient factual evidence, the Panel cannot but remain rather speculative on certain accounts. For instance, the Panel asserted that the import duty of 25% on car parts, decided on in 2004 and taking effect in 2005, is an internal charge (Article III:2) favoring the import-competing Chinese industry of motor parts. But for this to be true, it would have been relevant to investigate whether such an import-competing industry existed and whether it was benefited during the time that the Chinese applied their elevated import duty on parts. In the absence of such an industry, car assemblers in China would not be in a position to source from an alternative domestic supplier and would be forced to pay the higher import duty on car parts, squeezing their profits. This would not be in their interest, and that would leave us wondering why China would introduce such a measure. Follow-up questions that come to mind are: Who are the car assemblers in China? To what extent are they foreign firms or domestic firms? In other words, ownership matters in order to determine who carries the burden of the duties. Most importantly also: Who buys the assembled cars? Is it domestic Chinese consumers or foreign ones, and to what extent is the import duty passed through to the consumer in the form of higher prices? That in turn will depend on the demand elasticity for assembled cars, which is often correlated with overcapacity in the industry.

But before we enter a more systematic treatment of some of the questions above, we can ask ourselves why China imposed a higher tariff on the imports of motor vehicles than on motor parts before 2004 in the first place. It is true that, in the past, many great nations have pursued similar tariff structures for the purpose of building their own manufacturing industries using the dual tariff structure as a tool of industrial policy.[82] A country that makes the imports of complete motor vehicles relatively more expensive than imports of parts provides an incentive in favor of the shipments of parts and invites new investment in assembly activities. Additional investment in car assembly can occur through domestic entry or foreign investors keen on 'jumping' the high import duty on complete motors. One underlying reason for China to pursue such a policy could be that assembly activities generate technology spillovers and know-how that China would like to internalize rather than simply import from abroad. Additionally, it may also reflect a concern for creating domestic Chinese employment, since assembly is usually a labor-intensive activity. While China has not been violating any rules by setting its dual tariff structure on motor vehicles versus car parts at the time of entry into the WTO in 2001, it is undeniable that this gave rise to certain incentives for foreign suppliers, namely to ship more parts instead of complete motor vehicles. Hence, we expect the beneficiaries of the dual tariff schedule imposed to be the foreign suppliers of parts and the losers to be the foreign importers of complete motor vehicles. But an adversely affected importer of complete motor vehicles, faced with

---

82 M. Irish (2004), *The Auto Pact: Investment, Labour and the WTO*, Kluwer Law International.

a high import tariff of 25 %, can try to circumvent the duty by taking his complete motor vehicle apart, shipping the parts to China, and paying 10 % import duties, thus saving 15 % in duties. Economically speaking, the incentive to circumvent China's dual tariff structure was definitely present before 2004, and there is nothing in the case analysis to suggest that this did not actually occur. Indeed, history tells us that *circumvention* of high import duties through a strategy of disassembling products into parts is a distinct possibility and a strategy pursued by importers of final goods adversely affected by import duties.

A well-described example of this occurred during the 1980s when Japan was heavily targeted by European antidumping duties on its imports of consumer electronics into Europe. The Japanese tried to avoid the import duties by 'jumping' the duties by setting up assembly plants in Europe so that *they* could start shipping to Europe parts on which *they* did not have to pay duties; the parts were then further assembled inside the EU into consumer electronics and sold on the European market. The EU tried to put a stop to this through the 'screwdriver' cases by levying import duties on the parts similar to import duties on final consumer electronics. Academically, the causality between antidumping duties and Japanese 'antidumping' jumping is well documented[83] but from a legal point of view the import duties were not WTO-consistent, since they discriminated foreign parts against domestic parts and were considered an internal charge.

Is this what has been going on in China? Has there been an increase in the imports of car parts? Has there been an inflow of FDI during the time of the dual tariff structure, accompanying the increase in imported parts, which could be a sign of circumvention? If the objective of the Chinese government was to create its own car assembly industry by using trade policy as an industrial policy, did they succeed in doing that? Did the Chinese car-manufacturing sector grow during that time?

For a WTO Panel, it should be relatively easy to get access to this kind of data, if only because it can ask the parties involved in a dispute to supply the relevant information. While the questions above are not directly related to the object of the dispute, for an economist 'initial conditions' are important. There can be little doubt that the imposition of the dual tariff structure, with 25 % duties on imports of motor vehicles but only 10 % on the imports of parts, created certain incentives and dynamics in the car industry in China that laid out the foundations or 'initial conditions' in the light of which this dispute case should be considered.

Without access to firms' private information, we can only turn to the available public information in an attempt to get a better understanding of some of the allegations made in the dispute case.[84]

---

83 A. Blonigen (2002), 'Tariff-jumping antidumping duties', *Journal of International Economics*, 57(1); J. Haaland and I. Wootton (1998), 'Antidumping jumping: reciprocal antidumping and industrial location', *Weltwirtschaftliches Archiv*, 134(2).

84 The product level trade data set we use is UN Comtrade for imports and exports of complete motor vehicles (HS codes 8702, 8703, 8704) and motor vehicle parts (HS codes 8706, 8707, 8708).

Figure 1. Imports of complete motor vehicles and car parts

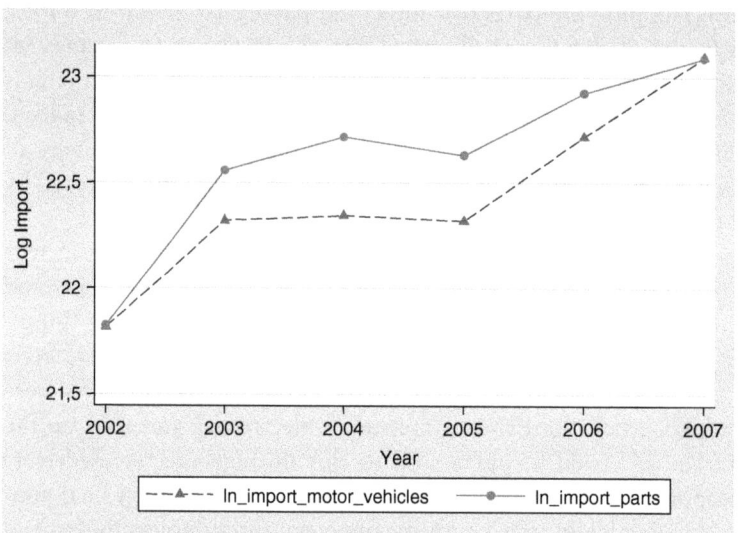

Source: UN Comtrade, imports reported in dollars.

We start in Figure 1 by examining the evolution of imports into China of complete motor vehicles as well as car parts to verify if the incentives that we believe to arise under China's trade policy are somehow reflected in the trade figures. Figure 1 shows that in 2002, right after China's entry into WTO, the imports of car parts equaled the imports of complete motor vehicles. But shortly after that, the imports of parts into China increasingly exceeded that of complete motor vehicles. This seems to suggest that the imposition of a dual tariff structure may indeed have created incentives for relatively more car parts being imported relative to complete vehicles. But after 2004, the gap between imports of parts and imports of complete motor vehicles narrowed, and they became equal to each other again in 2007. This seems to suggest that the measures after 2004 had taken effect. After an initial boost in the imports of car parts coinciding with an initially slower growth in imports of motor vehicles, imports in both types of activities converged again in 2007, possibly due to the circumvention policy on car parts that China pursued by that time, which again made imports of parts relatively less attractive.

In that same period, we also observe a substantial inflow of Foreign Direct Investment (FDI) in the car-manufacturing sector in China (in million USD). Table 1 shows that FDI especially increased before the years 2004 and 2005, but stabilized afterwards in the period that China imposed the circumvention duty that, under certain conditions, implied a similar duty treatment for parts as for complete motor vehicles. FDI inflows were highest in 2004 and 2005 but decreased again substantially in 2006. This seems to be consistent with the hypothesis that before 2005 there was a lot of tariff-jumping FDI taking place, and after the introduction of a high tariff on car parts, that kind of FDI inflow stopped.

Table 1. Inflow of foreign direct investment in
Chinese car manufacturing

Year	In million US$
2000	1089.9
2001	1017.6
2002	1226.6
2003	2003.4
2004	3352.5
2005	3404.9
2006	2140.9

Source: Ministry of Commerce of PR China.

At first glance, these facts could be consistent with a story of duty circumvention by foreign suppliers of car parts. But in order to assert that circumvention has taken place, there is a missing piece of the puzzle – i.e., *circumvention* assumes that the *same* suppliers previously shipping complete motor vehicles are the *same* ones setting up assembly plants in China and afterwards switching to shipping parts.

In this dispute case, no evidence was collected to verify that the ownership of the importing firms was the same as that of the FDI firms, thus distinguishing the EU screwdriver cases mentioned earlier, where the same Japanese firms were involved in first shipping complete goods and afterwards setting up plants in Europe and shipping parts instead of motor vehicles. The facts observed – i.e., increase in the shipment of parts relative to complete motor vehicles and inward investment – could just reflect different firms entering the car-manufacturing industry attracted by the incentives provided by the dual tariff structure.

Clear evidence on circumvention would have to show that the same firms previously supplying the Chinese market with complete cars were engaging in inward FDI in China and altering their shipments to China into parts rather than complete cars in response to the dual Chinese tariff structure in the initial years after 2001.

An alternative interpretation of the facts is that China deliberately used its tariff policy as part of an industrial policy. China may have used trade policy for the purpose of building its own car industry. The tariff-jumping FDI triggered by the dual tariff structure may have been anticipated and intended in order for the technology embedded in the assembly of cars to spill over from foreign investors to domestic car assemblers once foreign firms had invested in China. Academically speaking, the effectiveness of such an industrial policy is questionable, since the empirical results on FDI spillovers are ambiguous and inconclusive. At best, horizontal spillovers of FDI amongst firms engaged in the same type of activity are found to be weak. Similar types of firms act more as rivals and try to prevent knowledge spillovers to horizontal competitors. The only robust result emerging from the spillover literature is the presence of vertical spillovers, i.e. between a foreign multinational and its indigenous suppliers,[85] which could have given China a reason, in a second phase of its industrial policy, to pull up the import duty on car parts for the purpose of fostering local suppliers and to encourage vertical spillovers between the downstream FDI that had jumped the original tariff on complete vehicles and the local suppliers.

It is not unimaginable that China, through the phasing of its trade policy, tried to create its own car industry.[86] Introducing a high tariff wall on the imports of complete motor vehicles in a first stage favors domestic assembly of cars and stimulates foreign and domestic entry of car assemblers. Once the car assembly activity is well developed and foreign investors with their technology are in place, a higher tariff on the imports of car parts could constitute a second stage in China's industrial policy, where it aims to stimulate the domestic upstream production of car parts. Imposing a higher tariff on imports of parts favors 'local sourcing' to the benefit of the domestic import-competing car-parts industry but to the detriment of 'foreign sourcing' of parts, which brings us to the current dispute-settlement case under analysis. By pulling up the tariff on imported parts to 25%, imports of car parts will be adversely affected and car manufacturers inside China eager to save on costs are likely to switch suppliers and source from local suppliers (if present) that are not subject to the import duty.

The use of trade policy to build import-competing industries is a development strategy sometimes referred to as the 'infant-industry' argument for trade protection. However, by now we know that strategy is a fallacy. Baldwin showed that using trade policy is welfare-inferior to free trade.[87] A better way to build a domestic manufacturing industry is through the capital market that should provide the necessary financing and loans to facilitate the construction of new industries. This is far less distortive and is welfare-superior to trade policy to achieve that purpose. Of course, for the Baldwin argument to hold, capital markets should function properly. In China, however, there is evidence to suggest that credit markets do not function properly and are far less efficient than in most developed countries,[88] which may well explain China's incentive to revert to a relatively old way of constructing an import-substitution industry using trade policy.

The discussion above reveals that the incentive structure in this dispute case is 'open ended' in the sense that the rules in place undeniably give foreign suppliers an incentive to 'circumvent' the initial duty on complete vehicles (which is the

85 Beata Smarzynska Javorcik (2004), 'Does foreign direct investment increase the productivity of domestic firms? In search of spillovers', *The American Economic Review*, 94(3): 605–627.

86 In the original Panel Report, the Chinese delegation spoke of an industrial policy strategy.

87 Robert E. Baldwin (1969), 'The case against infant-industry tariff protection'; *The Journal of Political Economy*, 77(3): 295–305.

88 Sandra Poncet, Walter Steingress, and Hylke Vandenbussche (2008). 'Financial constraints in China: firm-level evidence'; CORE DP 2008/79; Alessandra Guariglia and Sandra Poncet (2008), 'Could financial distortions be no impediment to economic growth after all? Evidence from China', *Journal of Comparative Economics*, 36(4): 633–657.

Chinese stance in the dispute), although this remains unverified. At the same time, the Chinese government may also 'abuse' the higher tariff on car parts as a second phase in its industrial policy aimed at fostering its import-competing car-parts industry, which favors 'local sourcing' over foreign sourcing (which is the EU, US, and Canadian stance in the dispute) in the hope of benefiting from vertical spillovers coming especially from the foreign investors that previously jumped the high tariff walls on complete motor vehicles in the first phase of the industrial policy. This is a well-known development strategy used in the past by other countries, but it can be regarded as welfare-inferior to other domestic policies.

5.2   Four relevant questions related to the case

There are at least four relevant economic questions that were not addressed in the dispute case but that may have yielded a clearer understanding of the beggar-thy-neighbor policy content of China's trade policy.

Who bears the cost of the additional import duty?

A first relevant question would be whether the assembled motor vehicles in China were used for domestic sales to Chinese consumers or were meant for export destinations and consumers outside China. This is relevant in terms of who bears the ultimate extra cost of the surcharge on imported motor parts. If assembled cars are mainly for Chinese consumers, Chinese consumers are likely to pay a higher price for their cars as a result of the higher import duty on parts and Chinese trade policy would be carried domestically. If, however, the assembled cars are mainly exported, it is consumers in export markets that are likely to pay the additional price, but only if demand overseas is not too elastic, which is the second relevant economic question treated below. But let us first look at whether assembled cars are sold for exports or domestically.

Figure 2 below is derived from firm-level data[89] and gives us a peek at the importance of domestic sales versus exports of complete motor vehicles (2a) and car parts (2b). It appears that most complete motor vehicles are sold to domestic customers and a much smaller number is shipped for exports. While domestic sales remained relatively stable over time, exports continued to rise between 2004 and 2006. The only mention of exports in the dispute case under scrutiny is footnote 14,[90] which states that exports are *exempted* from import duties, which may

---

89 The firm-level data set we used is Oriana with variables on 200,000 firms in which we identify the firms in the car manufacturing sector and in car parts. Oriana does not use a product classification but a sector level classification NAICS. The correspondence with the HS codes suggest that the complete motor vehicles producers are in NAICS (2002) codes 336111, 336112, 336120, and 336214 while the car parts firms belong to NAICS (2002) 336211, 336312, 336322, 336330, 336340, 336350, and 336399. One of the serious limitations that we face is that we only have good quality data for 2003 to 2006. Another limitation is that firm-level data set does not have imports at the firm level. The exports values are firm-level, but are not split up by destination countries or by product.
90 Appellate Body Report.

Figure 2a. Complete motor vehicles

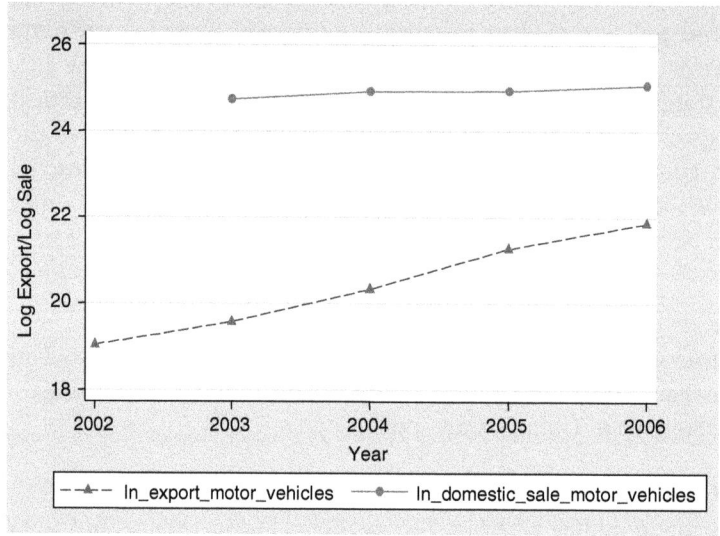

Figure 2b. Car parts

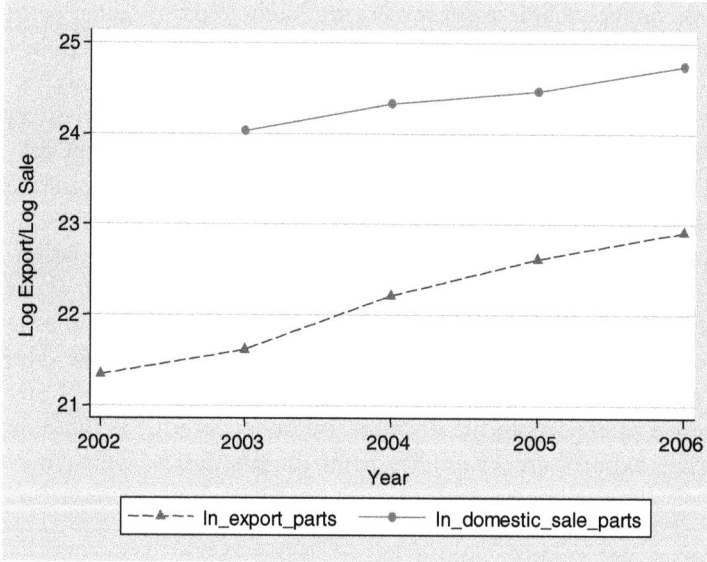

Source: Oriana firm-level data.

explain why they continued to rise. Figures 2a and 2b suggest that the import duties on complete car vehicles or car parts would mainly affect Chinese customers, given that domestic sales are more important than exports.

Figure 3. Profits of motor vehicle assemblers in China

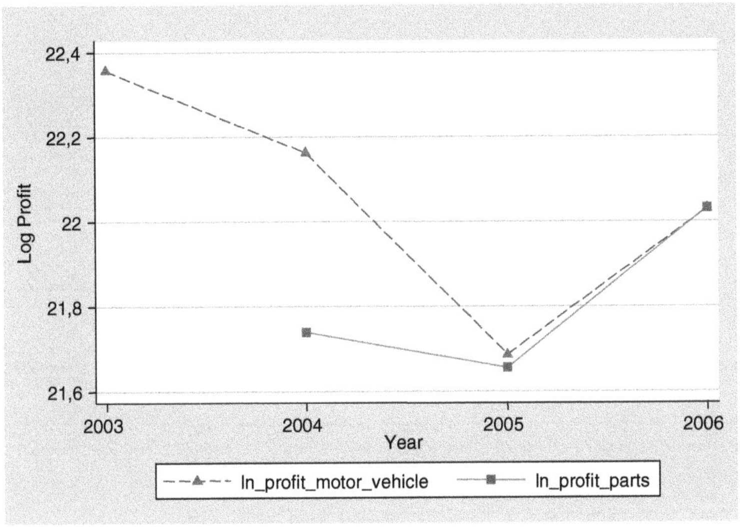

Source: Oriana firm-level data.

How elastic is the final demand for cars?

A second relevant question is whether or not the final demand for assembled motor vehicles is elastic. The demand elasticity determines the negative slope of the demand curve and reflects how consumers move away from buying a motor vehicle when the prices go up. This elasticity is indicative of the extent to which an increase in costs resulting from an extra charge on inputs used in the production process can be passed through to the consumer. Put differently, the demand elasticity captures how sensitive prices for assembled motor vehicles are. Car manufacturers may pass the higher import duty on to consumers by charging a higher price, but if demand is very elastic, this would imply a large drop in the sales of cars, and therefore car producers may prefer to absorb the duty even though it implies a squeeze in their profits. To estimate the elasticity of demand directly is not possible for us, due to lack of data on quantities sold and prices charged, but we can look at car manufacturers' profits over the years to see what happens there. Figure 3 shows that profits of both car manufacturers and car-parts producers in China were on a slide before the introduction of the new tariff structure, with profits for manufacturers of complete motor vehicles much higher than those for car-parts manufacturers. But after 2005, when the new tariff structure went into effect, profits for both types of firms rose again, suggesting that the tariffs benefited both. This is indicative that the additional costs from the import tariffs were passed through at least in part to consumers, resulting in price increases that did not affect sales too much, leaving the car sector with higher profits than before.

Figure 4. Investment in the Chinese car sector

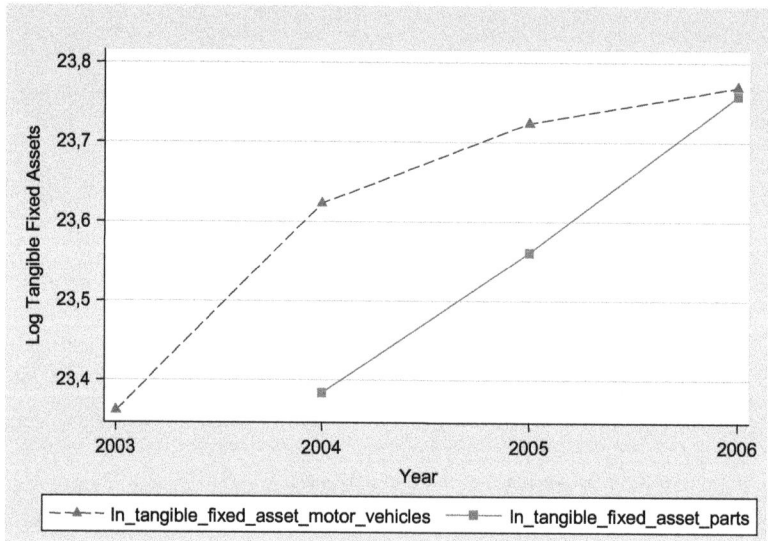

Source: Oriana.

Is there an import-competing Chinese car-parts industry?
The third question is on the existence of an import-competing domestic Chinese
motor-parts industry and whether it benefited from the higher tariff on car parts.
If there is such an industry, to what extent did the import duty of 25% benefit
them?

This is an important question, since the Panel's conviction of China on the basis
of Article III:4 assumes there is. Violation of Art III:4 implies that a country uses
trade policy to favor its local industry, since the underlying reasoning is that, when
car assemblers in China are faced with more expensive foreign parts, they are likely
to switch to domestically produced parts that have become relatively cheaper
because the duty does not apply to them. The existence and size of an import-
competing Chinese industry of parts is therefore important, since this would shed
more light on how substantiated the claim is that the high import duty on foreign
parts favors domestic parts suppliers.

We collected firm-level information on the group of firms in car manufacturing
and the group of firms in China reporting 'car parts' as their main activity.[91] One of
the variables of interest is firm-level investment in car assembly and parts. Figure 4
shows the evolution of fixed tangible assets of firms in China in the car sector,
which is generally regarded as a good proxy for investment. While both

91 See footnote 75 for more information.

Table 2. Number of firms in the car sector in China

	Number of firms	
Ownership type	Complete motor vehicles	Motor vehicle body and parts
Domestic	227	4,640
Foreign	60	1,236
Total	287	5,876

Notes: 'Foreign' includes: 'Foreign Invested Stock Limited Company', 'Sino-Foreign Cooperative Venture', 'Sino-Foreign Joint Venture', 'Wholly Foreign Owned Enterprise', 'HK, Macau or Taiwan Joint Cooperative Venture', 'HK, Macau or Taiwan Joint Venture', 'Wholly HK, Macau or Taiwan Invested Stock Limited Company', or 'Wholly HK, Macau or Taiwan Owned Enterprise'. The rest of the firms are defined as 'Domestic'.
Source: Oriana.

complete motors and car parts attracted investment, the growth in investment is more spectacular in the car-parts industry between 2004 and 2006, the period where the circumvention duty of the Chinese authorities applied. The investment in machinery, land, buildings, etc., grew so fast that the car-parts industry by 2006 had reached a similar level of assets as that of the motor-vehicles sector.

This sparse evidence already suggests two important facts that substantiate the claim made by the WTO Panel that the local industry was favored by China's trade policy. It shows, first, that an import-competing industry for car parts existed at the time, and, second, that it seems to have grown substantially over time at a higher pace than the car-assembly industry during the period the circumvention duty applied.

Who owns the car manufacturing industry in China?
A fourth relevant question is about ownership. To the extent that the entire car-parts industry is Chinese, the effects of a change in import duties on car parts would fall on Chinese shareholders. However, if there is a substantial amount of foreign ownership in that sector, the effect of an import duty on car parts would also be shared by them.

Ownership information is typically very hard to come by. While our firm-level data set has some information on ownership, it is time-invariant and is far from perfect. From Table 2 we observe that, based on our micro data, the foreign ownership in both the complete-motor-vehicle sector and in the car-parts sector lies around 20%.

Furthermore, it can be noted that in the more downstream industry of complete motor vehicles, the number of firms is around 287, making this a relatively concentrated sector. Concentrated sectors generally are less subject to competition, and firms have more market power.

Table 3. Nationality of foreign firms

| | Number of firms | |
Ownership country	Complete motor vehicle	Motor vehicle body or parts
China	26	48
US	7	25
Germany	3	16
France	3	7
Great Britain	2	3
Sweden	2	1
Italy	0	3
Canada	1	1
Japan	12	21
Korea	2	1
Hong Kong	3	17
Taiwan	1	2
Singapore	2	7

Notes: The sample used in this table includes firms that have information on their ownership AND have foreign owners. One firm can be owned by owners from different countries or regions.
Source: Oriana.

This is important for pass-through issues, as we know that more concentrated sectors are more likely to pass on adverse cost shocks to consumers. The total number of firms in the more upstream activity of the car parts is around 5,800 different producers, making this sector much less concentrated. Typically, competition in less concentrated sectors is stronger and market power lower. The pass-through to consumers is therefore likely to be more limited in car parts than in complete motor vehicles.

In terms of the nationality of the firms, we present in Table 3 the information available to us. The number of firms for which country of ownership could be retrieved is relatively small, but it gives us an idea of the proportions. Foreign ownership is relatively more common in the complete-motor-vehicle sector than in the more upstream car-parts industry. The largest group of foreign owners is the Asian countries (Japan, Korea, Hong Kong, Taiwan, and Singapore), followed by the EU, followed by North America (US and Canada). The presence of foreign firms in the Chinese car sector could reflect an outsourcing strategy where the purpose of foreign firms is to ship the goods they produce back to their country of origin. Or their presence could reflect 'horizontal FDI' for the purpose of serving the domestic Chinese market. In the first case, they would be far less affected by China's trade policy due to the exemption of exports (footnote 14 in the dispute case), i.e. goods produced for export markets are exempted from the high 25% duty on imports of car parts.

This can be verified in Figure 2, where exports continued to rise when domestic sales stabilized. In the second case, where FDI is of the 'horizontal type' for serving the domestic Chinese market, the import duties can adversely affect foreign firms' operations in China, depending on the pass-through to the Chinese customer.

Our gathering of factual evidence can only be regarded as indicative due to limitations in data, time, and manpower. Our main purpose was to raise questions rather than to pretend to answer them in full. But the many questions that the case leaves unaddressed suggest that the 'economic bone' is less straightforward to split than the legal one. If anything, the empirical facts that we gathered suggest that in the end the Panel most likely was right in ruling out the 'circumvention' hypothesis and embracing the 'industrial policy' hypothesis.

While the occurrence of 'circumvention' cannot be completely ruled out for reasons explained above, the facts pointing in the direction of China's use of trade policy as a tool of industrial policy are plentiful. The phasing of trade policy by China is almost a textbook case of an 'import substitution policy' pursued by other countries in the past. At the time of WTO entry, China first set a high tariff on the imports of motor vehicles to build manufacturing capacity in the upstream activity of car assembly, resulting in inward FDI and discouraging imports of complete vehicles. A couple of years down the road from WTO entry, China altered its trade policy by imposing a circumvention duty that raised the tariff on the imports of more upstream car parts, which are intermediates in the assembly of cars. This discouraged the imports of both car parts and complete vehicles and enhanced a spectacular increase in the investment in and capacity of the domestic Chinese car-parts industry. Furthermore, the exemption of exports from paying import duties on parts suggests that China combined its import-substitution policy with a well-known policy described by: 'import protection as export promotion'.[92] In a model where import protection raises the market size for a representative domestic producer, domestic sales for the domestic firm increase This allows the firm to lower its average cost curve and makes it more competitive, resulting in more exports. Hence, the Krugman model pointed out that import protection may actually stimulate exports.

While too little factual evidence is currently presented to formally accuse China of pursuing these 'beggar-thy-neighbor' policies, all we can say is that some of the facts, such as the spectacular growth in the Chinese car-parts industry after the 25% duty on parts was introduced, are consistent with it.

---

92 Paul Krugman (1984), 'Import protection as export promotion: international competition in the presence of oligopoly and economies of scale', in Henry Kierzkowski (ed.), *Monopolistic Competition and International Trade*, Oxford: Oxford University Press.

From an economic point of view, it is interesting to note that 'old' policy recipes appear to survive despite the fact that we know that trade policies can only be second best compared to other domestic instruments. Building industries behind tariff walls is less effective than investing in properly functioning capital markets.[93] Recent evidence also questions the ability to use import protection to raise exports when firms are heterogeneous.[94]

93 Baldwin, 'The case against infant-industry tariff protection'.

94 H. Kasahara and B. Lapham (2008), Productivity and the decision to import and export: theory and evidence', CESifo working paper no. 2240; J. Konings and H. Vandenbussche (2009), 'Antidumping protection hurts exporters: firm-level evidence from France', CEPR discussion paper no. 5678.

Appellate Body Report, *India – Additional and Extra-Additional Duties on Imports from the United States* (WT/DS360/AB/R, adopted on 17 November 2008)

PAOLA CONCONI

Université Libre de Bruxelles (ECARES) and CEPR

JAN WOUTERS

Katholieke Universiteit Leuven, Leuven, Belgium

Abstract: This paper critically reviews the main findings of the Appellate Body in the case *India – Additional and Extra-Additional Duties on Imports from the United States* (*India–Additional Import Duties*). This ruling sheds light on the interplay between two core provisions of the GATT, namely Article II GATT (Schedules of Concessions) and III GATT (National Treatment on Internal Taxation and Regulation). Linked to this demarcation, the question on the allocation of the burden of proof was a central point of contention in this dispute. The ruling also establishes the principle that WTO Members are allowed to use border tax adjustments, as long as the tax imposed on imports does not exceed the domestic tax. We argue that this principle can help to reconcile the objectives of the WTO with those of national governments.

Introduction

This contribution critically reviews the main findings of the Appellate Body (AB) in the case *India – Additional and Extra-Additional Duties on Imports from the United States* (*India–Additional Import Duties*).

Next to the interpretations developed in the *China–Auto Parts* case dating from the same year (2008), these findings shed light on aspects of the interplay between two core provisions of the GATT, namely Article II GATT (Schedules of Concessions) and III GATT (National Treatment on Internal Taxation and Regulation).[1] Remarkably, important questions on the delineation between these two 'cornerstones' of the GATT/WTO system were not only left open in the legal text, but also remained largely unexplored for more than 60 years in both the literature and GATT/WTO case law.

The authors gratefully acknowledge the exceptional assistance they received from Dominic Coppens in preparing this contribution, as well as the comments of Geert van Calster and Fernando González Rojas.

1 See AB Report, *China – Measures Affecting Imports of Automobile Parts* (*China–Auto Parts*), WT/DS339, 340, 342 (15 December 2008).

From a legal point of view, in the absence of clear guidance from previous case law, it should not come as a complete surprise that the AB came to a very different reading than the Panel on the demarcation question raised in this case, which crystallized around the interpretation of Article II:2(a) GATT. Linked to this demarcation exercise, the question on the allocation of the burden of proof – another important legal issue left open in the relevant legal texts (DSU) – was a central point of contention in this dispute.

From an economic point of view, the AB's ruling in *India–Additional Import Duties* establishes the principle that WTO Members are allowed to use border adjustments, as long as the tax imposed on imports does not exceed the domestic tax. We argue that this principle can help to reconcile the objectives of the WTO with those of national governments, and to achieve efficient trade and domestic policies.

The remainder of the contribution is organized as follows. Section 1 summarizes the *India–Additional Import Duties* dispute, describing the central facts of the case, the claims presented by the parties to the adjudicating body, and the findings of the AB. Section 2 discusses in detail the two main legal issues raised by this dispute, concerning the legal interpretation of Article II:2(a) and the burden of proof. Section 3 discusses the main economic issues related to this dispute: we first show that allowing countries to use border tax adjustments can counter fears that the trade pressures associated with WTO market-access commitments can lead governments to a 'regulatory chill' or a 'race to the bottom' in domestic regulations; we then discuss various problems involved in the use of border charges, and the implications of the AB ruling for the ongoing policy debate on carbon border taxes. Section 4 concludes.

1. Facts, claims, and findings

Before the Panel, the United States challenged two specific duties – the 'Additional Duty' and the 'Extra-Additional Duty'.[2] These duties were imposed by India at the border on imports of certain products and were charged in addition to the basic

---

2 We use the abbreviations employed by the AB. Shortly after the establishment of the Panel, India made significant changes to the Additional Duty and Extra-Additional Duty regimes, but the Panel decided that these were not included in its terms of reference and thus declined to rule on these modifications (see Panel Report, paras. 7.34–7.100; AB Report, paras. 130 and 136). Because these changes removed the Additional Duties, the European Communities decided to suspend a similar claim against India for which a Panel had already been established. However, according to the European Communities, several Indian states have reverted to discriminatory treatment of imported wines and bottles in violation of Article III:2 GATT since the suspension of the Additional Duty. Therefore, the European Communities launched a new case against India that is currently pending. See, for the suspended claim, *Request for Consultations by the European Communities, India – Measures Affecting the Importation and Sale of Wines and Spirits from the European Communities*, WT/DS352/1, G/L/804 (23 November 2006); for the pending claim, *Request for Consultations by the European Communities, India – Certain Taxes and other Measures on Imported Wines and Spirits*, WT/DS380/1, G/L/855, G/SCM/D79/1 (25 September 2008).

customs duties. The United States claimed that these duties are inconsistent with India's obligations under Article II:1(a) and II:1(b) GATT because they subject imports to ordinary customs duties (OCDs) or other duties or charges (ODCs) in excess of those specified in India's Schedule of Concessions.[3]

India responded that the United States mischaracterized these duties as OCDs or ODCs within the meaning of Article II:1(b) GATT. Instead, both the Additional Duty and Extra-Additional Duty are charges on the importation of products which are equivalent to internal taxes imposed in respect of like domestic products and therefore fall within the scope of Article II:2(a) GATT. In particular, the Additional Duty on alcoholic beverages is levied in the place of excise duties levied by states and the Extra-Additional Duty is imposed to counterbalance sales tax, VAT, and other local taxes or charges.[4]

Important to note from the outset is that details on the operation of these internal charges (e.g. which states actually levied such duties, the form and structure of duty rates) enabling a comparison with the (Extra-) Additional Duties did not come to the surface in the procedure. According to the United States, it was up to India to provide these details in order to underpin its alleged justification of the duties under Article II:2(a) GATT. India, on the other hand, claimed that the United States had to make a prima facie case that the charges do not fall within the scope of Article II:1(b) GATT and even explicitly neglected a written question from the Panel requesting details on the operation of certain internal charges.[5] It could only be inferred from the operation of the (Extra-) Additional Duties that they would in some cases result in charges imposed on imported products in excess of those imposed on like domestic products, but there was no concrete evidence whether this effectively happened.

The Panel came to the conclusion that the United States failed to meet its burden of establishing that both charges are not 'equivalent' within the meaning of Article II:2(a) GATT to internal charges and, as a result, failed to demonstrate that the duties are OCDs or ODCs within the meaning of Article II:1(b) GATT. Furthermore, the Panel offered no findings on the United States's alternative claim under Article III:2 GATT because the United States did not make an independent and separate analysis underpinning this claim.[6] Accordingly, the Panel made no recommendations under Article 19.1 of the DSU.[7] The United States's appeal

---

3 Panel Report, para. 7.5; AB Report, para. 3.
4 Panel Report, para. 7.30; AB Report, para. 4.
5 Panel Report, footnote 310; AB Report, footnote 409.
6 Panel Report, paras. 7.404–7.418.
7 Nonetheless, the Panel offered some 'concluding remarks' in light of the fact that India had made changes to the Additional Duty and Extra-Additional Duty after the establishment of the Panel (see above note 2). Because these changes were deemed outside its terms of reference, the Panel did not assess their impact on the consistency of the measures but, nonetheless, noted that: 'the Panel's disposition of the US claims under Article II:1(a) and (b) does not necessarily imply that it would be consistent with India's WTO obligations for India to withdraw the relevant new customs notifications or otherwise re-establish the *status quo ante*, i.e., the situation as it existed on the date of establishment of the Panel. By the same

mainly targeted the Panel's interpretation of Articles II:1(b) and II:2(a) GATT and the allocation of the burden of proof.[8] The AB fundamentally disagreed with the Panel's reading of Articles II:1(b) and II:2(a) GATT but did not accept the United States's claim on the burden of proof. The AB also refrained from making rec-ommendations to the Dispute Settlement Body but, nonetheless, formulated con-siderations about the potential application of the (Extra-) Additional Duties. The AB considered that the (Extra-) Additional Duties *would* not be justified under Article II:2(a) insofar as they result in the imposition of charges on imports in excess of internal charges that India alleges are equivalent to these (Extra-) Ad-ditional Duties; and, consequently, that this *would* render the (Extra-) Additional Duties inconsistent with Article II:1(b) to the extent they result in the imposition of duties in excess of those set forth in India's Schedule of Concessions.[9] How the AB arrived at this unusual 'conditional violation' is revealed in the next section.

2. Legal analysis

2.1 The interpretation of Article II:2(a) GATT and the delineation between Articles II and III GATT

The case thus revolved around the interpretation of Article II:1(b) GATT in relation to Article II:2 GATT. These paragraphs read:

1. ...

    (b) The products described in Part I of the Schedule relating to any contract-ing party, which are the products of territories of other contracting parties, shall, on their importation into the territory to which the Schedule relates, and subject to the terms, conditions or qualifications set forth in that Schedule, be exempt from *ordinary customs duties* in excess of those set forth and provided therein. Such products shall also be exempt from *all other duties or charges of any kind* imposed on or in connection with the importation in excess of those imposed on the date of this Agreement or those directly and mandatorily required to be imposed thereafter by legislation in force in the importing territory on that date.

---

token, in making this point, we do not wish to suggest that the entry into force of the new customs notifications necessarily implies that the [Additional Duty] on alcoholic liquor, to the extent it still exists, and the [Extra-Additional Duty] are WTO-consistent' (Panel Report, para. 8.2; see also below note 8).

8 The United States did not appeal the Panel's rejection of making findings under Article III:2 GATT. Conversely, India claimed before the AB that the Panel committed legal error by offering 'concluding remarks' (see above note 7) but the AB considered these as 'simple explanations of the Panel's conclusions, which are permissible'. India did, however, not appeal the initial decision of the Panel to disregard the changes made to the application of the duties (see above note 2). AB Report, paras. 130 and 136, paras. 222–230.

9 See AB Report, para. 231, (e), (f).

Figure 1. Panel's interpretation of Article II:1(a) juncto Article II:2 GATT 1994

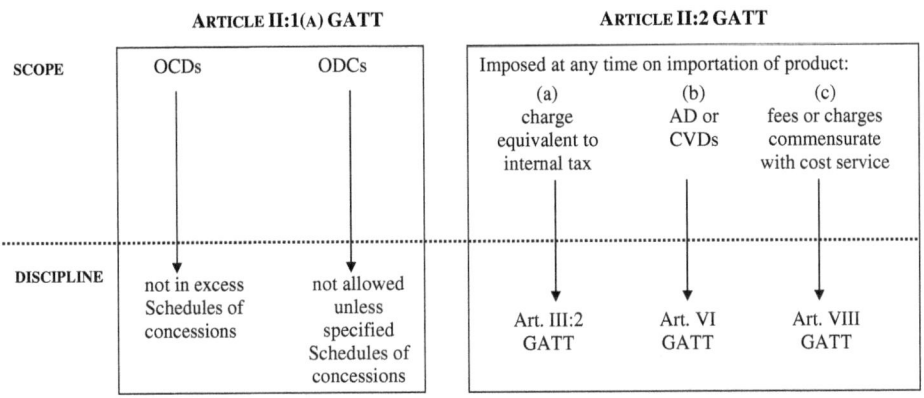

2. Nothing in this Article shall prevent any contracting party from imposing at any time on the importation of any product:

(a) *a charge equivalent to an internal tax imposed consistently with the provisions of paragraph 2 of Article III* in respect of the like domestic product* or in respect of an article from which the imported product has been manufactured or produced in whole or in part;

(b) any anti-dumping or countervailing duty applied consistently with the provisions of Article VI;*

(c) fees or other charges commensurate with the cost of services rendered.[10]

The Panel and AB reached a fundamentally different reading of Article II:2(a) GATT and its relationship with Article II:1(b) GATT. Although not always clearly or consistently articulated, their approaches seem to fit the structure set out in, respectively, Figures 1 and 2.

The AB agreed with the Panel that Article II:1(b) GATT draws a distinction between 'ordinary customs duties' (OCDs) and 'all other duties or charges of any kind' that are imposed 'on or in connection with importation' (ODCs) but the AB did not offer much guidance on how to interpret and delineate these charges left undefined in Article II:1(b).[11] At first sight, the AB also seemed

---

10 Emphasis added, interpretative notes not included.

11 ODCs are thus, by definition, not OCDs. According to the AB, these two sets of charges 'may, by their terms, not pertain to the same event of importation'. The AB continued that 'while in some instances, ODCs may be of a similar kind to OCDs, in other instances they may be of a different kind'. AB Report, paras. 151 and 157.

Figure 2. Appellate Body's interpretation of Article II:1(b) juncto
Article II:2 GATT 1994

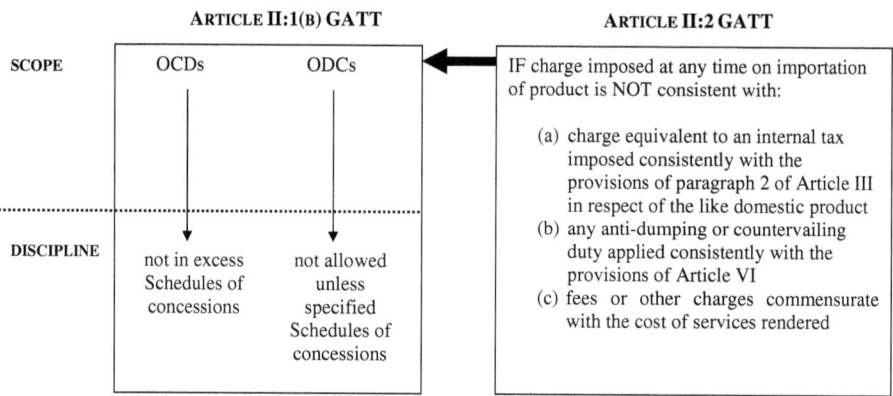

to confirm that both types of charges are subject to different sets of disciplines.[12]
While OCDs cannot be imposed on imported products in excess of those provided
for in that Member's Schedule of Concessions, ODCs are not allowed upon imported products in excess of amounts imposed on the date of entry into force of the
GATT,[13] as recorded and bound in that Member's Schedule of Concessions.[14]

However, the Panel and AB fundamentally disagreed on whether the scope of
Article II:1(b) could encompass charges on importation referred to under Article
II:2.[15] In order to grasp their different point of view, we need to recall that the
description of the items listed in Article II:2 could on its face be split into a part
defining the scope of the charge in question (e.g. charge equivalent to internal tax)
and into a part imposing substantive obligations upon that charge (e.g. imposed
consistently with the provisions of Article III:2). The Panel focused on the scope
and downplayed the substantive obligations imposed under Article II:2 itself (e.g.
imposed consistently with III:2), whereas the AB did not distinguish both aspects.[16]

In the Panel's view, charges falling within the scope of Article II:2 (i.e. charges
equivalent to an internal tax, AD/CVDs, fees or other charges commensurate
with the cost of the service) cannot fall within the scope of – and hence be disciplined under – Article II:1(b) but are disciplined under other GATT provisions

---

12 In light of the AB's conclusion, it might be doubted that the AB confirmed this understanding
(see below).

13 Or which are directly and mandatorily required to be imposed by legislation on that date.

14 See Understanding on the Interpretation of Article II:1(b) of the General Agreement on Tariffs and
Trade. AB Report, paras. 150–151.

15 AB Report, para. 153.

16 To be precise, there seems to be no clear distinction under Article II:2(c) between 'scope' and
'substantive obligation' as it refers to 'fees or other charges commensurate with the cost of services
rendered'. See also Panel Report, para. 7.136.

(respectively Articles III, VI, and VIII GATT) (see Figure 1). To reach this conclusion, the Panel had to make the following interpretations.[17] First, the Panel found a clear distinction between charges under Article II:1(b) (i.e. ODCs and OCDs) and charges under Article II:2 as the former 'inherently discriminate against imports' whereas the latter do not. Second, according to the Panel, the requirement that the charge should be 'equivalent' to an internal charge under Article II:2(a) should be distinguished from the obligation of 'consistency with Article III:2'[18] and is determined by whether the border charge and the internal charge have the same function, which does certainly not require that they are similar.[19] Such 'equivalence', which forms a necessary condition to fall outside the scope of Article II:1(b) by virtue of Article II:2(a), is thus a lower standard than the one imposed under Article III:2 (no taxation 'in excess').[20] Third, the Panel found that the element of 'consistency with Article III:2' is not such a necessary condition for the application of Article II:2(b). The reference to Article III:2 GATT in this provision simply makes clear that, 'in the view of the drafters of Article II:2(a), a border charge on the importation of a product which fulfils the same function as an internal tax on the like domestic product, should be, and is, subject to the provisions of Article III:2'.[21] A border charge equivalent to an internal charge falls outside the scope of Article II:1(b) and should instead be challenged under Article III:2 GATT. The question on whether such border charge on imported products is in 'excess' of equivalent internal charges on like domestic products will thus be addressed under Article III:2 GATT. More broadly, Article II:2 is included in Article II 'to make clear that some charges, even though they may look like ordinary customs duties, or "other duties or charges", are charges of a different kind and, as such, subject to different

17 In fact, the second and third interpretations spelled out below seem necessary to underpin the Panel's general view that charges equivalent to internal charges fall outside the scope of Article II:1(b) and within the scope of Article III:2. The delineation criterion of 'inherently discriminatory on imports' seems not necessary to reach this conclusion.

18 According to the Panel, 'equivalence' refers to the border charge, while the phrase 'imposed consistently with the provisions of (Article III:2)' refers to the internal charge. But, as the AB correctly observed, the latter phrase cannot exclusively refer to the internal charge, given that a determination under III:2 necessarily involves a comparison of a border charge with an internal charge. This clearly erroneous interpretation of the Panel is also reflected in confusing arguments set out in paras. 7.171, 7.184, and 7.209.

19 Panel Report, paras. 7.187, 7.192. The Panel considered that a determination of 'equivalence' seeks to establish whether separate charges on imported and domestic products 'when viewed together, can be considered to form a distinct whole within the relevant Member's customs duty and tax system', such that, 'the relevant function fulfilled both by the internal tax on the domestic product and the border charge is to impose a charge on a product qua product' and not qua domestic product or qua imported product (Panel Report, paras. 7.189, 7.190; AB Report, para. 168).

20 Panel, para. 7.198. The Panel emphasized that it is a necessary condition for the purpose of the Article II:2(a) inquiry only. Indeed, in the Panel's interpretation, charges within the scope of the other items of II:2 are also outside the scope of Article II:1(b).

21 Panel Report, para. 7.196. As the AB noted, 'we do not consider that the Panel preserved a role for evaluating "consistency with Article III:2" in the context of Article II:2(a)'. AB Report, para. 180.

disciplines'.[22] Given that Article II:2 simply clarifies in the Panel's view that those items are subject to other disciplines, the charges listed in Article II:2 are no exceptions to the obligations set out under Article II:1(a).[23] The Panel found support for its approach, inter alia, in a 1980 proposal of the Director-General, adopted by the GATT Council, concerning the introduction of a loose-leaf system for the Schedules of Concessions:

> I wish to point out in this connexion that such 'other duties or charges' are in principle only those that discriminate against imports. As can be seen from Article II:2 of the General Agreement, such 'other duties or charges' concern neither charges equivalent to internal taxes, nor anti-dumping or countervailing duties, nor fees or other charges commensurate with the cost of services rendered.[24]

Without much explanation, the AB found this statement of 'limited relevance', even though it seems to indicate agreement among GATT Contracting Parties that Article II:2 charges are not the sort of charges that could be recorded as 'other duties or charges' under Article II:1(b).[25]

Instead, the AB came to a different interpretation of Article II:2 and its relation to Article II:1(b) (see Figure 2). Although not explicitly formulated as such, Article II:2 was approached by the AB as an exception to the obligations set under Article II:1(b). The AB agreed with both parties that if a charge satisfies the conditions of one of the items of Article II:2, it does not result in a violation of Article II:1(b).[26] Conversely, in case these conditions would not be satisfied, such charges would fall within the scope and disciplines of Article II:1(b).[27] To arrive at this conclusion, the AB had to override the Panel's specific interpretations spelled out above, all of which were appealed by the United States. First, the AB disagreed that charges under Article II:1(b) could be distinguished from those set out under Article II:2 by relying on the concept of 'inherently discriminating against imports'. Charges under Article II:1(b) (i.e. OCDs and ODCs) could also be imposed without the rationale to inherently discriminate against imports (e.g. for raising revenue if no domestic production) and there is no textual basis in Article II:1(b) to limit its scope to inherently discriminatory charges.[28] Conversely, charges under Article II:2(b) and II:2(c) are exclusively imposed on imports and offer therefore no contextual support that charges under Article II:2 are 'universally non-discriminatory'

---

22 Panel Report, footnote 202.

23 Panel Report, para. 7.148.

24 Panel Report, para. 7.144.

25 AB Report, paras. 161–162.

26 To be sure, this would also be the case under the Panel reading because such charges would not fall within the *scope* of Article II:1(b) in the first place.

27 This can be inferred from paras. 214 and 221 of the AB Report.

28 The AB found that the label of 'inherently discriminatory' even suggested that tariffs are somehow 'unfair or prejudicial' and no legitimate instrument to accomplish certain policy objectives such as raising revenue. AB Report, paras. 158–159.

in respect of imports.[29] Second, the AB considered that the obligation of 'consistency with Article III:2' referred to in Article II:2 must not be distinguished from but 'read together with, and imparts meaning to' the requirement that a charge and internal tax be 'equivalent', which calls for 'a comparative assessment that is both qualitative and quantitative in nature'.[30] In particular, 'consistency with Article III:2' forms 'an integral part of the assessment' of 'equivalence'.[31] Third, as a logical inference, the AB also rejected the Panel's view that 'consistency with Article III:2' is not a necessary condition for the application of Article II:2(a).[32]

Accordingly, contrary to the Panel, the AB thus seems to draw a firm line between 'border charges', which are disciplined under Article II, and 'internal charges', which are disciplined under Article III.[33] Applied to the facts of the case, the AB observed that 'the Panel and the participants also agree that the Additional Duty and Extra-Additional Duty are *border charges* subject to the terms of Article II, and that they are *not* disciplined by the provisions of Article III as "internal taxes"'.[34] Nonetheless, the AB's statement seems incorrect insofar that it contends that this view was also shared by the Panel. The AB seems to overlook that, according to the Panel, charges equivalent to an internal charge – and the United States failed to demonstrate according to the Panel that the (Extra-) Additional charges do *not* constitute such charges – are disciplined under Article III:2 instead of Article II. Under both interpretations, the consistency of the border charge with Article III:2 should thus ultimately be assessed, but according to the AB this should be done under Article II:2(a).[35] Another difference between the two approaches is that the AB's reading does not mandate a Member challenging a border charge within the meaning of Article II:2(a) to formulate a separate claim under

---

29 AB Report, para. 160.
30 AB Report, para. 175.
31 AB Report, para. 181.
32 AB Report, para. 181.

33 Note that the concept of 'border charge' is not spelled out in Article II GATT. In *China–Auto Parts*, the AB also made the distinction between border charges and internal charges: 'It seems to us that an examination of whether a particular charge is an internal charge or a border measure involves consideration of all *three* types of charges, that is: ordinary customs duties under the first sentence of Article II:1(b); other duties and charges under the second sentence of Article II:1(b); and internal charges and taxes under Article III:2.' AB Report, *China–Auto Parts*, above note 1, para. 141.

34 AB Report, footnote 304 (emphasis added). The AB also held that 'contrary to what the Panel suggests, a complaining party is *not required to* file an independent claim of violation of Article III:2 if it wishes to challenge the consistency of a border charge with Article III:2' (para. 180, emphasis added). This seems, at first sight, to suggest that the AB does not require but leaves the option to challenge such a border charge under Article III:2. However, other aspects of the report question whether this option is indeed left open by the AB. First, the quote cited in the full text suggests that border charges are disciplined under Article II and not Article III. Second, as elaborated below, Article II:1(b) and III:2 impose different obligations. Third, the AB in *China–Auto Parts*, referring to its report in *India–Additional Import Duties*, also considered that the determination of whether a 'specific charge falls under Article II:1(b) or Article III:2 of the GATT must be made in light of the characteristics of the measure and the circumstances of the case'. AB Report, *China–Auto Parts*, above note 1, para. 171.

35 In the Panel's approach, this would be assessed under Article III:2 itself, whereas the AB would assess it under Article II:2(a).

Article III:2.[36] A border charge could (and should) be challenged under Article II GATT and not under Article III:2. This seems sensible given that a complaining party might, at least in theory, be unaware that a border charge to which its product is subjected is alleged to be counterbalanced by an internal charge.[37]

Nonetheless, the qualification of whether a charge is a 'border charge' subject to Article II or an 'internal charge' subject to III:2 is not always straightforward. As the AB acknowledged, *Ad* note to Article III might also come into play. This *Ad* note to Article III stipulates that Article III is applicable to any internal charge that applies to both domestic and imported products, but which is 'collected or enforced' in respect of the imported product at the time of importation. The delineation between such an 'internal charge' to which Article III:2 applies and a 'border charge' to which Article II:2(a) applies has to be assessed 'in the light of the characteristics of the measure and the circumstances of the case'.[38] Apparently, if a charge is imposed on domestic and imported goods (but for imported goods this charge is *collected or enforced* at the border), such charge is, pursuant to *Ad* note, deemed an 'internal charge' subject to Article III. On the other hand, if equivalent but different charges are imposed on imported and domestic products and the charge on imported products is imposed on importation, Article II:1(b) *juncto* II:2(a) is applicable for challenging such 'border charge'.[39]

Except for the clarification under which provision a claim should be formulated, what is the relevance of this disagreement between the Panel and AB? Indeed, the disciplines of Article III:2 would apply anyway: either directly as 'internal charge' under Article III:2, or indirectly, as 'border charges' to which Article II:2(a) applies. Procedurally, the allocation of the burden of proof might be different, as will be discussed in the next section. But also on a substantive level, the AB seems to give relevance to its holding that a border charge to which article II:2(a) applies is not disciplined directly under Article III but under Article II. After all, the AB concluded that the (Extra-) Additional Duties could not be justified to the extent they result in the imposition of charges on imports in excess of internal charges on domestic products and that this would render these duties 'inconsistent with Article II:1(b) to the extent that (they result) in the imposition of duties (on the product in question) *in excess of those set forth in India's Schedule of Concessions*'.[40] Such a border charge inconsistent with Article II:2(a) (because applied inconsistently with Article III:2) thus falls within the scope of Article II:1(b), but the AB left open whether it is disciplined under the first sentence (referring to 'ordinary customs duties', OCDs) or the second sentence (referring to 'other duties and charges', ODCs) of Article II:1(b). Three possible but

---

36 AB Report, para. 180.

37 Under the Panel's approach, the complainant would lose the case if it did not include an Article III:2 claim in its term of reference in case a functionally equivalent internal charge would be present.

38 AB Report, para. 304.

39 Obviously, imported products could, in addition, also be subject to the internal charge.

40 This quotation is derived from AB Report, paras. 214 and 221.

Figure 3. Appellate Body's interpretation of Article II:1(b) juncto Article II:2 GATT 1994 (elaborated)

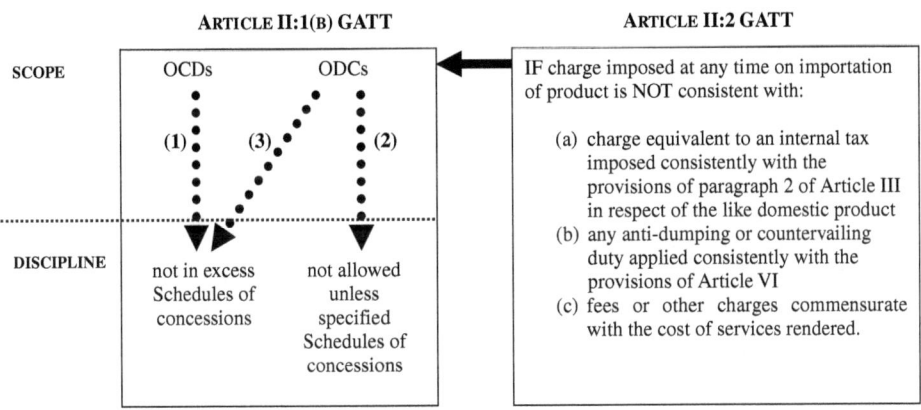

questionable explanations on the meaning of the AB's statement could be advanced (Figure 3).

First, the AB might have assumed that the (Extra-) Additional Duties fall within the scope of 'ordinary customs duties' (OCDs) but this would, at least, have required some substantive discussion on the definition of OCDs, as it seems more likely to bring such charges under the residual category of ODCs (1).[41] Second, the AB might have meant that such charges are a type of 'other duty or charge' (ODCs) under the second sentence of Article II:1(b) and are allowed insofar as their nature and level are recorded in India's Schedule of Concessions (2).[42] It might be doubted that the AB had this in mind because of the broader wording employed by the AB in its statement[43] and because the AB had previously observed that India had no recorded ODCs for the products in question.[44] Third, Piérola (2009) suggests that the AB might have implied that these charges are 'other duties or charges' (ODCs) but that such ODCs could be offered insofar as they do not lead to border charges in excess of the bound level for ordinary customs duties (OCDs) (3).[45] As Piérola (2009) rightly stresses, this interpretation would be problematic as it is generally understood that such ODCs are only valid if their nature and level was recorded. Yet, again, it seems doubtful that the AB had this

41 Recall that the United States claimed before the Panel that these charges are OCDs and only in the alternative that they are ODCs.

42 Insofar as also the conditions spelled out under note 47 are met.

43 The wording '*to the extent that it results in the imposition of duties* on ... in excess' does not fit with an interpretation that such an Additional Duty would only be considered allowed if its nature and level is scheduled.

44 AB Report, para. 120.

45 In the DSB meeting, India also understood the AB's statement in this way but considered it to be 'an inadvertent misstatement rather than a considered ruling', WT/DSB/M/259 (6 February 2009).

problematic interpretation in mind as it considered that OCDs and ODCs are 'two sets of charges ... described and *disciplined* in separate sentences of article II:1(b) and, may, by their terms, not pertain to the same event of importation'.[46] In sum, the AB's statement simply seems incoherent with other aspects of its report.

In a more recent case (*China–Auto Parts*), the AB unequivocally confirmed that ODCs 'are *permitted only* when their nature and level are recorded in a Member's Schedule'.[47] This would mean that charges referred to under Article II:2 but inconsistent with the stipulated obligations would be inconsistent with Article II:1(b) insofar as not recorded in a Member's Schedule (2)[48], unless, of course, they would be considered OCDs, which seems not very likely. Nonetheless, the Panel in *United States–Zeroing (Japan)* (*Article 21.5*) seems to have endorsed the interpretation that such 'Article II:2 inconsistent border charges' are not inconsistent with Article II:1(b) if they do not result in duties exceeding the bound level for ordinary customs duties (3).[49] After all, the Panel found a violation of Article II:1(b) because the United States had offered anti-dumping duties for the product in question *in excess of its bound level* and the excess amount could not be attributed to anti-dumping duties applied consistently with Article VI and could thus not benefit from the 'safe harbour' of Article II:2(b).[50]

In conclusion, the AB in *India–Additional Import Duties* clarified that charges inconsistent with Article II:2 fall within the scope of Article II:1(b). However, the

---

46 AB Report, para. 157 (emphasis added). The AB also held that the second sentence of Article II:1(b) stipulates further that 'such imported products shall be exempt from (ODCs), *to the extent* that such duties or charge exceed amounts imposed on the date of entry into force of the GATT 1994 ... as recorded and bound in the Schedules of Concessions annexed to the GATT 1994' (emphasis added). On the other hand, Piérola's interpretation of the AB's intention could find some support in para. 205, third sentence.

47 And if two other conditions are fulfilled: they do not exceed the level recorded in such Schedule, and they existed on the relevant date specified in the *Understanding on Article II:1(b) of the General Agreement on Tariffs and Trade 1994*. AB Report, *China–Auto Parts*, above note 1, footnote 209.

48 Insofar as the conditions listed above under note 47 are fulfilled.

49 It seems not likely that the Panel considered anti-dumping duties as falling within the scope of 'ordinary customs duties' (1). Panel Report, *United States – Measures Relating to Zeroing and Sunset Review – Recourse to Article 21.5 of the DSU by Japan* (*United States–Zeroing (Japan)* (*Article 21.5*)), WT/DS322/RW (circulated 24 April 2009), paras. 7.191–7.208.

50 The anti-dumping duties were thus included in the calculation of the applied duty rate. Panel Report, *United States–Zeroing (Japan)* (*Article 21.5*), above note 49, paras. 7.205–7.208. This reasoning implies that if the application of these anti-dumping duties would not have resulted in duties in excess of the bound rate, no violation of Article II:1 would be present. Of course, this does not foreclose that such anti-dumping duties could still violate Article VI GATT (contrary to Article II:2(a) charges – which seem to be exempted from the scope of Article III:2 in the AB's view, see above note 34 – there is no doubt that Article II:2(b) duties are subject to Article VI and are thus not only covered under Article II in the GATT). In most cases, the added value of invoking Article II as an additional claim to challenge anti-dumping duties or countervailing duties thus seems to be limited given that parties could directly jump to Article VI (or the AD or SCM Agreements). But, in this case, the Panel considered the Article II claim as relevant because the United States was still collecting anti-dumping duties on the basis of 'old' administrative reviews that were *previously* (in the original proceedings) considered WTO-inconsistent. Panel Report, *United States–Zeroing (Japan)* (*Article 21.5*), above note 49, para. 7.203.

substantive obligation imposed on these charges under Article II:1(b) is not yet clearly sorted out in the case law. In our opinion, such charges should fall within the scope of ODCs and therefore only be deemed consistent with Article II:1(b) in the improbable case that they are explicitly recorded (2).[51]

The AB's interpretation thus underlined the distinction between 'border charges', covered under Article II, and 'internal charges', covered under Article III. All 'border charges', even if they are imposed to counterbalance 'internal charges' (Article II:2(a)), fall within the scope of Article II. The delineation between 'border charges' and 'internal charges' was further clarified in the *China–Auto Parts* case, where the AB observed that 'whether a specific charge falls under Article II:1(b) or Article III:2 of the GATT 1994 must be made in the light of the characteristics of the measure and the circumstances of the case'.[52] In this respect, the AB was of the view that:

> a key indicator of whether a charge constitutes an 'internal charge' within the meaning of Article III:2 of the GATT 1994 is 'whether the obligation to pay such charge accrues because of an *internal* factor (e.g., because the product was *re-sold* internally or because the product was *used* internally), in the sense that such 'internal factor' occurs *after the importation* of the product of one Member into the territory of another Member.[53]

Hence, the obligation to pay an 'internal charge', covered under III:2, is triggered by an internal factor. For example, the obligation to pay internal charges referred to in *Ad* note to Article III accrues because of an internal factor and is merely *collected* for imported products at the border.[54] Conversely, the obligation to pay charges within the scope of Article II – so-called 'border charges' – accrues because of the act of importation. This fits with the Panel's observation in *India–Additional Import Duties* that also charges under Article II:2(a) are triggered by importation, even though 'the internal taxes to which the relevant charges are equivalent link liability to events other than importation'.[55]

2.2 Burden of proof

The allocation of the burden of proof was a deciding factor for the outcome of this case. Neither party offered evidence on the operation of the internal charges that would allow a determination of whether the (Extra-) Additional Duties effectively resulted in charges on imported products in excess of charges imposed on like domestic products. Obviously, for a claim under Article III:2, the burden would be on the complaining party to make a prima facie case of excess taxation and thus

51 It is indeed not very probable that Members recorded such charges given the Director-General's statement when introducing a loose-leaf system for the Schedules of Concessions (see above note 24).

52 AB Report, *China–Auto Parts*, above note 1, para. 171.

53 AB Report, *China–Auto Parts*, above note 1, para. 163.

54 AB Report, *China–Auto Parts*, above note 1, para. 162.

55 Panel Report, paras. 7.153 (footnote 198) and 7.248.

to advance details on the operation of the internal charges. However, what if 'consistency with Article III:2' is not addressed under Article III:2 itself but in an indirect way under Article II:2(a)?

Importantly, the United States agreed that the *ultimate* burden on whether the conditions under Article II:2 are met (i.e. consistency with Article III:2) rests on the shoulders of the complainant given that Article II:2(a), though an exception, should not be considered an affirmative defence.[56] But in the United States's view, it is up to the respondent to articulate a prima facie case that the charges fall within the scope and meet the conditions of Article II:2(a) in case the complainant has made a prima facie case under Article II:1(b). However, the Panel disagreed and held that the United States also had to make a prima facie case that the charges do not fall within the scope of Article II:2(a) to support its claim under Article II:1(b).[57] This position seemed to be inspired by the Panel's conclusion that Article II:2 does not set out *exceptions* to the positive obligations under Article II:1(b). Although the AB adopted a different approach on Article II:2(a) *juncto* Article II:1(b), it generally agreed with the Panel's conclusion on the allocation of the burden of proof but seemed to emphasize, somewhat stronger, India's responsibility in this respect. The AB observed that Article II:1(b) and II:2(a) are 'closely inter-related provisions' and that, in this case, 'the potential for application of Article II:2(a) is clear from the face of the challenged measures'.[58] In light of these circumstances, in order to establish *a prima facie* case of a violation of Article II:1(b), the United States had to also present arguments and evidence that the charges are not justified under Article II:2(a).[59] On the other hand, because India relied on Article II:2(a), it was also 'required to adduce arguments and evidence in support of that assertion'.[60] Yet, the AB did not give much guidance on when the complaining party would have met such a prima facie burden under Article II:2(a) as this 'will to some extent vary, depending upon the particular substance of the challenged measure and the extent to which a relationship between the border charge and the corresponding internal taxes is identifiable'.[61] Regarding

56 Panel Report, para. 7.164; AB Report, para. 183.

57 This is because a charge can only fall within the scope of Artcle II:1(b), as the United States claimed, if it falls outside the scope of Article II:2(a). Hence, the Panel did not accept that the United States could substantiate its claim that the charges fall within the scope of Article II:1(b) without demonstrating that they are not charges within the meaning of Article II:2(a). See Panel Report, paras. 7.148 and 7.160–7.164.

58 AB Report, para. 190. The AB indicated that the measures imposing the (Extra-) Additional duties stipulate that they refer to internal charges. AB Report, footnote 367. To be sure, the internal charges were not identified or listed in those measures, but only a general reference *in abstracto* was included.

59 The AB emphasized (para. 192) that 'not every challenge under II:1(b) will require a showing with respect to Article II:2(a)' but 'if, due to the characteristics of the measures at issue or the arguments presented by the responding party, there is a reasonable basis to understand that the challenged measure may not result in a violation of Article II:1(b) because it satisfies the requirements of Article II:2(a), then the complaining party bears some burden in establishing that the conditions of Article II:2(a) are not met'.

60 AB Report, para. 191.

61 AB Report, para. 193.

this particular case, the AB simply concluded that 'both parties had a responsibility ... to adduce relevant evidence at their disposal, both with respect to
Article II:1(b) and Article II(a)'.[62] Referring to India's refusal to provide details on
the charges upon the Panel's request, the AB reiterated its jurisprudence that 'refusal will be one of the relevant facts of record, and indeed an important fact, to be
taken into account in determining the appropriate inference to be drawn'.[63] The
AB even stressed that these 'were particularly important pieces of evidence at
India's disposal that should have been provided to the Panel' and seemed to hint
that the Panel should have attached more weight to India's refusal.[64]

The AB summarized its general approach to the burden of proof in WTO
dispute-settlement procedures, but failed to explain why this approach would, in
this case, support its conclusion to put the burden of making a prima facie case
under Article II:2(a) on the complainant. Instead, the AB grounded this interpretation on a new criterion ('closely inter-relatedness' of two provisions),[65] while it
seems that the same conclusion could have been reached on the basis of more
solid criteria developed in previous cases.

As the AB reiterated, the general principle for allocating the burden of proof
is that it 'rests upon the party, whether complaining or defending, who asserts
the affirmative of a particular claim or defence'.[66] Consequently, the burden of
proving a violation rests on the complainant's shoulders, whereas the burden
of proving an exception is put on the defendant. Nonetheless, the AB has
attempted in previous case law to distinguish 'exceptions', which establish an
exception to a rule, from provisions that exclude the application of other provisions (so-called 'excluding provisions') (Grando, 2006). With respect to such
'excluding provisions', the complainant has the burden of proving that 'the
defendant does not fall under the situation or has not complied with the requirements of a provision that excludes the application of the general rule' (Grando,
2006). The AB's understanding of Article II:2(a) seems to fit surprisingly well
in this category of 'excluding provisions'.[67] Paraphrasing AB statements from
previous cases, items listed in Article II:2 seem to be 'positive rules establishing
obligations in themselves' and not affirmative defenses.[68] If a Member complies
with Article II:2(a), Article II:1(b) 'simply does not apply' and, conversely, if
a Member does *not* comply with those obligations set out in Article II:2(a),

62 AB Report, para. 193.
63 AB Report, footnote 370.
64 AB Report, footnote 409.
65 Insofar as the measures call for the 'potential application' of the (exception-) provision in question.
66 'Where the complaining party has met the burden of making its prima facie case, it is then for the
responding party to rebut this showing.' AB Report, para. 185.
67 Because the opening phrase of Article II:2 ('nothing in this article shall prevent') suggests that it is
an exception, the AB might not have opted to disregard the application of this distinction in this case.
68 The United States also agreed that Article II:2(a) is not an affirmative defence. AB Report, *United
States – Measure Affecting Imports of Woven Wool Shirts and Blouses from India* (*US–Wool Shirts and
Blouses*), WT/DS33/AB/R (23 May 1997), at 16.

Article II:1(b) applies.[69] Indeed, this conforms to the AB's reading of Article II:2(a) *juncto* Article II:1(b) as sketched out above (see Figure 2): consistency with article III:2 should be assessed under the analysis of Article II:2(a) itself and, in case these obligations are not fulfilled, the charges fall within the scope of – and are disciplined by – Article II:1(b).[70]

Hence, the AB could have based its interpretation on previous case law instead of opting for a new criterion.[71] The choice for a new approach without linking it to previous case law adds a new layer of legal uncertainty to a field that urgently needs some coherence. To illustrate this point: Piérola (2009) wonders whether this new approach could be extrapolated to other provisions such as Article XX GATT in case the challenged measures call for the application of this provision. It is, however, well-settled case law that Article XX spells out affirmative defences, which put the burden on the defendant for formulating a prima facie case.[72]

3. Economic analysis

The need for border tax adjustments has long been recognized. Already David Ricardo noted: 'In the degree then in which [domestic] taxes raise the price of corn, a duty should be imposed on its importation ... By means of this duty ... trade would be placed on the same footing as if it had never been taxed' (Sraffa 1951).

As discussed above, in the case *India–Additional Import Duties* the AB ruled that the Additional Duty and the Extra-Additional Duty would not be justified under Article II:2(a) of the GATT 1994, insofar as they result in the imposition of charges on imports of alcoholic beverages in excess of the taxes applied on like domestic products (excise duties in the case of the Additional Duty and sales taxes, value-added taxes, and other local taxes or charges in the case of the Extra-Additional Duty) and insofar as this leads to the imposition of duties in excess of those set forth in a Member's Schedule of Concessions. In particular, a border charge under Article II:2(a) should be consistent with Article III:2, and this forms an integral part of the assessment of 'equivalence'. Hence, whether a border charge is equivalent to internal charges is based not only on a qualitative comparison of the function of a charge and internal tax, but also on quantitative considerations relating to their effect and amount.

---

69 AB Report, *Brazil – Export Financing Programme for Aircraft*, WT/DS46/AB/R (20 August 1999), paras. 139–140; *European Communities – Conditions for the Granting of Tariff Preferences to Developing Countries*, WT/DS246/AB/R (20 April 2004), para. 88; *EC Measures Concerning Meat and Meat Products (Hormones)*, WT/DS26/AB/R, WT/DS48/AB/R (13 February 1998), para. 104.

70 They are thus not necessarily inconsistent with Article II:1(b) GATT.

71 We do not imply that we fully agree with the distinction between 'exception' and 'excluding provision' but the AB should, at least, have integrated this case law in its analysis.

72 See, for example, AB Report, *US–Wool Shirts and Blouses*, above note 68, at 16.

The remainder of this section discusses three broad economic issues raised by the *India–Additional Import Duties* dispute. First, we argue that border tax adjustments may help to achieve efficient combinations of trade and domestic policies, allowing governments to internalize both terms-of-trade and domestic externalities. We then outline various problems associated with the use of border taxes. Finally, we discuss the implications of the AB's ruling for the ongoing debate on carbon tax adjustments.

3.1 WTO rules and efficient trade and domestic policies

The main goal of the GATT/WTO is to facilitate the exchange of reciprocal reductions in trade barriers. This goal is often perceived to clash with other policy interests of the Members. The fear is that governments may feel constrained from unilaterally raising tariffs because of GATT obligations, and may instead choose to lower domestic standards to improve the competitive position of their domestic firms. In particular, many labor and environmental groups claim that competitive pressures will lead either to a 'regulatory chill', with governments resisting the use of tougher regulations, or to a 'race to the bottom', with governments setting even less restrictive policies.

How can we reconcile the objectives of the WTO with the national objective of national governments? In an influential paper, Bagwell and Staiger (2001) argue that the answer to this question can be found in existing GATT rules, which are aimed at securing 'property rights over negotiated market access commitments'.[73] They consider a simple general equilibrium framework in which two countries trade two goods and governments make decisions over their trade policies (e.g. tariffs) and their domestic standards (e.g. labor and environmental standards) in pursuit of their own national objectives. The objectives of each government can be represented as a general function of its local prices and terms of trade, which are affected by both trade and domestic policies. Domestic policy instruments are imperfect substitutes for tariffs, implying that the same level of market access can be achieved by different 'policy mixes' (e.g. a low tariff and a weak labor standard, or a stricter labor standard and a higher tariff).

In this setting, governments' domestic-policy autonomy can interfere with the maintenance of 'reciprocity' – the balance of negotiated market-access commitments. In particular, a country could commit to reduce its tariff on a particular product and subsequently impose internal taxes on the sale of the product in a manner that favors domestic over foreign producers. Bagwell and Staiger (2001) argue that GATT's rules on 'nonviolation complaints' can be used to avoid the

---

73 Other papers that have recently examined the interaction between trade and domestic policies include Ederington (2001) and Horn (2006).

erosion of tariff commitments and a 'race to the bottom' in domestic regulations. As stated in Art. XXIII.1(b) of GATT:

> A valid reason for a complaint is that a Member considers ... that any benefit accruing to it directly or indirectly under this Agreement is being nullified or impaired or that the attainment of any objective of the Agreement is being impeded as the result of ... the application by another contracting party of any measure, whether or not it conflicts with the provisions of this Agreement.

Nonviolation complaints are based on the 'right to redress' and on the concept of 'nullification or impairment' of reasonable expectations of a benefit accruing from a negotiated concession and agreement. Under a successful nonviolation complaint, the complaining country is entitled to a 'rebalancing' of market-access commitments, whereby either its trading partner finds a way to offer compensation for the trade effects of its domestic-policy change (e.g. by lowering its trade barriers) or the complaining country is permitted to withdraw an equivalent market-access concession of its own.

Consider, for example, a government that is facing pressure from domestic producers to offer import relief in an industry where it has agreed, as a result of WTO negotiations, to hold tariffs low. The prospects of nonviolation constraints can deter this government from offering unilateral import relief to its producers by lowering domestic standards.

In our view, Bagwell and Staiger's (2001) view of the role of nonviolation complaints may be overoptimistic. As the authors themselves admit, nonviolation complaints have proven difficult to carry out in practice. Since the creation of the GATT, very few cases have centered on such complaints, and none of these explicitly involved labor or environmental standards. Moreover, in the very few disputes in which complainants have resorted to the idea of 'nullification or impairment', they have not succeeded in fulfilling the burden of proof. This is due to the difficulty for adjudicators in determining what the negotiating parties could have reasonably expected when they signed the agreement, as well as to the difficulty of assessing the trade effects of given changes in domestic standards (see also Horn, 2006).

We also somewhat disagree with Bagwell and Staiger (2001) on a more important point, which is directly related to the dispute between India and the United States considered here. In their paper, they argue:

> Importantly, however, this feat can only be accomplished if the subsequent change in domestic standards that each government desires would by itself *reduce* the market access that it afforded to its trading partner, so that it would then be induced to make compensating tariff reductions by the prospect of a nonviolation complaint. If, instead, subsequent to tariff negotiations a government wished to change its domestic standards in a way that would effectively grant *greater* market access to its trading partner at existing tariff levels, under WTO rules it would not have the flexibility to unilaterally raise its tariff so as to secure market

access at the negotiated level, and so in this case efficiency cannot be achieved by tariff negotiations. (p. 525)

Thus, in their view, efficient combinations of trade and domestic policies cannot be implemented if a government enters tariff negotiations with domestic policies that discourage access to its markets relative to efficient domestic policy.

We believe that this negative view may apply to domestic regulations that take the forms of *standards*, but not to domestic *taxes*. This is because in the latter case Articles II:2 and III:2, and their interpretation by the AB in its ruling on *India–Additional Import Duties*, can provide the necessary flexibility to allow Members to strengthen their domestic policies without affecting the balance of market-access concessions. For example, manufacturers in an importing country faced with the imposition of higher energy taxes, may argue that the resulting cost increase reduces their competitiveness *vis-à-vis* imported goods. In such circumstances, governments could offset this competitive disadvantage by using a corresponding border tax.

Thus, global efficiency can be achieved if countries negotiate tariff reductions – to internalize terms-of-trade externalities – and then use domestic taxes and equivalent border charges – to internalize negative domestic externalities.

Three important considerations are in order. First, in a standard two-country trade model like the one described by Bagwell and Staiger (2001), one of the two countries may wish to increase taxation on the domestic producers, as a result of an increase in the extent of (or in the awareness of) the negative environmental externalities associated with domestic-production activities. This more stringent domestic policy could be combined with the use of border taxation, so as to keep terms of trade unchanged. Notice, however, that the trading partner would be negatively affected by these policy changes, since they lead to a reduction in trade volumes. To keep the welfare of the trading partner unchanged, the border tax adjustment would need to be such that the terms of trade actually improve for the trading partner.

Second, Bagwell and Staiger (2001) consider a situation in which governments use *standards* rather than *taxes* to deal with the local externalities. From a legal point of view, it is not clear whether governments would be able to use border taxation to countervail the market-access effects of domestic standards. According to the AB's ruling on *India–Additional Import Duties*, Article II:2(a) allows border charges which are equivalent (and thus consistent with Article III:2) to domestic *charges*. The AB said that Members could, by imposing border charges, counterbalance domestic charges. But the AB did *not* say that Members are allowed to impose border charges so as to counterbalance non-fiscal charges on domestic products, which are disciplined under Article III:4. The text of Article II:2(a) might, on its face, not allow border charges on imported products to counterbalance domestic standards, since it does *not* read: 'charges on importation equivalent to domestic charges *or other domestic regulations* consistent with

Article III'.[74] Instead, Article II:2(a) refers only to 'internal tax' and to 'consistency with Article III:2' (not III:4). Thus, the exception under Article II:2(a) seems to require that there exist a domestic *charge* (e.g. not product standard) that is counterbalanced by a border charge.[75]

Our analysis above may thus only apply to when governments used taxes – rather than standards – to regulate negative domestic externalities. In this case, they would be able to optimally adjust their domestic policies to their national objectives, without distorting the balance of negotiated market access.

A third important consideration is that international trade negotiations alone – combined with domestic and border taxation – can only yield globally efficient outcomes in the absence of nonpecuniary externalities across countries. This is because in this case countries are not affected by each other's domestic policies directly, but only through the *trade effects* of such choices. If instead there are nonpecuniary externalities across countries, as in the case of trans-boundary pollution problems, global efficiency would clearly require coordinated policy efforts on both trade and environment (see also the discussion at the end of Section 3.3).

In conclusion, GATT rules of border tax adjustments can help to achieve efficiency of trade and domestic policies. Our analysis suggests that Articles II and III can help to counter fears that trade pressures associated with a country's WTO market-access commitments can cause a 'regulatory chill' or a 'race to the bottom' in domestic regulations.

3.2 Problems with border tax adjustments

The rationale for tax border adjustments is simple: they are a way to maintain the competitiveness of domestic industries, when responding to stricter domestic regulations. However, as discussed below, their application is often complex and can lead to abuses. First, border tax adjustments need to comply with the *National Treatment obligation* of Article III, which requires imported products to be treated no less favorably than 'like' domestic products. While there is no legal definition for 'likeliness', the Interpretative Note to Article III reads

> A tax conforming to the requirements of the first sentence of paragraph 2 would be considered to be inconsistent with the provisions of the second sentence only in cases where competition was involved between, on the one hand, the taxed product and, on the other hand, a directly competitive or substitutable product which was not similarly taxed.

---

74 Obviously, a violation of Article II GATT could still potentially be justified under Article XX GATT.

75 Of course, this observation only deals with border *charges* imposed on imported products to counteract standards imposed on domestic products. Domestic *standards* imposed on imported products are scrutinized under other provisions (e.g. Article III:4 TBT Agreement).

The interpretation of the concepts of 'like' and 'directly competitive or substitutable' products is far from obvious, as it refers to the extent of demand substitutability, which needs to be assessed based on econometric or other evidence. Another limitation of GATT rules on National Treatment is that they do not put any discipline on domestic instruments in cases where there is no 'like' or 'directly competitive or substitutable' domestic product.[76]

A second problem with the application of border taxes arises when the domestic excises tax is applied to an *intermediate good*, but it is the final good that is imported. For example, Poterba and Rotemberg (1995) stress administrative problems in the tax treatment of imports of final goods produced *using* intermediate goods that are subject to environmental taxes. In this case, border taxes are difficult to implement, since they require arbitrary assignments of intermediate-good inputs to final goods, for example on the basis of relative output weight or value. However, not taxing such imports would place domestic producers of final goods at a cost disadvantage and may encourage offshore production of these final goods.

In the case of *India–Additional Import Duties*, the United States argued that some of its products that are charged Extra-Additional Duty are subsequently used in India as inputs in the manufacturing of other products and are subject to state VAT, state sales tax, Central Sales Tax, and/or 'other local taxes or charges' in the same way as like domestic products.[77] As noted by the Panel, in the absence of a credit for the Extra-Additional Duty, these types of imports would be subject to duties 'in excess' of the internal taxes on like domestic products.

A third complication in the use of border taxes arises for countries characterized by a decentralized fiscal system, where charges tend to vary across constituencies and it is thus difficult to establish the correct rate for a common border tax. For example, under the Indian Constitution, excise duties on alcoholic beverages are established and collected by the individual states, not the central government, and the different Indian states are permitted to levy such excise duties at varying rates. Individual states are empowered to levy excise duties on alcoholic liquor 'manufactured or produced' in the relevant state. When different states levy varying rates of excise duty, it is by definition impossible for the government to fix a single rate for the border tax that is 'equal to the excise duty'.

As discussed in the previous section, one of the controversial issues with this dispute was the fact that India did not provide information on the various rates applied by its states and the methodology by which the central government averaged them in order to establish the corresponding border charge. Had this information been available, it is still not clear what kind of methodology to

---

76 See Horn and Mavroidis (2004) for a broader discussion of the difficulties involved in the interpretation of the National Treatment obligation and an analysis of case law involving violations of Art. III.

77 See Panel Report, para. 7.366.

compute border taxes would have been considered consistent with the National Treatment obligation of Article III.

3.3 Implications for the debate on carbon border taxes

Parties to the UNFCCC and the Kyoto Protocol are currently in talks designed to help shape a climate-change regime to follow the Protocol's first commitment period, which ends in 2012. At this point, the nature of that regime and the commitments it will entail are uncertain, but the emissions reductions needed will be significant.

In response to that challenge, a number of countries are pursuing or considering strong domestic action to address climate change. They are doing this either in anticipation of future regime obligations, as part of their obligations under the current treaties, or out of a desire to address the challenge of climate change irrespective of what might develop at the international level. In those countries, one of the key obstacles to such action is the fear that it may put their domestic industries at a disadvantage relative to producers in countries that do not take similarly strong action.

One policy option that has been repeatedly proposed to deal with such challenges is border carbon taxes, which are seen as a trade measure that would level the playing field between domestic producers facing costly climate-change measures and foreign producers facing very few.

The recent debate on border carbon taxes has been particularly heated in various countries. In the United States, two bills were proposed before the Senate,[78] both of which involve a cap-and-trade scheme and both of which foresee border taxes as part of the regime. Although they eventually failed to pass the Senate, these bills will likely inform whatever future climate-change legislation is passed. In Europe, similar proposals have been circulated. The EC-mandated High Level Group on Competitiveness, Energy and Environmental Policies has proposed the use of border carbon adjustments in its second report in 2006. Various politicians support the idea of imposing a carbon tax on goods imported from countries with no emission curbs under the Kyoto regime as part of the so-called EU's 'carbon equalization system'.[79]

While such measures increase the political feasibility of national climate-change legislation, they pose a serious threat to the international trading system and potentially violate international trade law under the WTO.

The *India–Additional Import Duties* case cannot really help us to assess whether or not the proposed carbon border taxes would breach WTO obligations.

---

78 S-1766, Bingaman-Specter Low Carbon Economy Act, and S-2191 Lieberman-Warner, America's Climate Security Act.

79 These proposals have been very controversial and have been opposed by various EU trading partners. For example, Ujal Singh Bhatia, India's ambassador to the World Trade Organization (WTO), has warned the EU of retaliation and litigation from its trade partners if the EU goes ahead with any trade-restrictive carbon border charges.

As discussed above, the AB ruling on this dispute establishes that, in the case of goods subject to indirect taxes (e.g. sales taxes and value-added taxes), border taxes are allowed under Article II:2(a) as a way to level the playing field between taxed domestic industries and untaxed foreign competitors. The extent to which they could also be applied to energy inputs of products, however, is unclear.[80]

To be compatible with GATT/WTO rules, carbon border taxes should not discriminate between domestic producers and foreign producers of like products – both should be treated similarly according to the National Treatment principle. Also, they should not discriminate between 'like' products based on the country of production, in line with the Most Favored Nation principle.

In the case of environmental taxation, goods that are 'like' from the point of view of their use may actually be considered very different because of the technology used to produce them: is a tonne of cement produced with solar energy 'like' a tonne of cement produced using coal?

While, as mentioned in Section 3.2 above, there is no legal definition for 'likeliness', the AB has ruled that likeness 'is, fundamentally, a determination about the nature and extent of a competitiveness relationship between and among products'.[81] Import restrictions on the basis of non-product-related process and production methods are generally not permitted. This would seem to mean that steel is steel, no matter how it is produced. Going further, likeness has been defined as being determined by four criteria: (i) the (physical) properties, nature, and quality of the products; (ii) the end-uses of the products; (iii) consumers' perceptions and behavior in respect of the products; and (iv) the tariff classification of the products.[82] It might be argued that consumers perceive 'dirty' steel as different from 'green' steel, but this would probably be something of a legal long shot, but a WTO dispute panel would probably consider the two products to be 'like'.[83]

Even if carbon border taxes were considered to be compatible with GATT/WTO rules, there are doubts about the effectiveness of such schemes. This would depend

---

80 Article II:2(a) GATT refers to a charge equivalent to an internal tax imposed consistently with Article III:2 'of the like product or *in respect of an article from which the imported product has been manufactured or produced in whole or in part'*. The question is whether energy inputs are considered as such an article. Moreover, Article III:2, to which Article II:2(a) refers, refers to taxes 'applied, directly or *indirectly*, to like domestic products'. Again the question is whether only inputs physically incorporated in the final product may be counterbalanced in case the final product is imported. The idea that carbon border taxes could be used by Members/Contracting Parties, if compatible with the national-treatment principle, was already put forward in the Panel Report *United States – Taxes on Petroleum and Certain Imported Substances* adopted on 17 June 1987. This concerned the GATT compatibility of the 'United States Superfund Amendments and Reauthorization Act of 1986', which had (re)-introduced an excise tax on petroleum at higher rates and a tax on certain chemicals, and imposed a new tax on certain imported substances produced or manufactured from taxable feedstock chemicals.

81 See *European Communities – Measures Affecting Asbestos and Asbestos-Containing Products*, Report of the Appellate Body, WT/DS135/AB/R (12 March 2001), para. 99.

82 Ibid., para. 101.

83 Moreover, Article II:2(a) GATT *requires* for a border tax to be consistent under Article II that there exist an internal tax on *like* domestic products. Hence, the argument that imported and domestic are not 'like' because of differences in PPM does not serve the defending party under Article II:2(a) GATT.

on whether they cover only basic materials (such as raw aluminum) or also cover manufactured products made from those materials (such as aluminum-frame bicycles). As described in the previous section, a broader scheme will be particularly difficult to manage, but a scheme that is more narrowly cast may have unintended adverse impacts. Specifically, it will raise the price of aluminum as an input good to domestic manufacturers of, say, bicycles, but it will not levy any charges on imported bicycles. Such a scheme would protect the aluminum sector from competitiveness impacts, but not the sectors that add value to aluminum.

A border carbon tax scheme could also be evaluated on the extent to which it might exert pressure on some countries to adopt stricter policies, or to take on tough treaty obligations. This potential will of course vary from country to country and sector to sector. In those cases where the percentage of a given good exported to the implementing country is particularly small, imposing a carbon tax will have little or no policy impact on the exporter.

Finally, as already mentioned in Section 3.1, GATT/WTO rules on tariff bindings and border tax adjustments can only help to achieve global efficiency when domestic policies affect foreign countries only indirectly, through their effects on market access. In the case of carbon emissions and other transboundary negative externalities, countries are affected by each other's domestic policies directly. In this case, global efficiency could only be achieved through trade and environmental negotiations.[84]

4. Conclusion

The case *India–Additional Import Duties* is the first to assess the validity of border tax adjustment under Article II:2(a) and of the GATT. Our analysis of this dispute raises some concerns about the legal reasoning of the Appellate Body, but we argue that the Appellate Body's economic reasoning was mostly correct.

In its ruling, the AB considered that charges inconsistent with Article II:2(a) fall within the scope of Article II:1(b) and hereby underscored the distinction between 'border charges', covered under Article II, and 'internal charges', covered under Article III. Unfortunately, the AB failed to reveal the substantive obligation imposed on these charges under Article II:1(b). In our opinion, such charges should be covered under 'ODCs' and therefore only be deemed consistent with Article II:1(b) in the unlikely case that they are explicitly recorded.

The AB also held that the burden of formulating a prima facie case under Article II:2(a) rests on the complainant in case the potential for application of Article II:2(a) is clear from the face of the challenged measure. At the same time, the AB also stressed the respondent's responsibility of underpinning any alleged justification under Article II:2(a). This could also be induced from the AB's strong

---

84 However, it is far from clear whether the WTO should be the forum for environmental negotiations, as stressed, among others, by Ederington (2001) and Conconi and Perroni (2002, 2005).

criticism of India's refusal to answer the Panel's written question regarding the operation of the internal charges. By formulating a new criterion to underpin its decision, the AB, however, raised more questions than it answered regarding its general approach to the allocation of the burden of proof. The Appellate Body's decision offers not much guidance on how to allocate the burden of proof in future cases.

We are less critical of the Appellate Body from an economic point of view. What its ruling on *India–Additional Import Duties* clearly establishes is that Article II:2(a) can be used as an exception to Article II:1(b), implying that Members can impose border taxes above their market-access commitments. However, they can only do so in a way that is consistent with Article III, implying that border taxes cannot be in excess of domestic taxes. We have argued that these rules may help to internalize both terms-of-trade and domestic externalities and to increase global efficiency.

References

Bagwell, Kyle and Robert W. Staiger (2001), 'Domestic Policies, National Sovereignty, and International Economic Institutions', *Quarterly Journal of Economics*, **116**: 519–562.

Conconi, Paola and Carlo Perroni (2002), 'Issue Linkage and Issue Tie-in in Multilateral Negotiations', *Journal of International Economics*, **57**: 423–447.

Conconi, Paola and Carlo Perroni (2005), 'Conditionality, Separation, and Open Rules in Multilateral Institutions', in E. Kwan Choi and James C. Hartigan (eds.), *Handbook of International Trade: The Economic and Legal Analysis of Trade Policy and Institutions, Volume II*, Oxford: Blackwell Publishing.

Ederington, Josh (2001), 'International Coordination of Trade and Domestic Policies', *American Economic Review*, **91**: 1580–1593.

Grando, Michelle T. (2006), 'Allocating the Burden of Proof in WTO Disputes: A Critical Analysis', *Journal of International Economic Law*, **9**: 615–656.

Horn, Henrik (2006), 'National Treatment in the GATT', *American Economic Review*, **96**: 394–404.

Horn, Henrik and Petros C. Mavroidis (2004), 'Still Hazy after All These Years: The Interpretation of National Treatment in the GATT/WTO Case-Law on Tax Discrimination', *European Journal of International Law*, **15**: 39–69.

Piérola, Fernando (2009), 'The Appellate Body Report in India – Additional and Extra-Additional Duties on Imports from the United States (DS 360) – Implications with Respect to the Interpretation of Article II and the Burden of Proof in WTO Dispute Settlement Proceedings', *Global Trade and Customs Journal*, **4**: 97–98.

Poterba, James M. and Julio J. Rotemberg (1995), 'Environmental Taxes on Intermediate and Final Goods When Both Can Be Imported', *International Tax and Public Finance*, **2**: 221–228.

Sraffa, Piero (ed.), with M. H. Dobb (1951), *The Works and Correspondence of David Ricardo*, Vol. IV, Cambridge: Cambridge University Press.

Comment

India – Additional and Extra-Additional Duties on Imports from the United States

FRIEDER ROESSLER

Executive Director, Advisory Centre on WTO Law

1. Introduction

Under the provisions of the GATT governing import charges and internal taxes, the Members of the WTO may levy internal taxes on imported products through their customs services. The relationship between the provisions governing import charges and those governing internal taxes was addressed for the first time by a panel and the Appellate Body in *India–Additional Import Duties*. I do not believe that this relationship was correctly analysed by the Panel. While the commentators describe correctly the rulings of the Panel and the modifications to those rulings by the Appellate Body, they do not provide an explanation of the function and interrelationship of the various provisions on import charges and internal taxes. I would like to complement their analysis by setting out my understanding of the function and interrelationship of these provisions in Section 2 below.

In the economic section of their paper, the commentators make a number of statements regarding the WTO rules governing border tax adjustments that I consider incorrect. In Section 3 below, I present my understanding of those rules and address those inaccuracies.

2. The relationship between the GATT provisions governing import charges and those governing internal taxes

The basic provisions of the GATT governing customs duties and other charges imposed on the importation of products of other Members are paragraphs 1(b) and 2 of Article II. The basic rules set out in Article II:1(b) read as follows:

> The products described in ... the Schedule ... shall, on their importation ... be exempt from ordinary customs duties in excess of those set forth and provided therein. Such products shall also be exempt from all other duties or charges of any kind imposed on or in connection with the importation.

265

The first sentence of paragraph 1(b) obliges WTO Members to exempt the products described in their Schedule of Concessions from ordinary customs duties in excess of those set forth in that Schedule (generally described as 'bound rates'). The second sentence obliges Members to exempt such products from 'all other duties or charges of any kind imposed on or in connection with the importation'. The two sentences of Article II:1(b) have different objectives. According to the first sentence, no customs duty may be levied that exceeds the bound rate. It is intended to protect the results of market-access negotiations. The second sentence obliges Members to reduce the number and diversity of import duties or charges by prohibiting, in principle, all duties and charges on bound items other than ordinary customs charges. It is intended to facilitate trade in bound items by simplifying customs procedures. It is thus not sufficient that the total of all duties and charges levied on or in connection with the importation of a bound item does not exceed the bound rate. Duties and charges of any kind other than ordinary customs duties are, in principle, prohibited whatever their level.

There are a number of important exceptions to the general prohibition of other duties and charges on the importation of products included in the Schedule of Concessions. The first is contained in the second sentence of Article II:1(b) itself. This provision permits other duties and charges that are not

> ... in excess of those imposed on the date of this Agreement or those directly and mandatorily required to be imposed thereafter by legislation in force in the importing territory on that date.

This exemption has been further elaborated in the Understanding on the Interpretation of Article II:1(b) of the GATT 1994. Paragraph 2 of the Understanding defines the 'date of this Agreement' as follows:

> The date as of which 'other duties or charges' are bound, for the purposes of Article II, shall be 15 April 1994. 'Other duties or charges' shall therefore be recorded in the Schedules at the levels applying on this date.

Paragraph 7 of the Understanding provides:

> 'Other duties or charges' omitted from a Schedule at the time of deposit of the instrument incorporating the Schedule in question into GATT 1994 ... shall not subsequently be added to it and any 'other duty or charge' recorded at a level lower than that prevailing on the applicable date shall not be restored to that level unless such additions or changes are made within six months of the date of deposit of the instrument.

The Panel in *Dominican Republic–Import and Sale of Cigarettes* noted that Members were required under the above provisions of the Understanding to record all other duties and charges as applied on 15 April 1994 within six months of the date of deposit of the instrument by which they accepted the WTO Agreement and that no further duties and charges could be recorded after that point in time.

The Panel concluded from this that Article II:1(b), second sentence read together with the Understanding meant that:

> imported products shall be exempted from all 'other duties or charges' of any kinds in excess of those as validly recorded in the Schedule of the Member concerned.[1]

The advantage of the Understanding is that each Member's Schedule now clearly indicates not only the maximum rates of ordinary customs duties the Member may levy in accordance with the first sentence of Article II:1(b) but also all other duties and charges that the Member may impose in accordance with the second sentence of that provision.

A further exemption from the general prohibition of other duties and charges on bound items is contained in Article II:2, which reads as follows:

> Nothing in this Article shall prevent [Member] from imposing at any time on the importation of any product:
>
> (a) a charge equivalent to an internal tax imposed consistently with the provisions of paragraph 2 of Article III in respect of the like domestic product or in respect of an article from which the imported product has been manufactured or produced in whole or in part;
> (b) any anti-dumping or countervailing duty applied consistently with the provisions of Article VI;
> (c) fees or other charges commensurate with the cost of services rendered.

Articles III, VI, and VIII of the GATT set out the conditions under which charges equivalent to internal taxes, and anti-dumping or countervailing duties and fees for services rendered, may be levied. This raises the question of why it was necessary to provide in Article II:2 for an explicit permission to levy charges consistent with those Articles. The answer is that, while Articles III, VI, and VIII regulated the levying of specific charges, they do *not* permit their imposition *as a condition on the importation* of products. For instance, while Article VI:2 states that Members 'may levy on any dumped product an anti-dumping duty', it does not exempt anti-dumping duties from the general prohibition of duties and charges other than ordinary customs duties on the importation of bound items set out in Article I:1(b). Given this general prohibition, the right to levy an anti-dumping duty on dumped products must be distinguished from the right to levy such a duty as a condition of importation. Articles III, VI, and VIII can consequently not be interpreted to imply the right to burden the process of importation with the collection of the charges they regulate. That right is conferred by Article II:2.

To summarize: Articles III, VI, and VIII permit Members to impose specific charges; the function of Article II:2 is to accord them the right to levy these charges as a condition of importation notwithstanding the general prohibition to burden

---

1 WT/DS302/R, para. 7.88.

the process of importation with the levying of charges other than ordinary customs duties set out in Article II:1(b), second sentence.

In respect of charges equivalent to an internal tax, Article II:2 has further functions. The application of internal measures is governed by the national-treatment provisions of Article III of the GATT. In respect of internal taxes, Article III:2(a) states:

> The products of the territory of any [WTO Member] imported into the territory of any other [WTO Member] shall not be subject, directly or indirectly, to internal taxes or other internal charges of any kind in excess of those applied, directly or indirectly, to like domestic products.

The Note *ad* Article III provides in relevant part:

> Any internal ... charge ... which applies to an imported product and to the like domestic product and is collected ... in the case of the imported product at the time or point of importation is nevertheless to be regarded an ... internal charge ... subject to the provisions of Article III.

This Note defines the scope of application of Article III. It makes clear that an internal charge is not turned into a 'border charge' subject to Article II:1(b) merely because it is collected in respect of imported products at the time or point of importation. However, the Note does not define the scope of Article III to comprise charges levied 'on the importation' of products equivalent to internal taxes on like products. Such charges are levied as a condition of importation – and consequently not on products already imported – and therefore fall under the general prohibition of other duties and charges set out in Article II:1(b), second sentence.

Moreover, the Note ad Article III covers only a 'charge which applies to an imported product and to the like domestic product'. It thus covers only charges on imported products that are identical to those on domestic products. However, in many instances, governments cannot apply to imported products the same charges that they apply to domestic products. For instance, a tax on domestic products that takes the form of a business turnover tax cannot be levied in that form on imported products because there is in respect of imported products no business turnover that could be the basis of taxation. To equalize conditions of competition in such a case, governments must be permitted to levy a charge upon importation that is economically equivalent but not identical to the domestic turnover tax. An additional function of Article II:2(a) thus is to exempt border charges that are not identical to internal taxes but economically equivalent to such taxes from the general prohibition of charges other than ordinary customs duties.

To summarize: an internal charge consistent with Article III may be imposed in respect of imported products 'at the time or point of importation' according to the Note ad Article III and a border charge that is equivalent to an internal tax consistent with Article III may be imposed according to Article II:2(a). WTO Members may thus use their customs services to collect their internal charges in respect of

Table 1. Customs duties and other charges on importation: basic principles as set out in GATT Articles II:1(b), II:2(a), and III:2

Charge	Principle	Main provisions
Ordinary customs duties	**Permitted** but must not exceed level of tariff binding	Article II:1(b) of the GATT
Other duties and charges	**Prohibited on bound items** except if validly recorded in Schedule	Article II:1(b) of the GATT and Understanding on Article II:1(b)
Internal charges collected or enforced at time or point of importation	**Permitted** provided the charge is consistent with Article III:2	Note to Article III of the GATT
Charges on importation equivalent to internal taxes	**Permitted** provided the charge is consistent with Article III:2	Article II:2(a) of the GATT

imported products and may make the importation of products conditional upon the payment of charges equivalent to internal taxes on like domestic products.

The principles explained above are summarized in Table 1.

3. The WTO law governing the application of domestic taxes and regulations to imported products and products destined for exportation

Under the provisions of the GATT and the Subsidies Agreement on national treatment, export subsidies, and restrictions on the sale for export,[2] a Member of the WTO may, in principle, apply to imported products the taxes and regulations it applies to domestic products and may exempt from its domestic taxes and regulations the products destined for export. The application of domestic taxes and regulations to imported products and products destined for export is optional: the Members have the right but not the obligation to impose the burdens borne by domestic products also on imported products. Equally, the Members may, but need not, apply to products sold abroad the measures applied to products sold domestically. As illustrated below and summarized in Table 2, a product exported from Member A to Member B could therefore be subject to four different forms of treatment:

- It could be exempted from domestic taxes or regulations by A upon exportation, and then taxed or regulated by B upon importation (taxation or regulation in the country of destination).
- It could be taxed or regulated by A and exempted from taxes or regulations by B (taxation or regulation at the country of origin).

2 See Articles II:2(a), III, including the Note to Article III, Note to Article XVI and XI:1 of the GATT and Note 1 to Article 1 and Annexes I–III of the Agreement on Subsidies and Countervailing Measures (SCM Agreement).

- It could be taxed or regulated both by A and B (taxation or regulation in countries of origin and destination).
- It could be taxed or regulated by neither A nor B (taxation or regulation in neither country of origin nor country of destination).

Table 2. Possible treatment of products entering international trade

		Importing member …	
		… taxes/regulates	… does not tax/regulate
Exporting member …	… does not tax/regulate	Taxation/regulation at *destination*	Tax/regulatory *exemption*
	… taxes/regulates	*Double* taxation/regulation	Taxation/regulation at *origin*

The WTO's system of border adjustment accords WTO Members wide policy options regarding the treatment of products entering international trade. This can perhaps best be illustrated with the example of two countries that apply special environmental taxes or regulations to different chemical products that cause pollution either at the time of production or at the time of consumption, or both.

Take first a product that causes pollution at the time of consumption. In this case, the exporting Member may wish to refrain from imposing fiscal or regulatory burdens on products destined for exportation because the pollution does not take place within its territory. The importing Member, however, may wish to apply its environmental taxes or regulation not only to domestic but also imported products so as to discourage the consumption of the product. The two Members would then follow the destination principle. If a product causes pollution only at the time of production, the country of production might wish to tax or regulate both domestic and foreign sales, while the importing country would have no reason to impose a fiscal or regulatory burden on that product. In this case, the origin principle would prevail. If the product causes pollution both at the time of production and of consumption, both countries may wish to apply the environmental tax and hence subject it to double taxation. Conversely, if neither the production nor the consumption of the product causes pollution, neither the exporting nor the importing country would have any reason to apply the tax. The product would then be exempt by both countries from fiscal or regulatory burdens. WTO law thus permits Members to adopt fiscal and regulatory measures affecting each of the chemical products that take into account their different environmental impact.

The above principles on border adjustment apply only to domestic taxes and regulations imposed directly on products, such as a tax on the sale of a product or a regulation prescribing the physical characteristics of products sold in the domestic market. Domestic taxes and regulations that do not affect products as such,

such as income taxes or a minimum-wage requirement, may not be offset through measures discriminating against products from other Members. Thus, WTO Members are, in principle, not permitted to impose fiscal burdens on products originating in countries with income taxes lower than their own[3] or to prohibit imports from countries with a minimum wage lower than their own.[4]

For the reasons set out above, I cannot agree with a number of the statements of the commentators on border tax adjustments. The commentators' conclusion that 'efficient trade and domestic policies may only be achieved [under WTO law] if governments use taxes – rather than standards – to regulate negative domestic externalities' is incorrect because the basic principles of WTO governing the application of domestic *taxes* to imported products and those governing their application of domestic *regulations* are the same.

The commentators also fail to take into account in their analysis that the basic GATT provisions governing the application of internal taxes and regulations to imported products are limited to taxes imposed on products and regulations affecting products. Those provisions do not permit Members to offset the competitive impact of internal taxes borne by producers (such as energy taxes raising the cost of transportation) and regulations affecting exclusively production (such as emission regulations increasing the cost of production). The commentators' conclusion that governments could use border tax adjustments to offset the competitive impact of high energy taxes faced by domestic manufacturers is therefore incorrect.

While import charges serving this purpose could possibly be justified under the General Exceptions of Article XX of the GATT, in particular paragraph (g) on measures related to the conversation of exhaustible natural resources, there is no equivalent exception in the SCM Agreement that would permit the reimbursement of energy taxes borne by producers in respect of products destined for exportation. Unlike the WTO rules governing restrictive import measures, the WTO rules governing export subsidies thus do not exempt measures serving specific policy purposes. Thus, even a broad interpretation of Article XX permitting border adjustments designed to offset the competitive impact of high domestic energy taxes borne by domestic producers could resolve the problem identified by the commentators only in respect of imports but not exports.

The commentators state that the WTO system of border tax adjustments presents difficulties for federal states in which the sub-federal governments levy value-added taxes (VAT) at different rates. If the federal government levies a charge on importation equivalent to the various VAT rates levied at the sub-federal level, a methodology would have to be developed to average them. This difficulty, so the commentators claim, could provide a new argument in favour of European tax harmonization.

3 This would be inconsistent with Article II:1(a) second sentence and/or Article I:1 of the GATT.
4 This would be inconsistent with Articles XI:1 and/or XIII:1 of the GATT.

These statements are based on incorrect assumptions. Under the national-treatment provisions of Article III of the GATT, each sub-federal government may levy on the imported products the taxes it levies on domestic products. There is consequently no need to levy sub-federal taxes on imported products at the point of importation. Furthermore, if a Member of the WTO were to decide to levy a charge on importation equivalent to the VAT levied at the sub-federal level, the question of the calculation of an average of the various VAT rates would not arise. As pointed out by a GATT panel, 'the national treatment provisions require contracting parties to accord to imported products treatment no less favourable than that accorded to any like domestic product, whatever the domestic origin. Article III consequently requires treatment of imported products no less favourable than that accorded to the most-favoured domestic products'.[5] If the imported and like domestic products may be sold in any of the sub-federal jurisdictions, which is normally the case, the charges on the imported product may thus not exceed the charges imposed on the domestic product sold in the sub-federal jurisdiction with the lowest VAT rate. If the charge on the imported product represented an average of the different VAT rates levied by all sub-federal governments, then imported products sold in the sub-federal jurisdictions with below-average VAT rates would be at a competitive disadvantage: domestic products would benefit from the below-average VAT rate in those jurisdictions while imported products sold in those jurisdictions would be subject to the average VAT rate. That would violate Article III:2 of the GATT. The complicated question of how to calculate an average VAT rate consequently does not arise under WTO law.

---

5 GATT Panel Report in *United States – Measures Affecting Alcoholic and Malt Beverages*, DS23/R, adopted on 19 June 1992, BISD 39S/206.

For EU product safety concerns, contact us at Calle de José Abascal, 56–1°,
28003 Madrid, Spain or eugpsr@cambridge.org.

www.ingramcontent.com/pod-product-compliance
Ingram Content Group UK Ltd.
Pitfield, Milton Keynes, MK11 3LW, UK
UKHW051008240426
470322UK00018B/567